THE FORGER'S SHADOW

Also by Nick Groom

The Making of Percy's Reliques (1999)

Thomas Chatterton and Romantic Culture (ed., 1999)

Introducing Shakespeare (2001)

NICK GROOM

THE FORGER'S SHADOW

How Forgery Changed the Course of Literature

PICADOR

First published 2002 by Picador
an imprint of Pan Macmillan Ltd
Pan Macmillan, 20 New Wharf Road, London N1 9RR
Basingstoke and Oxford
Associated companies throughout the world
www.panmacmillan.com

ISBN 0 330 37432 X

1 3 5 7 9 8 6 4 2

A CIP catalogue record for this book is available from
the British Library.

Typeset by Intype London Ltd
Printed and bound in Great Britain by
Mackays of Chatham plc, Chatham, Kent

For Michael Nath

scholar, friend, ally

Contents

The only form of lying that is absolutely beyond reproach is lying for its own sake, and the highest development of this is . . . Lying in Art.

Oscar Wilde, 'The Decay of Lying'

There are those who want a text (an art, a painting) without a shadow . . .; but this is to want a text without fecundity, without productivity, a sterile text. . . . The text needs its shadow: this shadow is a *bit* of ideology, a *bit* of representation, a *bit* of subject: ghosts, pockets, traces, necessary clouds: subversion must produce its own chiaroscuro.

Roland Barthes, *The Pleasure of the Text*

The noble Lord . . . made a rather astonishing point at the beginning of his speech, when he said that this book not only deals with adultery but deals with adultery that did not happen. That is the thing about fiction; it does not happen. That is something we have to bear very much in mind.

Lord Boothby, 'The *Lady Chatterley's Lover* Case'
(*Hansard,* 14 Dec. 1960)

Before

He wanted to dream a man: he wanted to dream him with minute integrity and insert him into reality.

Jorge Luis Borges, 'The Circular Ruins'

Can you imagine a whole new world? Can you even imagine one 'vast methodical fragment of an unknown planet's entire history, with its architecture and its playing cards, with all the dread of its mythologies and the murmur of its languages, with its emperors and its seas'? Or at the moment of genesis would you prefer to forge the poetry of an unknown place, and so bring a world into being as if it were merely the shadow of its own purest expression: as a mystery to be divined, and at your will?

To write such poetry is to craft an Adam from the dust, and breathe life and fire into his blood, and then hear him sing, as Prometheus moulded men out of clay, imitating their bodies from those of the gods. He inspired his children, and they awoke from the slime. Perhaps, as some Gnostic heretics compellingly recognized, the Biblical creation of Adam is a corruption of this old Hittite account of the poet, the maker, the trickster, because Prometheus was *plasticator* ('the maker') as well as being the more familiar *pyrphoros*, or 'bearer of sacred fire'.

The myth of Prometheus the Maker haunts the following pages as a story of making, a story of forging – and it has fascinated artists and poets too, particularly of the period I will be exploring. This book is about a certain dimension of making or forging – literary forgery – and about how various makers or forgers re-enact the myths of Prometheus in crafting persons and stealing fire to animate their dreams as believable realities.

Of Prometheus: he was the son of Iapetos, brother to Atlas, a non-moral being, subtle and cunning, a guardian of secrets, the 'forethinker'. Prometheus pitted himself against Zeus, tricking the god into accepting for sacrifice bones wrapped in fat, while reserving meat for the tables of men. Angry at being tricked, Zeus punished humanity by taking away fire; Prometheus stole it back. Hence Prometheus was venerated as a master craftsman and a master of craftiness, who copied from the gods to create his beings and then fired to animate them. He was himself imitated and worshipped by the potters of Athens, for his theft of fire provided them with the element of their own craft. Indeed, fire for the ancient Greeks was both corporeal and daemonic: of the body, and of the spirit. Fevers were called 'fires of the flesh', and the god of plague was also, like Prometheus, *pyrphoros*, 'fire bringing'. So the metaphor of making something in the forge – forging – blends ideas of craft and creation, body and soul, the tangible and the intangible: Prometheus is nothing less than a god of forgers.

In some versions of the Prometheus myth the theft of holy fire provoked Zeus to command Hephaestus, the daemon of fire and himself a skilled craftsman, to mould a woman from earth and water. This was Pandora, the bane of men and Zeus's revenge on Prometheus and all mankind for possessing fire. In other versions of the myth, however, the theme of sacrifice returns and undoes Prometheus. Like Orpheus, Prometheus is a pagan Christ, tortured and resurrected, who for his crimes against the thunderous Zeus was chained in fetters to a rock. Every morning, an eagle would come to tear out and dine upon the immortal liver of Prometheus; every night, the organ knitted itself together again in an infernal cycle of regeneration. And wherever Prometheus's blood dripped from the eagle's beak and talons as it soared away into the evening, the herb Promethean sprang up. This drug had magical, resurrective properties: Medea collected its dark juice when she called to the underworld to summon Brimo, the queen of the dead.

So the dead are here as well, haunting Prometheus and haunting the forge and haunting the literature. This is also, then, a book about ghosts – and stranger spirits too: shadows that shadow. In a sense, the literary forger is a shadow, forging what is already itself a fabrication, and thereby showing that literature, that most monumental fabrication, is no less forged than any shadowy literary forgery. The forger shadows authenticity, echoes echoes. Forgery haunts culture, spooking literature into disbelieving itself and throwing scholars and critics into curious fits because, like a secret told, forgery reveals the elusiveness of the mysterious ground on which fictions, stories, myths, poetry, and lies all dwell in varying measure. This literary ground is only mapped (in the sense of having order imposed on its unruliness) by non-literary cartographers, such as lawyers – but literary critics should take it back. Forged literature is, moreover, a realm of the fantastic, in which stories lie embedded within other stories, works unfold within works; in which fictions, dreams, and ghosts perpetually interfere with the order of things; in which time is forever unravelling backwards into a dark abysm in the fruitless search for origins; and of course in which, most fundamentally, uncanny doubles, copies, and counterfeits will stalk, shadow, and worry their supposed originals.

This book is to reaffirm, even rediscover, the delicious fictions of literature, not to despair over them; it is also to explain why authenticity legislates against forgeries. The history of authenticity is best understood by examining how forged writings have slipped down through time, as part of the ever-changing stories that societies tell about themselves – stories about authors and inspiration, theories of imagination and fables of creation, cultural myths and canons of aesthetic value. As poems and poets drift along, they leave behind a wake of ghosts: traces of older stories and the shadows of long-dead hands that once inscribed meaning, hands for whom the authentic was perhaps unstable or fluid. By recovering these disappearing traces, one begins to see past authenticity, and then to see right through it. For it is a contention of this book that literary forgers can be read as writers without sounding the tedious and incessant critical alarm in the word 'forgery'. To call a writer a forger is to dispossess them of the body of their own work, to attempt to exorcize them from the mainstream of literature. This book puts poetry back into literary forgery, and forgery back into poetry.

I was thinking of Prometheus the Maker, and of the ghostliness of forgery, when I visited Bristol on my thirty-second birthday, 19 February 1998. I was drawn there by Thomas Chatterton, the poet who grew up in Bristol, who mythologized Bristol in his writings, and who is now virtually forgotten in the city. I had already tried to retrace

Chatterton in London, but the traces simply vanish. All that remains in Brooke Street, where Chatterton died on the night of 24 August 1770 as the victim of arsenic and opium poisoning, is a plaque erected in the early nineteenth century. The memorial currently resides on the side of a branch of Barclays Bank, hovering incongruously in the contemporary bustle of High Holborn and Chancery Lane. It is tempting to reflect upon the irony that this distressed poet, who took his own life in the depths of poverty, starving, refused credit by the baker, should now be memorialized on a *bank* of all things and in a district that has become a financial centre . . . but all this is so much Romantic mythmaking (albeit impressive in its tenacity): as we shall discover, Chatterton was not starving to death, and neither did he commit suicide.

But he did die, cruelly young, and his body was autopsied at the Three Tuns public house, a few doors down from where he lived. The Three Tuns has also disappeared, leaving no trace, no living memory. Some of his friends apparently viewed the corpse before interment on 28 August, when Chatterton was given a pauper's burial in a mass grave in the burying ground of Shoe Lane Workhouse. In being buried in a cemetery, Chatterton's death was evidently not treated as a rational suicide. The century's public treatment of suicides was not a pretty sight, even if such post-mortem punishments were seldom invoked: bodies were denied common burial rights, could be dragged to crossroads and hanged by their feet from the gibbet, casually cremated or thrown into the sea. Instead, Chatterton was treated as a madman; the burial entry perhaps significantly gives the wrong name, a false name: recording him as 'William Chatterton Brook's Street 28'. Yet seek in vain for his remains. Chatterton did not rest in peace. The burying ground has long since disappeared, the bodies removed to an old graveyard in Gray's Inn Road and the City of London Cemetery at Little Ilford. A headstone has been erected in Shoe Lane, but the original site was built over by Farringdon Market and is now crossed by Farringdon Avenue. There are no graves there now, only stories that begin to creep about: a fanciful Bristol legend that Chatterton's body was packed up and sent home by his uncle, a carpenter by trade, and buried by night in the churchyard of St Mary Redcliffe: laid to rest in his father's grave. And there is also a more gruesome possibility: young bodies recently deceased were often dug up to be anatomized.

But anyway, his body has gone. I wandered across the remnants of eighteenth-century streets to catch the shadows of his life and death, guessing where lanes might have led before the tarmac roads and tiled underpasses came, finding odd alleys and rights of way, and, early in the morning, hearing the shouts of Smithfield Market. But no one called me to Thomas Chatterton.

So I didn't find Chatterton in London, and Bristol too tells the most meagre tale. There are only the scantiest of memorials. His home parish of Redcliffe is situated on the edge of Bristol, a poor, run-down, area of brutalist 1960s tower blocks. When I visited, children played, mothers hollered, and the wind blew icily around concrete edges. Here too, nearly all trace of the intricate network of eighteenth-century streets and alleys has disappeared. This makes sense – it was as poor an area in the eighteenth century as it is now: ripe for housing initiatives, ready for obliteration. Chatterton's impoverished family lived somewhere here on Redcliffe Hill, under the shadow of history. Just a single, incongruous element remains: a low rusticated development called Chatterton House. Obscure beginnings, forgotten endings.

Looking down from the hill onto the gigantic Gothic church of St Mary Redcliffe, there is likewise very little. Most of the memorials have been cleared from the churchyard, although a handful of Chatterton family gravestones have been left near the south porch: his father, Thomas Chatterton, died in 1752, aged thirty (the stone was recarved in 1853 and so there's nothing to touch here); his mother, Sarah Chatterton, died on 25 December 1791, aged sixty; his sister Mary Newton died on 23 February 1804, aged fifty-three, and her daughter Mary Ann Newton, last of the direct line, died on 7 September 1807, aged twenty-four. (This is not quite all, for one can still find bones, floating up from the mulch; perhaps some of these might be Chattertons – did I dare to take one?) Inside the church, there is only a recently inscribed and very bland tablet:

THOMAS CHATTERTON
of this parish
1752–1770
Poet

It is placed near the tomb of William Canynges, mayor of Bristol and patron of Chatterton's fictitious medieval poet, Thomas Rowley.

Canynges has two tombs, Chatterton has two memorials; but his body has gone, gone as if it never existed. But there used to be a nineteenth-century statue commemorating him; where has that gone?

I walked through to the north porch of the church. This harbours the remains of a shrine, once favoured by pilgrims and especially sailors (we are very close to the quay here). The porch is decorated with thick vegetative patterns and lively exploits from the 'Legend of Alexander the Great', an extravagant medieval adventure yarn, but I am looking for something else. Up a winding stair, above the vestry, over the porch, is a hexagonal muniment room. It was here, in an old chest, that Chatterton said he discovered the works of the fifteenth-century monk Thomas Rowley. Today, the room still contains long, dark chests – at least one of which dates from the eighteenth century – and there is a little wooden stool recognizable from old engravings of the treasure room. But the place is swept clean – the new brooms being as prominent as the old boxes. There is nothing else there at all. I paced about, in the footsteps of Oliver Goldsmith, Samuel Johnson, James Boswell, and many others. Nothing. Out of the narrow windows one now looks down onto a dual carriageway, and across the road to the remains of Pile Street School, Chatterton's birthplace. The old school is cut off from the parish, a remnant marooned in the middle of a car park. A Grade II listed building, it has been treated abominably, and one can only really visit it with permission from the current council tenant.

It is here that the scandal of Chatterton in Bristol becomes most acute. A genial museum worker occupies the building, but it is a dingy memorial. He leads me into an entirely bare room. 'This is the room in which Chatterton was born.' There's a formica table on which lies a damp, dismal visitors' book; the only other feature is a fireplace. I stare at it pathetically. The cosy 1760s, of pease pudding hot and pots of steaming tea, recedes, irretrievably. It is cold today. I dutifully inspect the book, which launches confidently in 1958 with the Lord Mayor leading a cavalcade of regular visitors, but they all peter out, disappear before I am even born. Something about a burglary. There have only been a handful of visitors this past decade (I recognize several of them, echoing footsteps, sidetracks). And now the house turns out to be an amalgam: the Georgian outer wall of the old school being re-erected as a baffle against the road. In other words, the building is a fake – and it's on the run as well. Chatterton's house has moved: it is now some 50 yards from where it was when Chatterton lived here, it has been reconstructed (to allow what? another car park?). The very ground is shifting. But then it turns out that this story is false too, like the transcript in biro of Chatterton's last verses I am shown: the verses were forged in the nineteenth century. The most real things here are the pitiful photocopies of his life story, offered to me in his own insubstantial house; they are taped to the back of a cornflakes packet.

But then, in an outhouse, languishing, I discover S. C. Fripp's statue of Chatterton as a bluecoat boy. The first stone of this pinheaded monument was laid on 13 November 1839; it was completed five and a half months later on 30 April 1840 and immediately attacked as mean and diminutive (although photographs show affecting affinities with Mark Wallinger's recent Trafalgar Square plinth-piece, *Ecce Homo*). Six years later, the statue was dismantled by the Revd M. R. Whish, the first in a line of St Mary Redcliffe vicars to question Chatterton's right, as a supposed suicide and forger, to be commemorated within sacred precincts (although apparently the church cat rests in consecrated ground in recognition of a righteous career spent in exterminating church mice). The statue was re-erected in July 1857, and then from the 1920s there were calls from the Chatterton Lodge of Freemasons for a new memorial – or at least repairs to the old one – and complaints about the shabby way in which Chatterton was being remembered (forgotten, rather). The Revd Cartwright finally responded in the 1960s by removing the statue entirely. It is now in a state of utter neglect, a lost icon. The face is badly eroded, the eyes sunk back like sockets in an ancient skull, of aeonic dereliction. Is this the head of Thomas Chatterton? Is this the genius who animated fifteenth-century poets and playwrights; the forger received by the Romantics as a modern Prometheus, cunning in craft and magnificent in ambition? Is this the poet who, one of the faithful declared, 'possessed an anvil of all work, and, with the same ease, could sharpen a needle, or mould a Colossus'?

No. Thomas Chatterton has flown from here, from everywhere. He lives in words, not deeds. And while surely one day Bristol will unshackle him, this book is no dead monument to the 'marvellous Boy'. It is an ember to raise new fires from what handfuls of dust remain.

'But cannot I create?
Cannot I form? Cannot I fashion forth
Another world, another universe,
To overbear and crumble this to naught?
Where is another chaos? Where?'

Saturn, in John Keats's *Hyperion*, bk 1

PART ONE

I. WRIGHT

I thought of Chatterton, the marvellous Boy,
The sleepless Soul that perished in its pride.

William Wordsworth, 'Resolution and Independence'

A biography of a Romantic poet was more than a biography
of an author and public figure. The Romantic poet *was* his
own hero. His *life* was poetry, and soon there developed a
canonical set of actions to be carried out by the poet.

Boris Tomaševskij, 'Literature and Biography'

That which we now call the world is the result of a number
of errors and fantasies, which came about gradually in the
overall development of organic beings, fusing with one
another, and now handed down to us as a collected treasure
of our entire past – a treasure: for the *value* of our humanity
rests upon it.

Friedrich Nietzsche, *Human, All Too Human*

What do modern readers generally know about Thomas Chatterton?

a) That he was an eighteenth-century or Romantic poet.
b) That he died young, like Keats.
c) That he committed suicide.
d) That he forged medieval poetry.
e) That he came from Bristol.
f) That there is a Pre-Raphaelite painting of him in the Tate
   Gallery.
g) That Peter Ackroyd has written a novel about him.

When asked to name a Chatterton poem, however, few readers find it possible. The life, rewritten as the archetypal Romantic myth, has completely overtaken the work.

And Chatterton's certainly was an extraordinary life and death, the fatal model for the Romantic, and later Pre-Raphaelite, poet: young, proud, and poverty-stricken; a mad, unrecognized, and suicidal genius. The myth became part of the very genesis of Romanticism: Samuel Taylor Coleridge's first published poem was 'Monody on the Death of Chatterton' (1794) and he reworked it throughout his life; Coleridge's friend and later poet laureate Robert Southey edited Chatterton's complete works; John Keats dedicated *Endymion* to his memory; Percy Shelley and Thomas De Quincey were avid admirers. Later, Henry Wallis painted a supine George Meredith posing as the dead poet in the iconic oil painting which now hangs in Tate Britain and is also reproduced as a mural in Pimlico, the neighbouring tube station. The Pre-Raphaelite poet and painter Dante Gabriel Rossetti was completely infatuated with the boy too: 'He was as great as any English poet whatever, and might absolutely, had he lived, have proved the only man in England's theatre of imagination who could have bandied parts with Shakespeare.' If there is any poet who discovered the limits of poetry, explored the extremity of Romanticism, and who toppled over the edge of the world, it is Chatterton.

More recently, Vita Sackville-West has written a Chatterton play, Serge Gainsbourg a Chatterton pop song, and Peter Ackroyd his Chatterton novel. They are among the hundreds of poets, playwrights, novelists, artists, composers, and ephemeral touts who have been moved by Chatterton to create something; and yet it is a strange and precarious legacy, underpinned by little more than two forbiddingly large, if invaluable, sources covering the life and works, and an amazingly persistent popular mythology forged around the poet's suicide. Moreover, until very recently there has been a quite pitiful dearth of criticism, and only scanty additional historical research. And it is also quite clear that surprisingly few of Chatterton's acolytes, let alone scholars and critics working in the field, have actually studied his writing; they remain seduced by biographical narratives: by the tales of his life and death.

The reasons for this lie deep in the mythography of Chatterton, and an examination of them should provoke a serious revaluation of Romanticism and a reassessment of our own value of authenticity today. The very clichés that come so easily to mind when describing his *marvellous* life are our direct inheritance of Romantic theories of authorship and creativity, in which the poet is marked out by genius, a genius confirmed not by producing striking poetry but by living an intemperate life, a life of 'limit experiences'. Put bluntly, the life gives authenticity to the art, and so the life replaces the art – and still does, whether we are dealing with the furore over writers like Binjamin Wilkomirski, who wrote a contested Holocaust memoir, or simply the authentically unmade bed of Tracey Emin submitted as a Turner Prize art installation. Authenticity is measured, then, by testifying to lived experience – whether social, gendered, and/or ethnic; or experimentation with sex, drugs, and/or radical politics (an often lethal cocktail); or merely by professing a profound and unaccommodating eccentricity. But evidently in all these instances, authenticity is located in the body of the artist.

Chatterton's life was super-authentic: he was a boy from the provinces, an autodidact, a vegetarian, an early opium eater, a libertine, a political radical, and an atheist, and he died tragically young. (Such a life was, in fact, so 'authentic' that it became unbelievable – at least less believable than his fictions.) Likewise, he wrote in a dazzling array of different styles: party-political satire, graveyard Gothic, fashionable journalist columns. He also wrote the works of Thomas Rowley, a fictitious Bristol cleric from the fifteenth century, whose writings were treated as genuine by some commentators for a dozen years after Chatterton's death. The works of Rowley consisted of a voluminous medieval archive of poems, plays, letters, maps, and antiquarian documents; texts that in their very material being and mode of production were medieval: in spelling, lettering, paraphs, curlicues, traced in faded ink on antique vellum. They reverberate with a weird poetry:

> In Virgyne the sweltrie sun gan sheene,
> And hotte upon the mees did caste his raie;
> The apple rodded from its palie greene,
> And the mole peare did bende the leafy spraie;
> The peede chelandri sunge the livelong daie;
> 'Twas nowe the pride, the manhode of the yeare,
> And eke the grounde was dighte in its mose defte aumere.

> 'An Excelente Balade of Charitie'

Chatterton provided a glossary to light the way through this obscurity – 'mees': meads; 'rodded': reddened, ripened; 'mole': soft; 'peede
chelandri': pied goldfinch; 'dighte': drest, arrayed; 'defte': neat,
ornamental; 'aumere': a loose robe or mantle (and 'Virgyne' is Virgo).
The verse has a distant and dreamy quality of an Edenic – indeed an
ethnic – Englishness. John Keats twice called Chatterton's language
the 'purest' English. It is like an incantation to resurrect history out
of nature. The 'Excelente Balade of Charitie', based on the parable of
the Good Samaritan, continues with a thunderstorm that shatters the
indolent heat:

> The sun was glemeing in the midde of daie,
> Deadde still the aire, and eke the welken blue,
> When from the sea arist in drear arraie
> A hepe of cloudes of sable sullen hue,
> The which full fast unto the woodlande drewe,
> Hiltring attenes the sunnes fetive face,
> And the blacke tempeste swolne and gatherd up apace.*

This poetic intoxication or 'fine frenzy' weaves the same atmosphere
as Keats's 'Eve of St Agnes' (written half a century later); it also gave
Wordsworth the metre for 'Resolution and Independence':

> I thought of Chatterton, the marvellous Boy,
> The sleepless Soul that perished in its pride;
> Of Him who walked in glory and in joy
> Behind his plough, upon the mountain-side:
> By our own spirits are we deified;
> We Poets in our youth begin in gladness;
> But thereof comes in the end despondency and madness.†

But unlike Wordsworth's 'Resolution and Independence', Rowley's
'Excelente Balade of Charitie' is called forgery and so Chatterton is
called a forger.

This book is about the problems of designating and defining and
being defined by 'forgery' (henceforth written without 'scare marks').

---

* 'Welken': the sky, the atmosphere; 'arist': arose; 'hiltring': hiding, shrouding; 'attenes':
at once; 'fetive': beauteous.
† Chatterton's metre, rime royal with a final alexandrine, is also used in 'Elinour and
Juga' and is itself taken from John Milton's 'On the Morning of Christ's Nativity'. Note
that Wordsworth is also alluding here to Robert Burns.

I am interested in writing's relationship with the real and how forgeries interpret the rules of representation to create a hybrid realism, both true and false. It is not enough to accuse forgeries of simply being deceitful and morally wrong; it is precisely by being able to break out into the real, to make the literary more real, that they can tell us a bit more about how literature works. Of course it could be argued that this book, by tricking away the authentic, is a part of the condition or crisis it is purporting to diagnose – which is doubtless the case – but my intention is really to encourage readers to read more poetry (and particularly to read Chatterton), and consequently to read some of the standard Eng. Lit. poems a little differently. I focus on the Romantic poets not merely because they are widely read and abidingly influential, but because the critical definition of literary forgery in Great Britain was fixed at the end of the eighteenth and the beginning of the nineteenth centuries. In other words, forgery waxed and waned at the same time as the Romantic movement, and is profoundly implicated therein. So Romanticism (for want of a better term) would have been very different without literary forgery – indeed it may not have recognizably existed at all. Already the material briefly quoted above begs the question: how could Chatterton's unbelievably authentic life produce so much deemed to be inauthentic, and yet remain powerfully attractive to poets who made a fetish of authenticity?

My answer is that the Romantic engagement with literary forgery not only produced a canon of forgers and maintained forgery as a site of inspiration but also provided the ideological means of disabling their work. Romanticism asserted the cultural rights of the individual artist and original creative genius over the impostor or forger. Since then, there has been only a tiny amount written about both Chatterton and the other writers I examine in the following chapters. James Macpherson, William Henry Ireland, and Thomas Griffiths Wainewright were all, like Chatterton, called forgers, and, like Chatterton, have been all but made to disappear from the cultural scene. They are like ghosts or revenants that have haunted the literary hinterlands, awaiting their enfleshings. These writers might not provide the answers to our current obsession with authenticity, but an investigation of them will at least explain how we came to be where we are.

✤ ✤ ✤

WORDS

'When *I* use a word,' Humpty Dumpty said in rather a scornful tone, 'it means just what I choose it to mean – neither more nor less.'

'The question is,' said Alice, 'whether you *can* make words mean different things.'

'The question is,' said Humpty Dumpty, 'which is to be master – that's all.'

Lewis Carroll, *Through the Looking-Glass*

Critical mastery shows itself to be rather shaky on forgery and its associated 'crimes of writing'. In the following pages I will unwind some key terms, words such as 'original', 'plagiarism', 'mimesis', 'imitation', 'copy', 'counterfeit', and 'forgery', in order to demonstrate the difficulties and occasionally the paradoxes of this dark corner of representation. The definitions are confusing and contradictory and all overlap because they have all shifted, but I want to propose at least a clear distinction between forgery and counterfeit. A counterfeit is a facsimile copy. Coins or notes can be counterfeited, and a counterfeit Picasso would be an exact copy of a pre-existent work. Forgery, however, has no actual original source; it conjures the illusion of a source. A forgery of a Picasso would be an original work, but located in Picasso's œuvre: it would be recognizably Picasso, a new Picasso, albeit painted by anyone except Picasso. In this sense, a forgery is like an impostor – or even a parasite. Or another way of considering the forgery is that it is potentially already there – 'Forgers', in Wyclif's preface to his translation of the Bible, 'treten forgeable thingis.'

Forged money, on this definition, would be a £3 note – a con rather than a counterfeit (indeed such frauds were popular among the shiftless because conning carried a lighter sentence than coining) – hence forgery and counterfeiting become distinct activities. They may also be contrasted with another exciting term, 'plagiarism', which is like counterfeiting, but only insofar as it makes an exact and invisible reproduction. A counterfeit coin must be so recognizable as to be entirely indistinguishable from other coins of the same denomination – it must be in a sense transparent: recognizable not as a counterfeit but merely as a sign, and it happily functions as legal tender until it is named counterfeit – whereupon its signification is radically altered and it becomes criminal evidence. The same is true of literary or artistic counterfeits. The act of naming a counterfeit effectively rewrites the text or repaints the picture, and makes any cultural transaction void. Forgery is also recognizable, but has prominence in its recognizability – declaring itself to be the same, but different. A forgery belongs to a recognizable œuvre (Picasso's blue period, Shakespeare's history plays, fifteenth-century poetry), or a recognizable scholarly field or taxonomy, but it presents itself as a contribution to that discourse, rather than as a repetition. Forgeries are finds – and paramount to the act of discovery is the *recognition* of discovery, although, as Thomas Hoving points out, 'Once a faker achieves a nest of pieces all in the same style, then scholars usually defend each new one by pointing to the body of others', and Orson Welles demonstrates in his wonderful film *F for Fake* (1973) that an entire period of an artist's work is probably easier to forge than individual scattered pieces.* Plagiarism, however, tells a different sort of story from both counterfeit and forgery: it is predicated on the *inability* of a reader or viewer to recognize any source.

These three terms, forgery–counterfeit–plagiarism, are often, in careless talk, treated as synonyms. They are, however, more like competitors. Each seeks supremacy over the other two, each endeavours to colonize the rabble of other terms that swarm about it, replicating their relationships and ambiguities (copy, fraud, imposture), and each aspires to master the code of representation through other discourses (for forgery it is the legal discourse, for counterfeiting the economic, for plagiarism the pedagogic). It might appear that it is precisely in this three-way relationship that the words assume their meaning, but the etymology of these words is much more bedevilled than one might imagine, although they do share a declining linguistic confidence. Only forgery, a sort of Romantic weed or inauthentic flower cultivated to hedge the Edenic garden of the imagination, retains any fragrance today.

---

* Hoving is here considering Han Van Meegeren, whose innovation was to paint Italianate Vermeers that would fill in a 'lost period' in the artist's œuvre and indicate an Italian tour.

Moreover, the following definitions are also a response to the earliest theories of authorship, in which literature is understood as being either imitative (making) or inspirational (prophesying). The combination of these two voices will become central to this book. The distinction occurs in the description of the genesis of poetry in Virgil's *Fourth Georgic*. The Muses sing to their father, Jupiter, of the earliest events of creation (the war between the Olympians and the Titans), and Jupiter rewards the Nine with the power to inspire men. Henceforth, this gift is considered authentic poetry, whereas human art is mere *technê* (distinguished by Aristotle in the *Nicomachean Ethics* as the production of objects through artistic craft). Sir Philip Sidney in his *Defence of Poetry* (written 1579–80) confirms the popular Renaissance position on this distinction:

> Poetry is of all human learning the most ancient and of most fatherly antiquity, as from whence other learnings have taken their beginnings; since it is so universal that no learned nation doth despise it, nor no barbarous nation is without it; since both Roman and Greek gave divine names unto it, the one of 'prophesying', the other of 'making', and that indeed that name of making is fit for him, considering that whereas other arts retain themselves within their subject, and receive, as it were, their being from it, the poet only bringeth his own stuff, and doth not learn a conceit out of a matter, but maketh matter for a conceit.

Forging as an inspirational craft is, I suggest, able to harmonize these two modes.

Original

The rote and orygynall fountayne of alle synne

'Bug' Bible*

Original means to arise, from the Latin *origo* (rise, beginning, source), and if its earliest uses are, not surprisingly, theological, the word was profoundly tainted by and indeed implicated in the Fall. It is as

---

* The 'Bug' Bible (1551) is so-called for rendering Psalm 91, v.5: 'Thou shalt not be afraid of bugges by nighte.'

'Original Sin' that original first arises in the fourteenth century, and
for centuries it was to remain deeply immured in sex, sin, and Satan's
wickedness. Chaucer's Pardoner (c.1386) uses the word as an analogy
to 'cause', specifically meaning cause of distress, lamenting:

> O cause first of oure confusioun!
> O original of oure dampnacioun;

suggesting here that the deadly sins of gluttony and drunkenness are
the *authors* of damnation. Perhaps not unconnected with this strong
religious sense and medieval thinking on the origins of the soul, the
origins of evil, the origins of human weakness and folly, original also
had a very early legal usage as an instigating writ, and so it is tempting
to use it as a word to connect the moral with the legal implications
of the Fall.

This is confirmed by the role of the Devil in the Old Testament,
who was simply a 'blocking agent', an authorized adversary: in the
Book of Job, for instance, he is a prosecutor. Satan's status as
the incarnation of evil was in fact moulded over a thousand years later
by St Augustine, who described his rebellion in *De civitate dei* ('The
City of God') and in doing so established the fall of the rebel angels
as the archetypal anti-story to Christianity. Satan's pride is partly his
lust to originate, to be original, independent of God. So the concept
of originality is primarily tied to human frailty, punishment, and the
degenerating career of the fallen angels, rather than to the order and
harmony of the celestial cosmology.

Such a reading is indeed tempting. But even at this medieval
moment, original was also being used to describe artistic and scholarly
sources, and, come the Renaissance, Humanists were able to cleanse
the word of much of its sinful tone. As word and concept, originality
was common to the activities of genealogy, antiquarianism, and etymology; textual criticism, editing, and translation; and also anatomy
and mathematics. In mathematics the word served as a term for a fixed
point, and so 'originality' might be said to be the Ptolemaic pole
towards which Keats is looking in his famous sonnet: 'Bright star,
would I were steadfast as thou art . . . still steadfast, still unchangeable.'
In any case, by a sort of deistic logic, the word was then used to
describe the science of the natural world and in particular natural
laws – a choice example coming in *A New Theory of the Earth* (1696),
in which William Whiston observes (with, I think, unintentional

wit) that 'Mountains are the principal Source and Origin of Springs and Fountains' (fountains being also sources as spring also means origin . . .). This interest in natural phenomena is also apparent in Locke's contemporaneous *Essay on Human Understanding*, which proposes a more secular epistemology:

> External material things, as the objects of sensation; and the operations of our minds within, as the objects of reflection; are the only originals from whence all our ideas take their beginnings.

So the original pejorative connotations of originality – that it was by definition a form of sin, the primal sin – were superseded first by attention to the allegory of Knowledge gained by eating the apple and therefore how best to develop experiential scholarly method, and subsequently by attention to the ecology of the Tree itself: naturalizing the phenomenon of originality in terms of experimental science and psychology – and thereby human identity. And by 1728, Edward Young in his essay 'On Lyric Poetry' could idealize the original source: 'Originals only have true life, and differ as much from the best imitations as men from the most animated pictures of them.'

Thus by the middle of the century, when Samuel Johnson variously defines original in his *Dictionary* (1755–6) as 'First copy; archetype; that from which any thing is transcribed or translated' and 'Primitive; pristine; first', the word had very little of its original force remaining and was gaining a sense of secular idealism, or the archetypal. It became a word that bestowed legitimacy on body and soul. If, to the late eighteenth-century aristocracy, one's *origins* (meaning where you came from) were *the* social necessity (and were powerfully mythologized by Edmund Burke in his *Reflections on the Revolution in France*), among more fluid orders it was something subtly different: originality, meaning financial flair, political acumen, indeed poetic genius, that promised success and influence; and 'an original' comes to mean a gentleman most singular and even odd. Eccentricity is seen as a pathological form of bourgeois individuality: a conceit in which identity is predicated on personal whim or excessive taste, instead of upon social mores.

This burgeoning concept of character, attached to notions of originality, also carried values of paternal legitimacy and patriarchal rights into artistic work: the originating author could have his likeness carried through generations. A single, early example will suffice at this stage.

John Bunyan defended himself in *The Holy War* (1682) against accusations of plagiarism by describing the fountainhead of his inspiration:

> Some say the *Pilgrims Progress* is not mine,
> Insinuating as if I would shine
> In name and fame by the worth of another,
> Like some made rich by robbing of their Brother.
> Or that so fond I am of being Sire,
> I'le father Bastards. . . .
>   It came from my own heart, so to my head,
> And thence into my fingers trickled;
> Then to my Pen, from whence immediately
> On Paper I did dribble it daintily.

But in likenesses we come to copying. The meaning of originality becomes as dependent on the sense of the copy, as the idea of copying appears to be upon the sense of an original.

Copy

> as where (before) you were abus'd with diuerse stolne, and surreptitious copies, maimed, and deformed by the frauds and stealthes of iniurious imposters, that expos'd them: euen those, are now offered to your view cur'd, and perfect of their limbes, and all the rest absolute of their numbers, as he conceiued them.
>
> John Heminges and Henry Condell,
> editors of Shakespeare's First Folio

Is copying really possible? A copy will never quite be the same: there is a degradation of the original, different materials, the copy inevitably occupies a different place in space and time. Perhaps it is an unattainable ideal, prompting wistfulness and nostalgia, perhaps it is uncanny – what Hillel Schwartz in *The Culture of the Copy* describes as 'peculiar':

> On the one hand, copying makes us what we are. Our bodies take shape from the transcription of protein templates, our languages from the mimicry of privileged sounds, our crafts from the repetition of prototypes. Cultures cohere in the faithful trans-

mission of rituals and rules of conduct. To copy cell for cell, word for word, image for image, is to make the known world our own.

The peculiarity comes, however, in inverting the expected hierarchy of original over copy. Schwartz is arguing that it is culture that gives rise to nature, and therefore the copy that gives meaning to the original – rather than the other way round. We inhabit a world of copies without fixed points of originality to coordinate the copies:

> Anything unique is at risk of vanishing. . . . An object uncopied is under perpetual siege, valued less for itself than for the struggle to prevent its being copied. The more adept the West has become at the making of copies, the more we have exalted uniqueness. It is within an exuberant world of copies that we arrive at our experience of originality.

The implications of reversing the relationship between original and copy ('originally' devised by Walter Benjamin) are far-reaching. For instance, Judith Butler uses the concept in gender and queer theory to argue that 'gay is to straight *not* as copy is to original, but rather, as copy is to copy. The parodic repetition of "the original" . . . reveals the original to be nothing other than the parody of the *idea* of the original.'

But copying is not merely independent of the concept of originality; it means, as Terence Cave has indicated, both imitation and plenitude: it is the one and the many – replication and profusion. *Copia*, from the Latin for abundance and multitude, riches and military strength and eloquence – and mastery. It gives us 'cornucopia', and the primary dictionary meaning of the English word 'copy' is fullness and plenty, especially in copiousness of language ('copiousness' of course derives from the same root). 'The copye of his loue', then, from Caxton's *Æsop* (1483), means an abundance of love, giving a festive sense of fertility and generation, and since the Middle Ages this meaning has existed alongside the common understanding of copy today – making a transcript or reproduction of an original.

There is, in any case, a possibility of exact copying under different cultural circumstances from our current materialism, especially if we consider the period just prior to the medieval. The notion of the copy was fundamental to Byzantine iconography, in which the archetype, such as a likeness of the Madonna and Child painted from life by St Luke, was copied as much by meditation as by technical expertise, and resulted in a full repetition of the divine likeness, complete with the holy powers of the original. Here it is the likeness rather than the object that is authentic, which is why impressions taken of the likeness were able to fulfil the same sacred role. As St Theodore the Studite phrased it in the ninth century:

> Every artificial image ... exhibits in itself, by way of imitation, the form [*charaktēr*] of its model [*archetupon*] ... the model [is] in the image, the one in the other, except for differences of substance. Hence he who reveres an image surely reveres the person whom the image shows; not the substance of the image. ... Nor does the singleness of this veneration separate the model from the image, since, by virtue of imitation [*mimesis*], the image and the model are one.

The iconic art object is transparent, at one with the archetype; moreover, as Gary Vikan has indicated, there is no hierarchy among icons: no superior or inferior examples, indeed no originals or copies – they are all copies and receive their sacred authority from relics, or in rare cases are relics themselves, such as the relic-icon Shroud of Turin. The point is that both icons and relics (most often bits of saints) are exemplars: such exhortations to lead a godly life do so by offering the acts and deeds of saints as iconic characters to be imitated. Indeed, it is worth noting in passing that as Ruth Padel points out in *Whom Gods Destroy*, *charaktēr* is a word first used in its present sense in tragedy (the genre of covering, costuming, masking) for the external appearance of a person (*persona* itself meant mask), but first described the sign scratched onto a coin to mark its value, its origin, and most importantly whether it was genuine or counterfeit.

But copies-as-exemplars are not confined to early Christian iconography. One of the meanings of 'copy' given by Johnson is 'The autograph; the original; the archetype; that from which any thing is copied', and there is a modern meaning of 'copy' as a text for the press, or as specimen, or 'hard copy' (printed out). So copy also has contemporary senses of reproduction *without* reference to any original, or as the *OED* puts it:

> Originally, the idea of 'transcript' or 'reproduction' was of course present; but in later use an original edition itself consists of so many 'copies'. In *fair copy*, *clean copy* of a writing, the idea of

'transcript' is distinctly present; but it disappears when the original draft is called the *rough* or *foul copy*. The word is much used in bibliography.

These senses come from an earlier usage, in which copy referred both to the reproduction and to what was copied – and at this point, 'copy' and 'original' begin dancing before one's eyes. If Johnson argued in *Rambler* 164 that 'When the original is well chosen and judiciously copied, the imitator often arrives at excellence', the early eighteenth-century portrait artist Jonathan Richardson had already pithily stated that 'He that works by Invention or the Life, endeavouring to Coppy Nature . . . makes an Original'. Evidently more precise terms, like mimesis and imitation, are required – especially in the arts and in art criticism (art criticism was another problem: Richardson also published score-cards showing how to award marks to paintings under various headings and hence determine whether they achieved sublimity or not). But Richardson's early aesthetic of an originality dependent on copying is an interesting gloss on the thirst for realism in painting. Among many similar *trompe l'œil* stories is that of Zeuxis, who painted bunches of grapes that tricked even the birds that fruitlessly pecked at them. Later, artists would learn by carefully copying the work of their predecessors, beginning with pencil copies of engravings and eventually progressing to the execution of exact, formal academy copies in oil – at once training in art practice and cultivating an instinct for the canon.

But do such copies recede from a sense of the truth? Locke, again, in his *Essay on Human Understanding*, warns that in law: 'Though the attested Copy of a Record be good proof, yet the Copy of a Copy never so well attested . . . [and] will not be admitted as a proof in Judicature.' As will become clear in my discussion of mimesis and imitation, there has been a philosophical embargo on copying cultural rather than natural models. The copy of a copy is a threat: it is illegitimate, breeding on itself; it is diabolical, and consequently a copy threatens the sense of the self, somehow unhinges being. This is seen in a gestural or performative sense in the (now obsolete) seventeenth-century phrase 'to turn one's copy', meaning to change one's style or behaviour, to assume another character, to masquerade or make-up (again, there are gender implications here). In other words, copying copies is a form of imposture, of being in someone else's place (which is inevitably the wrong place). 12½in × 15in paper is known as 'bastard' or 'double Copy' – an unintended (?) pun that seems to sum up these problems of primacy rather well. But if anything, copying is rhizomic: spreading in such a way as to repudiate models of 'source' and 'originality', thus introducing more transgressive forms of copying, such as plagiarism.

Plagiarism

> Gross plagiarism may consist with great originality. Sterne was a notorious plagiarist but a true genius.
>
> William Hazlitt, 'On Genius and Common Sense'

Plagiarism is a perversion of theories of origin: it is a narrative of discovery that seeks to disguise its origins and present itself without precedent. In a sense, plagiarism is an absolute veneration of the point of origin – more so than either forgery or counterfeit, which fetishize their supposed point of issue – but in its attentions plagiarism seeks to obliterate its origins entirely by moving them forward to the here and now. The plagiarized text is clearly designed to function under the same cultural laws of authenticity and composition as non-plagiarized texts – which is why it is potentially so subversive. It is like a virus that debilitates culture, a crash that can bankrupt cultural value, and it thrives in the mechanisms of cultural dissemination and reproduction: paper and pen, or printed book. 'Plagiarism', Stewart Home claims, 'is the negative point of a culture that finds its ideological justification in the "unique". . . . The plagiarist . . . recognises the role the media plays [sic] in masking the mechanisms of Power, and actively seeks to disrupt this function.'

Plagiarism is a snare, a trap for the unwary: 'How many be there . . . that, like Plagiaries, make it their trade to hunt and catch men?' A plagiary, from the Latin *plagiarius*, is one who forcefully possesses another, and *plagiarius*, deriving from *plagium*, is a net to entangle game. Plagiaries abduct slaves and steal children, disfiguring them to pass them off as their own; plagiaries are man-stealers and press gangsters; plagiaries are kidnappers, seducers, and of course literary thieves – stealing bodies and, as E. Cobham Brewer points out in his *Dictionary of Phrase and Fable*, 'Martial applies the word to the kidnappers of other men's brains.' They are the despised of literature, but uncanny too. In 1712 John Dennis called a plagiary 'but a scandalous Creature, a sort of spiritual Outlaw', and in 1751 Richard Hurd described them as

> those base and abject spirits, who have not the courage or ability
> to attempt any thing of themselves, and can barely make a shift,
> as a great poet of our own expresses it, *to creep servilely after the*
> *sense of* some other.

Although it is tempting to argue that plagiarism rose as printing technologies became more widespread – and indeed its first English usages are at the end of the sixteenth century – it is a concept evidently much older than the press: in the mid-seventeenth century, Sir Thomas Browne remarked darkly that 'Plagiarie had not its nativitie with printing, but began in times when thefts were difficult' (1646). Browne laments that plagiarism has a long criminal pedigree. It was in fact an ancient crime: the charge was so frequently made by Greek authors that the investigation of plagiarism, such as Macrobius's analysis of Virgil's debt to Homer, was a prominent feature of Alexandrine scholarship. And Anthony Grafton describes Porphyry's account of a dinner party with Nicagoras, Apollonius, Demetrius, and Calietes which degenerates into gossip about plagiarism (Porphyry in fact became a leading authority on forgery and pseudepigraphy, and for his attacks on the Bible was also beaten by the early Christians and had his books burnt). Clearly there was a distinction between plagiarism and conscious imitation or knowing allusion, but even on the stage, dramatists like Plautus and Terence acknowledged their sources in prologues to avoid accusations of plagiarism.

The most influential ancient use of the idea, however, is Horace's version of Aesop's fable of the borrowed plumage of the crow who disguises himself with peacock's feathers (itself, ironically, an adaptation). The image was deployed repeatedly in English criticism, for example by Robert Greene, who described Shakespeare in 1592 as an 'vpstart Crow, beautified with our feathers', by Browne again ('I wish men were not still content to plume themselves with others Feathers'), and later by William Wordsworth, who in 1816 criticized Thomas Gray for writing

> English Verses, as he and other Eton school-Boys wrote Latin;
> filching a phrase now from one author, and now from another . . .

if I were to pluck out of Grays tail all the feathers which, I know, belong to other Birds he would be left very bare indeed.

But if the charge of plagiarism was no more freely bandied about at the beginning of the nineteenth century than at the end of the sixteenth, it was of particular concern to the writers of the Romantic period. The severity of the accusation indicates an anxiety about originality that becomes an obsession, and the concomitant fears that the sacred well of individual genius can be poisoned or simply drawn dry by intruders. This itself can be seen as an ideological consequence of the rise of printing, the mass reproduction of texts, the deluge of copies, and the relative ease of theft. Plagiarism is a threat, a fear, a panic, a plague. And like other aspects of social abnormality, such as illness, madness, and death, it is imagined as despotic – contagious, sickening, unnatural, and terminal; to be guarded against only with the most vigilant surveillance. Hence William Hazlitt declared in a lecture, 'If an author is once detected in borrowing, he will be suspected of plagiarism ever after.' In its demonization, plagiarism has perhaps inhabited some of the space vacated by the word original, by being an irredeemably corrupt original; and as implied by Bunyan (above), plagiarism is a bastard offspring, an illegitimate child that enacts a primal crime: patricide (murdering its origin) followed by incest (breeding monsters out of its own flesh).

So plagiarism was – and undoubtedly still is – the severest charge that one writer could lay on another, and although nobody has yet been sent to prison for it (being at most a civil offence), it is arguably the defining ethical position of the writer, scholar, and critic, and of the profession of the humanities as a whole. Pope's swingeing satire on Grub Street literary life, the *Dunciad Variorum*, is riddled with plagiarists, including 'the phantom, More'. In a footnote on this insubstantial fellow, James Moore Smythe, Pope describes the anatomy of the 'Plagiary' thus:

> His case indeed was like that of a man I have heard of, who as he was sitting in company, perceived his next neighbour had stolen his handkerchief. 'Sir' (said the Thief, finding himself detected) 'do not expose me, I did it for mere want: be so good but to take it privately out of my pocket again, and say nothing.' The honest man did so, but the other cry'd out, 'See Gentlemen!

What a Thief we have among us! Look he is stealing my
handkerchief.'

Simple theft? Plagiarism proves rather unruly and ungovernable, and
yet phantasmic and even uncanny. During the games in book II of
The Dunciad, the Queen of Dulness arranges a booksellers' race for
a poet, a 'tall Nothing' and hence a ghost, whom the unspeakable
Edmund Curll seizes:

> A shapeless shade! It melted from his sight,
> Like forms in clouds, or visions of the night!
> To seize his papers, Curl, was next thy care;
> His papers light, fly diverse, tost in air;
> Songs, sonnets, epigrams the winds uplift,
> And whisk 'em back to Evans, Young, and Swift.

Simple theft again? – except that Pope himself took lines from Evans
for the 1743 *Dunciad* . . . and anyway the whole poem is an exuberant
rewriting of Dryden's *Mac Flecknoe* (which itself derives from Andrew
Marvell's 'Flecknoe'). Moreover, the work and its pseudo-scholarly
apparatus are assembled from layers and layers of parodic allusion,
imitation, and direct quotation. So what qualifies as an echo, an
allusion, a borrowing, a steal, a copy, a plagiarism . . . ? How do we
account for Pope's recycling of the works of others unless we reconsider
the idea of plagiarism (or propose Pope as a pioneering eco-poet,
recycling rubbish writing)? Do we excuse Pope's sophisticated mischief
by claiming that the cultural context of Augustan satire differs from
(by which we really mean, 'is inferior to') Romantic confession?
John Wilmot, Earl of Rochester, composed a cynical carnal love song
virtually entirely from lines taken from three of Francis Quarles's
devotional 'Emblemes'. Shakespeare, of course, lifted whole passages
from Chapman's *Homer*, North's *Plutarch*, Golding's *Ovid*, and Holinshed's *Chronicles*. Is this plagiarism? In music too, J. S. Bach's Goldberg
Variations conclude with a *quodlibet* of two popular songs of the time,
'Long Have I Been Away from Thee' and 'Cabbage and Turnips'.
Is there a cultural law operating that does permit the transformative
use of pre-existent elements? Samuel Taylor Coleridge was a notorious
'borrower' in his lectures on Shakespeare, in his *Biographia Literaria*,
and in many places elsewhere, but it was only after his death that
Thomas De Quincey 'exposed' him as a plagiarist, and the charge

has since tarnished Coleridge's reputation (it has been most recently prosecuted with singular fervour by Norman Fruman). Yet clearly it can be argued in defence of the Sage of Highgate that, copying Pope, he was perhaps imitating, rewriting, twisting, and parodying the language of German metaphysicians: recasting their old words in new, heretical ways – which is precisely what he succeeds in doing.

Bearing these problems in mind, it is worth noting that Johnson's definition of plagiarism is surprisingly mild for a man who lived by the efficacy of his pen, and he also adapts the familiar family image: 'Theft; literary *adoption* of the thoughts or works of another.'* It was, of course, a trap in which he was in frequent danger of being caught, first with the *Dictionary of the English Language* (1755–6) itself, and secondly with his compendious variorum edition of Shakespeare, which reprinted the commentaries of previous editors, most notably those of the ubiquitous Alexander Pope. Lexicographers and editors are plagiarists of a certain kidney: neither dictionary definitions nor illustrative quotations are newly minted for the occasion, but are meticulously gleaned from earlier scholars and writers. It is a form of collaboration with the dead (even if Johnson also had a half-dozen live Scotsmen aiding and abetting him on the enterprise). Hence too, perhaps, Johnson's charitable assessment of plagiarism in *Rambler* 143, in which he decides that a preponderance of parallel images is the only proof of the charge of plagiarism, and that chance is always a sure defence. Yet notwithstanding all this, Johnson was criticized in 1766 in John Bowle's *Reflections on Originality in Authors* for precisely that offence. 'Dictionary' Johnson, author of the homiletic *Rambler* papers and now editor of Shakespeare,

> seems to have made it his study to cull out others sentiments, and to place them in his works as from his own mint. This surely is an odd species of improvement from reading, and savours very little of Invention or Genius; It borders nearly upon, if it is not really plagiarism.

The problem of plagiarism looks insoluble because it is too easy to shuffle the meanings of artistic property, the reasons for that being that while the craft of 'imitation' remained a prevalent poetic technique in the eighteenth century, it was coming under intense pressure from

* My emphasis.

new legal and economic definitions of ownership and was eventually
squeezed into different shapes entirely. Ace literary card sharp of the
period is Laurence Sterne, posthumously attacked for incessantly
plagiarizing Robert Burton's *Anatomy of Melancholy* (1621–51) in his
vivaciously crack-brained novel *Tristram Shandy* (1760–8). At one point
in *Tristram Shandy*, Sterne's narrator himself bemoans the poverty of
literary composition:

> Shall we for ever make new books, as apothecaries make new
> mixtures, by pouring only out of one vessel into another?
> Are we forever to be twisting, and untwisting the same rope
> for ever in the same track – for ever at the same pace?

But of course when one realizes that these very remarks on plagiarism,
along with most of the rest of this chapter, are plagiarized from Burton,
Sterne has succeeded in squaring the circle of plagiarism and inverting
the whole problem into a delightful paradox.* Nevertheless, Sterne's
anticipation of critics who will cry wolf over plagiarism becomes a way
of forecasting an impending crisis of authenticity and the consequent
redefinition of the author: any writerly endeavour that fails to conform
to simplistic notions of single authorship provokes critical suspicion
and even stops being literature. It is at the same time deliciously ironic
that by the time Sterne wrote this, his novel had been both plagiarized
and pirated, and he was signing every copy as it came off the press
as an official endorsement to prevent counterfeits and unauthorized
continuations.†

Pope again had already parodied such an activity in his 'guarantee'
appended to the *Dunciad Variorum*, declaring '*every word, figure, point,
and comma of this impression to be authentic*', and the following chapter
will examine the implications of literary property and copyright laws;
but to understand how plagiarism is deployed to intensify cultural
property laws requires an obliquely historical approach, examining
classical modes of copying (mimesis and thence imitation) to introduce
the relevance of inspiration to the debate about originality and copying,
plagiarism and counterfeiting and forgery. These questionable terms

---

* Burton has, for example, 'As Apothecaries we make new mixtures every day, pour out
of one vessel into another.' Hazlitt, who censured Sterne for plagiarism, shares the
sentiment in *Conversations of James Northcote*.
† The accuracy of other books was attested by authorial signatures, such as John
Thomson's economic calculator, *Tables of Interest* (7th edn, 1804).

are all forms of shorthand for explaining away problems about where meaning comes from, where words, writing, where poetry comes from – and how it is to be assessed and valued. And as will become evident, the strategy by which later writers were able to authenticate the inauthentic was by figuring literary forgers within different theories of the imagination: forgers were dematerialized, they became shadows . . . This is what Jorge Luis Borges hints at in 'Pierre Menard, Author of the *Quixote*', describing a writer, who, emerging from a blur of inscrutable philosophical monographs, determines to write the novel *Don Quixote*:

> He did not want to compose another *Quixote* – which is easy – but the *Quixote itself.* Needless to say, he never contemplated a mechanical transcription of the original; he did not propose to copy. His admirable intention was to produce a few pages which would coincide – word for word and line for line – with those of Miguel de Cervantes.

Copying and inspiration may be superficially indistinguishable in their results, but, as Borges demonstrates, the identical texts will have profoundly different meanings.

Mimesis

Should all mimesis be prohibited?

Plato, *The Republic*

We shall return to the myths of textual illegitimacy shortly. But plagiarism was deployed as a counter to mimesis – it was a wrongful copying against which righteous copying could define itself, and is consequently discussed by 'Longinus' in his treatise *On the Sublime* (*Peri Hypsous*) – a late classical and often half-mystical treatise that had considerable influence on eighteenth-century and Romantic literary criticism.* Longinus argues that *mimesis* (the imitation of writers) is

---

* For example, on Pope, Addison, and Burke. John Hall published the first translation in 1652. The authorship and indeed the very existence of 'Longinus' has been questioned, although I use William Smith's translation of 1739 and consequently attribute the work to Longinus.

one of the characteristics of *noesis*, or the instinctive intellectual conception of the artist, which is a way of approaching the sublime. It is therefore a conscious – and inspirational – participation in a recognized tradition of expression.

> For hence it is, that numbers of Imitators are ravished and transported by a Spirit not their own, like the *Pythian* Priestess, when she approaches the sacred Tripod. There is, if Fame speaks true, a Chasm in the Earth, *from whence exhale divine Evaporations*, which impregnate her on a sudden with the Inspiration of her God, and cause in her the Utterance of Oracles and Predictions. So from the sublime Spirit of the Ancients there arise some fine Effluvia, like Vapours from the sacred Vents, which work themselves insensibly into the Breasts of Imitators, and fill those, who naturally are not of a tow'ring Genius, with the lofty Ideas and Fire of others.

Here, then, we begin to see the braiding together of copying and composing. Longinus gives some examples – such as Herodotus and Plato being 'Homeric' – and carefully distinguishes imitation from plagiarism: 'Nor is such Proceeding to be look'd upon as Plagiarism, but in Methods consistent with the nicest Honour, an Imitation of the finest Pieces, or copying out those bright Originals.' The artist's genius was announced in the ability to copy well. Greek poets and playwrights laid less emphasis on the originality of their material than on the posterity of their style, and (at least until Aristotle) were unwilling to break the flow of their text with references and acknowledgements to their sources. Truth spoke; truth sufficed. And predictably, Longinus's entire treatise is itself an exemplar – a model to be imitated.

Yet as a model to be imitated, and positing that the idea of mimesis has a resonant heritage, Longinus's *Peri Hypsous* is the johnny-come-lately at a perennial classical debate. Mimesis is twice discussed at length by Plato in the *Republic*, when the use of poetry and the arts is considered and then ultimately rejected from the ideal city state, and in consequence it is in the vanguard of Aristotle's counterattack, the *Poetics*. Later, Horace, in *Ars Poetica*, developed mimesis as a looser, more selective, and progressive interest, as did Quintilian in his lively elaboration of the 'hoard' of linguistic *copia* (translation, paraphrase, imitation), *Institutio Oratoria*. Finally, the Neoplatonist Plotinus rehabilitated Plato within an esoteric context and restored art to the ideal society. And although in these texts mimesis is commonly translated as 'imitation', it has persistently been argued that imitation is inadequate for the connotations of mimesis – which cover portrayal, representation, reproduction, copying, aping, and so forth – and that imitation (which in any case has its own technical meaning) also misses certain etymological implications: in an earlier form, mimesis was used in contexts of music and dance, as well as in mime and performance, and in that sense has a connection with the representation of the living body: in other words, it is a shadow.*

Strangely enough, Plato's own initial concerns with mimesis (which he uses in two senses: to represent generally and to impersonate specifically) seem at least partly provoked by another word that it is difficult to translate accurately: the Greek *pseudos* meant not only 'fiction' (stories, tales) but also 'lies' (fraud and deceit, and even the 'noble lie' of politics) – and this effectively sums up our problem in dealing with literature's necessary falsehood. Plato's objections to mimesis are twofold. First, he rejects low art: art should always be aspirational, and artists should only represent the highest qualities: 'the courageous, temperate, holy, free, and the like'; not women quarrelling, cowards, drunks, lunatics, smiths, and oarsmen (!) – 'Nor may they portray the neighing of horses, the bellowing of bulls, the murmur of rivers and roll of the ocean, . . . the noise of wind and hail, or the creaking of wheels, and pulleys . . . [neither] bark like a dog, bleat like a sheep, or crow like a cock. . . .' His lines rather betray his delight in such impersonation, in poetry.

But Plato's second notorious objection constitutes a part of his theory of ideas and is much more telling: 'all poetical representations are ruinous to the understanding of the hearers, unless as an antidote they possess the knowledge of the true nature of the originals.' Artists see only appearances; they are not able to perceive literally or physically the morality or essential truth of a subject. But the true artist 'would be interested in realities and not in mimesis'. In other words, Plato is contrasting the mental world of ideal forms with the lived, material world of shadows that we scramble through, seeing everything as

---

* Mimesis probably derives from the archaic for 'mime'. As I will be discussing imitation in its eighteenth-century context anyway, and in order to preserve the clarity of these definitions, I have adapted some of the translations from the Greek.

though through a glass, darkly. Art can only copy the shadows, those
fleeting copies of the absolute, which can themselves be no more than
mere copies of an artist's perspective. So if we already dwell in a mimetic
world, then art can produce only phantoms (*eidola* – what he calls in
the *Sophist* 'other') – it cannot represent essence. These copies of copies
of copies are therefore thrice removed from reality, and can have no
proper value or justification. And although this argument is primarily
an argument against the visual arts, by marrying the mimesis of painters
with that of poets, all artists are exiled from the state.

Socrates himself refuses to give a definition of mimesis, but notes
that 'the imitator is a long way off the truth' – as is implied in the
well-known simile of the cave. But Plato does admit here that art
might be of some utility. Comparing the plight of humans on earth
to a community of cave-dwellers, perceiving reality merely as a series
of shadows cast on a screen, he argues that true comprehension is akin
to walking out into bright sunshine – a dazzling revelation. So certain
works of art, while inevitably rooted in material phenomena, may help
to acclimatize the mind to the world of perfect knowing, as if by wise
premonitions. In Xenophon's comparable work *Memorabilia*, Socrates
argues that painters should draw from lexicons of idealized forms, but
Plato stresses that poetry and painting can never *mimeisthai* the ideal,
only 'resemble' actual Platonic ideas. This is one of the more obvious
points at which Plotinus offers a divine revision of Platonic philosophy.
In the *Enneads*, he argues that art is not about copying copies, but
constitutes the perception of ideal qualities embodied in an object:

> the arts are not to be slighted on the ground that they create by
> imitation of natural objects; for, to begin with, these natural
> objects are themselves imitations; then, we must recognize that
> they give no bare reproduction of the thing seen but go back
> to the reason-principles from which nature itself derives, and,
> furthermore, that much of their work is all their own; they are
> holders of beauty and add where nature is lacking.

Plotinus's Neoplatonist theory of art had considerable influence
on the Romantics, especially Samuel Taylor Coleridge. But clearly in
Plotinus's reading of Plato, art can aid spiritual growth only when an
absolute distinction is maintained between the real and its imitation –
which is precisely the distinction that is blurred by forgeries and
counterfeits (and is also the distinction that postmodern philosophers

such as Umberto Eco and Jean Baudrillard deplore as being dissolved
by simulation and hyper-realism). Platonically speaking, then, forgery,
and in particular forged poetry, would be the very worst form of
artistic endeavour. A copy of a copy of a copy of a copy masquerading
as absolute knowledge.

This may be what Plato himself is getting at in the unusually
exuberant dialogue *Ion* – which Longinus's *On the Sublime* itself imitates. Plato presents poets as inspired and irrational:

> the composers of lyrical poetry create those admired songs of
> theirs in a state of divine insanity, like the Corybantes, who lose
> all control over their reason in the enthusiasm of the sacred dance;
> and, during this supernatural possession, are excited to the
> rhythm and harmony which they communicate to men. Like
> the Bacchantes, who, when possessed by the God, draw honey
> and milk from the rivers, in which, when they come to their
> senses, they find nothing but simple water.

The idea of possession subsequently developed shares the same anxieties
as those debated in the *Republic*, in which art is imagined to multiply
the copies of copies; but in *Ion* a mood of hilarity prevails. The Muse
is compared to a magnet from which hang her artists (like strings of
compelled paperclips):

> not only does this stone possess the power of attracting iron rings,
> but it can communicate to them the power of attracting other
> rings. . . . And as the power of the stone circulates through all the
> links of this series, and attaches each to each, so the Muse,
> communicating through those whom she has first inspired, to all
> others capable of sharing in the inspiration, the influence of that
> first enthusiasm, creates a chain and a succession.

And so literally, 'Some poets are influenced by [suspended from] one
Muse, some by another; we call them possessed, and this word really
expresses the truth, for they are held.' Although this passage presents
the most ludicrous image – and might anyway be satirical – it nevertheless offers the figure of *furor poeticus* that was recognizable to Plato's
audience, to Longinus, to the Romantics, and still to us today. Indeed,
the significance in *Ion* of specifically Homeric possession will be seen
later in Macpherson's model of Ossianic bardic song, and the notion
of possession *per se* is crucial to William Henry Ireland's account of

Shakespearean inspiration. And anyway Plato is presenting here a much more suggestive model of inspiration than his later suspicion of the mimetic activity implies.

If Plato's student Aristotle only briefly and somewhat reluctantly discusses inspiration, mimesis is central to his thinking and he commences his answer to Plato's objections in the opening chapter of the *Poetics*. For Aristotle, the arts are precisely the *mimetic* arts, and as such they are the defining characteristic of humanity:

> First, there is man's natural propensity, from childhood onwards, to engage in mimetic activity (and this distinguishes man from other creatures, that he is thoroughly mimetic and through mimesis takes his first steps in understanding). Second, there is the pleasure which all men take in mimetic objects.

The latter point, the pleasure that is taken in mimetic objects, is surely crucial – and typically Aristotelian, for it permits men to enjoy the shadow-play in the cave without the imperative of having to get out into the light. Aristotle then proceeds by empirical reasoning. He distinguishes different mimetic objects by their various coordinates: their media, subjects, and various manners of representation, and is initially careful to claim, after Plato, that poets are called poets not because they are indulging in mimesis, but because they are writing in metre. He then makes a case for the craft (*technê*) of art, emphasizing its creativity and aesthetic judgement and its sense of insight: 'The artist is not a copier but a "maker" whose products can be best understood as imitations of human action, character, and emotion.' This is important, as it frees mimesis from Plato's meaning of either general copying or particular impersonation. Indeed, later in the *Poetics*, Aristotle condones the notion of mimetic 'image-making'. Horace too, although taking pleasure in verisimilitude, advised against slavish copying and advocated the poetic purposes of edification and delight, and it is Horatian mimesis that I will discuss below as 'imitation'.

By the English Renaissance, then, mimesis was a rhetorical term for imitation with the meaning of 'representation' in its modern and ideal senses. But, troublingly for Renaissance critical theorists, it also proved susceptible to being hijacked by other words: counterfeit, for instance, lurks here in perpetual ambush. In Henry Peacham's *Garden of Eloquence* (1577), mimesis is defined as 'an imitation of speech whereby the Orator counterfaiteth not onely what one said, but also his utterance, pronunciation, and gesture'. And Sir Philip Sidney defined poetry as 'an art of imitation, for so Aristotle termeth it in the word *Mimesis*, that is to say, a representing, counterfeiting, or figuring forth: to speak metaphorically, a speaking picture, with this end, to teach and delight.' Perhaps most confrontational is George Puttenham, in book III of *The Arte of English Poesie* (1589), describing the specific mimetic device '*Hypotiposis*, or the counterfait representation':

> The matter and occasion leadeth vs many times to describe and set foorth many things, in such sort as it should appeare they were truly before our eyes though they were not present, which to do it requireth cunning: for nothing can be kindly counterfait or represented in his absence, but by great discretion in the doer. And if the things we couet to describe be not naturall or not veritable, than yet the same axeth more cunning to do it, because to faine a thing that neuer was nor is like to be, proceedeth of a greater wit and sharper inuention than to describe things that be true.

While clearly the word counterfeit has a certain positive value here, the whole mimetic enterprise (i.e. poetry) runs very close to the pejorative because 'imitation' always has a sense of the ridiculous about it – it threatens to displace utterly the real by the fake, like some madcap Platonic caper in which everything is exposed as a copy of something else. Furthermore, the cognates of mimesis, like mime and mimicry (the latter admittedly deriving from Latin rather than Greek), illustrate its kinship with the more frivolous examples of culture: mimics, jesters, and buffoons, pantomimes and dumb shows. It is a performing or gestural art, it is an act.*

Romantic poets reacted against this imitative mode of making poetry, the Aristotle–Horace axis of neoclassical correctness in poetry and drama that had held sway for almost three hundred years, by devising a theory of the imagination in which the poet was an inspired medium. They did so by removing the neoclassical emphasis on the

---

* 'Mimic' (1598) in particular emphasizes the imitative as opposed to the real: 'Unlike its approximate synonyms, "counterfeit", "mock", "simulated", etc., the word does not now imply any deceptive intention or affect, being applied primarily to artistic or playful imitation, and usually suggesting that the copy is ludicrously diminutive or insignificant compared with the reality imitated' (*OED*). 'Act', meanwhile, is another problematic word, meaning both to do something and to pretend to do something.

materials and the materiality of poetry to leave the less tangible shadows of an inspirational discourse haunting verse. As a result, the definition of authenticity shifted from craft or *technê* (the productive skill and principles of literary knowledge) to the essential and individual and possessed brilliance of the poet himself (significantly, the poet was rarely herself). And so forgery – which is a heightened and secret form of imitation, of making, of *technê* – appeared to the Romantics less significant as a body of literary work to be read, and more telling as the unrestrained creation of a wayward genius.

Imitation

What oft was thought but ne'er so well exprest.

Alexander Pope, *An Essay on Criticism*

Definitions of 'imitate' (directly from the Latin *imitari*, 'to copy') are a case study in the impossibility of resisting pejorative connotations. Johnson writes a little history of representation by defining 'imitate' as first, 'to copy', and secondly, 'to counterfeit'. In the *OED*, the definitions collapse almost as rapidly, moving from 'after the manner of', to 'copy', thence to 'mimic', 'counterfeit', and 'ape', recalling the Musée Grévin's pun on *singe* (monkey) and *signe* (sign: the hall of this waxwork museum is filled with monkeys staring into mirrors and chattering at masks). Satan is of course the 'Ape of God', and so there is in effect a theological debate enacted here: it is as if words like imitate and copy are under constant siege from the diabolical – overtaken by meanings of falsehood rather than truth. 'Pressed too far, imitation', according to Bernard Dupriez, 'turns into *plagiarism*' (again, plagiarism is determined to be a trap), although Dupriez manages to find a disingenuous escape through literary theory, arguing for 'intertextuality'. One is tempted to propose 'the intertextuality of Christ'. . . .*

Nevertheless, imitation is a – or rather *the* – classical and neoclassical mode of literary composition, and had a huge influence from the Renaissance to the Augustans. Imitation is a liberating writing

---

* The Imitation of Christ has been a spiritual exercise since 1502, but even here the word is almost immediately defined as 'artificiel', 'a thing made to look like something else, which it is not', inevitably 'a counterfeit'.

philosophy because it acknowledges that literature is dependent on what has gone before, which in turn encourages the development of sources and canons (and hence scholarship), and ultimately provides aesthetic criteria. The historical value of a particular literary tradition is implied by its imitability – and the value of a work consists not in what is entirely new in it, but in how it reworks its sources. Or to phrase it slightly differently, the originality of an imitation depends on its degree of inspiration.

So imitation is not mere reproduction, and indeed simple copies are considered dead texts. The imitator (or rather, as Quintilian argues, the emulator) remoulds and reconstitutes and then animates the fragments of earlier writers: animates the discourse with *genius* – breathes into them. These metaphors of life and death and animation are clearly significant because they ultimately provide the terms for understanding originality, inspiration, and authenticity. The intangible effects of genius, the sense that a mind *breathes* through the written word, are effects that cannot be copied because they emanate from an authentic self, indivisible and impossible to replicate. Erasmus in *De duplici copia verborum ac rerum* puts the problem thus: 'If you want to express Cicero totally, you cannot express yourself. If you do not express yourself, your discourse will be a lying mirror.'

There is then a quasi-supernatural presence at work in a masterly text, a spirit that authenticates it. Terence Cave cites the example of Aristotle describing the language of Homer as 'animated' (*anima*: living and breathing and therefore oral, literally 'soul'), itself implicit in Homer's own invocation of 'winged words'. For a text to be authentic on such terms, it must convince the reader of these animated or spirited qualities, inflating itself by using oral or vernacular or extemporized constructions, by haunting itself with metaphysics or the supernatural, or by foregrounding the originality of the character of the poet, which may be authenticated in ways already outlined. Thus inflated, the text is literally *inspired.* And it is also worth noting that the figures, or *topoi*, of imitation and inspiration theory in the Renaissance run the gamut of corporeal and supernatural imagery. In digesting the appetizing concept of 'innutrition' from Quintilian's *Institutio Oratoria,* Joachim Du Bellay in his *Deffence et illustration de la langue Françoyse* (1549) vampirically describes imitation as a cannibalistic recipe: plump and ruddy authors must be 'devoured and, after having been well digested, converted into blood and nourishment' for those lean and hungry imitators in their wake.

Despite the commitment of Renaissance thinkers to theories of imitation, which encouraged confidence among poets and playwrights regarding the sensitivity of their readers and audiences to recognize sources, by the eighteenth century imitation had become more explicit, and was perhaps on its way to being condemned. Certainly something catastrophic happened to the idea between the eighteenth and nine-teenth centuries. The prevalence and popularity of 'verses in imitation of' in the first half of the eighteenth century (like Pope's *Imitations of Horace*) had almost completely vanished within two generations. Romantic poets evidently did not 'imitate', at least they did not imitate very much: Coleridge's verses of 1796 'Imitated from Ossian', Keats's Spenserian imitations, Walter Scott's inclusion of fourteen contem-porary imitations of ancient ballads in the three volumes of *Minstrelsy of the Scottish Border* (including pieces by 'Monk' Lewis, Anna Seward, and himself, 1802–3). Indeed, Coleridge's 'Rime of the Ancient Mariner' and Keats's 'King Stephen' could almost be called imitations. But Pope had imitated everyone and everything: Chaucer, Spenser, Waller, and Cowley, not to mention Horace (explicitly); Homer, Virgil, Spenser, Shakespeare, Milton, and Dryden (implicitly); and dozens of others in passing.

One way of reading this is to appreciate that Pope was engaging in continual and enriching dialogues with earlier poets, and it is worth stressing that imitation was, under the influence of Horace and Quintilian, considered 'a method of translating looser than paraphrase'. Dryden explained, 'In the way of imitation, the translator not only varies from the words and sense, but forsakes them as he sees occasion; and, taking only some general hints from the original runs division on the groundwork.' But there is another, more dismissive way of reading imitations. Edward Young, in *Conjectures on Original Composition* (1759), forced a false distinction between imitation and emulation that distanced Pope's imitative verses from readers oblivious to the traditions in which he was working: 'Imitation is inferiority confessed; Emula-tion is superiority contested, or denied; Imitation is servile, Emulation generous; That fetters, This fires; That may give a name; This, a name immortal.' And henceforth the very range of Pope's 'allusion' became troubling, even alienating, if the artistry of his imitation becomes obscured.

Pope himself offered one arch definition of imitation in the *Dunciad Variorum* in the words of Martinus Scriblerus, his pet pedant, who argues that the poem is a particularly fine example of imitation, which 'appeareth not only by its general structure, but by particular allusions infinite, many whereof have escaped both the commentator and poet himself'. Pope also parodied Longinus's *Peri Hypsous* in *Peri Bathos; or, Of the Art of Sinking in Poetry* (1728, penned at the same time as *The Dunciad*), which includes a chapter 'Of Imitation, and the Manner of Imitating'. In *Peri Bathos*, Pope suggests various hack writers as models of perfection (in fact those very writers pilloried and parodied in *The Dunciad*), and mischievously proposes that '*Imitation* is of two sorts; the first is when we force to our own purposes the Thoughts of others; the second consists in copying the Imperfections or Blemishes of celebrated authors.' In this context *The Dunciad* becomes an epic of true copying, in which the genius of Pope is certified by the rich nap of first-rank poets he knits into the text; moreover, by so skilfully imitating them, Pope ensures that these allusions also act as a prophylactic against his being numbered among the Dunces. It is also worth bearing in mind, however, that attempts to raise a copyright law and control piratical printers were at that time defining literary property rights and so redefining the activities of the writer. The work of the Ancients was, unlike that of the Moderns, common ground where all may graze, but as Henry Fielding argued in *Tom Jones* (1749), to steal from a living author is 'highly criminal and indecent; for this may be strictly stiled defrauding the poor (sometimes perhaps those who are poorer than ourselves) or, to see it under the most opprobrious colours, robbing the spittal.'*

The imitative or allusive mode of a mid-eighteenth-century poet like Thomas Gray, who claimed always to read Spenser before ever sitting down to write verse, was a reaffirmation of Quintilian and Longinan imitation – and therefore he made bold use of figures of wild inspiration such as 'the Bard', as well as deploying historical sources as authenticating devices. But the idea of originality had already drifted too far, had become too secular, too appealing to literary consumers to sustain the imitative mode. As early as 1751 Richard Hurd

---

* It is worth considering in passing whether Fielding was deliberately using a recently coined proverb, 'robbing the spittle [charity hospital]', or slyly alluding to the seventeenth-century poet Francis Quarles, who uses the phrase in *Divine Fancies* (1632).

was uneasy about this. His 'Discourse concerning Poetical Imitation', appended to his edition of Horace, begins:

> All *Poetry*... is, properly, *imitation*... every wondrous *original*... but a *copy*, a transcript from some brighter page of this vast volume of the universe. Thus all is *derived*; all is *unoriginal*.

There is a feeling of desperation as Hurd goes on, attempting a comprehensive defence of imitation and also defending poets against charges of indebtedness, by proposing that the critical term 'invention' be defined precisely as the philosophical term 'imitation'. He claims that imitation or allusion is inevitable, and offers the same nostalgic image of pastoral communality we have just seen above: 'The *objects* of imitation, like the *materials* of human knowledge, are a common stock.' This is evidently not a manifesto for modern, metropolitan poetry.

Hurd's next sally, 'A Letter to Mr. Mason on the Marks of Imitation' (1757), gives quasi-legal rules for the discovery of imitation, which, as Roger Lonsdale has noticed, now leave him disconsolate. Hurd is 'baffled' by the extent of his discoveries of borrowing, and crestfallen at the apparent poverty and second-handedness of the English tradition. Like Gerard Langbaine, however, who endeavoured to distinguish between classical imitation and modern literary theft, Hurd rallies himself with the category of 'learned *Allusion*' – in which thankfully 'even *Shakespear* himself abounds'.

In retrospect, Hurd's apologies for imitation look like a last-ditch stand, as two years later Edward Young published what has become a seminal treatise, *Conjectures on Original Composition*. Imitation is routed: it is at best repetition, at worst plagiarism:

> Originals are, and ought to be, great Favourites, for they are great Benefactors; they extend the Republic of Letters, and add a new province to its dominion: *Imitators* only give us a sort of Duplicates of what we had, possibly much better, before; increasing the mere Drug of books, while all that makes them valuable, *Knowledge* and *Genius*, are at a stand. The pen of an *Original* Writer, like *Armida*'s wand, out of a barren waste calls a blooming spring: Out of that blooming spring an *Imitator* is a transplanter of Laurels, which sometimes die on removal, always languish in a foreign soil.

Indeed Samuel Richardson, to whom Young's *Conjectures* was addressed, had already written *Clarissa* (1747–8), in which the villainous Lovelace's imitative letters – composed by patching together suggestive lines from plays and songs, and dubious argot – not only present him as a voice inauthentic, duplicitous, and dangerous, but are ultimately a sign of his satanic criminality. Gray was sufficiently concerned by this change of mood to acknowledge his sources; still, within a few years his 'learned allusions' were condemned as plagiarism – as were Hurd's – and uncovering anachronistic imitation in antique poetry like that of Ossian and Rowley became a way of detecting plagiarism and proving the verse to be forged.

Walter Scott refused to discuss ballad imitations in *Minstrelsy of the Scottish Border* with the observation, 'I ought in prudence to be silent; least I resemble the dwarf, who brought with him a standard to measure his own stature', and the word continued to lose ground in the nineteenth century. Coleridge, however, wrote well of imitation in *Biographia Literaria* (1817). Contrasting it with waxwork copying, the imitation breathes with its own life: 'imitation, as opposed to copying, consists either in the interfusion of the SAME throughout the radically DIFFERENT, or of the different throughout a base radically the same.' In the same year, Hazlitt proposed that imitation was not a repetition of the same idea, but the suggestion of new ideas.

Both were attempting to move eighteenth-century theories of imitation more into line with transcendental philosophy, but without much effect. The rise of industrial society and commodity culture caused imitations to be contrasted to the genuine or authentic, such as in the composition of manufactured luxury goods, and indeed the composition of fiction: 'Simulative, fictitious, counterfeit.' Even in the eighteenth century, Young (again) had decried imitations as 'a sort of *Manufacture* wrought up by those *Mechanics, Art,* and *Labour,* out of pre-existent materials not their own' and William Cowper had called imitation 'my aversion; it is servile and mechanical'. When Charles Dickens used the word 'imitative' in 1838, it was not to rekindle its literary and artistic force, but to keep it in the marketplace, where it has since denoted a particular bourgeois taste in consumer commodities: repro furniture, fake fur, an imitation fireplace – these are aspirational products, and so imitation ironically retains a degraded connotation of the elusive and intangible qualities that once fired it. But its literary sense has entirely disappeared. It is as if, come the

nineteenth century, imitations posed the same sort of threat to literature that Pope's apocalyptically dull dunces had done a century
before: imitations (implying unoriginality, inauthenticity, plagiarism,
counterfeiting) could drag fiction and tale-telling into a new Pandae-
monium. It was outlawed in aesthetics and rigorously policed in the
economy.

Counterfeit

False as his Gems, and canker'd as his Coins

Alexander Pope, *Dunciad Variorum*

Counterfeit (just one of its *copia* of forms, from *counterfaisance* to
counterfacture) has been haunting my discussion of words like copy
and plagiarism, mimesis and imitation. It creeps in the same sinister
manner as copying, lays the same traps as plagiarism, and exhibits the
same systole and diastole between pejorative and positive meanings as
imitation: the counterfeit is a craft, and like a craft may be an example
of technical expertise, or of cunning. In this it is also, of course, akin
to forgery. Historically, positive and negative uses of counterfeit existed
side by side, but eventually meanings of pretence gained ground, as if
the sign were less concerned with its object, and more and more
interested in itself and how convincingly it performed.

Before we even finish the word, it is enigmatic: the counter-/
contra- stem of counterfeit. Is 'counter-' meant as 'opposite' (opposite-
made?), as 'against' or 'in return' or 'upon', as one half of a binary, or
as an inversion . . . ? The Jesuit poet Gerard Manley Hopkins conjures
this mystery in his poem 'Pied Beauty':

> All things counter, original, spare, strange;
>   Whatever is fickle, freckled (who knows how?)

This is a radical prayer for salvation – 'All things counter, original,
spare, strange' are derangements of divinity; 'Whatever is fickle,
freckled (who knows how?)' is potentially devilish, the devil being
traditionally pied, or clad in motley: a maculate being. 'All things
counter' – like counterfeits – are as dodgy as 'All things . . . original'.

Counterfeit's primary meaning in the dictionary is something made in imitation of, against that which is original or genuine – in other words made in imitation of that which is *not* an imitation (or a counterfeit). Counterfeit, then, is a word that crosses boundaries, that is only half seen. An early example, in Gower's *Confessio Amantis*, shows the invisibility of the counterfeit, and the threat it poses to the real: 'This letter . . . Was counterfet in such a wise, / That no man shulde it apperceive.' It means transformed or disguised or degraded or adulterated ('Saffron is somtyme countrefetyd wyth a thynge that hyght Croco magina . . . the superfluyte of spycery'), and hence spurious or dishonest or deceptive or of course forged, or fictitious. John Wilmot, 2nd Earl of Rochester, disguised himself as 'Alexander Bendo' before presenting himself in the following words, casually swapping the meanings of counterfeit and original:

> If I appear to anyone like a Counterfeit, even for the sake of that, chiefly, ought I to be constru'd a true Man. Who is the Counterfeit's example? His Original, and that which he imploys his Industry, and Pains to Imitate, & Copy.*

Counterfeit also means a more tangible impersonation or impostor – unto the womb, counterfeit children being those fathered in adultery; or unto the grave – as Falstaff has it after he has escaped death at the hands of Douglas by playing dead:

> Counterfeit? I lie, I am no counterfeit: To die, is to be a counterfeit; for he is but the counterfeit of a man, who hath not the life of a man: but to counterfeit dying, when a man thereby liveth, is to be no counterfeit, but the true and perfect image of life indeed.

It also denotes semblance or pretence, and is used for ventriloquy.† And in Milton's *Paradise Lost* it means a false likeness, falsely represented:

> ire, envie and despair,
> Which marred his [Satan's] borrowed visage, and betrayed
> Him [Satan] counterfeit, if any eye beheld.

* Repunctuated.
† For ventriloquy, see Johnson's *Dictionary*: 'There have been some that could counterfeit the distance of voices, which is a secondary object of hearing, in such sort, as when they stand fast by you, you would think the speech came from afar off in a fearful manner.' He cites Bacon's *Natural History*.

To these senses of impersonation there is also a subsidiary meaning of counterfeit, used to describe possession in witchcraft trials, but also enacting the very confusion of possession. 'A possession counterfaited' confounds the understanding, because that word 'counterfeit' works both to indicate the wrongful nature of a devilish possession, while at the same time implying that the possession has, in common with all Satan's blandishments, no substance, no reality.* Satan is of course repeatedly referred to as 'the counterfaiter of God', endlessly deceiving: 'þus sal anticrist þan countrefette þe wondirs of God' (1340), and in Milton's *Paradise Lost*, again he is 'That false Worm, of whomsoever taught / To counterfeit Man's voice.'

Re-enter the Devil, then, on a twisted foot, limping. A seventeenth-century German handbill against the *Kipperer und Wipperer* (coiners and utterers of false coin) shows the Demon of Counterfeit with one foot scaly and taloned and the other a pegleg – except on closer inspection the pegleg is a disguise and a human leg is twisted back behind him. In fact, counterfeit does mean misshapen or deformed, further associating the word with the Devil and other asymmetical beings: 'I am lame, I am crooked, I am balde, I am a counterfeyte', but it also delineates a different sort of trickster. In *Figures in Black*, Skip Gates discusses the 'signifying monkey', a Hermes-like story-teller conjured up in Afro-American myths that capitalizes on the white racist image – blacks as simian, blacks as diabolical – and makes it positive, suggesting a punning playfulness with language, a cavorting trickster. The signifying monkey thus becomes a pivot in traditional Afro-American stories: a character who tells stories to other characters and consequently makes them act in certain ways. But the signifying monkey is more than a practical joker or a liar or indeed a counterfeiter: it is a mediator, through tricks, from another world, and so sometimes the monkey limps. This is what Carlo Ginzburg calls in *Ecstasies* 'asymmetrical deambulation' – the limper, like Loki, exists in different worlds – the divine and the material. Hence the diabolical riddling of the Monkey – and its fraternity with the Western tradition, in which limps and oracles have been pivotal since Greek tragedy and the Book of Revelation.

* Thomas De Quincey in his *Diary* (1803) describes meeting 'a fellow who counterfeited drunkenness or lunacy or idiocy; – I say *counterfeited*, because I am well convinced he was some vile outcast of society.'

The signifying monkey is, then, a metaphor for the act of interpretation, and interpretation that is quotidian and practical, if ludic: 'the trickster's ability [is] to talk with great innuendo, to carp, cajole, needle, and lie' and so forth – including authenticating gestures: 'technique of indirect argument', as Gates puts it. He continues:

> The Afro-American rhetorical strategy of signifying is a rhetorical act that is not engaged in the game of information giving. Signifying turns on the play and chain of signifiers, and not on some supposedly transcendent signified.

Signifying is therefore a way of speaking from the margin: a way of accepting the language of the oppressor but juggling with it, tinkering with it, amplifying its ambiguities, and deconstructing it in order to create a new narrative space. It is imitative but ironical speaking, counter-linguistic. And this, it strikes me, is precisely what those false signs – counterfeits – achieve in breaking the codes of representation, because the trickster is really, of course, analogous to the artist, who is in one sense an endorsed counterfeiter. Sidney remarked that poets are 'representing, counterfeiting, or figuring forth', and Puttenham described a poet as 'both a maker and a counterfaitor' – both early critics incidentally emphasizing then the *technê* of writing. And it transpires that this making or signifying sense of counterfeit is the latter part of an entirely non-pejorative constellation of meanings. Counterfeit could mean sincere and even authentic imitation, entirely without deceit: in Tyndale's Bible, the translator exhorts 'Be ye counterfeters of God' (though he later revised the word to 'followers') – and verily God is a good counterfeiter. The word can mean modelled upon, fashioned, or wrought: durable goods like 'Countrefeit basyns, ewers, hattes, brushes' were properly made, crafted. It was used for true likenesses in painting, a portrait 'counterfeited' the sitter. Finally, as indicated by Sidney and Puttenham, it was a positive literary term – John Lyly described the first part of his prose romance *Euphues* (1578) as his 'first counterfaite'. Yet counterfeit seems to have become sinister as the mirror-image of the word original, and as original became virtuous, so counterfeiting became vicious.

Most germane is the dovetailing of these meanings of counterfeit by the philosopher George Berkeley in his dialogue *Alciphron* (1732). He links 'Fabulous' with 'counterfeit writers'. This may come as no surprise – I have already proposed that forged literature is a realm of fantastic literature – but it requires that we clarify, finally, the meaning of forgery as the word that can best bind the protean problems of representation.

Forgery

> Forger: 1. One who makes or forms. 2. One who counterfeits any thing; a falsifier
>
> Johnson's *Dictionary*

Forgeries are cheats, pretences, cogs. So the daemon Hephaestus limps too. It is Hephaestus who makes tricks, Hephaestus (a.k.a. Vulcan) who forged the armour of Achilles, who fabricated mechanical maidens and animated Pandora and was venerated by craftsmen alongside Prometheus. Pope called him 'the Artist-god'.

Forgery, from the Old French *forgier* and Latin *fabricare* (fabric, fabricate – reminiscent of *texere*, weave, whence 'text') follows a similar pattern to 'counterfeit': it reiterates, mimics, indeed counterfeits the ambiguities of making and copying, of fabrication, of fictions, of poetry (which is from the Greek *poiein*, to make generally, and specifically to compose a literary text), of telling tales and inventing imaginary stories. But forgery is also different – it maintains its sense of creative vivacious trickery, oddly enough its humanism, in areas of deception where counterfeiting has become industrial and dehumanized; in other words, counterfeiting is industrial manufacture, forging is essentially a craft. The meaning of forge as construction has survived in ways that counterfeit has not – presumably because of the forge being persistently used to describe the smithy, blacksmith's hearth, or furnace, and also the attraction of smithying similes. The brain has been called the forge in which the speculations of the understanding are hammered out, likewise the heart has been imagined as a forge where wickedness is wrought, and Christopher Smart extended this to language: 'For my talent is to give an impression upon words by punching, that when the reader casts his eye upon 'em, he takes up the image from the mould which I have made.' Even Chatterton was complimented on his skill in 'melting down the Gold, Silver, and Brass of other Poets in the Crucible of his Brain, and producing from their Mixture a Metal of his own'. Moreover, these forges are not fully automated – they retain a sense of the craft of the hand, and what passes over the palm. Such forges were especially used for coining, and so coins struck are coins forged, and forgers are properly 'makers of money'.* In economic terms, then, true currency is struck, or minted, or specifically *forged*, whereas the counterfeit is the false, corrupt coin. There is a glimpse of Genesis in forgery, whereas the counterfeits, signs on the rampage, are Apocalyptic.

But still the two words are very closely identified. Like counterfeit, forgery means to make something in fraudulent imitation and pass it off as genuine. The forging, counterfeiting, or falsifying of a document (*crimen falsi*) is defined in Blackstone's *Commentaries* (1769) as 'the fraudulent making or alteration of a writing to the prejudice of another man's right', and this legal sense only came into full practice in 1552. But nevertheless, to forge has still maintained its fundamental meaning of making: John Wyclif declared in a sermon that 'Joseph was a forgere of trees, þat is to saie a wriȝte' (*c.*1380).† Like counterfeit, it means to frame or fashion or work, to contrive, devise, or invent. Like counterfeit, forgery has divinity: God, in Wyclif's translation of Ecclesiastes, 'is forgere of alle thingus', and two centuries later the prophet is described as 'forger of dreames' (Douay Bible, 1609: Deuteronomy). Forgery also has devilry – as late as 1685 forgers are described as 'that wicked Herd of perjured Satanists' – though significantly it does not have as much devilry as counterfeit. Like counterfeit too it has literary uses: to coin a word, to invent an imaginary story, which is exactly what poets and novelists and playwrights do – indeed forgery is used for authors or makers. It means to fable – in Chaucer's *Parson's Tale* (1387), 'In which delit they wol forge a long tale'; in Wordsworth's *Prelude* (1805), 'Forgers of lawless tales, we bless you then.' Like counterfeit again, forging is used figuratively for phrases of flattery.

Yet forgery remains in smithying and hammering and beating, and has escaped the exuberant excesses of counterfeit. Forgery is an extreme, but an extreme of invention. In literature, it is not satisfied by staying on the page. It goes beyond the confines of text, beyond the textual

---

* The forge also had curative properties: forge-water, in which heated irons had been cooled, was used as a medicine (1725).
† In Wyclif's translation of Exodus, the Lord asks, 'Who forgide the dowmbe and the deef, the seer and the blynde?'

entirely, into the realms of arts and crafts, performance and posture, fighting and murder – proving, somewhat surprisingly, that there is everything outside of the text.

> What the hammer? What the chain?
> In what furnace was thy brain?
> What the anvil? What dread grasp
> Dare its deadly terrors clasp?
>
> Tiger, tiger, burning bright
> In the forests of the night,
> What immortal hand or eye
> Dare frame thy fearful symmetry?

In William Blake's last revision of this poem (1806), the last line was changed to 'Forged thy fearful symmetry?'

MARVELLOUS

The marvellous fable includes whatever is supernatural, and especially the machines of the gods.

Alexander Pope, Preface to *The Iliad*

In *The Lives of the Artists*, Vasari tells the following story. Michelangelo, in his youth, once carved in marble a life-size figure of a sleeping Cupid. It was a beautiful work, that might have come from the hands of a classical master – indeed it was so remarkable that the Medici prince Pierfrancesco declared, 'If you buried it, I am convinced it would pass as an ancient work.' The Cupid confirmed Michelangelo's genius, but it also pitted Michelangelo's skills against the art market, for Prince Pierfrancesco went on, 'and if you sent it to Rome treated so that it appeared old, you would earn much more than by selling it here'. Having admitted the possible ghostly presence of an historical forgery, Vasari's story suddenly effloresces. In one version, Michelangelo distresses the statue of Cupid simply to show his genius at finishing marble; in another, Baldassare de Milanese buys the piece from Michelangelo, buries it in his vineyard in Rome, and sells it as an antique to Cardinal San Giorgio. There were yet more versions of the story, more owners of the statue, and more rumours. The provenance of the Cupid became impossibly tangled; it has now been lost. Michelangelo, on the other hand, made his reputation with the piece, and was immediately taken to Rome under the patronage of the Cardinal San Giorgio, of all people.

For Vasari, the story exemplifies the genius of Michelangelo, a Renaissance genius who could surpass the ancients. His originality is a way of transcending history (indeed, for Vasari, he is the 'divino' Michelangelo, a new messiah). But was Michelangelo involved in an elaborate hoax to ridicule the cardinal's antiquarian pretensions – a con that rewarded him with a year's patronage? Is this perhaps more a tale of Michelangelo's genius for cupidity, than for a lost Cupid? Is Michelangelo an inspired artist or an imitative craftsman – or for that matter a forger? What, in other words, would happen to Michelangelo today?

The unstable shifts in the meanings of authenticity and artistry make the question unanswerable. Moreover, competing theories of mimesis and imitation, copying and originality, counterfeiting and forging disrupt the narrative itself. The story splits into different versions, as the liar's path forks into the high road of fiction and the low road of forgery. Or rather the case spreads, rhizomically, back over itself, ravelling up the fraying threads of truth and falsehood.

But is there is an answer to the unanswerable question, an apparently final twist in this tale? What *would* happen to Michelangelo today, then? He has been enlisted as an honorary forger, canonized as a sort of patron saint, by none other than Eric Hebborn, maker of 'the finest art fakes of the twentieth century'. Hebborn too knows the story of the lost Cupid, and claims that it went from Duke Valentino into the collection of the Marchioness of Mantua before it disappeared: 'It's thought to be lost,' he said before he died. 'But it isn't. I recognised it because I've studied his sculpture so much. It's now catalogued as ancient Roman marble.' Hebborn knows that forgeries are unending stories, tales that lie awake, plotting, 'and it's a secret between me and Michelangelo'.

The final twist? Not quite: the story is still being told. In 1995, the

'Fifth Avenue Cupid' was sensationally spotted in the French Cultural Delegation, New York, by Kathleen Brandt, Professor of Art History at New York University. She attributed the statue to Michelangelo, as the same lost Cupid. The piece is damaged: its arms have been lost and the legs are snapped off below the knee, and in any case it is at best a poor Michelangelo: immature, disproportionate, and apparently derivative of his teacher, Bertoldo di Giovanni. (This Cupid is also wide awake and reaching for an arrow.) Brandt argues that these flaws tend to challenge the myth of instant genius that Michelangelo cultivated about himself throughout his *Life*, indicating that his artistry developed gradually . . . unless, then again, the 'Fifth Avenue Cupid' is a fake – as James Beck, Professor of Art History at Columbia University, claims. Beck argues that the statue was created to look like a damaged Michelangelo and dates from about 1900 – noting that its legs would be too long if it were restored. Beck, by the way, is also a defender of Michelangelo's instant 'super-creative' genius. And so it goes: artistry and genius are presented as oddly irreconcilable.

As already hinted by way of the above discourse on inspiration and composition, we need to tighten up theories of authorship. But there are problems. The biographies of literary forgers are too bizarrely complex to be guided by a single theory or critical orthodoxy – Chatterton was not alone in living an unbelievable, a fictitious life. Moreover, theories of representation do not account for the persistent literary fascination with forgery, as opposed to critical neglect – except possibly in the case of Borges, who weaves the most intricate fractals of authorship and repetition in stories and essays such as 'Pierre Menard, Author of the *Quixote*' and 'Borges and I'. To take my primary example: Chatterton was virtually deified by the succeeding generation of writers, for whom he acted as a figure of inspiration, and yet his forgeries – or actually any of his 'own' writings – were barely mentioned by those who deified him. For these critics, Chatterton's forged Rowley works were, like his other stuff, either simply not read, or by the same credulous process that mystified the life of the poet they became symbolic emanations of the 'purest' English. This Chatterton-being was not really a forger; he was barely a writer at all: the most authentic body with the most oracular voice had not really delivered outspoken testaments of inauthenticity, but had spoken from outside the usual distinctions of truth and lies.

There is, however, a possible solution to this paradox between the authentic and inspirational poet, and the inauthentic nature of the forged works produced. It may be possible to write a history of forgery that shadows the history of authority and authenticity in art, and Chatterton might be emblematic of this history. In doing so, the profound semantic confusion that arises between the terms associated with forgery (counterfeit, fake, fraud, plagiarism, fabrication, imitation, copy, and so forth) demonstrates the tangled thinking in this field. Chatterton – who trained as a copier, was accused of plagiarism and counterfeiting in the controversy over his Rowley works, was a maker and an imitator – embodies the immediate and passionate contradictions of poetry and forgery, and delivered them to later writers. And Chatterton delivered them – or rather his myth communicated them – under the guise of inspiration.

So it would be good to spend the remainder of this introduction stripping away the mytho-biographical layers to reveal the scene of Chatterton's writing. This enterprise is unfortunately extraordinarily difficult. Borges (after T. S. Eliot) says of Kafka that his precursors are subtly changed by him: what is written of a writer afterwards necessarily causes the revision of what came before. With Chatterton this temporal instability is particularly acute: not only are the posthumous writings about him so voluminous and the myth so insistent that the poetry is all but obliterated, but of course once we recover it, we discover that Chatterton's whole Rowley project was one of rewriting medieval literary history, and hence all history. André Breton once said, 'The work of art is valuable only in so far as it is vibrated by the reflexes of the future.' For a writer like Chatterton, the work is valuable only in so far as it is vibrated by the reflexes of the present masquerading as the prehistory of the future. So at this stage I will take another word, a single mythographic word, 'marvellous', to see where it leads. One day, I hope to be in a position to reread Chatterton's poetry and prose.

❦

Chatterton, we all know, was immortalized by William Wordsworth in the evergreen state of the 'marvellous Boy'. Let us follow this marvel. Marvellous is a good word here, for it is an audacious word, a word that offers a challenge to believe in the extravagantly implausible. Hence, '*The marvellous* is used, in works of criticism,' wrote Samuel Johnson, 'to express any thing exceeding natural power, opposed to *the probable*'; there is also an obsolete usage like 'fabulous', meaning a wonderful story or legend. Furthermore, the marvellous is used of the miraculous or prodigious, and therefore of the supernatural. Indeed, it seems peculiarly – almost *marvellously* – apt for the meteoric career of Chatterton: as dazzling as it was brief, and yet a portent of revolutionary cultural change. Chatterton was indeed, in Johnson's own formulation, a 'wonderful . . . whelp'. 'Marvellous' thus translates into a child prodigy, a sensational poet, a prolific Grub Street hack, an experimental drug user, and an adolescent suicide, all of which Chatterton might have been. But 'marvellous' also raises the banner of forgery – the shadow that hangs over Chatterton's reputation like a nightmare – for it is a word that invites disbelief even as it has done with describing something, and it is furthermore a word that is prey to preposterous inflation: a marvellous is also a fop. More revealingly pejorative associations may accrete in the word: 'marvellous' is a flag of surrender, an admission of expository defeat, a forlorn hope. It marks the boundary of belief, and exiles things like fables, fairies, forgeries, Chatterton himself, to an occult twilight. In other words, Wordsworth's line, which has become such a refrain for Chatterton and Chattertonians, also functions as a repudiation of his powers. To call Chatterton 'marvellous', let alone a 'Boy', is to label him an outsider.

This neglect brews a sort of hectic rage that troubles the Romantic myth. Read on: Wordsworth's next line is 'The sleepless Soul that perished in its pride', a line that makes Wordsworth's project quite clear: he is seeking to finish off Chatterton. The hissing sibilance of 'sleepless Soul', the plosive patter of 'perished . . . pride'; sss, sss . . . purr-purr. 'The sleepless Soul that perished in its pride' is a piece of imitative assonance and sympathetic magic, a binding spell to lay a ghost – a ghost that, precisely, *whispers* and *paces*.

The ghost is still abroad. Wordsworth wrote his lines as a warning to Coleridge, who was quite literally haunted by Chatterton, and Chatterton's realm, half-read, refused by critics, remains in dreams and visions. A recent apparition occurs in Peter Ackroyd's biography of Dickens, during 'A true conversation between imagined selves'. Chatterton's speech has become gnomic, meet for a spirit from the other side who casts such long shadows in the material world:

> I saw poets like craftsmen, like those builders of the great cathedrals. Like the stone masons who worked on the church

beside which I was born. How I longed to have my own signature imprinted on stone rather than upon vellum.

Before Ackroyd's Elysian vision fades, Chatterton's fatally ambiguous state becomes apparent: he realizes that he is 'Neither before nor after –'. As we will see later, this could be the definition of a ghost: neither properly before or after, but both – both prophetic and past. But soft. This is too neat, the edges too sharp. We can recover older, more transient routes.

ANOTHER BODY

> Moving on to relics, we've got shrouds from Turin, wine
> from the wedding at Cana, splinters from the true Cross . . .
> then of course there's all the stuff made by Jesus in his days
> in the carpentry shop. Pipe racks, coffee tables, cake stands,
> book ends, crucifixes, nice cheeseboard, waterproof sandals,
> fruit bowls; oh I haven't finished this one yet.
>
> Baldrick, 'The Archbishop', *The Blackadder*

Forgery, as is becoming clear, could be the critical state *par excellence*. In the next few chapters I will consider forgery as a way of making, that is a practised craft as opposed to a capitalist production, as a form of inspiration, and as the catalyst in intellectual revolutions in history, biography, and authorship. It is a cultural term, an economic term, a legal term; it resides with counterfeiting and plagiarism, with fraud, fake, and fiction, with hoax, pastiche, and imitation – as with literature and poetry. Can we clear any specific semantic space for forgery? Do we care to? Can forgery be defined without a debilitating recourse to words like real, true, or authentic? Certainly I stress that cultural history reveals the shifting contextual patterns that help to determine readings and responses to cases of literary forgery, but the cases are too complex to be guided by single critical theories, such as the economic (which treats literature as capitalist and forgery as criminal), or legal (which likewise seeks to make moral judgements based on authorial intention), or biographical (which might psychoanalyse the condition). What we are reading here is literature and it should be judged on aesthetic terms: whether it be good or bad, influential or indifferent.

As an example, consider the Turin Shroud, which has been – and is now – both authentic and inauthentic. Authenticity does not inhere in the object itself: it has no essence that we can reliably comprehend; rather, it is framed by different contexts or articulated by different discourses that give the object different meanings – indeed they make the same object a different object altogether. The Shroud is not a recent discovery. For at least half a millennium it has been venerated as a relic within the domain of the sacred, and has thereby been assured a certain authenticity in its status as a witness to the Crucifixion. Relics have for centuries come with certificates of authenticity under-written by the whole government of the Catholic Church, and so the Shroud's authenticity is validated by ecclesiastical law, and manifested in the restricted access allowed to it. It is worth noting, however, that the Shroud's historical provenance accounts for only 500 of the past 2,000 years, and that in 1359 Bishop Henri de Poitiers's report to the Pope condemned the relic as a forgery, quoted a confession extracted from the artist, and elicited the declaration by Clement VII that henceforth it was only to be exhibited as a secular work of art.

The greatest art faker of the twentieth century, Eric Hebborn, has discussed the difficulties in defining 'fake' to the point at which, like here, it becomes an unstable or slippery term:

> when we ask, what is a fake drawing or painting, we are assuming
> that drawings and paintings can be fake. Should this assumption
> be false then our question may be dismissed, never to be seriously
> posed again. But can drawings and paintings be fake? Surprisingly,
> the answer is no.

Hebborn's point, like that of E. H. Gombrich's comment in *Art and Illusion* that only statements and not pictures can be 'true' or 'false', is that 'it is the labelling, and only the labelling, of a picture which can be false, and contrary to popular belief there is not and can never be a false painting or drawing, or for that matter any other work of art'. One is reminded of John Berger's examples in *Ways of Seeing* of how a bit of writing, such as 'This is the last picture that Van Gogh painted

before he killed himself', will irrevocably alter the impact of a work.*
Similarly, an authoritative attribution, 'Leonardo da Vinci (1452–1519)',
or perhaps better still, a price tag, '£38m' – as opposed to the dismissive comment, 'Twentieth-century fake' – will help to determine the
response to the work. Behind the money there is also a more profound
point regarding the nature of representation: St Augustine asks *unde
vera pictura esset, si falsus equus non esset?* 'How could it be a true
picture, unless it were a false horse?'

The point is that when these contexts change, whether gradually
through time, such as in an increasingly secularized society that subor-
dinates the church to science and technology, or suddenly and
catastrophically, such as by forensic analysis like carbon-dating, then
the object's signification is completely changed. Although the object
does not alter in its physical composition and in fact remains somewhat
incurious to revaluations of itself, it does keep metamorphosing. The
Sudarium Taurinensis ('sweat-cloth of Turin') has been treated as the
2,000-year-old winding sheet of Jesus, a medieval forgery, the veil of
St Veronica, the first three-dimensional photograph (a self-portrait
of Leonardo, of course), the after-image of either a crusader or a Jew
crucified in mockery of Christ, and the blasphemous idol of the
Knights Templar. And the Shroud is now all of these true things,
and simultaneously all of the false as well; historical and prophetic,
transcending human explanatory logic – and a self-evident tourist
attraction. Even since the Carbon-14 dating of the Shroud has con-
signed it to 1260–1390, sindonologists have continued to weave ever
more intricate arguments proving its authenticity – from the scientific
adviser to the Vatican, Professor Luigi Gonella, who declared that 'The
tests were not commissioned by the Church and we are not bound by
the results', to Ian Wilson, who argues that a 'bioplastic coating' on the
Shroud has caused its radiocarbon readings to be over 1,000 years out.
The Shroud has since been exhibited again.

One could continue ravelling up this cat's cradle of claim and
counter-claim, but it is worth pointing out how attention continues
to focus on the iconic object: there is little analysis by sindonologists
of the role of the artist or of artistic intentions. Perhaps this goes

---

* Chatterton's 'Excelente Balade' is likewise read as evidence of a pre-suicidal state of
mind; in fact, it was probably composed twelve months before he arrived in London and
only prepared for publication there.

without saying: if the Shroud is genuine, there is no author except God, who authored the piece in the same way that He authored the world – or perhaps, like some theories of the camera, it is a reproduction without human agency – and a very wraith-like and intangible reproduction at that. Roland Barthes for one has remarked on this Shroud-like quality of the camera: 'Photography has something to do with resurrection: might we not say of it what the Byzantines said of the image of Christ which impregnated St. Veronica's napkin: that it was not made by the hand of man, *acheiropoietos*.'* If the Shroud is forged, on the other hand, then it was not properly an author but a forger with criminal intentions who fabricated the object. But if the Shroud was made by the equally iconic Leonardo, then he is a self-evident genius, the proto-typical Renaissance Man; and clearly only a genius who had already invented helicopters, submarines, and bicycles could take a photograph of himself in the Renaissance. So Pierre Barbet has declared: 'If this be the work of a forger, he must have been a super-genius as an anatomist, a physiologist and an artist, a genius of such unexcelled quality that he must have been made to order.' There is an alarming imbalance here: why are the creative powers of the forger not straightforwardly ranked with those of the genius or with God? I will be arguing in this book that in fact they often are – but in ways that are usually very well disguised. Forged work has not been treated with the respect bestowed upon a Leonardo because in the early nineteenth century authenticity became so crucial to Romantic aesthetics that it profoundly redrew the map of literary culture and we are still living with its assumptions today, particularly in the ways in which we consider the author and issues of authorship.

The example of the Turin Shroud also suggests a more basic problem posed by forgeries: forgeries challenge the ground on which one comes to a work, they upset canons, queer the pitch. In the case of the Vinland Map (the 1440 map showing the Americas fifty years before Columbus's voyage), the historical identity and therefore validity of the United States is in question. And in less than fifty years the map has been respectively proved authentic, faked, and now seems to be being rehabilitated again. George Painter argues of the map that

---

* Barthes is probably thinking here of the Mandilion of Edessa, a cloth showing Christ's face that supposedly contributed to the conversion of King Abgar and was venerated in Asia Minor until it disappeared in 1204.

'Humanism appealed in its own bankruptcy to science which gave the right answers to the wrong questions': there have been disputes over the efficacy of scientific tests, further forensic evidence based around matching-up worm-holes in the map's leaves and boards, and a revision of historical understanding – all of which makes the authenticity of the map more plausible. This is E. D. Hirsch's point in *The Aims of Interpretation*. He argues that the first and all-important step in interpretation constitutes the actual validation of criticism – 'How do I know that I'm reading this correctly?':

> What Heidegger called the priority of pre-understanding is described by experimental psychologists as the primacy of the schema; by Gombrich, in art history, as the primacy of the genre; by cognitive theorists (particularly those concerned with scientific knowledge) as the primacy of the hypothesis. . . . For that which we are understanding is itself a hypothesis constructed by ourselves, a schema, or genre, or type which provokes expectations that are confirmed by our linguistic experience, or when they are not confirmed, cause us to adjust our hypothesis or schema.

The forged work is only acceptable and therefore conventionally readable, then, when its pre-condition is met and it is recognized as a 'forgery' – at which point it must stop, in some way, being a 'forgery' – or, for that matter, being a conventional work of art. Indeed, Hirsch's comment does imply why undeclared forgeries might be so alarming to readers: forgeries refuse this priority of pre-understanding or primacy of genre and so put the reader on his or her mettle – or in the same sort of hopeless condition in which it becomes quite possible to mistake a shopping list for an Imagist poem. And in the same way it seems that in contemporary art, as the art becomes less easy to recognize, the claims of authenticity become more crucial.

In any case, forgeries are generally ignored by critics and not often considered worthy of literary anthologies or art shows. A reason for this is suggested by a critical tempest in a teapot some years ago. Raymond Picard denounced Roland Barthes's work in *Nouvelle Critique ou nouvelle imposture* (1965), to which Barthes responded in *Critique et vérité* (1966). At one point he draws an analogy between criticism's rejection of the avant-garde, and the exclusion from culture of that which it considers fraudulent. Both transgressions offend critical taboos, and Barthes analyses Picard's escalating language to argue that a form of criticism based on verisimilitude is very fond of 'evident truths':

> These evident truths are, however, essentially normative. By a habitual process of confused logic, the unbelievable proceeds from the forbidden, that is to say from the dangerous: disagreements become divergences, divergences become errors, errors become sins, sins become illnesses, illnesses become monstrosities. As this normative system is very narrow, a mere nothing can go outside it: rules appear, perceptible at those limits of verisimilitude which one cannot transgress without coming up against a sort of critical *anti-nature* and falling into what is then called 'teratology' [which is a marvellous tale of prodigies or freaks].

Criticism's presumptions also become clear, I would venture to add, when it discovers an apparent forgery: this is a supposed transgression against its rules; it acts with exaggerated astonishment and claims that all deviations from its codes are alarming, monstrous, pathological – and precisely not literary. It is a rather ironical footnote that Alan Sokal and Jean Bricmont's tedious rehash of Picard's position in *Impostures intellectuelles* (1997) begins with the tale of an imposture by Sokal, who submitted a piece of gibberish to a theoretical journal and had the thing accepted. The same mechanism is evident: the imposition of normative language (in this case scientific language), the refusal to allow critical boundaries to be transgressed, and the ensuing assertion that theory is fraudulent. It is worth adding that in this critical theatre, theory, or avant-garde criticism, is considered fraudulent in the wrong way, whereas hoaxes perpetrated by Alan Sokal are proposed as fraudulent in some sort of right way because they appear to expose charlatanism. In other words, Sokal's proposition that one does not approach a theoretical journal with any pre-condition but that it is a hatful of frauds becomes self-fulfilling when he himself submits spoof articles.* The difference between Sokal and the forgers I will be examining in this book is that the text of the hoaxer or the prankster is a like a time-bomb: the text has some inbuilt feature that will cause it to self-destruct. This may be in the form of a jolly funny name ('Batson D. Sealing', 'A. R. de T.', 'Nat Tate'), deliberate error (Sokal's use of

---

* Some intellectual renegades have been approvingly citing Sokal's 'Transgressing the Boundaries: Towards a Transformative Hermeneutics of Quantum Gravity', *Social Text* 46/47 (1996), 217–52.

physics), something more spectacular like Tom Keating painting in white lead a message on the canvas that would show irrefutably under X-ray – like the word 'fake', or simply a bathetic admission of culpability. In these cases, the work is unfinished until it has been exposed: its coda is a narrative of revelation and the most intentional element in the work is its creator's repudiation of it. Hoaxes are intellectual exercises designed to show the mastery of the hoaxer over the hoaxed; the forged work, however, maintains its integrity and is not designed to implode. It is more seductive than that.

In discussing literary forgery, however, I deliberately avoid such an approach, arguing that authorial intention becomes wholly irrelevant, and that a fruitful reading of forged texts sidesteps the more legal elements of intention: of 'malice aforethought', if you like. In any case, it is a common defence by art forgers that they never *intended* to deceive: they merely painted; the signatures were added later by dealers or restorers or other forgers, the forgery that arose was not a deliberate act – as the following and doubtless entirely true story about Eric Hebborn's apprenticeship as a 'restorer' shows.

Hebborn remembers that an aristocratic picture dealer whose 'whole being contrived to suggest a fashionable survival from the late eighteenth century' came one day into the Haunch of Venison Yard studio. He was an expert on late eighteenth-century English portraits.

> The canvas under his arm was not, however, a portrait, a landscape, a still-life, or for that matter anything else – it was completely blank. Nor did the blank canvas belong to England or even the eighteenth century. It had an original Dutch seventeenth-century stretcher, a Dutch seventeenth-century canvas, and a Dutch seventeenth-century ground. All it lacked was a Dutch seventeenth-century picture to make it worth a small fortune.

Hebborn notes ruefully that he appeared to be the only one to notice the want of a picture, and that negotiations continued as normal:

> 'Aczel, old boy, I've made an exciting discovery, what do you think of this Vandevelde?'
>
> 'Very interesting. Very interesting indeed. Looks like a job for Mr Hebborn here. What do you say, Eric?'

> 'Uhm, very, uhm, interesting. What did you say it was, Vanden what?'
>
> 'It, Eric, is a *Vandevelde*, and a very fine one I should say, wouldn't you.' He addressed the dealer.
>
> 'Not too fine, not too fine. Something for the small collector I imagine. After all it needs fairly extensive restoration . . .'*

Hebborn (with assistance from others in the studio) produced a Vande-velde pastiche, signed it, distressed it, and was subsequently instructed to 'add the highly important, but also highly improbable attribution to Jan Brueghel' which was painted over the name 'Vandevelde' which Hebborn had been instructed to 'discover' on the canvas earlier (thus do forgers lay traps and plots, weave narratives). The doubly fake signature 'Jan Brueghel' was a double bluff to ensure that the 'Vande-velde' attribution would be accepted.

In this episode, the idea of intention becomes refracted (literally, *bent*) through a ludicrous game or surreal performance, and inevitably it does become irrelevant. What is the 'intention' here? To paint a ship accurately? To paint a Vandevelde? To explore certain colour effects using a seventeenth-century palette? To make money? To express one-self? Hebborn complains that he was not allowed to paint the entire picture – 'I was enjoying the work and looked upon the Vandevelde as my creation' – and so another restorer painted certain passages to prevent a single style being impressed upon it too deeply. And where is that 'Vandevelde' now? Hanging in an apartment on Fifth Avenue . . . ? In forgery, economic and criminal intentions have achieved such complete supremacy over aesthetic and textual concerns that the work of art is no longer a work of art but a piece of evidence – unless it remains undisclosed, in which case it can function with the freedom of an objet d'art. As with the Turin Shroud, a succession of shifting discourses can magic entire objects into something else.

Finally, then, to return to literary forgery. Some of these issues in theorizing forgery through authorship can best be demonstrated through examples of critical approaches to the charge that Thomas Chatterton was a forger. The first response is (and indeed was) flatly denying that Chatterton was a forger at all and to insist that all the

---

* A worthless seventeenth-century Dutch painting had presumably been stripped away to leave the ground which, importantly, maintained its original and authenticating surface crackle.

texts are authentic. This bracing argument has been comprehensively demolished by medieval scholars. So how does scholarship *prove* anything? By weight of comparable evidence: by building an archive and measuring likenesses and differences, by developing a taxonomy – indeed by all those Renaissance techniques based on a positive understanding of originality. In any case, however, the argument in question stalls the myth of Chatterton: he becomes an oddball who discovered medieval verse rather than the writer who actually composed it. The opposite, equally destructive argument, is to condemn the forger as a criminal and refuse to treat the works as literature at all; proposing instead a legal or psychological profile of the felon, whose malignant motives become far more important than the work itself, which is reduced to forensic evidence: Exhibit A. Convicted literary forgers are expunged from the canon, and their work enters an anecdotal category outside literature, where they are regarded as mere cultural curiosities.

This critical approach, fuelled by a legal rhetoric, exposes or perhaps 'outs' forgeries. The activity tends to aggrandize the critic, who becomes the privileged adjudicator of moral and cultural values and a connoisseur of artistic truth. Indeed the arbitrary connoisseurship of the good 'eye' or 'ear' finds itself in an unlikely partnership with meticulous historical research in order to establish the precise material status of the work under authentication: what is the manuscript's provenance or the painting's history of ownership? Can it be traced to a study or studio? Is its existence corroborated by letters, receipts, or other archival documents? Are paper, ink, paint, all correct? Does it have a signature? Indeed, it is worth noting here the implicit relationship between author, authority, and authenticity.*

Such a reading of the material production of a work, and the ideology of bourgeois connoisseurship that it generates, clearly designates forgery as a potentially subversive, even revolutionary activity. Forgery is taken as a straightforward attack on capitalist aesthetic values, otherwise there would not be dozens of scholars confirming the material progress of paintings and manuscripts through history: the

---

* The word 'author' (medieval *auctor*) is derived from a constellation of Latin verbs and the Greek noun *autentim*, meaning authority, which became the Latin *auctoritas*, used by the early Church to indicate God as the authoritative origin and hence justifying His entitlement to worship. The associated verbs are *agere* (to act or perform), *augere* (to grow), *auieo* (to tie).

activity of these scholars is precisely to prevent forgeries getting into galleries and libraries, or going to sale and messing up the market – one important reason why commercial interests are permitted to sit in judgement over definitions of authenticity. But forgery also mimics the production of authenticity and like a virus, it exposes an artistic aura as a fallacious illusion. On a more positive note, the fabrication of authenticity in forging provenance, ownership history, supporting texts like receipts, paper, ink, paint, signature, and so forth allows the forger to become an artist of more than mere text or image, and also to efface himself entirely from the work. In this case, forgery becomes an imaginative production of the past that rests only ironically on material evidence, and which shows the forger as a story-teller *par excellence*. The forger is an artist of more than mere texts or images – the forger is an artist of the hybrid.*

Indeed, the concern for authenticity over the past few years has advanced critical disinterestedness into the realms of empirical forensic science, with some interesting results: stylometry (the computerized analysis or 'fingerprinting' of literary style) has proved for the time being that Thomas Middleton revised our text of what we have been calling Shakespeare's *Macbeth*. Dozens of Rembrandts (including one purchased for the National Gallery by Henry Moore) have recently been reattributed to his workshop or pupils. In such cases, issues of authenticity take on the character of a war of attrition. Do we really want to have *Macbeth* decommissioned from the battery of great Shakespeare tragedies? The point being that Shakespeare, that poet with barely any biography at all, is less an author than an 'author-function': to put it crudely, he is a trademark, a franchise under which *Macbeth* has, for almost 400 years, been licensed. The stage history of *Macbeth* is Shakespearean, as is its place in the repertoire, its printing history, its critical tradition, its cultural and educational status. Simply by keeping such good company it has been canonized, and also reciprocally influenced what is held to be 'Shakespearean'.

To counter this, the more sophisticated liberal critic might then defend forgery as an historical concept, claiming that there are no absolute standards of authenticity in culture, that boundaries between artworks and faking are in constant flux and are therefore unreliable.

---

* For example, the Vermeer forger Han van Meegeren has been considered as brilliant a chemist as he was an artist (although I think his 'Vermeers' are ridiculously overrated).

Like the ebb and flow of the sea upon the seashore, the secret ministry of forgeries has helped to create the body and practices of English literature: they have determined the canon, defined the idea of the poet, and influenced national identity. This admirably relativistic argument is useful because it reminds us of the necessity for theories of authorship and genre – just before it dissolves all aesthetic and cultural history into uncertainty. The western canon is constructed from named writers producing œuvres of works characteristic of themselves, their genres, and their period, and so recognition, inherently conservative, becomes a form of critical training: one checks up on the artist or author before making a critical decision.

Variations on this approach could argue, say, that exposed forgeries are peepholes into the history of taste, or even into the history of truth and falsehood. But society is reluctant to allow that truth might merely be an ideological special effect, and so fixes it as an abstract ideal, outside history. This is why criticism is then compelled to condemn forgeries. Life is true, and art is all illusion: falsehoods, lies. This has certainly worried cultural commentators for centuries. Bacon called poetry 'nothing else but *feigned history*' – drawing attention in 1605 to the inherent falsity of literature. In *A Defence of Poetry*, Sidney defended poets against this Platonic condemnation, that it is 'the mother of lies' by declaring: 'A Poet never lyeth because he never affirmeth.'* And so a secondary system has been formulated, in which art is identified with the artist and offered as at some level truthful, to be contrasted with forgeries (lies, impersonation). The work of art takes on some of the transcendent lustre of truth, while the definition of forgery is left fugitive. But forged works are extreme manifestations of the accepted techniques of fiction – extreme to the point of being unacceptable, and they mark the limits of literature. All poets are liars; some are better liars than others; those who lie with most effrontery are called forgers.

This is how forgeries break the unwritten laws of criticism. Literary analysis is not like analysis in other academic disciplines, because of the characteristic difference between the humanities and the physical sciences: criticism lacks what Geoffrey Strickland calls a 'method' to

---

*   It is a common Renaissance critique, based partly on the difficulty of reconciling quotidian literature with a theory of originality, that poets are liars. In his essay on verisimilitude, the structuralist critic Tzvetan Todorov also accused poets of lying.

which one could attribute a 'result' – except, of course, in that persistent exception forgery. In other words, forgery recasts criticism as a demonstrable and closed discourse, rather than as an open one. It also makes profound disagreement possible – even likely – which is a rather rare condition in criticism.

So, how does one define forgery without referring to authenticity? Forgery, I have shown, is a historical concept, and the story of forgery reveals it to be an art of making, a pre-industrial literary craft or *technê* rather than a legal or economic cultural practice. It is furthermore often a craft of the raw material (the manuscript) rather than the production of a commodity (the printed book). And forgery can also produce something that in a sense works, at least as far as literature itself actually 'works'. Twentieth-century notions of authenticity are predicated then on the Romantic reception of forgers, a reception that dematerialized them through a model of inspiration. This elevated the inspired art of the mind (the immaterial) over the physical craft of the hand (imitating verse), and set the terms of inauthenticity, such as forge, counterfeit, and plagiarize, against each other.

Thomas Chatterton was foremost a *forger* (I now use the word advisedly) – not a mere poet. The posthumous debate over his fifteenth-century works that took place between 1777 and 1782 – known as the Rowley Controversy – demonstrates how forgery was ultimately defined not as an issue of the law or economics, nor even of the intellect or the imagination, but as literary manual labour. Craft was downgraded to make the creative original pre-eminent – and this is seen too in the shift in the definition of 'genius' from the Augustan to the Romantic. Literature therefore became a system of managing the body, of regulating the work of the hand against that of the head. The expenditure of the body is assessed, and the productions of the hand are treated with scepticism or distrust (a point I will be developing ultimately with reference to Charles Dickens). Forgery rebels against such literary management and regulation – breathing new spirit into another body of literature.

II. VILLAIN

... if ever I should be brought to the gallows for forgery ...

Tobias Smollett, Roderick Random

Forger Rodney Amos was arrested in Indianapolis after trying to pay a taxi driver with a fifty million dollar bill.

The Week, 10 July 1999

The value of money has been settled by general consent to express our wants and our property, as letters were invented to express our ideas; and both these institutions, by giving more active energy to the powers and passions of human nature, have contributed to multiply the objects they were designed to represent.

Edward Gibbon

The execution of John Prince, for forgery, at the 'triple tree' gallows, Tyburn:

> On the morning of execution, when put in the cart, he appeared intent on his book, and regardless of any thing that passed around him ... When brought to the tree, he seemed calm and chearful; and owned that he was very easy. And being asked, whether he now acknowledged the justice of his sentence? he answered, there was no fraud intended, nor forgery committed; but as his king and country had found him guilty, he submitted ... The usual proper devotions being performed, in which he joined and also the surrounding people, he looked round with a calm countenance, but seemed to want words; he then said. 'The peace of God

be with you all; I wish you more grace than I have had, and not to come to this sad end which *I have brought myself to.*' Then having received the last benediction, he quietly resigned his life and suffered his sentence.

John Prince was a country lad who had gone to seek his fortune in London. He worked as a footman and porter to a print dealer, where he unaccountably made enough money to set up business as a draper, and then equally unaccountably had sufficient fortune to buy a mill in Surrey for dealing corn to the City. It was there, however, that his unaccountable successes were in part accounted for as the profits of petty but sustained larceny: he had been '*so and so in London*', his erstwhile business partners muttered, 'and was now come down to cheat *the country*'.

John Prince sold up and returned to London as a dodgy property speculator, now more blatantly involved in sundry frauds and forgeries, in particular passing counterfeit securities to take possession of effects and estates. It may have been crooked practice, but it was also good business – and like many sharp operators since, Prince seemed blind to any illegality. He maintained that all his clients were eventually paid, and anyway he'd never been caught misbehaving. All that changed on 13 September 1763, however, when Prince was arrested for obtaining by false pretences a parcel of silk hose – about £13 worth. He made energetic claims that he was simply the hosier's debtor, and 'he had no right to consider me as a thief'; nevertheless, Prince was remanded in custody by the magistrate, and ordered to return to court two days later.

The magistrate who had remanded him was the famous Sir John Fielding, half-brother to the novelist Henry Fielding, and stone-blind to boot. Appropriately perhaps, things now took a novelistic turn: as one contemporary observed, John Prince's affairs were like a mine ready to be sprung, and ready to bury the miner in the ruins. A man named Robert Mackoun, who was by chance reading a newspaper in a coffeehouse, was drawn to the report of Prince's forthcoming hearing. Robert Mackoun had been trying, without success, to cash a bill of exchange given to him by Prince as part of a property deal: to be precise, as a £100 deposit for a country estate at Long Ford, Middlesex. But Mackoun now suspected the bill to be forged, and so he attended the hearing and brought the bill with him.

When the case reopened, then, Sir John was presented with another, much more serious prosecution against Prince. Prince attempted to talk his way out of this predicament too. The bill was signed by Bricklen & Co., whom he claimed were brandy merchants; then he changed his story and said that Bricklen was in fact an outlawed liquor smuggler – although his credit money was still sound. 'It is no forgery,' declared Prince to the blind Justice of the Peace, 'but a good bill, and would have been paid had it been demanded when due; but it was never demanded.' Of course, one of the reasons it was never demanded was because Bricklen & Co. could never be found, whereupon Prince argued that Bricklen had by now gone to Yorkshire.

Sir John, somewhat exasperated by the loquacious evasiveness of Prince, gave him nine days to contact the elusive Bricklen, and then cross-examined Mr Orcherton, an innkeeper who had countersigned the suspect bill. It soon became clear that Orcherton, a one-time crony of Prince's, had since turned his coat against him – indeed, Prince seems to have made a habit of alienating business partners. He now laid open all of Prince's frauds. Orcherton had countersigned Prince's forged bills with his own real name; these bills were to raise money for Prince to buy Orcherton's house, which would then be remortgaged to honour the bills of exchange that were banked – although many would not be called, perhaps ever. It was a subtle and ingenious fraud, based on the observation that the economy ran through keeping confidence in paper money and postponing debt, meaning that bills of exchange tended to circulate in the economy like notes, rather than being instantly cashed into hard currency. Consequently, it was at the ambiguous point between *promising to pay* and actually *paying* that buccaneers of the alternative economy could thrive. Forging false names such as 'Bricklen & Co.' to the bonds was the only thing that made the project demonstrably illegal.

On hearing Orcherton's damning testimony, Prince began quarrelling with him, and Orcherton said that as he had gone bankrupt with the scheme, and was moreover now likely to go to prison, he would be very satisfied to see Prince hanged – to which Prince swiftly appealed that this was sufficient grounds to invalidate Orcherton's evidence. The truculent Prince was then searched, however, and a paper 'teeming with secret practices and dark deeds' was found upon him – a document that tended to confirm Orcherton's evidence.

Prince's excuses were running thin. At his next appearance in court, no Bricklen & Co. having been traced, Prince was now remanded to the infamous Newgate Gaol. His health declined, he caught prison fever and looked unlikely to be well enough to be tried, but in January tried he was, and, there being still found no hide nor hair of a Mr Bricklen, John Prince was found guilty of forgery. He absolved himself by saying mysteriously, 'I was unfortunately connected with a set of bad people, and had but a *light character,* and it was determined that some one must die, and I *am singled out to fall a sacrifice.*'

The case of John Prince exemplifies a number of characteristics of eighteenth-century forgery trials: the aspiring social ambitions of the lower middle-class, the white-collar crime that leaves almost no trace, the subverting of property, even the spectral spirit merchant; then the performance in court, the weight given to varieties of textual evidence, the refusal to accept intention, the severity of the sentence, the politeness of the execution, and even Prince reading a book in the fatal cart and the enigmatic remark that this is a martyrdom of sorts – all these features have literary implications that will be unwound in the following pages.

But the case reminds us primarily that forgery, counterfeiting, plagiarism even, are legal terms. The last chapter outlined the cultural ambiguities of these words throughout history, and proposed that a counterfeit should properly be considered as a facsimile copy without a necessary source, a plagiarism as a facsimile copy mistaken for an original, and a forgery as an original work within an unoriginal, or rather a pre-existent, context. These distinctions are borne out by examining the legal uses of the words in the eighteenth century, but culturally these words were actually only ever quasi-legal. No one was ever imprisoned, let alone hanged, for purely *literary* misdemeanours, which were ethical issues – despite often being described in heavily loaded terms: 'highly criminal', as the magistrate Henry Fielding described plagiarism. Of course, plagiarism was not at all 'highly criminal', and indeed if Alexander Pope, for instance, had really thought that plagiarism was comparable even to the theft of a handkerchief, he would have been endorsing the 'Bloody Code' of capital statutes that would have punished such a crime by sending the plagiarist to the gallows – it was a capital offence to pickpocket a single shilling. Plagiarism had no legal standing, and neither did literary forgery – unless perhaps in civil suits, or in the satirical *Grub-Street Journal* – but they nevertheless provoked the most intemperate anxieties. This, then, is an area in which cultural authority comes into conflict with legal authority, during a particular period in which the status of the author is being professionally codified and determined.

It may be a commonplace to declare that the eighteenth century witnessed a rapid growth in literary forgery – the fake Formosan traveller George Psalmanazar, William Lauder's hoax that Milton was a plagiarist, James Macpherson's Celtic bard Ossian, the 'marvellous Boy' Thomas Chatterton's medieval monk Rowley, William Henry Ireland's Shakspeare papers – but the facts are striking. The period was obsessed with authenticity, and arguably this not only coloured every aspect of writing but also created opportunities for experimental literature, some of which was called forgery. In the field of scholarship too, charges of forgery and plagiarism dogged (and often helpfully clarified) the development of editorial protocols and historical criticism in literatures as diverse as the Bible, Shakespeare, the classics, and old English ballads. And these episodes also occurred in a literary milieu saturated with the law. The law was a subject for literature in trial reports, rogues' histories and confessions, as well as learned commentaries and reports, but it was also the object of literature in cases of copyright infringement, pirate printing, and literary property debates.

The coincidence of terms like forgery and counterfeit across law and literature is no accident, then, but rather the telling indication of a fight for supremacy in deciding who should define the words and what they should mean. The question is really whether on the one hand literature can be legislated against, or on the other whether the law is made of words, mere words. And it is predominantly in the very act of forgery that literary and legal definitions of artistic craft and notions of authorship, whether of a poem or of a crime, most violently collide. Artistic invention remains an endorsed form of lying, of defrauding an audience by bewitching with illusions that blur the sense of emotional or psychic reality. The question lies at the heart of as influential a play as *Hamlet* – it is precisely what so disturbs Hamlet after he has been rehearsing the players:

> Is it not monstrous, that this player here,
> But in a fiction, in a dream of passion,
> Could force his soul so to his own conceit,
> That, from her working, all his visage warm'd;
> Tears in his eyes, distraction in's aspect,

A broken voice, and his whole function suiting
With forms to his conceit? And all for nothing!
For Hecuba!
What's Hecuba to him, or he to Hecuba,
That he should weep for her?

– or that the audience should weep with him?

Moreover, are readers of immoral books or audiences of immoral plays at all implicated in the offences they experience; is reading a species of crime? The infamous forger and thief Mary Carleton was depicted by Francis Kirkman in *The Counterfeit Lady Unveiled* (1673) as reading novels at too early an age: 'believing all she read to be true . . . and supposed herself to be not less than a *heroina*'. Conversely, can you be somehow 'lying' or 'not yourself' when you propose and even commit a crime: can a defence be that it was done 'all for nothing' (this of course becomes another dilemma for the rogue and peasant-slave, Hamlet)? And what implications might these problems have for conceptions of authorship, and even human subjectivity, not least when they are presented by a character who is such a dab hand at forgery himself – as Hamlet himself is, when he forges the death warrant of Rosencrantz and Guildenstern?

Although the lion's share of this book will be about forgery and inspiration, arguing that they develop alongside each other as ways of testing authenticity, it is important to place the legal situation in the cultural foreground: not least because my final forger, the poisoner Thomas Griffiths Wainewright, was indeed convicted of forgery (although he literally got away with murder). As will become apparent in the penultimate chapter, in Wainewright's case as in Oscar Wilde's, the law eventually did succeed in imposing a certain sort of criminal character on a defendant, and by doing so legislated where the boundaries of artistic work should lie. The legal pathology of the author begins in the eighteenth century.

In any case, the period saw a sharp increase in criminal cases of forgery and counterfeiting. On the face of things, these instances of financial fraud have less to do with the development of concepts of intellectual property and the establishment of copyright, than the growth of the national economy and an increasing reliance on paper credit, and the necessity of consumer confidence; in fact, though, as is apparent from the trial of John Prince, cases of financial fraud created conditions and responsibilities for all forms of authorship: effectively turning a text into the scene of a crime, replete with evidence of its execution – 'a paper, teeming with secret practices and dark deeds'. In cases of literary forgery, this site (more often than not a manuscript, jealously guarded) becomes the central concern of criminological critics. But the literary forgers examined in the ensuing chapters all played a 'Get Out of Jail Free' card and presented their work within the mystic frames of inspiration, making texts both authentic and other, making claims of authenticity entirely independent from the forensic, and forcing contradictory demands on their readers. And subsequently, dramatizing the source for a work as supernatural has been used to justify the nonsense of any number of tortured artists: they can insist that a text is both me and not me by claiming that it was somehow weirdly inspired, and in doing so, they have helped to draw attention away from literary merit and towards some peculiarity of the artist's being, some abnormal tendency.

The confusions between copying, imitating, counterfeiting, and forging explored in the last chapter are roughly settled in the eighteenth century, with counterfeit losing its sense of positive making and being redefined by the law to mean an unendorsed and potentially fraudulent copy, something whose true nature is disguised, whereas forgery maintains its sense of craftedness (or craftiness), and is used particularly for fabricating authority (signatures, provenance, forensic details, and so forth). But despite the speed with which copyright and anti-forgery laws multiplied in these hundred years, such legislation remained wholly financial: as with plagiarism, no writer was ever in the dock for literary forgery, and copyright infringement and piracy charges against booksellers and printers were civil rather than criminal offences. On the other hand, many felons were hanged for forging economic bonds. But there is, I think, an evident legal attempt to establish some sort of control over these slippery words and their multiple definitions: counterfeiting becomes coining, a straightforward currency crime, and plagiarism is legally translated into copyright infringement: a material rather than an intellectual theft, policed by booksellers. The authorial implications of plagiarism were handled by the literary and academic establishment, and the whole definition of a good author and a good critic becomes intimately connected with reputation and professional integrity – as it remains today. Thus eventually we see the complete collapse of imitative composition, and the brief but influential displacements of cultural authority by writers such as Macpherson, Chatterton, and Ireland that ultimately enable a literary definition of authenticity to evolve. Even so, forgery continued to be contested by both the literary and legal camps throughout the century, because it persisted in questioning the meaning and representation of authenticity and authority.

COPYRIGHT

A Bill for the Encouragement of Learning, by Vesting the Copies of Printed Books in the Authors, or Purchasers, of such Copies, during the Times therein Mentioned

8 Anne, cap. 19

The first English copyright legislation was passed in 1710, but debate about literary property ran from concern over the licensing of the press, about which John Milton famously wrote *Areopagitica* in 1644, to the ultimate House of Lords ruling on the 1710 Act in 1774. It was inevitably a subject on which writers became particularly agitated, and it would be no exaggeration to say that copyright laws and the ensuing advent of the professional author made the very literature of the period possible.

In 1667 John Milton, arguably the first professional writer outside the theatre, received £20 from Samuel Simmons for *Paradise Lost*: £5 on delivery, £5 when the first edition sold out, and two further payments of £5 for second and third editions. In 1694, John Dryden received £200 in four £50 instalments from Jacob Tonson for his translation of Virgil (£200 then is equivalent to about £50,000 today). Tonson had meanwhile acquired half rights to *Paradise Lost* in 1683 and in 1695 published *The Poetical Works of Mr. John Milton*, in which he had sole rights. In 1697, he published Dryden's *The Works of Virgil*, and the Tonson firm also had possession of the works of Shakespeare for most of the eighteenth century. It is possible to see the genesis of a canon in the literary holdings of the Tonsons, and although the market was not by any means sewn up by them, or for that matter any other bookseller, the higher echelon of prestige booksellers (the Tonsons, the Dodsleys) decided what constituted serious Literature.* The broadside ballads and chapbooks that rolled from the St Paul's Churchyard presses were dismissed as pulp fiction.

But the market took a while to settle, and in 1715 Alexander Pope made about £3,000 on his translation of Homer's *Iliad*. This was an extremely ingenious and lucrative deal in which Pope sold his copyright to Bernard Lintot for 1,200 guineas and made another £1,800 or so from selling subscriptions (which were advance payments for each volume in return for which the subscriber's name would be printed in the book itself); it enabled Pope to become financially and artistically independent. In 1746 Samuel Johnson received a princely £1,575 from five respectable publishers for the *Dictionary of the English Language*, out of which sum he employed six amanuenses; he supplemented his income by moonlighting – writing the *Rambler* and *Adventurer* essays in the evenings. Thirty years later, and by now in receipt of a pension, Johnson asked for only 200 guineas from a cartel of thirty-six booksellers for the *Lives of the Poets*, although in the event he received twice that amount. If, as he once famously declared, 'No man but a blockhead ever wrote, except for money', Johnson still maintained a professional pride and was not positively avaricious.

Author–publisher relationships shifted, therefore, in response to the law, the market, and the emergence of a professional ethic. Milton's contract, the first such extant, shows that the poet had property in his poem and was able to sell it, and also had some immediate control over, and benefit from, reprintings. It is also a complex enough document to suggest that such deals were a recognized aspect of the booktrade, although Milton never struck another deal with this particular bookseller. With Tonson, we see a bookseller planning for long-term profits by making a serious investment in a major contemporary poet, and also selectively acquiring earlier properties. Pope, however, took advan-

---

* 'Booksellers' in the eighteenth century meant publishers, as well as retailers of books and publishing rights.

tage of the 1710 copyright legislation to position the author as the
central market force and dictated his own terms, to the extent, it has
been suggested, that he virtually defrauded his publisher – but Pope's
works were such hot commodities that he struck a similar deal with
the same bookseller for *The Odyssey* soon after. The stabilization of the
market and consequent establishment of the professional writer is
confirmed by Johnson's career, in which his major works were spon-
sored by cartels and terms were settled by careful negotiation. This
shift in the mode of literary production, the historical materialist might
argue, creates the conditions for Romanticism, in which market forces
are internalized in the entrepreneurial individuality of the poet – a
plausible yet nevertheless tedious reading. A much more interesting
way of understanding how the author is repositioned through these
five generations is to focus less on the means of literary production,
and rather on the process of literary representation: in other words, by
considering how literature talks to itself about problems like originality,
plagiarism, and forgery in the context of the booktrade.

Since the Middle Ages, the monopoly of book production had been
regulated by the Crown and the Stationers' Company, which afforded
some literary protection to authors. But such regulation was really a
means of controlling the press, and the Stationers' Company was
founded in 1556 precisely as a mechanism of censorship to oversee the
registering and hence the licensing of books. When in 1637 the number
of licensees was reduced to twenty master printers, who were obliged
to relicense their properties, Luther's *Table Talk*, Foxe's *Book of Martyrs*,
and the Geneva Bible were all effectively banned by being refused
new licences. The Crown's need to control the press, the consequent
establishment of the Stationers' Company, press licensing – these
restraints were then seized upon by booksellers for commercial advantage: they could take sole responsibility for printing certain works, and
hence reap sole profits, and John Feather has suggested that the whole
concept of copyright was therefore an accidental by-product of censorship: licensing 'confirmed the idea that a copy was unique and that
the right to print it was also unique'.*

---

* Feather also argues that 1814 was the first real copyright act, as practices that went
back at least as far as the sixteenth century were properly codified.

Only members of the Stationers' Company were legally entitled to
print, and by the regulations of the Company booksellers were required
to register themselves as owners of 'copy' (both the manuscript or
'printer's copy', and also the right to copy) – which in 1643 became
enshrined in law: no book could be printed unless it was entered in
the Stationers' Register. The Company also enjoyed the protection
of the Crown. Throughout the seventeenth century, printing was
assumed to be a royal prerogative anyway and royal grants were made
for the right to print new books, but even after the 1710 Copyright
Act it remained possible to apply for Letters Patent for the sole privilege
of producing certain books – usually for a period of fourteen years.
William Warburton, for instance, successfully applied for Letters Patent
for his edition of Pope in 1759. Although there was an unwritten law
that an author's consent was required before publishing, it was the
booksellers who were almost solely responsible for their books – and
they who would suffer the pains of illegal publishing. Punishments
ranged from cropped ears and slit noses, to being hanged, drawn, and
quartered for treason.

In 1644 John Milton challenged this monopoly over writers,
readers, and books in *Areopagitica*, a work published in response to
the parliamentary reinstatement of licensing. In this polemic, Milton
argues that it is the author who is rightly responsible for books, which
are written for the benefit of both the individual reader and the reading
community, or national culture, in general, arguing that the new act

> will be primely to the discouragement of all learning, and the
> stop of Truth, not only by the disexercising and blunting our
> abilities in what we know already, but by hindering and cropping
> the discovery that might be yet further made both in religious
> and civil Wisdom.

For Milton, all writing carries with it the divinity of the Biblical Word,
and the writer, particularly the good writer and the poet, therefore
partakes in this divinity. He famously warns,

> as good almost kill a Man as kill a good Book; who kills a Man
> kills a reasonable creature, God's Image; but he who destroys a
> good Book, kills reason it self, kills the Image of God, as it were
> in the eye . . . a good Book is the precious life-blood of a master

spirit, embalmed and treasured up on purpose to a life beyond life.

Condemned books were burned by the hangman, and so in law there was already a notion that books could be executed. But of course this resonant passage is not merely expressing indignation at the intrusion of the law into learning. Milton takes the legal implication that books live, to argue oxymoronically that books lead both tangible and intangible lives (they are the blood of a spirit), that they are sacred relics to be venerated (itself an intriguing comment from a radical Protestant), that they are 'a life beyond life'. Milton removes books from worldly commerce and makes them shimmer with such otherworldliness that they become inspired and inspirational.

But Milton failed to revoke the Licensing Act, and similar laws, regularly renewed throughout the Interregnum and Restoration, continued to protect publishers for the next half-century. Eventually, in 1695, the renewal of the Act was prevented by a political and philosophical opposition that had been brewing for some years. John Locke, for instance, fought to end licensing. The chapter 'Of Property' in his second *Treatise of Government* (1690, subtitled 'An Essay Concerning the True Original, Extent, and End of Civil Government' – note the exaggerated anxiety in the adjectives 'True Original') is clearly an argument for an author's rights over a literary property:

> every Man has a *Property* in his own *Person*. This no Body has any Right to but himself. The *Labour* of his Body, and the *Work* of his Hands, we may say, are properly his. Whatsoever then he removes out of the State that Nature hath provided, and left it in, he hath mixed his *Labour* with, and joyned to it something that is his own, and thereby makes it his *Property*. It being by him removed from the common state Nature placed it in, it hath by this *labour* something annexed to it, that excludes the common right of other Men. For this *Labour* being the unquestionable Property of the Labourer, no Man but he can have a right to what that is once joyned to, at least where there is enough, and as good left in common for others.

This model, applied to literature, presents a model of craft: the work of the hand is to be rewarded, as opposed to the mysterious movement of a spirit.

Following attempts to revive the Licensing Act in 1707 and 1709, the Queen Anne copyright Bill was drafted in 1709 (and passed in 1710).* This law regulated the practices of the Stationers' Company by stipulating that copyrights belonged either to an author, or to the bookseller who had bought the right, and that such a copyright would entail for twenty-one years if a book was already in print, and fourteen years for a book not yet published. That right would then revert to the author (if still alive) after the term had expired, for another opportunity of a fourteen-year copyright. It was a significant innovation that authors could retain copyright, and were entitled to profit from the ongoing copying and dissemination of their work. The Act, as Mark Rose indicates, 'marked the divorce of copyright from censorship and the reestablishment of copyright under the rubric of property rather than regulation'.

This rubric of property, derived from Locke, was enthusiastically bruited during the passage of the bill. Both Joseph Addison and Daniel Defoe published articles supporting author's rights, and compared book pirates to the most savage robbers or, extending the model of property into patriarchy, to kidnappers. Addison was fascinated by the connotations of kidnapping in biographies and especially in obituaries, and Defoe argued in his *Review* (2 February 1710):

> A Book is the Author's Property, 'tis the Child of his Inventions, the Brat of his Brain; if he sells his Property, it then becomes the Right of the Purchaser; if not, 'tis as much his own, as his Wife and Children are his own – But behold in this Christian Nation, these Children of our Heads are seiz'd, captivated, spirited away, and carry'd into Captivity, and there is none to redeem them.

It is worth pointing out that much of Defoe's writing is critically concerned with issues of authenticity: in the veracity and reliability of pseudo-autobiographical narrators like Moll Flanders and Robinson Crusoe, the details regarding the apparition of the ghost of Mrs Veal, the provenance of his supposed manuscript for *Memoirs of a Cavalier*, and even in poems such as 'The True-Born Englishman', which satirizes national purity by describing the genesis of '*That vain ill natured thing, an* Englishman' among an 'Amphibious Ill-born Mob'.

---

* Originally titled 'A Bill for the Encouragement of Learning and for Securing the Property of Copies of Books to the Rightful Owners thereof'. The earliest use of 'copyright' had come in 1701.

But despite the Copyright Act, and the comparable legislation of 'Hogarth's Act' in 1735 that extended copyright to engravings, the precise nature of literary property continued to be debated throughout the century as booksellers argued that their perpetual copyright had survived the 1710 legislation as common law. It was not until 1774 that the Act was finally asserted. The Tonsons had successfully retained their copyright in Milton's *Paradise Lost* in 1736, and, more alarmingly perhaps, defended their effective copyright in Shakespeare through price wars and other aggressive market practices.

The literary property debate also helped to clarify the legal position of authors and literature, and a notable pamphleteer on the subject was Pope's literary executor William Warburton, who joined the fray in 1747 with *A Letter from an Author to a Member of Parliament concerning Literary Property*. The significance of this influential tract lies in Warburton's extension of Lockean ownership to literary composition, by superseding the craft of the hand with the more rarefied work of the mind. He argues that property is either moveable or immoveable: moveable properties are either natural or artificial, and artificially produced moveables are products of the hand or of the mind, things like a utensil or a book:

> For that the Product of the *Mind* is as well capable of becoming Property, as that of the *Hand*, is evident from hence, that it hath in it those two essential Conditions, which, by the allowance of all Writers of Laws, make Things susceptible of Property; namely common *Utility*, and a Capacity of having its Possession *ascertained*.

According to Warburton, property produced by the hand is 'confined to the individual Thing made', but property produced by the mind (such as 'a *Book* composed') is 'not confined to the Original MS. but extends to the *Doctrine* contained in it: Which is, indeed, the true and peculiar Property in a Book'. This is an important point, for it proposes that an author's property in his or her work is quite unlike and indeed far superior to the 'Thing made' by the hand. In other words, authors are defined as producers of something immaterial, 'the Product of the Mind'. In terms of forgeries, which are as much materially as mentally crafted, Warburton's argument demonstrates that the literary property debate instinctively reflected the growing need to define literature as an indefinable but inspirational discourse ('the *Doctrine*'), henceforth distinguished from other forms of fiction writing.*

Under the terms of the Act, authors could now be as litigious as printers. In 1741, Pope sued the pirate bookseller Edmund Curll for publishing his correspondence without permission, and in doing so set a precedent that the copyright of personal letters remained with the writer. Indeed, Mark Rose sees the case as a transitional moment in the history of authorship, authors' rights, and literary property, arguing that the decision of *Pope v. Curll* involved 'an important abstraction of literary property from its physical basis in ink and paper' – precisely the distinction later argued by Warburton.† Crucially, the author was no longer regarded as the mere inventor of a thing (such as a manuscript), but as the producer of meaning. The law had helped therefore to dismiss the Renaissance artist-artisan model of literary composition, and literary works were increasingly judged on those intangible qualities that transcended the physical conditions of production – whether manuscript or printed book. 'The *writer*', as Martha Woodmansee puts it, 'becomes an *author*' (*auctor*: originator, founder, creator), and so in effect, authorial genius was being measured by inspiration, rather than by physical craft. Moreover, these changing attitudes towards literary property also run alongside Young's *Conjectures on Original Composition*, which, as pointed out in the last chapter, argued that poetic genius was natural and organic – 'An *Original* may be said to be of a *vegetable* nature; it rises spontaneously from the vital root of Genius; it *grows*, it is not *made*' – and imitation, in contrast, was a form of literary industry: 'a sort of *Manufacture* wrought up by those *Mechanics*, *Art*, and *Labour*, out of pre-existent materials not their own'.

The 'unspeakable Curll' was not of course the only illegal publisher working in London. Michael Treadwell has researched the twilight world of false imprints, and discovered a small group of more edifying specialist publishers who would publish and distribute controversial

---

* Ironically, Warburton was later accused of plagiarizing from Milton the concluding paragraph of his essay on miracles.

† It transpired that Pope had in any case actually tricked Curll into publishing his correspondence in 1735 by anonymously leaving him copies of the letters, and so the whole exercise was a way of excusing the vanity of a gentleman like Pope subsequently producing his own authorial edition of correspondence in 1737. Pope explained in his preface to this edition that he feared his letters would be forged.

material in order to disguise or protect authors. Such imprints were
particularly expedient around the time of the Popish Plot and the
Exclusion Crisis, and consist of spoof names, common names, or false
names, coupled with vague geographical locations: 'near the Pall-Mall',
'near Holborn', 'near St. Paul's Churchyard', or they give no address
or bookseller's sign at all. The most notorious user of a false imprint
was, again, Alexander Pope, in his first publication of *The Dunciad*
(1728). This originally appropriated the name 'A. Dodd' and purported
to come from Dublin; another issue exists with 'A. Dod', and a 1729
pirated edition of the work has 'A. Dob' on the title-page: a doubly
mendacious claim. A Scottish pirate of Pope's translation of Homer's
Odyssey published in 1760 carries the jocular imprint 'Printed for A.
Horace, P. Virgil and T. Cicero, in Pater-noster Row, J. Milton in St.
Paul's Church-Yard and D. Plato and A. Pope in the Strand', but even
such audacious wit had a dark side to it – exposing the imprint as a
mere stamp, effectively another part of the text that could be rewritten,
another part of the story. Authenticity was not really real: it merely
comprised yet more representation. This was not to everyone's taste.
Despite his friend Pope taking typical advantage of this textual condition, Jonathan Swift considered the practice to be a variety of forgery:

> A forgery [he writes], in setting a false name to a writing, which
> may prejudice another's fortune, the law punishes with the loss
> of ears; but has inflicted no adequate penalty for doing the same
> thing in print, though books sold under a false name are so many
> forgeries.*

Except that Swift did not write this after all. It was that man Alexander
Pope again.

What booksellers feared, though, was not so much the clandestine
printers in London and elsewhere, as the legalized piracy in Dublin
and Scotland. Dublin, deployed by Pope in his fraudulent imprint to
imply that *The Dunciad* might be from the hand of Swift, no less, also
acted as a reminder to London booksellers that that city printed with
complete impunity works copyrighted in England. The Scottish book
trade too lived by its own laws. Things came to a head in the late
1760s. In 1766, the printer Andrew Millar, to whom James Thomson
had sold *The Seasons* (1726-30), and whose copyright had apparently

---

* In Lilliput, fraud was treated as a greater crime than theft.

lapsed in 1758 (after two terms of fourteen years), sued a rival for printing the work in 1763. Thomson's *Seasons* was the best-selling poem of the century and therefore a valuable piece of property. Millar narrowly won the case, but shortly afterwards it blew up again, and this time the House of Lords marginally found in favour of allowing a cheap reprint of the poems. The common law right to perpetual copyright was finally overturned in 1774 (although some university presses were granted perpetual rights to certain books in 1775), and the works of dead authors like Shakespeare and Milton and indeed Thomson were now, like the classics, common property. In response, they now began appearing in voluminously annotated variorum editions to compensate the booksellers for their immediate loss of property.

It is important to stress that these were booksellers, not authors, fighting cases of copyright. Although as indicated above, writers like William Warburton did meddle in the law, the perpetual copyright was broken on an issue of a cheap reprint of a popular work that benefited readers rather than authors (who were dead) or for that matter booksellers (who had already accrued profits). What is worth noting in passing, however, is that the possession of copyrights by major booksellers determined whose work would be included in the canon-forming anthologies published at the beginning of the nineteenth century. Roger Lonsdale has argued that such considerations skewed the eighteenth-century canon for almost two centuries, as later anthologies were simply compiled from these first showcases in which booksellers had exhibited their properties.

The ongoing debate about literary property, which continued to fill journals such as the *Gentleman's Magazine* in the late 1760s, now developed into a debate about the role and occupation of the writer. Lord Camden, for instance, notoriously pronounced that genuine authors did not write for money:

> I speak not of the Scribblers for bread, who teize the Press with their wretched Productions; fourteen Years is too long a Privilege for their perishable Trash. It was not for Gain, that *Bacon, Newton, Milton, Locke,* instructed and delighted the World: it would be unworthy of such men to traffic with a dirty Bookseller for so much as a Sheet of Letter-press. When the Bookseller offered *Milton* Five Pounds for his Paradise Lost, he did not reject it, and

> commit his Poem to the Flames, nor did he accept the miserable
> Pittance as the Reward of his Labor; he knew that the real Price
> of his Work was Immortality, and that Posterity would pay it.

It is a revealing passage. Camden, who at this stage was one of the
advocates of the authenticity of Thomas Rowley's poetry (Chatterton's
medieval forgery), presents the author as a genius necessarily outside,
or rather beyond, the market, completely rejecting the model of the
professional author. His author was guided, of course, by the prompt-
ings of inspiration.

If, as Thomas Mallon suggests, 'The history of copyright actually
has more to do with piracy than plagiarism', plagiarism and copyright
were intimately connected throughout the period, and questions of
literary property were seldom far behind those of lawful printing rights.
And although writers accused of plagiarism were not tried under the
Copyright Act, it is evident from Defoe's remarks ('these Children
of our Heads are seiz'd, captivated, spirited away, and carry'd into
Captivity'), that plagiarism and illegal printing went together like
parrots and pirates.

FORGERY AND COINING

> The faking boy to the crap is gone,
> At the nubbling chit you'll find him;
> The hempen cord they have girded on,
> And his elbows pinned behind him.
> 'Smash my glim!' cries the reg'lar card,
> 'Though the girl you love betrays you,
> Don't split, but die both game and hard,
> And grateful pals shall praise you!'
>
> The bolt it fell – a jerk, a strain!
> The sheriffs fled asunder;
> The faking boy ne'er spoke again,
> For they pulled his legs from under.

And there he dangles on the tree,
That soul of love and bravery!
Oh, that such men should victims be
Of law, and law's vile knavery!

Jack Fireblood, 'The Faking Boy'

The law against forgery (by which I mean economic rather than literary
forgery, of course) was severe. First codified in 1413, it was developed
by the court of Star Chamber, and a statute of 1562–3 made the forgery
of deeds and documents relating to the acquisition of property, chattels,
and annuities punishable by the pillory, imprisonment, forfeiture of
all possessions, and the loss of ears; on a second conviction, it became
a capital felony. Within seventy years (1634) certain first offences had
become capital crimes, and in 1729, possibly in response to the case of
'Japhet Crook' (a.k.a. Sir Peter Stranger: the last man in England to
lose his ears for forgery) all economic forgeries became capital offences.
By the end of the eighteenth century forgery was policed by over
400 separate statutes, each one drawn up in response to a particular
infringement and all potentially punishable by death. Transportation
for fourteen and seven years respectively was reserved for such offences
as forging stamps and hallmarks, using the same stamps more than
once, and for posing as corporate glaziers and fraudulently fitting
windows.

William Blackstone, in his *Commentaries on the Laws of England*
(1762–3), described the proliferation of forgery statutes since the
English Revolution as a consequence of the paper-credit economy, and
listed a selection of offences.* He defined forgery as 'the *crimen falsi* . . .
the fraudulent making or alteration of a writing to the prejudice of
another man's right', and describes the forgery of deeds and wills,
marriage licences, bank bills, notes, or other securities, promissory
notes, invoices and delivery notes, South Sea bonds, East India bonds,
lottery tickets, and army or navy debentures or the impersonation of
seamen (the forgery of sailors' papers was particularly widespread
because of their protracted absences during the wars, and later included
taking wages, pay, prize money, bounties, pensions, and so forth).
It was also an offence without the benefit of 'clergy', which offered a

* Blackstone's entry was later annotated at length by John Taylor Coleridge, the poet's
brother, in his edition of Blackstone's *Commentaries* of 1825.

pardon from capital punishment to those able to read – the most explicit example of English law privileging the educated and also incidentally saving the Elizabethan poet and playwright Ben Jonson from the gallows. Forgery was almost by definition a crime of the literate. 'I believe', Blackstone concluded with satisfaction after pages of statutes, 'through the number of these general and special provisions, there is now hardly a case possible to be conceived, wherein forgery, that tends to defraud, whether in the name of a real or fictitious person, is not made a capital crime.' Of course, many more statutes were to follow, but, crucially, despite the profusion of offences, literary forgery had *not* entered the statute books, although the principle of impersonation and false representation for fraudulently acquiring profit runs very deep in Blackstone's *Commentaries*. Yet as he wrote in his opening chapter, Blackstone defined forgery as a crime against social, rather than natural, rights: it was a crime against civil society.

Moving from theory to practice and examining a contemporary compendium of crimes and popular trials such as *The Bloody Register* (1764), one is struck by the savagery of sentences for forgery. Among the murderers, robbers, pirates, highwaymen, traitors, rapists, footpads, and sodomites, there are several forgers: Frederick Schmidt, who forged a banknote for £100 (hanged), William Smith, who forged a bill of exchange for £45 (hanged), William Baker, who forged a warrant for the delivery of three chests of tea (hanged), John Rice, who forged South Sea stock (hanged), and our man John Prince, who forged a bill of exchange for £125 (hanged). These are in contrast to the comparatively mild sentences reported for coining, clipping, and 'uttering', or circulating debased coin: Sir Richard Blackham for counterfeiting Dutch skillings (forfeited all goods, chattels, lands, and tenements and imprisoned for life), Thomas Hill for counterfeiting stamp duty (death, but jury sought His Majesty's mercy), Thomas Panting for uttering light guineas (£200 fine and three years' imprisonment), and Abigail Newstead for coining (sentenced to death but afterwards transported).

Why were forgers treated in such an extreme fashion? Forgery was not simply a crime to be punished: it posed a threat to the stability and indeed the economic vitality of the entire nation. Historians such as Douglas Hay and Clive Emsley have commented on the severity of forgery statutes, arguing that the expanding capitalist economy at the beginning of the century created a rise in the use of promissory notes, and consequently a sudden increase in statutes against fraud. While there was no immediate evidence that forgery was to become a serious problem, it became an increasingly common offence as the law was deployed to protect commercial interests. In 1785, the philosopher William Paley argued that forgery threatened the 'circulation' of the economy, as if cash were some life force nurturing the body of the country – effectively making the capital punishment of forgers a requirement for the wellbeing of the market. But it is important not to lose sight of the associated crime of counterfeiting or coining in analysing the legal meaning of forgery. Coiners tended to receive comparatively lighter sentences than forgers (fines, imprisonment, or transportation); it was specifically the inventive forgery of economic and legal instruments that was so objectionable. Coins had as much a symbolic value as paper credit, and Peter Lamborn Wilson goes so far as to suggest that the earliest coins were 'detachable bits of holy power, made of substances at once chthonic (under-ground) and celestial (sun/moon, gold/silver) – an exchange not between humans but between humans and spirits' – but they also had an inherent material value depending on which precious metal they were struck from. The value of paper credit was, in contrast, entirely dependent on the fortunes of the national economy.

The Crown had had the prerogative in minting coin since Henry II, although the law itself went back to Ethelred. Athelstan had passed anti-counterfeiting laws in the tenth century that carried the penalty of the loss of the guilty hand, but counterfeiting and clipping had still periodically disturbed trade, for example in the mid-thirteenth century when Henry III ordered 'all persons guilty of this crime who were found in the kingdom to be suspended on gibbets and exposed to the winds'; and by the fourteenth century, when imports and exports of sterling were banned, counterfeiting gold and silver coin became a form of treason. The country had recently weathered a potentially catastrophic currency crisis: for years the integrity of the coin of the realm had been diluted by clipping, or by irresponsible monarchs mixing gold and silver with base metals, and as early as 1464 when a new mintage was introduced there had been rumours that the new gold was alloyed and not so good as the old money. But in any case, clipping, counterfeiting, and adulteration were at an endemic level by the late seventeenth century. Charles II having been restored, he struck a new, pure, and Stuart guinea mintage in 1662, in which the coins adopted the French style of milled or inscribed edges to make clipping impossible and counterfeiting much more difficult: the coins actually carried the motto *Decus et Tutamen*, meaning 'a decoration and a safeguard', which is once again on pound coins today. These new coins were, however, of such a high quality that they were melted down and exported to the continent, where their metal content commanded a higher price than their face value in England, and so the old, degraded silver coins remained. There was a run on guineas, and a loss of faith in silver coinage, and clipping silver rocketed after 1686: the public loss on all the clipped and light counterfeit coins then current was estimated to be at least 45 per cent of money in circulation, or £2¼ million.

In a drastic measure, the newly formed Bank of England resolved to replace the entire coinage: in January 1696 coins were completely devalued, and then withdrawn as a new silver mintage with milled edges was gradually introduced (for a limited period they could be used to pay taxes or make loans to the king). But by the summer, markets had become anarchic and, unsurprisingly, barter was rife – the majority of the population had lost their purchasing power and there were insufficient quantities of new coins to sustain the economy. Into the crisis then stepped none other than Isaac Newton, newly appointed by the chancellor, Charles Montague, as warden of the Mint at the handsome annual salary of £400. Newton reorganized the national Mint, established provincial mints, and raised the rate of production – and by 1698 the crisis had been averted, although it had cost the government the equivalent of a year's revenue. Meanwhile, Newton became a scourge of seventeenth-century counterfeiters: hunting them down and attending their executions: nineteen in 1697, eight in 1698, and, satisfyingly for Newton, none in 1700.

After the enthusiasm of 'the Great Recoynage' and despite Newtonian principles being brought to bear on the money supply, coinage laws were only slowly supplemented during the eighteenth century, and sentences now lightened. One would only expect to be imprisoned for, say, gilding shillings and sixpences to make them look like guineas or half-guineas, and likewise counterfeiting ha'pennies and farthings carried a sentence of just two years. Even in Roman times, counterfeiting had been a capital offence, and it usually took the form of covering copper coins with a thin layer of silver (Pliny even claims that some numismatists specialized in collecting counterfeits!) – but for a number of reasons, clipping, coining, and uttering were not treated as savagely as forgery in the eighteenth century. First, it was extremely easy to clip: shaking a few gold coins in a bag would render a little dust – indeed the Philadelphia Mint discovered a few years ago that $5 was lost by abrasion every time a million dollars' worth of gold coins was handled – by which it meant lifting the bags into a truck. Counterfeiting was also extremely easy by the mid-century: the last George II ha'pennies, for instance, had been coined in 1754, the first George III ha'pennies were not struck until 1770, and so pieces were by then very badly worn. The process was simple too: the trial of Abigail Newstead describes the accused making a mould for a shilling from plaster of paris, filling it with tin, engraving the edges of the counterfeit coin once set, scouring it with sand and salt, and ageing it by rubbing it on her clogs. Furthermore, Leon Radzinowicz suggests that coining was not policed with particular assiduity, because the thief-takers were less concerned in catching small fry than they were in keeping the minor crimes flourishing in order to lead them to a master criminal. Coiners were effectively lower-class artisans, members of an underworld society who kept a melting pot ready for stolen jewellery and silver plate, and in turn supplied makers of trinkets, utterers, and the small change of the criminal fraternity at large. In terms of any reward received, it was often more profitable to take in utterers than counterfeiters, though the biggest rewards were reserved for forgers: as late as 1819 the Committee on Criminal Laws reluctantly sanctioned the reward of large bounties to help break forgery rings.

Moreover, there was a sense that fraud was a civil rather than a criminal offence: indeed, canny coiners would often make deliberate errors on their coins so as to be less likely of being accused of counterfeiting and so be tried for fraud instead.* Until 1757, obtaining property by false pretences was only a crime if a person had obtained money or chattels by false tokens or counterfeit letters, and cheating was a common law offence only if it was generally injurious to the public, such as through false weights or measures. As Sir William Holdsworth reported, in 1702 'when A got money from B by pretending that C had sent him for it, Lord Holt grimly asked "shall we indict a man for making a fool of another," and bade the prosecutor to have recourse to a civil action'. Finally, counterfeiting was at one level sanctioned by

---

* This still happens today in the Netherlands, with conmen asking tourists to change 2,000 guilder notes: the bill is a fake denomination.

the government: it was one of the less salubrious forms of foreign policy. In 1796 the British government struck Louis d'Or gold coins in Birmingham and printed millions of false French assignats in London as an economic weapon against the Revolution.*

It was not until the end of the century that the tide changed, when the legal reformer Patrick Colquhoun compiled a list of 130 coiners working in London (many of whom were subsequently convicted) and in 1796 drafted a bill against counterfeiting. Colquhoun argued that the laws relating to counterfeiting were obsolete and that the proof required to convict coiners was impractical: 'it is not to be wondered at, where the profit is so immense, with so many chances of escaping punishment, that the coinage of, and traffic in, counterfeit Money has attracted the attention of so many unprincipled and avaricious persons.' He estimated that of the annual £2 million cost of London crime, £310,000 was attributable to coining, and £250,000 to forging and swindling – both typical urban crimes. And convictions for forgery had continued to increase despite the very high chance that a conviction would lead to execution: indeed, on the Western Circuit 1804–15, a convicted forger was more likely to hang than a convicted murderer. Clive Emsley merely argues that this suggests that 'the judiciary had accepted the need to protect commercial interests with a rigorous deployment of the law', but it looks more as though a panic had at last taken hold.

But Colquhoun's measures were as much preventative as they were punitive. In chapter seven of his *The Police of the Metropolis* (1805), he analysed the production and distribution of counterfeit coin and proposed making possession of counterfeiting tools and machinery illegal, as well as developing the preventative measures that eventually became encoded in the very fabric of the monetary system. Eighteenth-century forgers often used a chemical to erase all the handwriting on a cheque except the signature: the trial of Frederick Schmidt, for one, describes how he washed the word 'twenty' from a bill, carefully dried it, and added (from his ability to 'write twenty sorts of hands'), the words 'one hundred'. But when printers started using permanent inks to print cheques, bills, and promissory notes, the crime clearly became impossible to commit in this way. This is the beginning of our own

---

* Both the Allied and the Axis powers planned similar enterprises in the Second World War.

counterfeit deterrents in cash and credit cards: security features in dollar bills currently include cotton and linen paper with red and blue threads, polymer embedded in the paper which under ultra-violet light glows yellow or red depending on the denomination, colour shifting ink which appears green when viewed head on but black when viewed at an angle, micro-printing of tiny words, and of course the watermark; while on credit cards now one often sees a holographic version of the Droeshout portrait of William Shakespeare to guarantee authenticity and value.*

What the laws against coining suggest, then, is that coins are ultimately their own guarantor by virtue of the metal they are made from, if handlers should beware; whereas paper money has no inherent value – it is merely a sign of one's right to gold coin. But Locke had argued that gold coin, '*a little piece of yellow Metal*', had no intrinsic value either – it is just that it does not spoil, is accepted as currency by a common consent, and difficult to counterfeit (or so he claimed – supporters of paper credit argued that printed paper was more secure against fraud). Like a banknote, gold has value only when it is in circulation, is visible, and has an owner: gold and paper are both then simply signs of value for an economist in the eighteenth century. The distinction between bullion and paper credit is made therefore not by any essential difference in their physique or modus operandi, but by codifying the transgressions against them: that is to say, by classify-ing counterfeiting as far less serious an offence than forgery. Hence William Blackstone describes the proliferation of forgery statutes since the English Revolution as a consequence of the paper-credit economy which replaced the (apparently) inherent value of a minted coin with a guarantee, a signed promise, rather than value *per se*. So for Black-stone, forgery is presented as a crime against the *principle* of a paper credit economy – an *ideological* crime against what was in any case a new and unsettling financial world – whereas counterfeiting was just sharp practice that nevertheless maintained the traditional principles of both market and coinage. This distinction was itself, of course, an

---

* It is also worth noting, in light of Eric Hebborn's comments above about not being permitted to finalize his Vandevelde painting, that traditionally many artists, many different hands, worked on the engravings of bank notes and bonds.

illusion maintained in the interests of developing a paper-credit economy, against which threats (forgeries) were treated with much more severity than those misdemeanours that challenged the 'inherent' value of coin. The point was made explicitly in the trial of John Rice for forging South Sea shares, in which The Bench censured the felon thus:

> 'for considering your crime, and its consequences, in a nation where there is so much paper credit, I must tell you (said the Lord Chief Justice) I think myself bound in duty and conscience to acquaint his Majesty you are no object of his mercy.' Adding, 'that all public companies concerned in paper credit, should take caution from this instance, as no doubt they will, to examine strictly all letters of attorney, and papers, wherein there can be any suspicion of fraud.[']

Forgery did indeed pose a vast potential threat to the aristocratic and landowning classes. If rural sabotage such as arson, cattle-maiming, the destruction of trees, and so on had increased to such an extent that it demanded the introduction of the 'Black Act' in 1723, such attacks on authority were actually very localized in effect and served more of a symbolic function than one that hinted at imminent peasant insurgency. Even anonymity was a crime: any person who 'shall knowingly send any letter without any name', or with fictitious names, 'demanding money, venison, or other valuable thing' would be guilty of a felony without benefit of clergy. Forgery, however, could apparently execute its direst threats against the wealthy and influential and utterly dispossess them: it could deprive the nobleman of inheritance and the landowner of land, and specific noblemen and landowners at that – it was not a victimless crime like passing counterfeit currency. And even if tales of aristocrats pauperized by forgers owed more to contemporary folklore and paranoid delusions than to reality, forgery was still potentially theft on a scale that could replot the power structures of the country. As Douglas Hay puts it, only in one area were landlords really exposed to the danger of substantial financial loss: 'Their largest possession was land. The only way it could be taken from them illegally was by forgery – and it is significant that forgery was punished with unmitigated severity throughout the century, by death.' In the case of John Prince described at the head of this chapter, it seems that properties could indeed be shuffled with apparent ease among base-born

miscreants. Even Adam Smith was to claim that 'nobody complains
that this [capital] punishment is too severe [for forgery], because when
contracts sustain action property can never be secure unless the forging
of false ones be restrained'.

In fact Smith, the herald of industrialism, productivity, and free
enterprise, was quite wrong – or perhaps just well behind the times.
There was considerable public sympathy for the middle-class criminal
forger, as is shown by the preliminary essay to *The Malefactor's Register*
(1779), like *The Bloody Register* another proto-*Newgate Calendar*:

> Forgery, enormous as the crime is, in a commercial state, might
> perhaps be more effectually punished and prevented than at
> present, by dooming the convict to *labour for life* on board the
> ballast-lighters. Forgerers [*sic*] are seldom among the low and
> abandoned part of mankind. Forgery is very often the last dreadful
> refuge to which the distressed tradesman flies. These people then
> are sensible of shame, and perpetual infamy would be abundantly
> more terrible to such men than the mere dread of death.

This sympathy is for the educated tradesman caught in a pickle; it
appeals to bourgeois readers, and it is also a sympathy that, with
certain permutations and additions from the literary forger, continued
for another century or so. But there was very little sympathy across
social classes – aristocratic judges were often bent upon swinging such
felons: they feared that forgery was itself becoming a trade.

Certainly by the mid-eighteenth century, forgers were helping to
change the hellish culture of the gallows at Tyburn's triple cross (so
named for its triangular gallows) into a more, um, *elevated* experience.
These offenders constituted a new class of villain becoming the 'fruit
of the gibbet': educated, respectable, polite, and often dandified – this
was the type of the forger. None other than James Boswell described
the hanging of the forger James Gibson in 1768:

> Mr. Gibson was indeed an extraordinary man. He came from
> Newgate in a coach . . . He was drawn backwards, and looked as
> calm and easy as ever I saw a man in my life. He was dressed in
> a full suit of black, wore his own hair round and in a natural
> curl, and a hat. When he came to the place of execution he was
> allowed to remain a little in the coach. A signal was then given
> him that it was time to approach the fatal tree. He took leave of
> his friends, stepped out of the coach, and walked firmly to the

cart . . . When he was upon the cart, he gave his hat to
the executioner, who immediately took off Mr. Gibson's cravat,
unloosed his shirt neck, and fixed the rope. Mr. Gibson never
once altered his countenance.

Finally, with a stunning demonstration of sangfroid, 'He refreshed his
mouth by sucking a sweet orange.'

William Smith too, mentioned above for going to the gallows for
forging a bill of exchange for £45, was considered to be a man of a
seductive but fell genius. 'His capacity may be easily gathered from his
writings published in the daily papers. . . . But unhappily for him,
his abilities only served to aggravate his guilt, and gave him opportunities of doing mischief, and entering into wicked plots, and
contrivances, that a man of less genius would not think of.' He was a
silver-tongued con-man, who on one occasion visited an eminent
doctor, drew a pistol on him and threatened to blow out his brains if
he did not hand over five guineas. The doctor refused, so Smith
changed his tactics, fell to his knees, and lamented his distressed state;
whereupon the doctor offered him three guineas' charity, which Smith
instantly took up and made off with. Indeed, in considering such cases,
Lincoln Faller goes so far as to suggest that forgers, as a new kind of
'economic individualist', took over from freebooting highwaymen as
the 'great crooks of the latter part of the eighteenth century', whose
trials and executions

> prompted much more special pleading about the law than the
> hanging of even the most sympathetic thieves, and seemed greater
> social embarrassments. . . . If it had once seemed that anyone
> might take to the highway, so much more it seemed that
> anyone, in a pinch, might alter a note or bond.*

But this middle-class identification with the plight of the forger actually
obscures a more subtle shift in opinion: it was the crime of those who
aspired to be gentlemen. William Wynne Ryland, engraver to George
III and a forger of bills of exchange, was hanged in 1783, and although
the last forger was hanged in 1829 and the law was abolished in 1837,
that was the year in which the former art critic of the *London Maga-*

---

* Paul Baines notes that in 1732, James Patterson considered the 'reigning vices of the
age' to be swearing, perjury, and forgery, the latter two being moreover essentially the same
crime: '*Forgery* is doing with the *Pen*, what [Perjury] commits with the *Tongue*.'

zine, Thomas Griffiths Wainewright, was transported to Tasmania for forging a Bank of England bill. He escaped the gallows by the skin of his teeth. A connoisseur like Ryland, Wainewright had blown his fortune on the most extravagant peccadilloes.

In addition to the orange-sucking James Gibson, notable forgery cases included the Perreau brothers, hanged for forging a bond on the testimony of the *femme fatale* Margaret Rudd, and Dr William Dodd, also hanged for forging a bond. Samuel Johnson was only one of many who defended the 'Macaroni Parson' Dr Dodd: he ghost-wrote speeches and sermons for Dodd, he wrote letters under his own name to the Lord Chancellor and other worthies, a petition from Dr Dodd to the King (and one from Mrs Dodd to the Queen), he wrote observations for the newspapers – but all in vain.* None of the efforts of Samuel Johnson at the height of his powers could save Dodd. It was an open and shut case: the jury took just ten minutes to return a guilty verdict. George III had established a ghastly precedent by condemning the Perreau brothers the previous year, and so the 'Unfortunate Doctor' was refused a royal pardon and executed on 27 June 1777.

Dodd's case, coinciding with the publication of the basilisk Margaret Rudd's memoirs, was considered a national disgrace and helped to swing public opinion conclusively against the death penalty for forgery. The case also ran concurrently with the Rowley Controversy (the debate about Thomas Chatterton's forgeries): Rowley's poems were published the day after Dodd was arrested.

---

* Among his literary publications Dodd had written a new book of Pope's *Dunciad* (1750) and an anthology of *The Beauties of Shakespeare* (1752); during his trial, the *Gentleman's Magazine* published a letter from 'Verus' claiming that as Dodd had commenced work on an edition of Shakespeare, he should be pardoned (1777).

CRIME WRITERS

Their life a general mist of error.

John Webster, *The Duchess of Malfi*, IV. ii

Still, the gallows was an appropriate place for a forger to end up: it was treated as a site of authenticity and therefore of truth. The scaffold, even more than the dock, was a stage for confessions and speeches and final words before thousands of witnesses. The hanging was also a ritual of sacrifice and renewal, and the execution was a moment when the representations of truth – criminal exploits, trial transcripts, confessions – perfectly, if briefly, meshed with the stuff of reality itself. In the case of forgers, those felons convicted for undermining the veracity and authority of legal and economic texts, death symbolized the reassertion of legitimate truth, order, and power. And yet at the same time there is a confusion in such executions. The legal record in collections such as *The Bloody Register* constantly insists on testimony, forensic matter, and confession to restore the order of the everyday after the disruption of crime; it relies upon the very models of realism that forgery mimics and makes inauthentic. Thomas Panting was indicted when parcels of guineas, pairs of scales, and guinea weights were discovered in his rooms, and 'they found also a paper, upon which there seemed to appear, among some dust, something to shine, as if there had been in it some filings of gold, or some other metal'. Even in its final assertion, authentic evidence was in a hopeless and perpetual embrace with its own unreal, fictitious reflection. The execution of the forger became as futile as it was inescapable: it was performed to confirm the authority of the law, but the law was derived from an empirical definition of truth upheld only by the very permission of the inauthentic.

This strange doubleness is entirely characteristic of the accounts of forgeries in *The Bloody Register* and other Tyburn calendars, which are insistent on the reality of the events described, but both forgers and prosecutors are playing the same knowledge game: establishing proof by hard forensic evidence, such as signatures on bank notes, although the forger does it by shadowing the real. Crime writing declares the truth of its own physical utterance: it consists of true accounts, news, verbatim speeches – a discourse constructed of 'particulars', 'circumstance', 'explanation', 'occurrence'. It is made of solid objects like promissory bills and silver buckles and recognizable environments like shops and streets; it records facts and historical events, and catalogues with an obsessive zeal the properties of goods and bodies. Moreover, criminal biographies made outrageous and sordid claims of authenticity – advertisements for such books might declare that booksellers had affidavits signed by their felons shortly before execution to confer publishing rights, and in at least one case the hangman, it was said, was prepared to testify that on the very scaffold itself his charge had told him to which bookseller he had given the authentic account of his life. Meanwhile James Macleane, 'The Gentleman Highwayman', was incapable of saying a word at his sentencing, but 'a Copy of what he had intended to say, if Sorrow had not deny'd him Utterance' was still printed, 'taken from his own Hand-writing'. And yet these horrid attempts to authenticate crime texts do actually demonstrate how easy it is to fabricate the printed page: crime writing is a genre of literature – it is fictitious, a form of fantasy, a set of conventions and protocols. The same sorts of authenticating techniques might be found in John Foxe's *Acts and Monuments* (1563, 1570), Bunyan's *Mr. Badman* (1680) – which Bunyan claims is based on 'True stories, that are neither *Lye*, nor *Romance*', or Daniel Defoe's *A True Relation of the Apparition of one Mrs. Veal* (1706), in which Defoe uses sensual and empirical evidence such as names, places, dates, events, and testimony to prove the extrasensory – a typical characteristic of apparition narratives. On the other face of this counterfeit coin, it is also worth noticing how sensational true-crime narrative and 'authenticated' rogues' histories patterned the lives of the forgers – not just those who were swinging from the triple tree, but more importantly the myths and legends that accrued around Macpherson, Chatterton, Ireland, and Wainewright. Horace Walpole had already written in 1778 that he believed that 'All of the house of forgery are relations'.

The potential and crippling fictiveness of all this 'empirical' evidence is furthermore apparent in the textual strategies deployed by scholars in the eighteenth century. During the debate between the 'Ancients' and the 'Moderns' over classical learning, the modernist

Richard Bentley argued that classical works should not be treated as a Parnassian field of universal and decontextualized human wisdom, but needed to be rigorously historicized and prosecuted with a legal zeal. Bentley was in fact extraordinarily effective in exploding the myths of the classical canon, one of his early successes being to detonate by a relentless historical logic the forged *Epistles of Phalaris*. It was against Bentley's garrulously digressive and fabulously learned method that Swift's *Tale of a Tub* (1704) was written, and Pope too has a Bentleian commentary running throughout the *Dunciad Variorum*. But Bentley was also fantastically misguided, and his approach proved witlessly fertile on hare-brained projects such as his edition of Milton's *Paradise Lost* (1732). This was a madcap exercise in applying to a modern epic the techniques of textual transmission he had perfected on classical texts. Certainly Bentley was right in positing that poems written in the last fifty years might be corrupt, but it required an extravagant speculation to demonstrate they were as corrupt as those composed fifty centuries ago. He nevertheless proposed that Milton's amanuensis and printer had miscast the poet's lines, made unsubstantiated revisions, and even interpolated their own verses into the poem. The poor blind poet was obviously disabled from correcting his proofs and remained ignorant of the forgery. It was up to Bentley to mend the text.

At his most decent, Bentley was trying to exemplify the role of the modern editor. 'Parallelist' editions of Milton, such as by Thomas Newton, and books on Spenser and Pope, by Thomas and Joseph Warton, respectively, tended to trace references, allusions, borrowings, and imitations – if not plagiarisms. But Shakespeare editing, particularly in the hands of Pope, had tended to be bracing and unafraid to fiddle with the texts of the Bard, and Lewis Theobald's assault on Pope's Shakespeare was very much a Bentleian attack on loosely argued emendation. It was not until Richard Farmer's *Essay on the Learning of Shakespeare* (1767) that source-hunting really became an established feature of Shakespeare editing as well. Bentley therefore offered his Milton as a model of 'Sagacity and happy Conjecture', in order to create what Marcus Walsh calls 'an ideal Milton, who might and should have written the ideal poem that Bentley's emendations and, at last, re-writings, seek to reconstruct' – and in such a relationship of poet and editor he was echoing the communion of epic poetry with God's creation. While at one level Bentley's achievement is laughably inept,

William Empson has notably (albeit eccentrically) used it as a way of mapping potential fault-lines in Milton's poem: reading Bentley can strip away 200 years of Miltonic veneration, put one in dialogue with an erudite and pugnacious editor, and force one to justify one's taste. That in itself is a lesson to be learned; but in the context of this chapter, Bentley's method should also be seen as a vanguard attempt to establish scholarly canons of English literary authenticity based on physical evidence – or the lack of it. It may be of immense significance that he should have failed so spectacularly, but today it should remind us to approach canonical texts, most notably those invented Shakespeare plays such as *King Lear* we take completely on trust, with extreme caution. Pope, unafraid to rewrite lines of Shakespeare, characteristically parodied the work of such scholars as a crime: these 'Haberdashers of Points and Particles' are counterfeiting '*our* Glorious Ancestors, Poets of this Realm, *by clipping, coining, defacing the images, mixing with their own base allay, or otherwise falsifying the same; which they publish, utter, and vend as genuine*'. The obsolete term 'utter' ignites at this point.

Pope's remarks against scholars are doubtless to be expected, but curiously the coining metaphor was also used in a religious sense – which is again of relevance to Milton. The so-called 'pious fraud' of, say, the tenth-century Aquitaine monks who sought to canonize Martial created what Richard Landes calls 'a counterfeit apostolicity more reprehensible than counterfeit coinage because it debased God and his saints'; it also consequently ruined their leading impresario, Ademar. In the eighteenth century, Christopher Smart wrote in *Jubilate Agno* that 'God has given us a language of monosyllables to prevent our clipping', and so the day-to-day crimes of urban life here become an aid to meditation on the holiness of language, and incidentally confirm the diabolical associations of counterfeiting. Oddly, Milton, who was in any case venerated as being almost heretically original, was also the victim of another accusation of literary fraud in 1747. William Lauder, a Jacobite who had managed to lose a leg on a golf course, began publishing essays under the name of 'Zoilus' in the *Gentleman's Magazine*, essays that were collected and published separately in 1750 as *An Essay on Milton's Use and Imitation of the Moderns, in his Paradise Lost* – the title itself a one-legged jibe at Falconer's 1741 *Essay upon Milton's Imitations of the Ancients in his Paradise Lost*. Lauder argued that Milton had plagiarized modern Latin poets for *Paradise Lost*, the case being 'proved' by quoting doctored passages from the work of mid-seventeenth-century poets such as Grotius and Andrew Ramsay, in which lines from a 1690 Latin translation of *Paradise Lost* were interpolated. Samuel Johnson, who as we shall see never much liked Milton anyway, was sufficiently pleased by Lauder's performance to write a preface to the book, but the forged plagiarisms were inevitably soon exposed.

If Milton was doubly imposed upon, Samuel Johnson, the consummate professional writer, appears at the dead centre of many eighteenth-century arguments about literary forgery. He furiously attacked James Macpherson for Ossian and in his mid-sixties hared off on a tour around the Scottish islands with the cantankerous energy of a man intent on disproving the validity of the work. Chatterton's Rowley poetry was read at his Literary Club and he was soon out and about in Bristol to inspect the remains there. In both cases, the respective supporters of Ossian and Rowley resisted Johnson's hotfooted attempts to chair the debate, though his judgements have nevertheless prevailed. Curiously, though, Johnson was devoted to a drinking partner who styled himself one 'George Psalmanazar', a sort of cross between a performance artist and a crypto-ethnographer who in 1704 had published *An Historical and Geographical Description of Formosa*, by 'a Native of the said Island, now in *London*'. Psalmanazar insisted, by a combination of exotic anecdotes, gibberish, autistic draftsmanship in spinning a curious alphabet, and an alarming raw diet, that he was a native 'Formosan'. It was a performance of 'otherness' that set contemporaries agog: Swift mentions 'Sallmanaazar' in *A Modest Proposal* (1729) and is clearly indebted to the *Description of Formosa* for *Gulliver's Travels* (1726). The episode remains intriguing today. Nevertheless, Psalmanazar exists almost within a tradition of deception: from Herodotus to Bruce Chatwin, travel writing and imposture have enjoyed a fertile relationship, and so at one level Psalmanazar's *Description* is a hybrid of travelogue and rogue's history. But there is still something quite arresting in the pseudo-Formosan's work. In the preface to the second edition of the *Description* he answers his critics with a do-or-die double-bluff:

> You do me more Honour than you are aware of, for then you
> must think that I forg'd the whole story out of my own Brain . . .
> he must be a Man of prodigious parts who can invent the Descrip-

tion of a Country, contrive a Religion, frame Laws and Customs, make a Language, and Letters, etc. and these different from all other parts of the world; he must have also more than a humane memory that is always ready to vindicate so many feign'd particulars, and that without e'er so much as once contradicting himself.

This level of self-assurance is approaching the mystic otherworldliness that Hillel Schwartz congratulates in impostors: 'they are not deranged but faithful to a lifelong project that oscillates toward [*sic*] the spiritual'. Such profound impersonation clearly goes far beyond the brief deception of posing as a veteran soldier in order to take a pension; the case of Psalmanazar goes directly against the grain of emergent bourgeois individualism. He insisted on being buried in an unmarked grave.

The complexity of the term 'forgery' within the overlapping, entangled contexts of literature and law (and also of counterfeit and coining, plagiarism and copyright, mimesis and imitation), clearly resists any simple diagnosis. Instead, forgery shadows other cultural formations – issues of authorship and literary work, freedoms of the press, the transformation of the literary marketplace, as well as theories of originality, inspiration, and authenticity. Once detected, forgery is reduced by law, in a sense, to a means of classification: as soon as a work is identified as forged or plagiarized, it is stripped of its literary status and its author becomes a mere writer, and then a criminal exiled to anecdotal literary history. But a rehabilitation of forgers needs to situate writing practices both inside and outside the orthodox understanding of authorship, to show how forgers escape the confines of conventional authorship. Moreover, forgery recognizes that in literature, truth is represented by the same techniques as fiction, which runs the risk of making truth a culturally-specific phenomenon. Thus Charles I's *Eikon Basilike* ('the King's image', 1649), which went into over forty editions and was anyway probably written by John Gauden, attempted to intervene in contemporary historical process and avert the beheading of the monarch. It failed. In a more sinister example Titus Oates, who masterminded the Popish Plot, attempted to change the course of the succession by forging the 'Windsor Letters' to support his murderous claims. He too failed.

But is there a more salutary social history here, an accommodation of failure? And can there be any redemption for the hundreds of forgers who ended their lives with a 'hemp necktie'? Perhaps. The next chapters will move inwards, from body to soul. Despite the recurrent presentation of writing as a physical witness, which we will see in the crafted manuscripts of Chatterton and Ireland, one writer, James Macpherson, explicitly eschewed the physical for a fresh comprehension of authenticity in the uttered word. For eighteenth-century authors writing in the shadows of forgers – those whose fatal crime was to write the wrong thing – Macpherson offered the inspired, singing, ghostly voice of the afterlife.

PART TWO

III. GHOST

The Sun, the Moon, and the Stars, Clouds and Meteors, Lightning and Thunder, Seas and Whales, Rivers, Torrents, Winds, Ice, Rain, Snow, Dews, Mist, Fire and Smoke, Trees and Forests, Heath and Grass and Flowers, Rocks and Mountains, Music and Songs, Light and Darkness, Spirits and Ghosts . . .

Ossian's similes, from Hugh Blair's *Critical Dissertation*

The ancient Poets animated all sensible objects with Gods or Geniuses, calling them by the names and adorning them with the properties of woods, rivers, mountains, lakes, cities, nations, and whatever their enlarged & numerous senses could perceive.

William Blake, *The Marriage of Heaven and Hell*

*¶ (*b*)=‡∗∗&,//://†(*p*)=∗∗xy.

Vet. Inscript. ap. GRONOV.*

Death stalks the forger, either literally as capital punishment or culturally as censorship; can literature raise the dead? Some writing, like spells and necronomica, is explicitly devoted to conjuring ghosts; memorials, testaments, biographies, and histories also try to 'bring their subjects alive', and *per se* all writing might be considered as evasive action against mortality. Such literature is inspirational, then, because

---

* This epigraph appears on the title page of the satirical pamphlet *Gisbsal, An Hyperborean Tale: Translated from the Fragments of Ossian, the Son of Fingal* (1762).

it cheats the grave, and the trope is familiar in the morbid poetry of
John Keats and other Romantics:

> This living hand, now warm and capable
> Of earnest grasping, would, if it were cold
> And in the icy silence of the tomb,
> So haunt thy days and chill thy dreaming nights
> That thou wouldst wish thine own heart dry of blood
> So in my veins red life might stream again,
> And thou be conscience-calm'd – see here it is –
> I hold it towards you.

If, as I am arguing, literary forgery is accommodated within Romanticism as inspiration, is forgery the literature that characteristically
raises the dead?

Inspiration is arguably the great unacknowledged mode of
eighteenth-century writing, and at least partly accounts for the century's
relative downgrading in the English literary canon. Pope, Behn, Defoe,
Richardson, Fielding, Johnson: these are not writers whom one thinks
of as inspired. They are satirists, dramatists, journalists, novelists, even
hacks – they are professional writers. They wrote brilliantly and ener-
getically – for money. They escaped the confines of patronage, they
wrote for the press, they forged careers in writing, they made a living
by their pens: they are among the most profoundly important and
influential writers that this culture has ever produced, and yet they
remain eclipsed by Romanticism and its dogmas of sincerity, originality, and inspiration. (Disgracefully, some Eng. Lit. survey courses still
march without breaking step from Milton to Blake.) But in the middle
of the eighteenth century, the revival of inspirational theories of
authorship starts to rise in a ghostly crescendo in the bardic songs
of Ossian, and reverberates throughout the Romantic movement and
beyond. Inspiration is a form of composition that guarantees the authenticity of the poetic self precisely because it lies outside that self, in
some other region. In journeying to such a place, a writer 'loses' him
or herself, or writes as if 'possessed' by another, and it is the transit
between these two states of self and other that then authenticates the
poet. But by being alien, inspiration is in a sense inauthentic – necessarily so – and perhaps literary forgeries (as inauthentic) can be read
as radical examples of this inspiration, and therefore inspirational
in themselves. Hence the culture of composition shifted precisely in

response to forgery, because literary forgery was so extreme. And in the case of Ossian, his poems were read as manifestations of all the resurrectionist tendencies mentioned above – to an extent that some could only describe as criminal.

So, we begin with one of the most preposterous confrontations that (n)ever took place in the history of Western culture. In the blue corner is Samuel Johnson, the greatest man of letters of the eighteenth century: an elderly, elephantine, scrofula-scarred, half-blind manic depressive with an irrepressible desire (and ability) to out-argue all comers; in the red corner is James Macpherson: a tall and proud, thickset and leather-booted, fiery-haired Scotsman enjoying a rip-roaring success as a translator and historian. 'Mr. James Macpherson,' wrote Johnson on 20 January 1775,

> I received your foolish and impudent note. Whatever insult is offered me I will do my best to repel, and what I cannot do for myself the law will do for me. I will not desist from detecting what I think a cheat, from any fear of the menaces of a Ruffian.
>
> You want me to retract. What shall I retract? I thought your book an imposture from the beginning, I think it upon yet surer reasons an imposture still. For this opinion I give the publick my reasons which I here dare you to refute.
>
> But however I may despise you, I reverence truth and if you can prove the genuineness of the work I will confess it. Your rage, I defy, your abilities since your Homer are not so formidable, and what I have heard of your morals disposes me to pay regard not to what you shall say, but to what you can prove.
>
> You may print this if you will.
>
> SAM. JOHNSON

Johnson had recently written *A Journey to the Western Isles of Scotland* (1775), in which he attacked both the honesty of Macpherson's work and his character as a gentleman (this had in fact been going on for a while: a dozen years before Johnson had said of the man, 'Why, Sir, when he leaves our houses, let us count our spoons'). But the story goes that these two writers were not content simply to debate with each other: they very nearly did literally fight – and not in any aristocratic duel. Macpherson, in his big boots, with his hot temper and savage manners, was out to *see* Johnson, if he thought he was hard enough – and who at sixty-five was a mere twenty-five years or so older than the Scot. Johnson responded by acquiring a gigantic truncheon, almost as tall as a caber – 'an oak-plant of a tremendous size' – six feet long and topped with a weighty head, which 'he kept in his bed-chamber, so near the chair in which he constantly sat, as to be within reach' – within reach indeed when he penned the above letter. Macpherson, like all bullies, ran away.

This anecdote amounts to a fable – a fake, even – but it has been extraordinarily tenacious in literary mythology, and has done a great deal of damage to Macpherson's subsequent reputation. A forger is bad enough, but a Scottish scoundrel who would beat an old man, and the greatest Englishman of the century to boot? And despite the archival work done to show that Johnson made at least six copies of the letter to circulate to his cronies (although he claimed that there was only one copy he had since lost), the stage-handling of this melodrama has still not been fully appreciated. The legend was fixed by Boswell, who used it to head a digression on Johnson's great strength and fearlessness, and for whom striding into the middle of dog fights, keeping gangs of muggers at bay until the watch arrived, throwing impudent fellows into the theatre pit for sitting in his chair (the chair, it has to be said, went as well) – in between compiling dictionaries, editing Shakespeare, and holding forth at the dinnertable – was all in a day's work for the consummately professional English writer.

Of course, Johnson's persistent carping about the Scots – like horses, he decided in his *Dictionary*, they dined upon oats – was precisely what Macpherson had taken umbrage at. Some sort of trumped-up form of national honour was ostensibly at stake, and the oak-plant is clearly a branch of ethnic English propaganda. But Johnson was also making a more serious point about what he thought Macpherson had been up to, and his purchase of his cudgel is an emblematic moment in Boswell's *Life of Johnson* that could rank with his notorious refutation of Berkeley's philosophy:

> After we came out of the church, we stood talking for some time together of Bishop Berkeley's ingenious sophistry to prove the non-existence of matter, and that everything in the universe is merely ideal. I observed, that though we are satisfied his doctrine is not true, it is impossible to refute it. I never shall forget the

alacrity with which Johnson answered, striking his foot with mighty force against a large stone, till he rebounded from it, 'I refute it *thus*.'

As Berkeley's philosophy is refuted by showing that he is not living in the real world, and is therefore a fake philosopher, Macpherson is dealt with as a criminal, and therefore an illicit writer – essentially a forger.

But what had Macpherson done to provoke the wrath of the 'Great Cham'? He had translated and edited, or written, or indeed forged, depending on one's point of view, one of the most extraordinary poetic works of the age: the lost epics of a third-century Celtic bard. The *Fragments* of Ossian's poetry had been published in 1760, when Macpherson was just twenty-three years old. This pamphlet was followed by two epics and a collected edition (1765) recently re-edited in 1773 – the year in which Johnson had visited the Hebrides to go Ossian-hunting. As he had fully expected before he left, Johnson found nothing there to convince him that the epics could be anything but an utter fabrication. Gaelic was an illiterate language and so there were no manuscripts more than a few years old; hence there could be no literature.

> I look upon Macpherson's 'Fingal' [he said to Boswell] to be as gross an imposition as ever the world was troubled with. Had it been really an ancient work, a true specimen of how men thought at that time, it would have been a curiosity of the first order. As a modern production, it is nothing.

Rather ironically, Johnson then hit the nail on the head: 'He has found names, and stories, and phrases – nay, passages in old songs, and with them has blended his own compositions; and so made what he gives to the world as the translation of an ancient poem.' Which is pretty much what contemporary Ossianists have agreed.

Macpherson, an itinerant and impoverished scholar who had changed universities three times for both intellectual and financial reasons (and yet still managed to leave without a degree), eventually secured a precarious living as a charity schoolmaster and began collecting traditional Gaelic verse. All this might have been innocent enough, had he not encountered a dashing playwright named John Home, who discovered what Macpherson was collecting and translating, and desperately desired to see some samples. Macpherson overcame his initial reluctance and handed Home some pieces, who then immediately passed them around the literary salons of Edinburgh as the poetic remains of the lost culture of the Scottish Celts. Copies were sent to Horace Walpole, Thomas Gray, and other connoisseurs in England, and Macpherson's fate was sealed. The *Fragments* were published, and whipped up a veritable storm. The reading public, already intoxicated by the neurotic fiction of sentimentalism (typified by Samuel Richardson's *Clarissa*), went wild over the *Fragments'* strange raptures. Macpherson was now dispatched to the Highlands and Islands to collect more materials, and scoured the country for six months: loading his ponies with manuscripts, rescuing scraps of paper from the scissors of tailors, and jotting down riddling tales from the memories of old Highlanders. He then took up residence with Hugh Blair, Professor of Belles-Lettres at Edinburgh University, and in less than four months he had translated and annotated *Fingal,* a 19,000-word epic, and various other poems. It has to be said that this industriousness was very much in Johnson's own style, and indeed there are similarities between the two – Macpherson was a terrifically hard worker: he later translated *The Iliad* in under twelve weeks. Anyway, *Fingal* was published in December 1761; *Temora,* another epic, followed in 1763.

It was a meteoric ascent, but at this point Macpherson's biography, strangely like other writers who appear in this book, turns from the extraordinary to the fantastical. The Ossian debate was abruptly curtailed by the political intervention of the Prime Minister, the Earl of Bute. Bute had seized on the popularity of Ossian to bolster his unstable government (indeed, *Fingal* was dedicated to him), but when support for Macpherson began to waver in 1764, he decided to appease his opponents by sacrificing the turbulent scholar-poet. He offered Macpherson the post of provincial secretary to the governor of West Florida – and the translator of Ossian left for the Everglades.

This American sojourn lasted little more than a year, however, and fifteen months later Macpherson was back and working as a political lobbyist for the Tory governments of the late 1760s: writing anonymous newspaper letters and articles to rally government support. He published an *Introduction to the History of Great Britain and Ireland* in 1771 and his prose *Iliad* in 1773, two more *Histories* in 1775, and a sharp rebuttal of the declaration of American independence in

1776.* Macpherson's next project was to lobby against the East India Company for an Indian prince: Mohammed Ali, the nabob of Arcot. Macpherson defended the nabob in a book attacking the company (1779), and became his London agent. The prince supplemented Macpherson's now substantial government pension with frequent and lavish gifts, and, moreover, bought a parliamentary seat for him in 1780. Macpherson was MP for Camelford, Cornwall, for the remaining sixteen years of his life – despite various political scandals accusing him of financial speculation and conflicts of interest – and in 1785 he was considered of sufficient standing to be shortlisted for the office of poet laureate. He died in 1796, leaving five children (he never married), and willing money to finance a commemorative monument to himself, his funeral and burial in Westminster Abbey, and a vindication of Ossian. The controversy re-ignited on his death.

Macpherson's posthumous hope to establish Ossian did, to an extent, succeed – there were editions published nearly every year between 1800 and 1830. Moreover, his treatment of Ossianic myth and popular folksong was not so very different from, say, Elias Lönnrot's crafting of the Finnish *Kalevala*, first published in 1835. Lönnrot wrote a 22,000-line poem based on traditional oral poetry from the Karelia region of Finland, a poem now considered by the Finns to be their national epic – they even celebrate Kalevala Day on 28 February to commemorate the first appearance of Lönnrot's text. Like Macpherson, Lönnrot collected extant remains, which included taking recitations by dictation, and then forged a national identity out of these fragments. Macpherson really did collect manuscripts and transcribed traditional songs, and *Fingal* and *Temora* were in a large part derived from these remains. But he also fashioned his own interpolations to fill gaps or lacunae, or to replace obscure or inconsistent readings, and so his 'translation' was effectively a paraphrase, carefully adapted to the tastes of his eighteenth-century readers. Such freedom is typical of the bardic tradition itself, and Macpherson was virtually composing as a 'bard': reworking Ossianic stories, themes, and language into an epic to celebrate the mythic past and clarify the identity of post-Jacobite Scotland. In other words, Macpherson was 'reinventing' Ossian by developing a new poetry of contemporary myth. The charge of forgery

---

* *The Rights of Great Britain asserted against the Claims of America* was gratifyingly more influential than Johnson's pamphlet on America, published the previous year.

is just too flippant an explanation, but it does reveal the writerly values that Johnson was committed to uphold.

In fact, it is difficult to object to Macpherson's techniques of poetic recreation. He might have blurred distinctions between history and literature, fact and fiction, by boldly attributing his pieces to the third century, but what precisely was that distinction? Only a decade before Ossian, Henry Fielding had called himself a 'historian' in his novel *The History of Tom Jones*, in which he also described Homer and Milton as 'historians' – indeed, up to the end of the sixteenth century 'history' was used to describe epics, such as *The Faerie Queene*, and also dramatic tragedies. Samuel Richardson, moreover, called himself the 'historian' and 'editor' of *Clarissa* (1747–8), and when William Warburton wanted to preface that novel with a declaration that the whole work was a fiction, Richardson took offence because he considered himself a moral truth-teller. Many early eighteenth-century novels called themselves 'histories' or 'lives' and were framed with prefaces disengaging the writer from the work, or claiming that a manuscript had been 'found' (usually in a peculiar place), or that the work had been edited from the papers of a friend. The tradition continued throughout the nineteenth century in the work of writers as diverse as Thomas Carlyle, Edgar Allen Poe, and William Hale White (who hid behind two pseudonyms, as 'Mark Rutherford' edited by 'Reuben Shapcott'); even today, Umberto Eco and Ferdinand Pessoa (who wrote under seventy-two different personae – properly 'heteronyms' rather than pseudonyms) play just such games with fiction. But if in 1760 Hugh Blair was still calling novels 'Fictitious Histories' and the philosopher David Hume could describe poets as 'lyars by profession', by the nineteenth century things had been straightened out a little. Alexander Carlyle wrote to Henry Mackenzie on 9 January 1802, deciding that Macpherson had 'laid himself too much open to the critics by attempting, in his Dissertations on Fingal, to unite two things that must ever remain separate, viz. poetical fiction and historical truth'. But it is precisely the way that Macpherson is able to articulate his double-tongued 'poetical fiction and historical truth' that creates the Ossianic. Poetical fiction becomes inspiration and historical truth becomes memory, and the two are entirely merged together, as indistinct as water is in water.

Macpherson's literary integrity is in any case surely proven by the considerable fascination he exercised over writers across the western

world: Blake certainly saw something in his unique vision; Wordsworth, Coleridge, and Byron wrote 'Ossianics' and borrowed phrases
and images and moods, as did Scottish writers like Robert Burns (who
called him one of the 'glorious models after which I endeavour to form
my conduct'), Walter Scott (especially in *The Lay of the Last Minstrel*,
1805, and *Waverly*, 1814), and James Hogg (*Queen Hynde*, 1824). In
Wales, Iolo Morganwg (a.k.a. Edward Williams) launched his own
Celtic revival by unearthing and restoring and fabricating the culture
of the bards. And everywhere, the sublimely morbid Ossian also helped
to install in the unconscious of readers what was to become the
machinery of the Gothic novel: tangled plots of bitter political hatreds;
obscure rivalries between lovers that inevitably culminate in some
hideous irony of blasted hopes; scenes obsessively revolving around
dark memories of bloody death inspired by omnipresent spirits and
set beside ruined tombs in miserable storm-ravaged landscapes –
and nearly everything of significance in Ossian happens at night. Quite
simply, these are compelling ghost stories.

Macpherson also had a stunning success on the continent, if his
own celebrity was rapidly eclipsed by Ossian's. The works were swiftly
translated into Italian, and in German they established a school of
bardic poetry led by Friedrich Gottlieb Klopstock which later helped to
create the *Sturm und Drang* aesthetic. Versions followed in Bohemian,
Danish, Dutch, French, Hungarian, Polish, Russian, Spanish, and
Swedish. They were a ready source for writers, painters, and composers:
Johann Wolfgang Goethe transcribed Ossian's entire 'Songs of Selma'
at the end of *The Sorrows of Werther* (where they would have been
read by Frankenstein's monster), Jean-Dominique Ingres painted *The
Dream of Ossian*, Franz Schubert set a handful of songs, and Felix
Mendelssohn composed *Fingal's Cave*. It was a favourite of politicians
and monarchs too: Thomas Jefferson read Ossian every day, and Vic-
toria and Albert visited Fingal's Cave at Staffa, read Gaelic, and were
keen amateur Ossianists. Such was the titanic reputation of Ossian
that Macpherson might have influenced history more than even he
could ever have imagined: Napoleon carried two books with him into
every battle he fought: *The Sorrows of Werther* and the collected works
of Ossian. 'I like Ossian,' he said, 'but for the same reason that I like
to hear the whisper of the wind and the waves of the sea.'

Nevertheless, despite its clear influence on later writers, Samuel
Johnson's condemnation has survived for two centuries and either

discouraged scholars and critics from taking much interest in Ossian, or simply encouraged them to peddle pea-brained prejudices. Johnson's disgust for the poems of Ossian is so absolute that it has bludgeoned any coherent debate, and Ossian is only gradually being read and discussed again. This is because Ossian threatened not only Johnson's being as a writer, but also what became his lifelong project as the architect of an English literary canon, principally via the writers cited in the great *Dictionary* and his edition of Shakespeare. He would soon be crowning his canon-making with the fifty-two prefaces or 'Lives' of the English poets, commissioned in 1777 and published from 1779 to 81 in no fewer than sixty-eight volumes. Here, he stressed the professionalism of canonical writers (and indeed their biographers): the literary life should 'tell us his studies, his manner of life, the means by which he attained to excellence, his opinion of his own works, and such particulars'. *The Lives of the English Poets* was a testament to Johnson's meticulousness as a close reader, his famously gargantuan appetite for books and reading, and his doggedness in untwisting previous biographical sources: all critical practices that are performed best in the library, sitting at a desk with paper and pencil to hand. Ossian, a mysterious bard of the oral tradition who, up in the Highlands, had as yet left no palpable impression whatsoever on subsequent culture, and moreover replete with the vaguest, most imprecise images, ran directly counter to Johnson's conception of authorship – and threatened to muddle the distinctions between real lives and fictional lies that Johnson was promulgating. Although in 1775 he probably had no inkling that he would be writing any lives of any English poets, he did fervently believe that writing literature and criticism was an activity of application rather than inspiration, of judgment rather than rapture, and of morality rather than fantasy. As we will see, there is little to offer such a reader in the poems of Ossian. The only thing that both Johnson and Macpherson could agree upon was the necessity to fight for what they believed in, the need to assert a physical sense of being alive: to be a working, writing body, rather than a historical fiction, a 'walking shadow', a mere echo of oneself, a ghost.

❧ ❧ ❧

GHOSTS

By the side of a rock on the hill, beneath the aged trees, old
Oscian sat on the moss; the last of the race of Fingal.

Ossian, *Fragment VIII*

Ossian is blind, his beard blows in the wind; he sings of graves,
barrows, stone circles, and ghosts. His poetic prose is archaic and
inarticulate, reminiscent more of Old Testament prophecies than of
the fashionable effusions of eighteenth-century 'primitive' verse; his
phrases are suffused with a smothering sense of antiquity and its most
melancholy associations – decay, death, loss. It is almost unremittingly
dark and dismal, describing millennial battles of a lost age, ghostly
and silent, shadowy and blurred. This is the distant murmuring of a
mystical race. 'Fragment II' (a piece later adapted as 'Carric-Thura'),
reads as follows (it is best read aloud):

> I sit by the mossy fountain; on the top of the hill of winds. One
> tree is rustling above me. Dark waves roll over the heath. The
> lake is troubled below. The deer descend from the hill. No hunter
> at a distance is seen; no whistling cow-herd is nigh. It is mid-
> day; but all is silent. Sad are my thoughts alone. Didst thou but
> appear, O my love, a wanderer on the heath! thy hair floating on
> the wind behind thee; thy bosom heaving on the sight; thine eyes
> full of tears for thy friends, whom the mist of the hill had
> concealed! Thee I would comfort, my love, and bring thee to thy
> father's house.
>
> But is it she that there appears, like a beam of light on the
> heath? bright as the moon in autumn, as the sun in a summer-
> storm, comest thou lovely maid over rocks, over mountains to
> me? – She speaks: but how weak her voice! like the breeze in the
> reeds of the pool. Hark!
>
> Returnest thou safe from the war? Where are thy friends, my
> love? I heard of thy death on the hill; I heard and mourned thee,
> Shilric!

> Yes, my fair, I return; but I alone of my race. Thou shalt see
> them no more: their graves I raised on the plain. But why art
> thou on the desert hill? why on the heath, alone?
>
> Alone I am, O Shilric! alone in the winter-house. With grief
> for thee I expired. Shilric, I am pale in the tomb.
>
> She fleets, she sails away; as grey mist before the wind! – and,
> wilt thou not stay, my love? Stay and behold my tears? fair thou
> appearest, my love! fair thou wast, when alive!
>
> By the mossy fountain I will sit; on the top of the hill of
> winds. When mid-day is silent around, converse, O my love, with
> me! come on the wings of the gale! on the blast of the mountain,
> come! Let me hear thy voice, as thou passest, when mid-day is
> silent around.

One's immediate sense is of insistent repetition: 'I sit by the mossy
fountain; on the top of the hill of winds. . . . By the mossy fountain
I will sit; on the top of the hill of winds . . . It is mid-day; but all is
silent . . . when mid-day is silent around.' The howling wind, the rising
gale, the dark disruption despite the noonday sun, the retreat of natural
order in the shape of the deer – a creature legendary for its perception
of the supernatural, the silence, the mist, and the confusion of inner
and outer worlds (tears and fountains, tombs and grey mist), even of
night and day ('bright as the moon in autumn, as the sun in a summer-
storm'). The ghostliness of the heath, of the wind, of the tomb ('the
winter-house'), the weakness ('like the breeze in the reeds of the pool'),
the paleness, the intangibility, the eeriness, the repetition of love and
death, of love and death . . .

The images gather claustrophobically, as if hemmed in by the walls
of a tomb. And coming afterwards, like a train of ghosts, one glimpses
the 'floating hair' of Samuel Taylor Coleridge's 'Kubla Khan', one
catches the breath of Catherine on the moor in Emily Brontë's
Wuthering Heights (1847), even tastes the red mist of Wagnerian
slaughter that suffuses John Boorman's film *Excalibur* (1981). The
ensuing 'Fragment III', opens with the impression of the passing of
time, passing because time has already just been evoked in precisely
the same terms: 'Evening is grey on the hills. The north wind resounds
through the woods.' And yet time, it transpires, does not pass so much
as swirl, eddy, and ebb.

Ossian is haunted by the question, 'whither the dead?', haunted by the dead who won't lie down. Ghosts are everywhere: on the weeping wind, on the airs that Ossian draws from his lyre, on the waves and storms and tempests. The ghosts outnumber the living, indeed Ossian is the last of his race and keeps company only with the dead, with memories that remind him of the futility of his persistence: a living bard with dead characters and a dead audience, whose song seeks to summon the dead, whose song seeks to emulate nature, to become indistinguishable from the murmur of the breeze or the clatter of water, and whose dead are likewise indistinguishable from nature and song.

The ghost of Crugal that haunts *Fingal* emerges almost imperceptibly from a false dawn:

> My hero saw in his rest a dark-red stream of fire coming down from the hill. Crugal sat upon the beam, a chief that lately fell. He fell by the hand of Swaran, striving in the battle of heroes. His face is like the beam of the setting moon; his robes are of the clouds of the hill: his eyes are like two decaying flames. Dark is the wound of his breast.

Likewise, Aldo in 'The Battle of Lora' is a 'thin ghost . . . on a rock, like the watry beam of the moon, when it rushes from between two clouds, and the midnight shower is on the field'.

It is an explicit role of the bards to summon ghosts, a re-membering from a fragment of a person, but such powers are not confined to the bards. In *Temora*, set by the Lake of Lego, the haunt of the dead, sleep becomes a metaphorical '*hill of ghosts*', a realm where the ghosts may visit the living. In his commentary, Macpherson muses on the superstitions of the Highlands of Scotland, where ghosts foretell death, and it is worth emphasizing that many of the Ossianic ghosts are lovers, kith and kin, and as such are benign memories to remind characters of duties and responsibilities. Macpherson also notes, however, that it was thought that storms were raised by ghosts, and that whirlwinds and sudden squalls of wind were caused by restless spirits moving themselves hither and thither. Hugh Blair went so far as to claim that 'Ossian describes ghosts with all the particularity of one who had seen and conversed with them, and whose imagination was full of the impression they had left upon it.' It is an important, if passing, remark – a weird claim of authenticity.

❧

Such an otherworld appealed, of course, to William Blake, who admitted 'I own myself an admirer of Ossian equally with any other Poet whatever.'* His own life was a visionary experience spent among ghosts and angels, and the supernaturalism of Ossian asserts itself through the cadence of the Prophetic Books, such as *The Book of Ahania*:

> The lamenting voice of Ahania,
> Weeping upon the void
> And round the tree of Fuzon.
> Distant in solitary night, but no form
> Had she: but her tears from clouds
> Eternal fell round the tree,
>
> And the voice cried . . .
> 'I lie on the verge of the deep.
> I see thy dark clouds ascend,
> I see thy black forests and floods,
> A horrible waste to my eyes.'

There is much in this lament, in the imagery and cadence, that one recognizes from Ossian, but there is also an anti-Ossianic activation of vocabulary that makes Blake's verse quiver gigantically – even when it is immobile – rather than tarry, beset by ghosts. And in the succeeding *Book of Los*, this kinetic power propels Blake's poetry away from Ossian and towards Milton:

> The Immortal stood frozen amidst
> The vast rock of Eternity – times
> And times, a night of vast durance:
> Impatient, stifled, stiffened, hardened;
>
> Till impatience no longer could bear
> The hard bondage: rent, rent, the vast solid
> With a crash from immense to immense
>
> Cracked across into numberless fragments. . . .

This is not the haunting of a ghost but the emergence of a giant, as

---

* The influence is apparent in early work, such as 'Gwin, King of Norway'; and see also 'The Couch of Death' and 'Contemplation'.

if Ossianic spirits are too intangible and need to be enfleshed as vast creatures – titans, angels, devils: 'Names anciently rememberd!' as Blake would put it, 'but now contemn'd as fictions.'

In *Paradise Lost* the Titans were specifically identified with the Celts, and the analogies Macpherson made with Milton's poem in his notes to *Fingal* most frequently linked the Celtic warriors with the fallen angels. Furthermore, one of Macpherson's footnotes to *Temora* describes his pity for Milton's Satan – anticipating the Romantic enthusiasm for the Devil's party. But it is important to stress that Ossian could only provide the ghost of an inspiration to Blake, who was fiercely committed to absolute originality, and once declared, 'Englishmen rouze yourselves from the fatal Slumber into which Booksellers & Trading Dealers have thrown you Under the artfully propagated pretence that a Translation or a Copy of any kind can be as honourable to a Nation as An Original . . .' Ossian's ghosts were shadows cast by the past, but Blake's spirits are vital and creative forces that drive the present into the future. Ossian's ghosts too are oddly unoriginal – repetitions or fragments of dead people; in fact, the principle of repetition animates the entire project, and is symptomatic of Ossian's form and function as a phantasmic bard. Here too, it will transpire, Blake and Ossian diverge.

BARDS

A poet laureate is a 'Pretender, Pseudo-Poet, or Phantom'

Alexander Pope, *Essay on Man, Epistle II*

When the teenager James Macpherson began collecting traditional Gaelic poetry in 1756, a few ancient bards still survived. Once, each Highland clan had maintained a bard, who preserved and honoured the history and exploits of his kinsmen, and marked special occasions such as births, deaths, and marriages with poems and songs. It is a familiar, if romanticized, image, but one which was all the more evocative of a lost age after the dissolution of the clans and the suppression of Gaelic culture following the Battle of Culloden in 1746. And although the word has been loosely applied to poets and singers, from Shakespeare ('The Bard of all Bards was a Warwickshire Bard,' as David Garrick so eloquently phrased it) to Robert Plant of the rock band Led Zeppelin, Macpherson, a gifted classicist, had a specific Homeric meaning in mind when he began to mould Ossian – who was called by Voltaire 'the Homer of Scotland'. And it is meet to begin a bardic voyage with *The Odyssey*.

The blind bard of the Phaeacians is Demodocus (in book VIII of *The Odyssey*), whom the Muse has blinded but blessed with sweet song. He sings of gods and of men: of Ares and Aphrodite and the limping craftsman and forger Hephaestus, and of recent history in a version of *The Iliad*. Demodocus is much respected and honoured, and though his songs are conventional and formal recitations, central to court order, they nonetheless bring tears to Odysseus's eyes. As Charles Segal explains, the bard was neither a wandering minstrel nor a hired hand, but a 'permanent fixture in the royal establishment and has a respected place and regular duties there'. The Homeric bard is a singer rather than a maker, *aoidos* rather than *poietes*, 'because he is the voice and the vehicle of an ancient wisdom . . . [however] if the poet's powers are divine, they are not irrational.' Odysseus himself is quick to praise Demodocus, hospitably carves him the choicest cut of meat, and declares that he has been taught not only by the Muses but even by the presiding god of poetry and music, Apollo himself. Such poetic skill is precisely Apollonian: it is not a divine rapture that possesses the poet in a frenzied madness, not even the heady inspiration described by Plato in *Ion* or *Phaedrus*. The Muses called upon for Homer's invocation to catalogue the ships that sailed to Troy in *The Iliad* are 'present and know everything', but they communicate such information with discretion rather than through rolling eyes and foaming mouth.

A clear example of this occurs at the end of *The Odyssey* (book XXII) when Phemios, another bard, pleads with Odysseus during the slaying of the suitors to save his life. Yes, he has been singing for

the suitors, but then that is literally his employment: he is a professional
bard, and claims a privilege against his execution.* In Pope's translation:

> O King! to mercy be thy soul inclin'd,
> And spare the Poet's ever-gentle kind.
> A deed like this thy future fame would wrong,
> For dear to Gods and Men is sacred song.
> Self-taught [*autodidaktos*] I sing; by heav'n, and heav'n alone
> The genuine seeds of Poesy are sown;
> And (what the Gods bestow) the lofty lay,
> To Gods alone, and god-like worth, we pay.
> Save then the Poet, and thy self reward;
> 'Tis thine to merit, mine is to record.

Phemios is not simply repeating what he has learnt from a teacher –
as an autodidact his skills come from himself, and yet simultaneously
his inspiration is divine. But the Muse (or the god Apollo) is the
lightning rod or medium of inspiration – keeping distant events fresh,
filling in gaps in knowledge, and cultivating his voice. 'At such
moments,' says Segal, the bard 'is like the warrior into whom the god
breathes *menos* at the height of battle': Homer uses the same term,
ενεπνευσε, meaning 'breathed into' or 'inspired', for both.

The public character and social responsibility of the bard described
by Homer is clearly evident in eighteenth-century accounts of ancient
societies such as 'Estimate' Brown's *Dissertation on Poetry and Music*
(1763) and John Macpherson's *Critical Dissertations* (1768).† Brown was
an avowed supporter of Ossian, in which he saw evidence of the time
when bards were no longer legislators, yet still retained their 'Power
and Dignity in full union'; whereas John Macpherson regarded the
bard as a cultural prophet:

> The poet and prophet are congenial souls. Their professions are
> nearly allied. . . . As it is the prophet's business to utter predictions,
> so the poet assumes the same character occasionally, and asserts
> that he speaks the language of the Gods.

This latter notion – quite un-Johnsonian – was later pursued by
Thomas Carlyle in 'Heroes and Hero-Worship' to equate the bard with
the 'vates', a Latin word used by Caesar to describe the rather mys-

* The twentieth-century analogy being: 'Don't shoot me, I'm just the piano player.'
† James Macpherson appears to have helped his cousin John write these *Dissertations*.

terious soothsayers and herbalists he encountered in Gaul, and soon after adopted by Virgil for the public poet or bard.* Indeed, Virgil also bestows the title on Proteus, whose multiplicity represents the variety of earthly forms, and uses it for the Sybil as well. There was falsehood here too: Hildegard von Bingen, for instance, coined the word *Falschin* for vates, to distinguish the false from the true prophets. Sir Philip Sidney defined the vates as a poet or prophet, whereas Chambers suggested that 'The *Bardi* were the Poets; the *Vates*... were the Sacrificers, and Naturalists'. Whatever they were, the word did blossom into some rich English forms: Caxton has 'vaticinant' (1490) for prophesying and predicting; 'vaticinate', 'vaticination', and 'vaticinator' were used throughout the seventeenth century. It also seems to have been favoured by the Cambridge Platonists; Henry More in his *Song of Soul* (1647) deploys the word gorgeously: 'The soul is said to be in a vaticinant or parturient condition, when she hath some kind of sense, and hovering knowledge of a thing, but yet cannot distinctly and fully... represent it to herself.' But although Pope describes the 'unspeakable Curll' as a 'caitiff vaticide', usage of the word and its cognates declined in the eighteenth century and the concept was absorbed into the general idea of the bard.

This implicit connection between bards and Druids is worth teasing out a little more. According to Raphael Holinshed in *The First Volume of the Chronicles of England* (1577), there was originally little difference between bards and Druids, at least until the bards degenerated 'to be minstrelles at feastes, droncken meetings, and abhominable sacrifices of Idols'. Druids (the word is derived from the Celtic) are equivalent to the Gallic 'druidae' of Caesar's description – magicians, wizards, or diviners. Although in Ireland early Christian saints were often called Druids, the indigenous kind were rumoured to be a tricky lot. Caesar described Druidic sacrifices of giant wicker men in which human victims were burnt alive, Pliny the Elder insisted that the Druids were cannibals, and there was a general consensus that Stonehenge and other stone circles had hosted their beastly rites and slaughters. A. L. Owen outlines the Druidic day's work thus:

> The Druids raised storms, laid curses on places, killed by the use of spells, declared auspicious occasions, and created magical

* Strabo too describes the vates as soothsayers of the second rank of the Druidic hierarchy.

obstacles. Their persons were sacrosanct, and they were therefore employed as ambassadors. They were physicians, and they investigated crimes.

These powerful and frightening figures became icons of English poetry. Andrew Marvell, for instance, considered himself to be a 'Druid', as did the poetaster Leonard Welstead, mainly because he enjoyed a drink. Druids doubled as poeticisms for priests, poets, and singers, and proved popular with Milton (in *Lycidas*), with William Collins, and of course with Blake. Thomas Warton originally intended to introduce his *History of English Poetry* with an allusion to the lost poems of the Druids. Indeed, the antiquity of Druidism meant that eighteenth-century antiquarians tended to associate them with the origin of language, of worship, and of humanity itself. Blake claimed in *A Descriptive Catalogue of Pictures* (1808) that Druidism flourished before Adam, and that the Jews had received from the Druids 'a tradition, that Man anciently contain'd in his limbs all things in Heaven and Earth'. Even their terrifying form of human sacrifice found a defence in the gentle satire of Thomas Love Peacock's novel *The Misfortunes of Elphin* (1829). Peacock suggested that it was no worse than hanging felons for (astoundingly) *forgery*:

> If one of these old Druids could have slept, like the seven sleepers of Ephesus, and awaked, in the nineteenth century, some fine morning near Newgate, the exhibition of some half-dozen funipendulous forgers might have shocked the tender bowels of his [the Druid's] humanity as much as one of his wicker baskets of captives in the flames shocked those of Caesar.

No less surprising is Wordsworth's persistent interest in them – he mentions Druids more often than any other English poet and christens himself one, but seems confused whether they represent a twilight Ossianic darkness or, for example in his *Ecclesiastical Sonnets*, the dawn of Christianity. They appear in *The Prelude* first as a nightmare haunting Salisbury Plain with the 'dismal flames' of wicker men, before almost instantly metamorphosing into 'long-bearded teachers' conducting their classes to the soft muzak of Ossianic winds:

> . . . while breath
> Of music swayed their motions, and the waste
> Rejoiced with them and me in those sweet sounds.

Like Ossian, they mediate between past and present, dreams and wakefulness, the ether and the earth.*

But apart from enigmatic stone circles, there were no Druidic remains – no literature or language for their secret tongue was never committed to paper, it was said, and so was extinguished with them, and there were no archaeological sites of oak groves and mistletoe, or finds of silver sickles. Rather, Druidism lay in the land. The ancient text of these mountains green, pleasant pastures, and clouded hills might be completely illegible by the eighteenth century, but in the verse of James Thomson and William Cowper, Blake and Wordsworth, there is a sense that one is at least in the presence of a glorious natural language. 'Ah what shall Language do?' asks Thomson in 'Spring', from *The Seasons*,

> Ah where find Words
> Ting'd with so many Colours; and whose Powers,
> To Life approaching, may perfume my Lays
> With that fine Oil, those aromatic Gales,
> That inexhaustive flow continual round?

So it is precisely Ossian's incoherent and primitive way of reading the world that created such an awesome atmosphere for contemporary readers. Ossian, who has outlived the Druids and outlasted primitive religion, is an outcast from the unknowable Druidic mysteries, is forsaken by even the cruellest gods. Yet his poetry still repeats the Druidical creed by tracing meaning in oaks and glades and Cyclopean rocks. Fingal himself is described as a storm: 'He came like a cloud of rain in the days of the sun, when slow it rolls on the hill, and fields expect the shower'; and Ossian answers the bard Carril by describing his plaintive song as if it were composed of the natural eddies of the air: 'sit thou on the heath, O Bard, and let us hear thy voice. It is pleasant as the gale of spring that sighs on the hunter's ear; when he wakens from dreams of joy, and has heard the music of the spirits of the hill.' Like the Druids, the mighty who have passed leave their traces sighing on the wind, remembered in the twist of a tree, or a scattering of rocks, in the glittering sun, or dancing rain. Hence at the death

---

* Despite his later scorn for Ossian, Wordsworth wrote several poems exhibiting a direct Ossianic influence: 'Glen Almain', 'Effusion in the Pleasure-ground on the Banks of the Bran', 'The Earl of Breadalbane's Ruined Mansion', 'The Highland Broach', 'Written in a Blank Leaf of Macpherson's Ossian', and the four 'Cave of Staffa' sonnets.

of Ossian's son Oscur: 'He fell as the moon in a storm; as the sun from the midst of his course, when clouds rise from the waste of the waves, when the blackness of the storm inwraps the rocks of Ardannider.'*

Nature is also, however, a political discourse. The oak is Druidic, but it is also quintessentially English, and furthermore a Jacobite symbol (Charles II having hidden in one). Macpherson was only nine years old when he witnessed his Jacobite kinsmen overrun the local Castle of Ruthven and march to join the Pretender, Bonnie Prince Charlie, to restore the Stuarts to the throne; he also witnessed the bloody remnants of the Jacobite army fleeing back from the Battle of Culloden, pursued by 'Butcher Cumberland'. Macpherson's teenage years were spent in a Scotland subject to harsh English colonial rule: clan chieftains were outlawed, their houses razed, their estates forfeited; kilts, tartans, the carrying of traditional weapons, even playing the bagpipes, were banned. English replaced Gaelic in schools; troops were barracked at garrisons; new roads divided the remote Highland wilderness – in short, the English attempted to destroy the clans and eradicate Gaelic culture. So it is possible to read Ossian as an attempt to reforge the Scottish nation after the massacre of Culloden, a crucial text in the reconstruction of national identities both inside and outside Great Britain.

Historians, however, are liable to become excitable in politicizing the Highlands, finding a Jacobite in every acorn-cup. Oaks, it transpires, also have a specific vatic quality, independent of the Druidic culture, and far removed from political upheavals. Socrates in *Phaedrus* mentions a tradition of the temple of Dodona, that oaks first gave prophetic utterances: 'The men of old, far simpler than you sophisticated young men, deemed that if they heard the truth even from "oak or rock", it was enough; whereas you seem to consider not whether a thing is or is not true, but who the speaker is and from what country the tale comes.' The question 'Who is speaking?' is irrelevant to Socrates; his opinion returns us to the issue of authenticity and authority in voice.

Ossian, as the embodiment of a 'natural' oral tradition, shares the

---

* Notwithstanding this, some contemporary reviewers still thought the works too polished: 'I am convinced that his original was a Wilderness; but, it was a Wilderness of beauties: Perhaps it would have been as well, had they been produced in their primitive disorder' (Anon., *Fingal Reclaimed*, 1762).

Socratic, and anti-Johnsonian, distrust of letters: they are destructive
to memory and therefore truth – the Muses were in fact the daughters
of Mnemosyne, or Memory. Ossian effectively proposes then a
version of authenticity differently calibrated from that of the written
text. It may be modish, but it is quite mistaken to worry more about
the teller than the tale. This position that not only justifies bardism,
but also releases literary forgery – and literature more generally – from
intentionalist and biographical criticism.

Elsewhere, in *Phaedrus*, Socrates himself calls on the Muses, and
he becomes moderately inspired in comparing four kinds of madness: prophecy, purification by mysteries, poetry or the inspiration of
the Muses, and love. Prophecy and poetry are both 'a possession of the
Muses; this [possession] enters into a delicate and virgin soul and
there inspiring frenzy, awakens lyric and all other numbers; with these
adorning the myriad actions of ancient heroes for the instruction of
posterity'. Socrates's apparent willingness to surrender himself to the
blandishments of the Muses is characteristic of Platonic philosophy
and also of Neoplatonism, as we will see presently. But, like vatic
inspiration, this is a measured congress with the Muses, rather than a
wild possession. In fact, it is worth comparing this way of generating
poetry, in which female Muses are decorously courted by male minds,
with Virgil's hallucinatory account of how the female Sybil receives
her oracular information from the male god.

The Sybil lives in a 'spacious cave' full of doors and thresholds,
filled with echoing voices:

> before the place,
> A hundred Doors a hundred Entries grace:
> As many Voices issue; and the sound
> Of Sibyl's Words as many times rebound.
> Now to the Mouth they come: Aloud she cries,
> This is the time, enquire your Destinies.*

In response, the god overtakes her and she is physically transformed:

> Her Colour chang'd, her Face was not the same,
> And hollow Groans from her deep Spirit came.
> Her Hair stood up; convulsive Rage possess'd
> Her trembling Limbs, and heav'd her lab'ring Breast.

---

* I have used John Dryden's thrilling translation.

> Greater than Human Kind she seem'd to look:
> And with an Accent, more than Mortal, spoke.
> Her staring Eyes with sparkling Fury rowl;
> When all the God came rushing on her Soul.

The sense of physical possession here is in stark contrast to the fragrant inspiration of the Homeric Muses. The Sybil is not so much kissed by the creating breath of the god, as overpowered and inseminated, raped to the point of orgasm:

> Strugling in vain, impatient of her Load,
> And lab'ring underneath the pond'rous God,
> The more she strove to shake him from her Breast,
> With more, and far superior Force he press'd:
> Commands his Entrance, and without Controul,
> Usurps her Organs, and inspires her Soul.

Like bursting hymens the doors of her cave fly open and her prophetic voice is carried on a shuddering hurricane:

> Now, with a furious Blast, the hundred Doors
> Ope of themselves; a rushing Wirlwind roars
> Within the Cave; and Sibyl's Voice restores.

It is a startling passage: the Muses too were female, with fertile imaginations in which their thoughts were conceived, their words pregnant with meaning. Romantic Neoplatonist thinking, however, would make inspiration and indeed authenticity an entirely masculine enterprise, presided over by angels and daemons, all of whom were male.

Despite the profound difference in tone, there are in fact many similarities between Virgil's Sybil and Macpherson's Ossian – the echoes, the wind, the confusion of voices, the implicit passivity of the medium – and such a model of rapture did generate a reading that Homer was so inspired: hair streaming, beard blowing in all directions, blind eyes rolling about in the head. Thomas Blackwell, for instance, an influential thinker whose *Enquiry into the Life and Writings of Homer* was published in 1735, argues that the Homeric Bards (ΑΟΙΔΟΣ) are like the Dionysian bacchante, working themselves into the frenzy of 'rhythmus', a form of inspired primeval chanting:

> While he was personating a *Hero*, while his Fancy was warming,
> and his words flowing; when he had fully entered into the *Measure*,

was struck with the *Rhythmus*, and seized with the *Sound*; like a Torrent, he wou'd fill up the Hollows of the Work; the boldest Metaphors and glowing Figures wou'd come rushing upon him, and cast a *Fire* and *Grace* into the Composition, which no Criticism can ever supply.

Blackwell has in fact has been considered as one of the principal influences upon Macpherson's concept of oral poetry* – indeed, he was Principal of Marischal College while Macpherson was a student there – and Blackwell's Homer was certainly an influence on such things as Thomas Gray's haggard creature 'The Bard' (1757),

> Loose his beard and hoary hair
> Streamed, like a meteor, to the troubled air.

But Ossian is entirely different. He sits down on hills in the rain and bemoans his fate, rather than shrieking from lightning-racked mountain tops. Although contemporaries like Gray may have confused the two, Macpherson, brilliant classicist that he was, may have been rather sceptical of Blackwell's inspired Homer.

Ossian, then, is inspired by the Homeric Muse, as opposed to the Blackwellian rhythmus: his knowledge derives literally from the daughters of Memory (Mnemosyne) who 'know everything', and his social functions are (or at least were) to attend kings, mourn and remember the dead, maintain the historical record, and effectively legislate culture, not to be gripped by fits of divine madness. This again distinguishes Ossian from Blake, who in annotating Joshua Reynolds's *Discourses* (Discourse III), quoted Milton's specific condemnation of such a form of inspiration:

> A work of Genius is a Work 'Not to be obtain'd by the Invocation of Memory & her Syren Daughters, but by Devout prayer to that Eternal Spirit, who can enrich with all utterance & knowledge & sends out his Seraphim with the hallowed fire of his Altar to touch & purify the lip of whom he pleases.' MILTON

In Ossian, it is ghosts that do the work of the Muses. Indeed, the only society that Ossian can enjoy is ghostly.

Malcolm Laing, in his super-sceptical edition of Ossian published in 1805, complained among many other things (such as that Mac-

---

* Not least, ahem, by me.

pherson was a plagiarist of Virgil, Homer, and Milton) about this 'intermix' of the quick and the dead, of the past in the present. But the poems constitute a vast memento mori, in which predestined defeat has an analogy with human mortality. As Matthew Arnold was to lament, quoting from 'Cathloda': 'They went forth to the war, *but they always fell.*' Ghosts are a necessity, and cloudiness or ghostliness is a prerequisite of renown for, in the Virgilian epigraph on the title-page of *Fingal*, 'fortia facta patrum': the book celebrates 'brave deeds of the forefathers'. It explains why Ossianic society seems to converse, live, and love in blood, why killing is the sole intimacy of the culture, and why Ossian, a survivor, is so bereft. He has failed, because he still lives. As William Hazlitt put it in one of his lectures on the English [*sic*] poets:

> Ossian is the decay and old age of poetry. He lives only in the recollection and regret of the past. There is one impression that he conveys more entirely than all other poets, namely the sense of privation, the loss of all things, of friends, of good name, of country – he is even without God in the world.

The ghostly Ossianic Muse also conforms to Plato's standards of Homeric possession described in the simile of the magnet in *Ion*, from which hang chains of imitators, and also to Longinus's version of inspiration in which many authors 'catch fire' from the example of another, archetypal poet. Early admirers of Ossian either raved about its beauties or produced imitations in both prose and verse.

> I am gone mad about them [said Thomas Gray on 20 June 1760]. they are said to be translations (literal & in prose) from the Erse-tongue, done by one Macpherson, a young Clergyman in the High-lands. he means to publish a Collection he has of these Specimens of antiquity, if it be antiquity: but what plagues me is, I can not come at any certainty on that head. I was so struck, so *extasié* with their infinite beauty, that I writ into Scotland to make a thousand enquiries ... this Man is the very Demon of Poetry, or he has lighted on a treasure hid for ages.*

---

* Robert Anderson, in his 'Life of Gray', remarked: 'It is observable, that sublimity of genius has been generally attended with a strong affection for the demonry of the ancient northern fable. Milton was particularly fond of it. It was the study of his youth and the dream of his age. This passion seems natural.'

Similarly, Andrew Erskine wrote to Boswell after reading *Fingal*:

> It is quite impossible to express my admiration of his Poems; at
> particular passages I felt my whole frame trembling with ecstacy;
> but if I was to describe all my thoughts, you would think me
> absolutely mad. The beautiful wildness of his fancy is inexpressibly
> agreeable to the imagination.

For both, reading Ossian was an *ecstatic* experience – *ekstasis* meaning
to stand outside oneself – and therefore seemed to be a displacement
or translation of the self by another force. There was an attempt to
theorize such an enraptured response by the critic John Gordon, who
introduced a passage from Ossian thus: 'Who then can look at the
following description, and not forget almost, that he is reading words?
– so naturally do the real objects themselves rise to our view!' He
argues that the words are so close to the objects they represent that
they work as a summoning – which is striking when one considers the
prevalence of ghosts in the poems: how naturally can *they* rise to view?
But this strange conjuring effect does, however, look forward, like so
much of Ossian, to 'Kubla Khan', 'in which', as Coleridge claimed, 'all
the images rose up before him as *things*.

Imitations of Ossian were published so rapidly that Macpherson
almost seemed to have inaugurated a new genre of writing, and this
quality to inspire others swiftly drew Macpherson's own relationship
with the late Ossian into the discussion. It is implicit in Gray's
important comment, 'this Man is the very Demon of Poetry', which
attempts to explain Macpherson by elevating him to a figure of daemonic inspiration. But Macpherson continued to present himself as a
translator and editor. Herbert Croft (of whom more later) could not
understand it: 'They abuse Macpherson for calling them translations.
If he alone be the author of them, why does he not say so, and claim
the prize of fame. I protest *I* would.'

As it was, the *Fragments* began unequivocally: 'The public may
depend on the following fragments as genuine remains of ancient
Scottish poetry', and Macpherson was referred to as the 'translator'
throughout. For the revised and collected edition of 1773, however,
Macpherson had decided that 'A translator, who cannot equal his
original, is incapable of expressing its beauties', and he substantially
revised the work. Genuine poetry was, however, like gold: it 'loses
little, when properly transfused; but when a composition cannot bear

the test of a literal version, it is a counterfeit which ought not to pass current.' Some Ossianic critics today see in the complexity of translation the activities of interpretation and mediation between Gaelic and English, between oral and literate culture, between the Highlands and Lowlands, and Peter Murphy notes that the poems, by calling themselves 'translations', include connotations of movement and transfer. But translation in this sense is a specialist theological word:

> it can describe the transport of a person to heaven without death, or (of Ossianic relevance) it can describe the moving of mortal remains from one place to another. It can also describe a sort of rapture, a figurative use derived, one supposes, from 'translation' to another state of being.

Which is certainly what Gray and Erskine felt (and, for that matter, the Sybil). And the act of translation itself deploys, as Adrian Poole and Jeremy Maule indicate, metaphors of resurrection. Like biography, translation has been condemned not only as a form of body-snatching (or plagiarism), but also of occult reanimation. Translators have been compared to Aesculapius, who is supposed to have breathed life into a dismembered corpse, as well as to alchemists transfusing and mixing spirits. Friedrich Nietzsche, in *The Gay Science*, goes even further. He argues that 'translation was a form of conquest', and antithetical to a sense of history. Hence the Romans could confidently, recklessly seize Greek works, declaring

> Should we not make new for ourselves what is old and find ourselves in it? Should we not have the right to breathe our own soul into this dead body?

Translation was also the technical term for the migration of charters and relics – physical objects that conferred authority on people and institutions. Things like a stone used to beat St Stephen, part of the column of Christ's flagellation, a tooth of St Zeno, the tibia of St Peter, the skull of St James the Less, were all translated to St Mark's in Venice as talismans that gave a sacred sanction to the secular activities of the church: absolute power was translated into a handful of macabre fragments in an act of repetitious mourning not unlike Ossian.

✤ ✤ ✤

REPETITIONS

> ... if there were no repetition, what then would life be?
> Who would wish to be a tablet upon which time writes
> every new inscription? or to be a mere memorial of the
> past? ... If God Himself had not willed repetition, the world
> would never have come into existence. ... Repetition is
> reality, and it is the seriousness of life.
>
> Søren Kierkegaard, 'Essay on Repetition'

Blind Ossian cannot receive new impressions, his poetry depends
upon age-old repetition, and this dereliction perhaps makes Ossian a
symptom of history who exhibits the linguistic symptoms of senile
dementia, as Luce Irigaray famously described them: 'Spoken more
than speaking, enunciated more than enunciating, the demented person
is therefore no longer really an active subject of the enunciation.
... He is only a possible mouthpiece for previously pronounced
enunciations.' Ossian's language is confused, repetitive, a bewildering
combination of a tiny vocabulary and a cabbalistical catalogue of names
and genealogies, spoken as if an alien language, spoken as if on the
verge of collapse. The quality of Ossianic repetition is less, then, like
the echolalia of the idiot-savant who repeats any language but is
incapable of rational discourse, and more like the murmuring delirium
of a mind dissolving into mist.

Indeed Horace Walpole found the disintegrating language of
dementia characteristic of his aesthetic of the Gothic – it was a
linguistic version of the Burkean sublime. As he wrote to George
Montagu:

> Visions, you know, have always been my pasture, and so far from
> growing old enough to quarrel with their emptiness, I almost
> think there is no wisdom comparable to that of exchanging what
> is called the realities of life for dreams. Old castles, old pictures,
> old histories, and the babble of old people make one live back
> into centuries that cannot disappoint one.

The letter was written on 5 January 1766, just a few months after the
publication of the collected Ossian, and Walpole's language is redolent
with Ossianisms: visions, pastures, emptiness, dreams, age, babble. It
makes sense too of Johnson's remark of Ossian: 'Sir, a man might write
such stuff for ever, if he would *abandon* his mind to it.'

But the later Romantic translation of Ossian into a figure of
inspiration found less in dementia and more in translating the congress
of the Muses into an aesthetic of repetition. It was a way in which the
art of imitation could be practised, not as 'imitation' in the neoclassical
sense of the word, but instead as sublime echoes or shadows. Repetition
is central to Samuel Taylor Coleridge's philosophy, in which imaginative creativity was 'a repetition in the finite mind of the eternal act
of creation', but his most enticing account of repetition comes in *The
Friend*. It is worth quoting the passage at length:

> [T]here is one excellence in good music, to which, without mys-
> ticism, we may find or make an analogy in the records of History.
> I allude to that sense of *recognition*, which accompanies our sense
> of novelty in the most original passages of a great composer. If
> we listen to a Symphony of CIMAROSA, the present strain still
> seems not only to recal [sic], but almost to *renew*, some past
> movement, another and yet the same! Each present movement
> bringing back, as it were, and embodying the spirit of some
> melody that had gone before, anticipates and seems trying to
> overtake something that is to come: and the musician has reached
> the summit of his art, when having thus modified the Present
> by the Past, he at the same time weds the Past *in* the Present to
> some prepared and corresponsive Future. The auditor's thoughts
> and feelings move under the same influence: retrospection blends
> with anticipation, and Hope and Memory (a female Janus)
> become one power with a double aspect. A similar effect the
> reader may produce for himself in the pages of History, if he will
> be content to substitute an intellectual complacency for pleasur-
> able sensation. The events and characters of one age, like the
> strains in music, recal those of another, and the variety by which
> each is individualized, not only gives a charm and poignancy to
> the resemblance, but likewise renders the whole more intelligible.
> Meantime ample room is afforded for the exercise both of the
> judgment and the fancy, in distinguishing cases of real resemblance
> from those of intentional imitation, the analogies of nature,

revolving upon herself, from the masquerade figures of cunning and vanity.

In a single chord, Coleridge harmonizes the melody of history with a 'female Janus' (the two-faced god, looking both forwards and backwards), who through the marriage of Hope and Memory herself recalls the Muses. This gives truth and symmetry to history whenever a shared trait is disclosed, but not when there is a mere extrinsic copying. Repetition in this passage is ultimately a form of revelation.

In the year of Macpherson's death (and coincidentally the year of William Henry Ireland's Shakspeare forgery), Coleridge published *Poems on Various Subjects*. His first collection included among its 'Effusions' one 'Imitated from Ossian' and another titled 'The Complaint of Ninathoma', and in the preface to the second edition (1797) Coleridge explicitly referred to Ossian – as he had done in his lecture 'On the Present War' in 1795. At the same time he was also considering writing an Ossianic opera, 'Carthon', and was planning a 'History of English Poetry' to include a 'Series of True Heroic Ballads from Ossian' (note the word 'Ballads' that was to become so pivotal in his and Wordsworth's career with the publication of *Lyrical Ballads* in 1798). And 'Kubla Khan' (1797) too breathes the dying air of Ossian in the defeated half-rhyme of the couplet,

> And 'mid this tumult Kubla heard from far
> Ancestral voices prophesying war!

Most characteristically, Coleridge's Ossianic imitations, or rather *repetitions*, miniaturize the crashing storms and sublime mists, focusing perhaps upon a single flower caught in an Ossianic gale, witness to some faithless tryst; and indeed his first conversation poem, 'The Eolian Harp', also first published here, translates the dim power of Ossian into a domestic setting. The harp of the title is a stringed instrument hung in a window to hum with the wind:

> Such a soft floating witchery of sound

that then summons ghostly memories:

> Whilst thro' my half-clos'd eyelids I behold
> The sunbeams dance, like diamonds, on the main,
> And tranquil muse upon tranquillity;
> Full many a thought uncall'd and undetain'd,

And many idle flitting phantasies,
Traverse my indolent and passive brain
As wild and various, as the random gales
That swell or flutter on this subject Lute!

These lines may be philosophically far superior to anything within Macpherson's ken, but they are an echo, a repetition of the Ossianic breeze. And so Coleridge's reading and writing of Ossian is like a form of translation here: the transferral of power from one place to another, carrying for Coleridge both the living and the dead.

Macpherson had his own figure for this melancholy whisper: '*the voice of the dead*' – a supernatural way of dying, in which a soul in distress is called away by the ghosts of ancestors. This is clearly reminiscent of the Irish tradition of the 'bean sí' or banshee: a solitary female spirit or 'otherworld woman' whose plaintive, keening cry is heard to lament when a family or clan death is imminent, and thereby inspire poets. Sabine Baring-Gould described her lilting, Ossianic song thus:

When the banshee loves those she calls, the song is a low, soft chant giving notice, indeed, of the proximity of death but with a tenderness of tone that reassures the one destined to die and comforts the survivors; rather a welcome than a warning

– which is perhaps how Thomas Gray understood it:

Ghosts ride on the tempest to-night:
Sweet is their voice between the gusts of wind;
Their songs are of other worlds!

Did you never observe (*while rocking winds are piping loud*) that pause, as the gust is recollecting itself, and rising upon the ear in a shrill and plaintive note, like the swell of an Aeolian harp? I do assure you there is nothing in the world so like the noise of a spirit.

The banshee (the anglicized word is first recorded in 1771) weaves together song, families, and death; or, to put it another way, it blends the oral tradition with historical bloodlines and ghosts. It is an expression, female, of the immanence of the past within the present, it is a spirit of place and history: a genius loci.

Hence repetition is more than a secret gate through which the

Ossianic comes within Romantic poetry; repetition is a way of translating the inauthentic into the authentic. And it does so by ordering female figures of inspiration and art: distinguishing, as Coleridge says, the 'charm and poignancy . . . [of the] analogies of nature, revolving upon herself, from the masquerade figures of cunning and vanity'.

When Coleridge revised 'The Eolian Harp' twenty years after its first publication for the perhaps significantly titled *Sybilline Leaves* (1817), he added another eight lines, confirming how profoundly the Ossianic vortex of air, soul, and music had been maintained in his philosophy. Purified, if inauthentic, Ossian had become the abiding taste of a heavenly mingle of sense and sensuousness:

> O! the one Life within us and abroad,
> Which meets all motion and becomes its soul,
> A light in sound, a sound-like power in light,
> Rhythm in all thought and joyance everywhere –
> Methinks it should have been impossible
> Not to love all things in a world so fill'd;
> Where the breeze warbles and the mute still air
> Is music slumbering on her instrument.

Coleridge's delightfully domestic conversation poems were, however, to have less immediate influence than the Prometheanism inspired by Ossian's Celtic twilight. If Coleridge was content to find divine immanence

> Where the breeze warbles and the mute still air
> Is music slumbering on her instrument,

John Keats recast these lines to redefine poetry:

> A drainless shower
> Of light is poesy; 'tis the supreme of power;
> 'Tis might half slumb'ring on its own right arm.

Keats's *Hyperion* was begun the year following Coleridge's *Sybilline Leaves* in the autumn of 1818, after a walking tour of Scotland and attendance at Hazlitt's lectures. Keats had visited Fingal's cave at Staffa, and had already written lines on it in a letter to Thomas Keats, 23–6 July 1818, before he sat down to his epic. Like Robert Southey, who told Grosvenor Bedford that to write his epic *Madoc*, 'I shall study three works ... the Bible, Homer, and Ossian', Keats seems to have had his trinity too: Shakespeare, Milton, and again Ossian.

Keats's reading of Ossian is evident from the outset. Macpherson's 'Fragment III' commences with a typical Ossianic fugue:

> Sad, by a hollow rock, the grey-hair'd Carryl sat. Dry fern waves over his head; his seat is in an aged birch. Clear to the roaring winds he lifts his voice of woe.

Keats, meanwhile, opens *Hyperion* (in lines that were repeated in *The Fall of Hyperion*), with a translation of this image back to the genesis of the Celts and the fall of the Titans, the subject of the poem:

> Deep in the shady sadness of a vale*
> Far sunken from the healthy breath of morn,
> Far from the fiery noon, and eve's one star,
> Sat gray-hair'd Saturn, quiet as a stone,
> Still as the silence round about his lair;
> Forest on forest hung about his head
> Like cloud on cloud.

But despite the familiar setting the Ossianic air is entirely absent from this primal scene:

> No stir of air was there,
> Not so much life as on a summer's day
> Robs not one light seed from the feather'd grass,
> But where the dead leaf fell, there did it rest.
> A stream went voiceless by, still deadened more
> By reason of his fallen divinity ...

For the reader alive to the music of Ossianic voices and Coleridge's wind-thrummed harp, the chilling silence of these lines achingly captures the calamitous state of Saturn. More hopeless still, it also shows that in the beginning, there was no word, and that the ghostly sounds echoing out of the Celtic void are all laments for this first founding, crushing defeat.

---

* It is worth noting Keats's use of the word 'vale'. He wrote in a marginal note to his copy of Milton's *Paradise Lost*: 'There is a cool pleasure in the very sound of vale – The english word is of the happiest chance. Milton has put vales in heaven and hell with the very utter affection and yearning of a great Poet. It is a sort of Delphic abstraction a beautiful thing made more beautiful by being reflected and put in a Mist.'

Two paradigmatic examples of writing about ghosts and shadows, Augustan and Romantic, braid inspiration with ghosts, nature, sleep, dreams, and authenticity. Following his encounter with the Sybil, Aeneas descends into Hell to visit the Shades and Death, ranging over a surreal topography of roosting dreams and delusion, which in Dryden's translation reads,

> Full in the midst of this infernal Road,
> An Elm displays her dusky Arms abroad;
> The God of Sleep there lies his heavy Head:
> And empty Dreams on ev'ry Leaf are spread.

Mission accomplished, Aeneas exits through the ivory gate:

> Two Gates the silent House of Sleep adorn;
> Of polish'd Iv'ry this, that of transparent Horn:
> True Visions thro' transparent Horn arise;
> Thro' polish'd Iv'ry pass deluding Lies.

As Pope says, 'Virgil dismisses Aeneas through the gate of falsehood. Now what is this, but to inform us that all he relates is nothing but a dream, and that dream a falsehood?'

What then? That the landscape of ghosts, dreams, and 'Deep Frauds' is all lies, or rather all parts of the anatomy of one perennial lie? Coleridge, however, in quoting a Jean-Paul Richter poem, reversed the relationship of dream and reality:

> If a man could pass through Paradise in a Dream, & have a Flower presented to him as a pledge that his Soul had really been there, & found that Flower in his hand when he awoke – Aye! And what then?

What then, indeed? Could you recognize such a token, would you know? The experience is a challenge to transcend authenticity – indeed it receives its very truth from its impossibility. It is not an unfamiliar position to argue that the prime necessity for the Romantic imagination is impossibility – witness the craving Promethean ambition of everyone from Blake to Byron – but there is also a necessary inauthenticity in Romantic writing. Literary forgery helps to make this possible: as an extreme inspirational and inspiring discourse, but also as a straight counter-intuitive challenge to find the most perfect truth in a lie. But there is another point as well. Both Aeneas and Richter are describing journeys – voyages through dreamlands – as is Ossian, as is Rowley, whose works are in part a travelogue of medieval Britain. 'Writing', as Gilles Deleuze and Félix Guattari have suggested, 'has nothing to do with signifying, but with land-surveying and map-making, even of countries yet to come.' And so in the hands of Thomas Chatterton, in the poems of Thomas Rowley, we encounter another traveller from an antique land to hold us.

IV. LUNATIC

O, for a draught of vintage!

John Keats, 'Ode to a Nightingale'

Raving in the Lunacy of ink.

Thomas Chatterton, 'The Whore of Babylon'

I essentially am not in madness,
But mad in craft.

William Shakespeare, *Hamlet*, III. iv

Thomas Chatterton, 'the most extraordinary young man' Dr Johnson had ever heard of, was a charity-educated boy and apprentice scrivener from Bristol with precocious poetic pretensions. He began writing and publishing poetry at the age of eleven – verse that ranged from fables to elegies, from descriptive pastorals to vitriolic satires, coffee-house journalism, and oriental exoticism. His fortunes changed, however, when he discovered a chest in a church storeroom containing the literary papers of a fifteenth-century monk called Thomas Rowley. Here were poems, plays, letters, notes and sketches, and memoirs that hinted at a far more lavish Bristol heritage than anything hitherto described by medieval chroniclers. Despite his time-consuming apprenticeship, Chatterton found time to transcribe and annotate a large selection of these papers, thereby revealing Rowley as a fabulously significant, but previously lost poet, playwright, and antiquarian historian. Rowley's literary works were gorgeous and rich and quite beyond anything else of the fifteenth century (as one critic has put it, 'it was Rowley who first taught later poets their trade'), and his notes on the history of Bristol, from its earliest Saxon glory to the height of its medieval grandeur, were of stupendous importance to provincial historians: Rowley was to Bristol what William Camden had been to Britannia. Local antiquarians, notably William Barrett and George Symes Catcott, fostered Chatterton's transcription and annotation, and before his untimely death he provided them with generous materials. After two decades' work Barrett published his *History of Bristol*, replete with facsimile Rowley papers, in 1789.

Or, to put it another way, Thomas Chatterton was a forger. In less than a year a fifteen-year-old boy invented a mock-medieval language, imagined in extraordinary detail the history and cultural life of Bristol city through a Dark Ages millennium, fabricated a mass of authenticating documents, maps, and drawings, and against this background composed over a score of major poems, including two attempts at an epic on the Battle of Hastings and a play on the Bristol hero, 'Ælla'. As if this wasn't enough, the writings were not confined to the works of Rowley, but included the identifiable hands of William Canynge, John Iscam, Sir Thybbot Gorges, and John Ladgate, plus an earlier poetic chronicler of Bristol, Ralph Cheddar, and the Saxon poet Turgot.

It is unbelievable. A row raged for five years over whether a fifteen-year-old, bluecoat, provincial, urban teenager could have had the time, the resources, or the wit to fabricate fifteenth-century literature, as is clear from an exasperated letter to the *European Magazine* in 1782:

> Sir, Dr. Glynn says, 'It is an insult to reason and common sense to suppose that the poems of Rowley were the productions of that d—n'd shitten arse boy Chatterton'. Notwithstanding this illiberal, and no less inelegant mode of expression, some respect may perhaps be due to Dr. Glynn's opinion.

And this a dozen years after Chatterton had died.

The debate was furious, and dominated conversations over High Table at Oxbridge colleges, in coffeehouses and at club dinners, in the chambers of lawyers and professional historians, at society parties in London and Bath and of course Bristol; it also filled column inches in newspapers and journals, was the subject of a dozen pamphlets and books, and the occasion of elegies, plays, paintings, and monuments – by which time the Rowley works were indeed deemed to have been forged by Chatterton. And yet it is fantastically unhelpful to pigeonhole the Rowley works as forgeries. It explains nothing, it removes them from the canon of literature into the realm of cultural anecdote, and it prevents Chatterton's extensive other work from being read as literature: everything else – poems, letters, life – becomes so much supporting evidence for the crime of forgery. In fact, as Chatterton's superlative editor Donald Taylor has indicated, the Rowley works constitute less than twelve months' activity out of a creative career of over six years, but the emphasis on forgery has both distorted his œuvre and declassified it as literature. As if this were not enough, the myth of Chatterton is at least as powerful as the insistence in treating him as a forger (and it is a myth that I have just succumbed to again by calling him 'unbelievable'). So Chatterton is caught in a double-bind. But, as suggested above in the introduction, some of the threads of this marvellous myth can be unpicked to see how they run through the work of later writers. As with Macpherson, then, I will be searching for evidence of the transcendent in Chatterton: tropes of inspiration that drive his work into the arms of the Romantics.

Mentioning James Macpherson raises questions about the fraternity of the two writers – indeed, Chatterton's imitations of Ossian were among his most publishable works. For Johnson, the entire Rowley Controversy was an inexplicable (or demented) repetition of the Ossian affair:

> I think this wild adherence to Chatterton more unaccountable
> than the obstinate defence of Ossian. In Ossian there is a national
> pride, which may be forgiven, though it cannot be applauded. In
> Chatterton there is nothing but the resolution to say again what
> has once been said.

Johnson reluctantly acknowledges the national interest implicit in Ossianic defences, but this is something he cannot discern in Rowley's provincial Bristolian pride: in other words, for Johnson there is literally no ground, no territory on which to have this debate.

But there is also an anxiety here, a worry about illegitimate succession, like the hatching of an anti-canon, emphasized by Johnson's mismatched pair 'Chatterton' and 'Ossian'. Indeed, such a dynasty of forgers was later versified by William Mason, whose 'four forgers' were Lauder, Macpherson, Chatterton, and Ireland. Or as the anonymous author of 'The Ossiad' put it:

> Chatterton, poor misguided Youth,
> Foe to himself, as well as Truth,
> Work'd hard where nothing could be got,
> Whether he gain'd Belief or not.
> Few in this Age so weak are found,
> To cultivate another's Ground;
> And their own just Pretensions drop,
> By planting to disown the Crop:
> Yet thus we learnt old Rowley's Name;
> Thus started Ossian into Fame!

Other commentators saw Macpherson as the bearer of a curse. As early as 19 June 1777, Horace Walpole had written to William Cole, 'I believe Macpherson's success with Ossian was more the ruin of Chatterton than I', and fifty years later Wordsworth, in a foolish fit of bad temper, claimed that the poems of Ossian had no worth and that their only influence had been malign: 'No succeeding Writer appears to have caught from them a ray of inspiration; no Author in the least distinguished, has ventured formally to imitate them – except the Boy, Chatterton, on their first appearance.'

But despite the Macpherson–Chatterton or Ossian–Rowley axis so frequently referred to by contemporaries, there are serious problems in equating the two, and Macpherson's more recent defenders have rightly complained that, despite a decade of Ossianic and Rowleyan revisionism, a startling level of critical misconception prevails whenever Macpherson and Chatterton are simplistically yoked together. My own coupling of these two writers is not, I hope, facile, but rather an attempt to acknowledge the identification made by their contemporaries, and especially their later readers. Haunting and deliria are as much features of Chatterton's writing as they are of Ossian's, but here they are transcendent, giving rise to fateful and prophetic readings of nascent divinity that power his myth. The following account begins with a careful consideration of Chatterton's life, that should begin to make the inflections of myth all the more glaring – and hence perhaps reveal their purpose.

✤ ✤ ✤

LIFE

The wild Expences of a Poet's Brain
Chatterton's 'Will'

He came from humble beginnings. The Chattertons (the name was also spelt Chadderton) had for many generations enjoyed the shelter of the church of St Mary Redcliffe in Bristol, an enormous Perpendicular Gothic pile, where they worked as sextons, or at least as odd-job men. Chatterton's father, however, Thomas Chatterton senior, had significantly improved his lot by diligent application and had raised himself to the position of writing master of the church and neighbouring free school. He was an eccentric man who absent-mindedly roamed around the city of Bristol talking and gesticulating to himself, and was considered, perhaps because of his unusual behaviour, to be a bit of a boozer. But he was also very proud, and eager to rescue his family from historical obscurity.

When he was out of the school house, Chatterton senior was pursuing a promising amateur career as a local historian and antiquarian. His interests ranged widely: he had a large trove of Roman coins, and he was bewitched by magic and necromancy and the writings of Cornelius Agrippa, but his most treasured possession was a little archive of fifteenth-century manuscripts. Over the north porch of the Church of St Mary Redcliffe there was (and of course still is) a 'muniment' room, which in the eighteenth century contained several large chests of deeds, bills, receipts, and church accounts. William Canynge, a wealthy merchant and five times mayor of Bristol between the reigns of Henry VI and Edward IV, had left his papers in the largest chest – 'Mr. Canynge's Cofre' – and had ordered them be inspected annually. Eventually, this practice declined, the chests were forgotten, and the keys lost – but in 1727 'Mr. Canynge's Cofre' and the other six chests in the muniment room were officially broken open and pillaged for manuscripts. Some of this historical booty ended up in city archives, much remained scattered about in the muniment room. Fifteenth-century deeds and documents were still covering the floor of the room twenty-three years later when in 1750 Chatterton senior helped himself to a basketful – indeed, there were still bits left in 1767 when his son Thomas Chatterton junior explored the north porch, and even a decade later when Michael Lort visited St Mary Redcliffe: 'What remained in the north porch, and which I saw there, were slips of dirty illegible parchment law writings and probably about Cannings time . . . Dr. Goldsmith I am told, filled his pockets with such.'*

Chatterton senior used these fifteenth-century parchments for his own genealogical researches in establishing the history of his family's connection with St Mary Redcliffe. While the Pile Street pupils played with the old green wax parchment seals, their writing master locked up some of the manuscripts in a couple of wooden boxes saying that they were very valuable, claiming that he had learnt from them that persons of the name of 'Chadderton' had been employed by the church, to use his own phrase, 'Time out of mind'. That done, any remaining parchments were disposed of in the school. Waste paper was a valuable commodity in the eighteenth century, and the old manuscripts might have been used for covering books, for tailors' patterns and thread papers, for scouring windows and cleaning cutlery, for lining pie dishes, or for wiping one's arse and lighting fires. All this happened before Thomas Chatterton the younger, the poet, was born, however, and by the time of his arrival on 20 November 1752, his father had already been dead for three and a half months. The remaining family – mother Sarah, daughter Mary, and Tommy – decamped from the school and moved up Redcliffe Hill.

Thomas Chatterton's early life was spent fatherless and in poverty. He was sent away from his late father's own Pile Street Free School for being backward, and his mother had to teach him to read. Despite the doting attention of her and his older sister, he was unresponsive until, as Mary later recalled, he began to take an interest in some old paper their mother was cutting up for dress patterns and book covers:

---

* Oliver Goldsmith, author of *The Vicar of Wakefield* and *She Stoops to Conquer*, had foraged there in 1771.

> My brother was dull at learning, not knowing many letters at
> four years old, and always objected to read in a small book. He
> learnt the Alphabet from an old Folio music book of father's my
> mother was then tearing up for wast paper, the capitals at the
> beginning of the verses.

His mother was able to teach him his letters from this old book: 'He
fell in love with the illuminated capitals', and Chatterton then began
to read avidly the family's massive black-letter church bible. After his
disaster at Pile Street, Chatterton fared rather better at Colston School,
which he entered on 3 August 1760, aged seven and three quarters.
Colston School had been established in 1708 by the merchant and
philanthropist Edward Colston, and was modelled on London's Christ's
Hospital – although it provided a more ascetic and less rigorous
intellectual training. The boys wore Tudor bluecoats adorned with the
brass badge of a dolphin, and had their heads tonsured in monastic
fashion. Chatterton now became a voracious reader. Aged ten, he
joined Samuel Green's circulating library, and within two years he had
compiled a list of seventy books he had read, including Shakespeare,
Milton, and possibly a black-letter Elizabethan edition of Chaucer
(perhaps Speght's of 1598 or 1602); Mrs Green afterwards said he was
'very fond of reading black letter print particularly old Poetry'.
Chatterton usually read in St Mary Redcliffe, perched by William
Canynge's tomb, and his sister remembered he often climbed 'the
towers of the church', where he would read further, ascending to
the Middle Ages. He also began to write his own poetry – sombre
devotional verse, but also brisk modern fables derived from John Gay,
dealing with midnight appearances of sprites and ghosts haunting
graveyards.

   Chatterton left Colston's aged fourteen on 1 July 1767 and was
apprenticed to John Lambert to be trained as a legal scrivener (a
copier). His indentures demanded that 'Taverns he shall not frequent,
at Dice he shall not play, Fornication he shall not commit, Matrimony
he shall not contract'. He was punctual and efficient, working a twelve-
hour day at Lambert's and spending most evenings with his mother
and sister, returning at 10 p.m. to lodge with his master. But at least
twice a month Chatterton met of an evening in a tavern as part of a
group of teenage apprentices with literary ambitions: the 'Spouting
Club', whereupon he may have stayed out all night, extemporizing

verse, frequenting taverns, flirting and committing fornication, if not actually contracting matrimony.

As it turned out, Chatterton found he had very little to do at Lambert's: his time was supposed to be spent copying legal precedents, but sometimes there was less than two hours' work a day. Then a discovery was made that would change his life. One evening, his mother was dressmaking, using for thread papers and patterns some scraps of the manuscript parchments her husband had taken from the St Mary Redcliffe muniment room. In an uncanny repeat of the experience that inspired him to start reading, Chatterton was immediately arrested by these fifteenth-century scraps of illuminated Gothic lettering. He demanded to know where they had come from, and he was shown the two boxes of manuscripts his father had collected. Chatterton was ecstatic, telling his mother 'that he had found a treasure and was so glad nothing could be like it'. He took all the manuscripts, visited the muniment room for any remains still there – and found four more. His mother recalled,

> he was perpetually rummaging and ransacking every corner of the house for more parchments, and from time to time carried away those he had already found by the pocketsful. One day, happening to see Clarke's History of the Bible covered with one of these parchments, he swore a great oath and stripping the book, put the cover into his pocket, and carried it away.

The sudden discovery of this manuscript hoard enabled the fifteen-year-old Chatterton to give a medieval shape to his imagination. He began to explore the history and culture of fifteenth-century Bristol, regaling his friends and family with inspired tales of the old city. But not content with imaginative reconstruction, he actually began to construct the physical remains of fifteenth-century Bristol: the teenager began forging fifteenth-century parchments. The hoard from the muniment room provided an indisputable provenance for any further manuscripts he might produce, and he could find old strips of vellum in Lambert's scrivening office, even if it meant snipping margins from the edges of old documents. He concentrated on producing the works of a monk, Thomas Rowley (c.1400–70), which he claimed had been recovered by his father from St Mary

Redcliffe.* Rowley was the confidant, resident poet, and cultural odd-job man for William Canynge, Chatterton's sepulchral companion during his reading and of course the actual donor of 'Mr. Canynge's Cofre'. But the Canynge Chatterton recreated was not merely a businessman and civic mayor of Bristol: he was the Maecenas of his age, a benefactor of St Mary Redcliffe, the patron of Rowley, and the centre of a group of writers, ecclesiastics, architects, and medieval literati – all of whom Chatterton invented. When Rowley wasn't writing poems and plays, translating historical treatises from Latin, or travelling the country on antiquarian jaunts, he worked as the scribe and business associate of Canynge, allowing Chatterton to forge an immense range of material corroborating his fifteenth-century vision: business memoirs, accounts, research notes, pedigrees, heraldry, maps, correspondence, and coterie verse.

Lambert had a small but useful library for the Rowleyan background: Camden's *Britannia*, Baker's *Chronicles*, Chaucer's works, *Charters of Bristol*, and Willis's *Cathedrals*. Chatterton could not afford to purchase any such books himself, but he still haunted the city's bookshops for anything of interest. One bookseller afterwards reported to William Henry Ireland that Chatterton used to read, copy, and borrow books: 'he did not confine himself to any particular head, but perused promiscuously books on religion, history, biography, poetry, heraldry, and in short the most abstruse treatises on every subject'. He also practised copying the lettering from the parchment remains, and learnt how to age manuscripts. One friend said that Chatterton held vellum over a candle flame to blacken it and shrivel the parchment; another said that he would rub streaks of yellow ochre, rub it on the ground, and then crumple it in his hand: 'That was the way to antiquate it.' But this is too easy: there is surprisingly little evidence of his more sophisticated ageing techniques, which often resulted in manuscripts being left completely illegible – and hence allowed Chatterton to make comprehensive 'transcriptions' from these unreadable scraps.

He began an immense Rowley enterprise, and by September 1768

* He took the name 'Rowley' (originally he deliberately misspelt it 'Ronlie') from a brass of Thomas Rouley, bailiff 1466–7 and sheriff 1475–6 (when William Canynge was mayor) in St John-in-the-Wall, and the name may well have occurred in some of the very muniment fragments.

was ready to go public. A new bridge was being opened in Bristol, so Chatterton forged an eyewitness account of the pomp and pageantry that had attended the opening of the old bridge in 1247. The account was published to considerable acclaim in a Bristol journal on 1 October 1768, and Chatterton, still only fifteen, immediately came under the scrutiny of an antiquarian book collector, pewterer, and local celebrity, George Symes Catcott. Catcott interrogated Chatterton about the provenance of the printed manuscript, who claimed that it had come from his father's collection, gleaned from the chests in the muniment room of St Mary Redcliffe. Keen to assess the hoard, Catcott demanded to see more examples, and Chatterton produced 'The Bristowe Tragedie', a long ballad he had written to elaborate a brief fragment of Bristol lore. Catcott introduced the young lad to William Barrett, a retired surgeon who was working on a history of Bristol, and Chatterton was given the run of Barrett's library: 'He would catch hints and intelligence from short conversations, which he would afterward work up, and improve, and cover in such a manner that an attentive and suspicious person only could trace them back to the source from whence he derived them.' But others were not so credulous. Chatterton tried, unsuccessfully, to woo the London publisher James Dodsley and – famously – the Gothic aesthete Horace Walpole with his Rowley works. Dodsley rejected them, and Walpole, despite his initial enthusiasm, consulted with Thomas Gray and William Mason, who divined the forgery. Walpole wrote back and gently admonished Chatterton:

> I wrote him a letter with as much kindness and tenderness, as if I had been his guardian; for though I had no doubt of his impositions, such a spirit of poetry breathed in his coinage, as interested me for him: nor was it a grave crime in a young bard to have forged false notes of hand that were to pass current only in the parish of Parnassus.

Although Walpole later – rather vaingloriously – blamed himself for Chatterton's subsequent fate, Chatterton may have been disappointed but was quite unabashed by the encounter. Rowley did not constitute his sole literary output. He had also been writing love poems to order, for a friend of his who had emigrated to Charlestown, in addition to light local eulogies, descriptive verse, elegies, and the first of his Ossianic imitations – and he was already a published author. It is true that he wrote little more Rowley after the encounter with Walpole, but that may be attributed to his projected move to London and his widening literary horizons. And anyway only a tiny proportion of the Rowley corpus was published in his lifetime; it was Chatterton's Ossianics that were the most immediately successful of his works – six of the seven were published before his death, and one a month after.

Chatterton mastered the Ossianic form: his pieces ranged from the sixth to the twelfth centuries, from Saxon homilies based around Bristol to a complexly allusive conflict on the Isle of Man.* There is considerable historical allusion and local legend – in one, Ethelgar jumps off a cliff, is saved by St Cuthbert, and so becomes a monk. Chatterton dispensed with the Ossianic company of ghosts, the prose is more sprightly, swifter moving, and richer in flora and fauna than Ossian, and Chatterton patterns the Ossianic voice in a structural refrain rather than as obsessive repetition. The twelve-line opening sentence of 'Kenrick' neatly demonstrates this – it is rather wittily erected on the observation 'Kenrick . . . prepared himself for war':

> When winter yelled through the leafless grove; when the black waves rode over the roaring winds, and the dark-brown clouds hid the face over the sun; when the silver brook stood still, and snow environed the top of the lofty mountain; when the flowers appeared not in the blasted fields, and the boughs of the leafless trees bent with the loads of ice; when the howling of the wolf affrighted the darkly glimmering light of the western sky; Kenrick, terrible as the tempest, young as the snake of the valley, strong as the mountain of the slain; his armour shining like the stars in the dark night, when the moon is veiled in sable, and the blasting winds howl over the wide plain; his shield like the black rock, prepared himself for war.

Most significantly, though, there is no Ossianic figure of the bard, no authenticating matter, no prefatory or introductory material, even.

The next year was characterized by the perfection and subsequent abandoning of Rowley, and increasingly ambitious forays into popular writing: more descriptive verse and elegies, more Ossianics, a burletta, the first of his mock-heroic satires (the most notable of which is the

---

* 'Ethelgar', 'Kenrick', 'Cerdick', and 'Gorthmund' were the Saxon pieces (the latter with a Danish subject), 'Godred Crovan' was Manx, and the two 'Hirlas' pieces Welsh.

food-fight epic, 'The Constabiliad', soon revised into 'The Consuliad'), political letters, and the first of the remarkable 'African Eclogues'. Within a year of the Walpole exchange, the seventeen-year-old Chatterton had published thirty-one titles in seven different journals, five of which were London publications.

Despite this prodigious achievement, it is as Rowley begins to wane that rumours of incipient suicide wax: another key to unlock the secrets of his soul. There are stories of Chatterton threatening to commit suicide, supposedly carrying a loaded pistol about in his pocket and often putting it into his mouth and saying he wished he could persuade himself to draw the trigger. A letter was found on his desk at Lambert's describing his 'distresses', and that 'on Mr. Clayfield's receiving that letter, he [Chatterton] should be no more'. Lambert discovered the letter, panicked, sent for Barrett, and the two of them talked Chatterton out of suicide, which would assuredly have damned his soul for eternity. But Chatterton had evidently seen an opportunity to rid himself of his indentures and be free to make his fortune in London. On Easter Saturday 1770, shortly after the first letter had been found, Chatterton's 'Will' was discovered by Mrs Lambert. It gave the date of his death as the following day: Easter Sunday (15 April 1770). It is remarkable that this admittedly self-parodic and by no means self-annihilatory mock-will should have been taken at all seriously – not least because the mock-will was a minor literary genre of the time – but Chatterton was instantly released from his apprenticeship, having served two years and nine months. And as he was dead within four months of writing it, the 'Will' has been treated as a grimly prophetic testimony, rather than a brilliantly rash and irresponsible satire that lambasts Bristol antiquaries, mocks himself for being lunatic, draws up elaborate plans for the monument that should be erected to his memory in St Mary Redcliffe, and bemoans his existence with a reference to Yorick, the eternal jester of *Hamlet* and the nom de plume of the late fashionable writer Laurence Sterne: 'Alas! poor Chatterton.'

Chatterton made plans to leave as soon as he could. In his last days in Bristol he wrote to a number of London publishers and journals to prepare the ground for his freelancing, and a week before he left he sold Catcott the most ambitious of his Rowley works: the play 'Ælla'. But still the dark rumours persist in representing the move to London

as doomed. His friend James Thistlethwaite, for instance, asked him
what he would do in London. Chatterton allegedly replied:

> My first attempt shall be in the literary way: the promises I have
> received are sufficient to dispel doubt; but should I, contrary to
> my expectations, find myself deceived, I will, in that case, turn
> Methodist preacher: Credulity is as potent a deity as ever, and a
> new sect may easily be devised. But if that too should fail me,
> my last and final resource is a pistol.

Anyway, as he was successful enough at the first, he was not obliged
to establish his own sect. . . .

He left for London on 24 April 1770, distributing gingerbread (his
favourite comfit, also a supposed aphrodisiac) among a gaggle of friends
who had gathered on the steps of St Mary Redcliffe, then boarding
the coach and going to seek his fortune. After travelling through a
snow storm, Chatterton arrived in the metropolis and wasted no time
in visiting publishers and editors of journals; he wrote to his mother
– 'Here I am, safe, and in high spirits'; he was lodging with a relative,
one Mrs Ballance, in Shoreditch. The aspiring writer had, however,
forgotten a red pocket-book containing his Rowleyan glossary, and was
unable to prepare any Rowley works for publication without it: his
letters home constantly requested that it be sent to him, and when it
finally arrived he was able to complete his medieval fable of the Good
Samaritan, 'An Excelente Balade of Charitie', in early July 1770.* In
the meantime, he quickly signed contracts for several pieces of journalism, and for a 'voluminous' history of England, to be serialized in
the autumn, during the compilation of which he expected to visit
Oxford, Cambridge, Lincoln, Coventry, and elsewhere. Although he
was instantly making plans to leave London, he felt secure in his
chosen profession, and was utterly confident of success. He assured
his mother, 'No author can be poor who understands the arts of
booksellers.'

Chatterton's literary output increased further, now concentrating
on profitable political letters and extensive anti-government satires,
fashionable prose narratives, drafts of burlesque plays and burlettas,
and more of his anti-colonial 'African Eclogues'. Some of his writing

* Surprisingly, this was one of his few publishing failures: it was rejected from the *Town
and Country Magazine*, and not published until 1777.

proved particularly lucrative. 'The Revenge', a burletta possibly performed in Marylebone, made five guineas, enabling him to buy a box
of presents for his family: china for his mother, two silk fans for his
sister, and herb snuff and tobacco for his grandmother.* But despite
his successes with 'Patriot' Opposition papers and a fruitful introduction to John Wilkes, it is the 'African Eclogues' that are the firmest
indication of a post-Rowley direction. These three† loosely linked
poems are effectively different episodes in the same myth cycle of love
and war, describing demi-gods and heroes, thunderbolts and flood,
enacted in a boiling landscape against the background of European
colonialism:

> On Tiber's banks, where scarlet jasmines bloom,
> And purple aloes shed a rich perfume:
> Where, when the sun is melting in his heat,
> The reeking tygers find a cool retreat;
> Bask in the sedges, lose the sultry beam,
> And wanton with their shadows in the stream.

In the cut-throat world of metropolitan journalism, Chatterton
was, then, a qualified success and making a living from his work.
In June, he moved from Mrs Ballance to lodge with Mrs Angell, a
dressmaker in Holborn, and for the first time he had the privacy of
his own room. He thrived in London: even catching a cold in the
capital was a worthwhile experience, as he put it to his sister, 'I have
a most horrible wheezing in the throat; but I don't repent that I
have this cold; for there are so many nostrums [quack remedies] here,
that 'tis worth a man's while to get a distemper, he can be cured so
cheap.' Ten days later, the cold had gone. He had a hare-brained
scheme to travel to Senegal as a ship's doctor, and wrote to Catcott in
August to ask after Barrett for a reference. The city was stimulating
his imagination to wild and exotic new horizons. And then suddenly
he was dead: poisoned by arsenic and opium.

---

* Ironically, the manuscript of 'The Revenge' was lost, rediscovered several years later
as wrapping paper in a cheesemonger's.
† 'An African Song' is also sometimes included among the Eclogues.

DEATH

Cin: I am Cinna the poet, I am Cinna the poet.
4. Pleb: Tear him for his bad verses, tear him for his bad
verses.

William Shakespeare, *Julius Caesar*, III. iii

Chatterton's death overpowers the life, just as his literature is under-
mined by charges of forgery. We all know that he committed suicide
out of pride, desperation, poverty, and neglect. The traditional view is
that Chatterton had been gradually starving, unable to make his living
as a London writer. He could not return to Bristol in disgrace, he
would not allow himself to dine with Mrs Angell (although she said
he had not eaten for two or three days), the baker refused him a loaf
on credit – and so he immediately committed suicide: he perished in
his pride. This account was subsequently confirmed by the discovery
of an Inquest Report: in this, Mr Angell stated that on the afternoon of
22 August, Chatterton returned to lodgings in a passion about the
baker's wife, who had refused him bread until he paid the three shillings
he already owed her. As he was still agitated on the 23rd, Mrs Angell
had inquired, 'What ails you?' Chatterton replied 'Nothing. Nothing.
Why do you ask?' Around 10 o'clock on the morning of the 24th he
left with a bundle of papers, saying he would put them somewhere
safe lest they should meet with an accident. Mr Cross the apothecary
saw him at 11.30, when he stopped to ask for some arsenic, which he
requested for an experiment he wished to conduct. He did not return
to the house until 7 p.m. Pale and dejected, he spent the evening with
the Angells, muttering rhymes in an unintelligible language until he
went to bed. He was never seen alive again, and nobody knows how
he spent the last afternoon of his life or what he did with the mysterious
papers. Although the floor of his room was covered with scraps of
paper when his body was found, his 'Last Verses' were beside him.
Death was due to poisoning by arsenic in water, taken on 24 August
and proving fatal the following day. Barrett reported that Chatterton

took 'a large dose of opium, some of which was picked out between his teeth after death, and he was found the next morning a most horrid spectacle, with limbs and features distorted as after convulsions, a frightful and ghastly corpse'. Opium, however, might cause death but would not cause convulsions – possibly it was taken to deaden the pain of the arsenic.

There is some convenience in ascribing Chatterton's death to arsenic: he had recently mentioned arsenic poisoning in a short melodramatic story, 'The Unfortunate Fathers', and whether circumstantial evidence or mere coincidence, such a tendency to see the death prefigured in the writing has twisted Chatterton's œuvre into a medical disposition, the symptoms of psychiatric derangement. Louise Kaplan, for instance, has suggested that he was suffering from bipolar manic depressive disorder, indicated by 'imposturousness' and suicidal tendencies, and it is possible to turn much of his later writing into a series of 'last goodnights': every mention of death, poison, suicide, despair becomes inflated. Such readings help to give Chatterton's life the symmetry of a parable: he is mythologized, and his poetry becomes incidental to an empathetic identification with his precocity, brilliance, furor, poverty, and extremity – rather than reading his work as a hyperactive creativity driven by sleep deprivation, righteous starvation, and possible opium addiction. In any case, he was buried in a cemetery: Chatterton's body was not disposed of as a suicide's, whose remains were dragged to crossroads and hanged by the feet from gibbets, or casually cremated, or thrown into the sea, denied common burial rights – although possibly it was an act of mercy to declare him *non compos mentis* so as to avoid such dreadful indignities. Mr Cross the apothecary later confirmed this to Michael Lort:

> Mr. Cross says he had the Foul Disease which he wd cure himself and had calomel and vitriol of Cross for that purpose. Who cautioned him against the too free use of these, particularly the latter. He loved talking about religion and to argue against Christianity, saying that he meant to turn Mahometan. This circumstance Cross turned after his death to some account, for being found dead in his bed and to all appearance poisoned, when the Jury sat on the body Cross urged this among other things to prove he was out of his senses.

At the very least, the idea of Chatterton threatening to turn 'Mahometan' suggests that he was prepared to make all sorts of wild remarks to impress people – not least by threatening to extinguish himself a few times.

But clearly the account of the suicide I have given contains not just a few ambiguities – it is plainly at odds with the evidence. Chatterton was not impoverished: he had been making a decent enough living from his journalism and fashionable writing. The Hamiltons, for example, who were journal editors for whom Chatterton some-times worked, were interviewed in 1777 and were adamant that 'he did not die for want' – they themselves had forwarded payments to him. Chatterton did not leave a suicide note, despite signalling his earlier 'threats' in letters and the 'Will': his 'Last Verses', written on his deathbed and concluding,

> Have mercy, Heaven! when here I cease to live,
> And this last act of wretchedness forgive!

turn out to be a forgery by a later biographer, John Dix. Dix also forged a suicide letter, and other sensational Chatterton manuscripts. The Inquest Report detailing the last hours of his life is a Dix fake: reread my summary and notice how it lays the possibility of further 'discoveries' of Chattertoniana via the 'bundle of papers' that must be kept so safe.

In fact, other potential forgeries from Chatterton's lost 'bundle of papers' might be pointed out. Chatterton never admitted on paper that he was responsible for Rowley's works, and only reluctantly half-admitted the fact to his mother and sister. He generally avoided discussing the authenticity of the trove of manuscripts: on 20 July 1769, for instance, he wrote to a Mr Stephens, possibly a relative who had expressed his scepticism of Rowley, and towards Chatterton's writing generally:

> You may inquire if you please for the Town and Country Maga-
> zines wherein all signed D B. and Asaphides are mine. The Pieces
> called Saxon are originally and totally the product of my Muse
> tho I should think it a greater Merit to be able to translate Saxon.*

With regard to the falling out with Walpole, he simply states, 'I differed

---

* Note the classical use of the word 'Muse' here that has brought Chatterton knowledge of a dead language.

from him in the age of a MS.' In other words, Chatterton admits that the Saxon Ossianics are his, but is evasive about Rowley. This casts doubt over the famous lines he apparently composed at almost exactly the same time to Walpole – 'Walpole! I thought not I should ever see'. In this short verse, Chatterton compares Rowley with Walpole's Gothic novel, *The Castle of Otranto* (1764), which had been first issued with a title-page claiming that it was translated from an Italian romance:

> Translated by WILLIAM MARSHAL, Gent. From the Original
> ITALIAN of ONUPHRIO MURALTO, CANON of the Church
> of St. NICHOLAS at OTRANTO.

Walpole also composed a preface going into some detail about the provenance of the supposititious 1529 printed version, and moreover analysed internal evidence to argue that the story was originally written between 1095 and 1243. He offered to reprint the 'Original' Italian, and hoped that future researchers might identify the actual castle in which the scene is set. It later transpired that all this was part of the fiction.

So is Chatterton claiming that Rowley is simply a similar sort of literary *jeu* to *The Castle of Otranto*?

> thou mayst call me Cheat –
> Say, didst thou ne'er indulge in *such Deceit*?
> Who wrote Otranto ?*

Nowhere else does Chatterton admit that Rowley is an example either of contemporary genre fiction, or a 'Deceit'. These lines were again first published by John Dix; they too are likely to be forged.

The point is that two of the founding documents in the way we think we 'know' all about Chatterton and therefore the way that we use and read Chatterton – his admission that Rowley is a fake and his suicide notes – were forged by a mythographer. It might be ironic that the life of a forger, plagiarized by a biographer, is then counterfeited and passes successfully as cultural currency for centuries, but we should also ask whether we actually *prefer* the version of history in which Chatterton committed suicide – and what need such a sacrificial desire fulfils.

So what killed him?

---

* My emphasis.

Cross's statement mentions the 'Foul Disease', which, from the details of the medication taken, would appear to be the pox. It would be no surprise to learn that Chatterton had contracted a venereal disease, indeed possibly the distemper mentioned in the letter to his sister quoted above was such – which might explain the need to take a 'nostrum'. Mrs Angell, his landlady, appears to have been more a madame than a dressmaker, and certainly charged Chatterton for sexual favours. A bawdy letter from Catcott, who had asked 'Since you are got under the Tuition of an Angel, shou'd be glad to be inform'd whether he belongs to the Prince of Darkness, or the Regions of Light', elicited the reply from Chatterton four days later (12 August 1770):

> Angels, according to the Orthodox Doctrine, are Creatures of the Epicene Gender, like the Temple Beaux: the Angel here, is of no such materials; for staggering home one Night from the Jelly house, I made bold to advance my hand under her covered way, and found her a very very Woman. She is not only an Angel, but an arch Angel; for finding I had Connections with one of her Assistants, she has advanced her demands from 6s. to 8s.6. per Week, assured that I should rather comply than leave my Dulcinea, and her soft Embraces.

As Cross mentions, Chatterton was consequently dosing himself for the clap with vitriol (probably 'red arsenic' – a preparation of arsenic and sulphur) and calomel (mercurous chloride or 'horn-quicksilver'). But note too Cross's admission that he had supplied the poison, his pains to emphasize that he 'cautioned him against the too free use' of it, and his specious arguments to the inquest that Chatterton was mad and suicidal. Cross is absolving himself of any responsibility for the accident, but doing what he can to prevent any further distress by trying to get Chatterton buried, rather than disposed of like a felon.

What, then, of the opium, used to deaden the pain of the arsenic, thereby implying a suicidal intention? The grains of opium found in his teeth suggest that Chatterton was not taking the common pain-killer laudanum (opium grains dissolved in alcohol), but was taking opium in its raw state: a coarse powder made into sticks or flat cakes, and this preparation could be endured only by an experienced user. Was Chatterton perhaps an opium eater: was he taking the drug recreationally as Thomas De Quincey and Samuel Taylor Coleridge would in later years? Perhaps the nostrum he enjoyed so much was a mild opiate, such as laudanum, which he started taking for his cold, and did not stop when he recovered. Was he inspiring himself with a poetic hallucinogen? Can the sultry exoticism of his 'African Eclogues', written about this time, be seen as the heady intoxication of poppies?

Well, critics can find many things in a poem, but in this case there is, most surprisingly, some forensic evidence to boot. A deep stain in the pocket book found on his body has been chemically analysed and shown to be that of an opium alkaloid. So, was Chatterton administering arsenic as a cure for the pox, and deadening its pain with opium? Or was he a habitual opium eater who by mixing it with his venereal medication created a lethal cocktail? Was Chatterton's death a dreadful accident rather than a romantic suicide?

This speculation at least underlines the shortcomings of reading Chatterton's life and work as a suicidal trajectory, and also alerts us to the fateful mythology that quickly established itself, whether by local anecdote, or through forged documents like the Inquest Report and the activities of his mythographer, John Dix. One story claims that 'walking in a church-yard a few days before writing [to his mother], he had quitted the path, and wandering among graves, he suddenly found himself on his face in one, by stumbling; but he added, in his humorous way, "it was not the quick and dead together;" for he found the sexton under him, who was digging a grave' (Dix again, now turning Chatterton into Hamlet). Another, more melancholy version of this episode has Chatterton again stumbling into a fresh grave in St Pancras churchyard. A friend hauls him out of the grisly hole with the remark that he was glad to be present at the resurrection of a genius, but Chatterton smiles, 'My friend, I feel the sting of a speedy dissolution. I have been at war with the grave for some time, and find it is not so easy to vanquish it as I imagined; we can find an asylum to hide from every creditor but that.' If we believe this story, three days later his debt to death was called in and this time he stayed in the grave – at least for a little while longer.

The myth of Chatterton is animated, it appears, by this marginal existence between life and death. The myth projects Chatterton as a sleepless soul, a being who is so mythologized in death he refuses ever to die: he abides at this margin between living in the grave and dying on his bed. In Henry Wallis's famous oil painting of the death of

Chatterton, he refuses even to lie down properly. As Chatterton
approaches the fatal night, his life is dematerialized, he evanesces, and
a ghostly logic of mystery and disappearance draws over him: where is
his body? Oddly, this ghostliness is an ineluctable presence in Chatterton's own poetry as well, and this in itself makes Chatterton a haunting
writer, like a revenant struggling to return on the wings of the muse.
Or even a Christ figure. . . .

The resurrection began within days of his death. The news about
the lost works of the fifteenth-century poet Thomas Rowley had begun
to circulate outside the circles of Bristol antiquarians, and in the very
month Chatterton died, Dr Thomas Fry of St John's College, Oxford,
visited Bristol in search of Rowley and intending to patronize Chatterton as the discoverer – or possibly as the author – of his works.
Cruelly, he was too late, and instead took copies of Rowleyan work
from Barrett and Catcott. In Fry's wake came his friend and colleague,
Dr Francis Woodward, who on 30 November asked Catcott for a copy
of 'The Bristowe Tragedy'. The news was spreading, and the chattering
classes pricked up their ears.

Rowley was so erudite, so sophisticated, and such an accomplished
poet that it was absurd to consider that a mad wastrel could have
forged his works. The supporters of the authenticity of Thomas Rowley,
or 'Pro-Rowleyans', spent as much time deriding the education, intelligence, and morals of Chatterton as they did championing the learning,
wit, and morality of the monk Rowley, and Catcott and Barrett made
plans to publish. Throughout the 1770s, a selection of Rowley's works
was read in literary salons, Catcott and his cronies entertained potential
patrons in Bristol, Chatterton's London garret became a grisly tourist
attraction, and a few more pieces made it into print, including the
inaugural Rowley ballad, *The Bristowe Tragedy*, which was published
in 1772.

Chatterton had hardly shown the Rowley works to anyone while
he was alive; now he was dead, everyone was obsessed with them –
and with him too. On Monday, 29 April 1776, Samuel Johnson met
Catcott at a Bristol inn, declaimed some of Rowley's verses, paid a
visit to Barrett, inspected some of Rowley's manuscripts, and climbed
up to the St Mary Redcliffe muniment room. Johnson was in good
humour but short breath as Catcott pointed – '*There*! *There* is the
very chest itself.' After this 'ocular demonstration', as Boswell drily put

it, there was nothing left to be said.* Johnson was impressed, but not at all convinced, deciding 'This is the most extraordinary young man that has encountered my knowledge. It is wonderful how the whelp has written such things.'

With the publication in 1777 of *Poems, Supposed to have been Written in Bristol, by Thomas Rowley and Others, in the Fifteenth Century*, edited by Thomas Tyrwhitt, the storm really broke. Tyrwhitt reproduced pivotal Rowley texts such as 'Ælla' and 'An Excelente Balade of Charitie'. The edition quickly went into a second, then a third reprint, sales hastened, no doubt, by Tyrwhitt's sudden – and very public – change of mind about the authenticity of the poems. His edition was swiftly followed in 1778 by John Broughton's edition of *Miscellanies in Prose and Verse*, which set Rowley alongside Chatterton's journalism. It was an incongruous, even unsettling, juxtaposition, and provoked even more vigorous discussion in public and private. Next came Herbert Croft's novel *Love and Madness: A Story Too True*. This sentimental epistolary novel was based on the sensational murder of Lord Sandwich's mistress, Martha Reay, by the desperately lovelorn Revd James Hackman. Hackman shot her in the head as she left the theatre and then tried to kill himself. His pistol misfired. He was arrested, tried, sentenced, and executed – by which time his passion and dignity and desperate plight had inspired great public sympathy. Croft had no access to Hackman's supposed correspondence with Reay and simply made up the letters. Except that, as a fan of suicides and eager to make a name for himself, he had visited Bristol in July 1778, calling on Catcott and Barrett, and then visiting Sarah and Mary Chatterton. He paid the dead poet's mother and sister a guinea and a half just to read Chatterton's letters – before disappearing with them. Following a brief correspondence with the man, the Chattertons heard no more until their letters appeared in print two years later in *Love and Madness*, where they were gratuitously inserted into one of Hackman's fictional epistles. The reading public was, not surprisingly, scandalized, and Johnson attacked Croft for this inextricable mingling of fact and fiction (a real letter is stolen and printed as part of a fake letter

* It is worth pointing out the allusion perhaps to Othello's 'ocular proof' in Boswell's phrase 'ocular demonstration'. *Othello* is a triply appropriate reference: Chatterton used the play as the basis of his play, 'Ælla'; it hinges on a piece of fraudulent evidence, the handkerchief; and souvenir handkerchiefs were sold commemorating Chatterton's death – which was how John Clare first came to read him.

describing a real event . . .), but a second edition of the novel was announced within five weeks. All the distressed Chattertons received was a further £10 from the egregious Croft.

The controversy surrounding Chatterton and Rowley intensified in ferocity, reaching its peak in 1782: letters to newspapers and journals, pamphlets for and against, books, new editions, parodies, a play, and even souvenir handkerchiefs and a hastily erected monument in Bath's fashionable Lansdowne Crescent. 'Rowleiomania' was not just a publishing phenomenon: it was a major cultural event. Every major scholar participated: Horace Walpole desperately defended himself against the accusations of those who held him personally responsible for Chatterton's cruel death; Thomas Warton devoted a chapter of his epoch-making *History of English Poetry* to disproving Rowley, and subsequently published a lengthy pamphlet on the subject; Edmond Malone, in the middle of editing Shakespeare, suspended his labour to attack the authenticity of the works.

On the other side, the President of the Society of Antiquaries, Jacob Bryant, compiled a vast 600-page variorum of mystic antiquarianism – a mound of half-baked erudition and a monument to over-interpretation – to defend Rowley, and the Dean of Exeter, Jeremiah Milles, published the *Rowley Poems* in a beautifully sumptuous and woefully misguided edition. It was the critical debate of the century. Barrett entered the lists somewhat late in the day. His *History of Bristol*, finally published in 1789, made extensive use of Rowley manuscripts – for which it was roundly condemned. All this huffing and puffing by superannuated antiquarians had blown out the storm by then, although works occasionally emerged throughout the nineteenth century with ingenious new theories about Rowley. Chatterton was left to biographers, myth-mongers, and Romantic poets.

His mother never recovered from his death; she died in poverty in 1792. His sister married Thomas Newton, a glass-cutter, in 1777, and had four children, three of whom had died by 1785, as had her husband. She was eventually provided for by a charity edition of Chatterton's works published in 1803 by Robert Southey and Joseph Cottle, respectively the friend of Wordsworth and Coleridge and later poet laureate, and the publisher of *Lyrical Ballads*. She died in 1804, however, leaving £300 for her daughter, Mary Ann (Marianne) Newton, who died at the age of twenty-four three years later.

❧ ❧ ❧

OTHER

Now I want
Spirits to enforce, art to enchant

William Shakespeare, *The Tempest*, Epilogue

Of the various Thomas Chattertons constructed by myth's rewriting
of history, let us select one: Chatterton was a neurotic freak who
affected a 'sullen and gloomy temper' and a vegetarian who believed
that meat would poison his imagination. He often refused dinner
because 'he had work in hand, and he must not make himself more
stupid than God had made him'*, and he often stayed up all night
writing by the light of moon – by which he claimed he could better
compose poetry. But that wasn't all. Very late one dark and stormy
night, his master Lambert discovered him not writing poetry at all
but attempting to raise spirits using Cornelius Agrippa's *De Occulta
Philosophia.*† The book had belonged to his father. Was this a Faustian
appeal for supernatural aid in attempting to create the shadowy paternal
figure of Rowley? Or just another exaggerated anecdote?

Whatever the case, Chatterton's poetry is haunted by a profusion
of ghosts and spirits; he is fascinated by the mysteries of things outside
trying to get in, and in writing about such teeming supernatural figures
he gives his verse a quality of anticipation, as if it is on the threshold
of some ghastly reversal of fortunes that will allow the train of spirits
free egress to the material world. Often he is extremely droll in his use
of supernatural machinery, but it is sometimes shocking and occasionally awesome. And of course this morbid repetition of self-haunting,
of the ghostly return, makes his writing susceptible to the sort of *post*

---

* He would not eat meat steaks – offal was excepted – and was very abstemious, living
mainly on bread and water, although there is evidence that his diet included fish, oysters,
tarts, tongue, tea, water, and gingerbread (his favourite).
† Chatterton senior possessed Agrippa in a seventeenth-century edition (including the
spurious fourth book). He also wrote the ages of the moon next to the births of his
children, Mary and Giles Malpas, recorded in his copy of *History of the Holy Bible.* The
first son, Giles Malpas, born 12 Dec. 1750, died at four months.

hoc interpretations that see death and particularly the 'suicide' being prefigured all over the place.

One might usefully compare Chatterton here, as so often, with Keats. Keats coughed up arterial blood and recognized that it was his 'death knell'. Thereafter, his poetry has an intense sense of human frailty and inescapable doom about it – but that is not its only quality, and it would be a mistake to read it as if it is tubercular verse that can be appreciated only in the physiological and biographical know-ledge that he was under a fatal sentence. How important is it for us as readers of Keats to know that he knew he was dying and eventually died, and how important was it for readers throughout the nineteenth century? Is the death of Keats ultimately more significant than his poetry? And is Chatterton perhaps the first major writer whose biog-raphy, real or otherwise, succeeds his work: an archetype for Keats and subsequent literary celebrities like Arthur Rimbaud?

In one of Chatterton's earliest poems, composed when about eleven years old, a 'dark infernal sprite / A native of the blackest Night' alights upon 'Sly Dick' and tempts him to mischief, and in one of his last pieces, an Ossianic, Gorthmund is terrorized by the nightmarish ghosts of the lovers he has raped and slain: 'The howl of Hubba's horrid voice swelled upon every blast, and the shrill shriek of the fair Locabara, shot through the midnight-sky.' Their shrieks may be 'all a vision', but they portend Gorthmund's own death: he dies with the exultant howls of Hubba and Locabara echoing in his ears. Ghosts and the super-natural infest Chatterton's writing, often with the most uncanny results. The first version of Chatterton's 'Elegy to Phillips' includes an angry and frustrated attempt to claw back his friend Thomas Phillips:

> Ah could I charm by negromantic Spells,
> The Soul of Phillips from the deathy Tomb!

Perhaps the tales of Chatterton's Frankenstein-like spell-casting from Agrippa lend these lines a biographical force, but bizarrely in this case, having finished his elegy, Chatterton learnt that accounts of Thomas Phillips's death had been exaggerated. He was still alive – as if verily Chatterton had clutched him back. The verse had somehow unwound time for a few days, even if Phillips soon died again and the second time remained dead.

Chatterton's poetry is actively haunted by a fear of its own potential, as if it thirsts for a physical embodiment of the spirit of poetry as a way of binding it – which itself might explain the material manuscripts of Rowley. This unruly spirit might also be felt in the eerie presence conjured at the sound of sacrificial Druidic chanting in 'Elegy, Written at Stanton Drew', 'Whilst the troubled Spirit near / Hovers in the steamy Aire'*, or the hyper-acute memory of the tiger-slaying African hero Gaira. He cannot escape the cursed glimpse he had of his lover, Cawna, chained and enslaved by the pallid race of European colonists: he is literally possessed by it –

> Reflection maddens to recall the hour
> The Gods had giv'n me to the Dæmons Power.

Most tellingly here, it is the white man's very insubstantiality that makes him so threatening. They may be 'The palid shadows of the Azure Waves' in 'Heccar and Gaira' or 'the pale children of the feeble sun / In search of gold' in 'Narva and Mored', but this intangibility is an asset in the fervid heat:

> Swifter than hunted Wolves they urge the race
> Their less'ning forms elude the straining Eye
> Upon the Plumage of Macaws they fly.

The invader and slaver and colonizer does not come as a conquering god, rather as a ghost from elsewhere – seeking to possess.

Ghosts, or rather 'sprytes', are also surprisingly populous in the Rowley poems – most notably in 'The Parlyamente of Sprytes', a historical array of builders beginning with Nimrod (architect of the Tower of Babel) and concluding with Canynge (benefactor of the spire of St Mary Redcliffe). The spirited pageant is hosted by Queen Mab:

> Whan from the Erthe the Sonnes hulstred,
> Than from the Flowretts straughte wyth dewe
> Mie Leege Menne makes yee awhaped,
> And Wytches theyre Wytchencref doe –
> Then ryse the Sprytes ugsome ande Rou,
> And take theyre Walke the Letten throwe.†

---

* Donald Taylor rather charmingly sees this as a highly sexualized poem: 'from fantasized foreplay, through violent copulation and orgasm, to postcoital languor'.
† Chatterton did not gloss these stanzas himself, which gives the lines a feeling of Lewis Carroll's 'Jabberwocky'; the more difficult words are, however, 'hulstred': hidden, secret; 'leege': loyal; 'awhaped': astonished; 'ugsome': terrible; 'rou': horrid, grim, ugly; 'letten': churchyard; 'bordelier': cottager; 'ethie': easy; 'deft': neat, handsome; 'immengde': mingled; 'flanched': arched; 'asyde': beside.

Similarly, Canynge's dream in 'The Storie of Wyllyam Canynge' describes a roused spirit, which in this case whisks Canynge away on a fantastic voyage:

> As when a Bordelier on ethie Bedde
> Tyr'd wyth the Laboures maynt of sweltrie Daie
> In Slepeis Bosomme laieth hys deft Headde
> So Senses sunke to reste mie Boddie laie
> Eftsoons mie Sprighte fromme Erthelie Bandes untyde
> Immengde yn flanched Ayre wyth Trouthe asyde.

In this instance, the muse that Chatterton has in mind is not so much a lurking ghost or even a classical divinity, but a Robin Goodfellow. It arrives incongruously, not from medieval witchery but from an eighteenth-century popular fiction that is full of reveries in which writers are commonly swept through feeble literary allegories by elfin genii and pixieish daemons. In George Colman and Bonnell Thornton's journal *The Connoisseur*, there is such a dream of the traffic across an Ocean of Ink:

> While I stood contemplating this amazing scene, one of those good-natured Genii, who never fail making their appearance to extricated dreamers from their difficulties, rose from the sable stream, and planted himself at my elbow. His complexion was of the darkest hue, not unlike that of the *Dæmons* [apprentice boys] of a printing house. . . .

This marvel is dressed like a book, armed with a proofsheet and a quill, and introduces himself as the Genius who will conduct 'Mr Town', the dreamer, through an allegorical landscape of literary fame. Chatterton's spryte in 'The Storie of Wyllyam Canynge' voyages through time rather than space, presenting a historical perspective that briefly puts Canynge in his place:

> Strayt was I carry'd back to Tymes of yore
> Whykst Canynge swathed yet yn fleshlie Bedde
> And saw all Actyons whych han been before
> And all the Scroll of Fate unravelled
> And when the Fate mark'd Babe acome to Syghte
> I saw hym eager gaspeynge after Lyghte.

Elsewhere, Chatterton does use the playful conceit of the gnat-like

genius buzzing through one's dreams like a flea in the celestial ear –
and in an even more sprightly fashion than the exotic vision of *The
Connoisseur.* In 'Journal 6th' (a verse epistle to his friend John Baker),
he writes:

> After fasting and praying and grunting and weeping
> My Guardian Angel beheld me fast sleeping
> And instantly Capering into my Brain
> Relieved me from Prison of bodily Chain
> The Soul can be every thing as you all know
> And mine was transform'd to the shape of a Crow

– whereupon he embarks on a not un-Blakean day-trip to hell. The
vicious satire of 'The Whore of Babylon' too is comprehensively
haunted, or rather pestered, by ghosts inconsiderately raised by Samuel
Johnson: 'a walking Spirit of the Press / Who knocks at Midnight at
his Lordship's Door', the Cock-Lane Ghost, the spectre of Shakespeare,
and the ghost of Johnson's own genius (which is eventually pickled in
vinegar). Even more ridiculously, Chatterton's mock 'Will' presents a
mechanism to allow his ghost to continue dedicating publications,
and insists that any ladies he has consorted with 'need be under no
Apprehensions from the Appearance of my Ghost for I dye for none
of them'.

These ghosts are all different, projections of separate literary
moments, quotations from different books and genres, and this is the
most un-Ossianic thing about them. In Ossian, ghosts are the presiding
population and give meaning to the present through their repetitive
lamentations; but Chatterton's miscellany of sprytes does not summon
the dead as enigmas echoing through aeons, as manifestations of cloudy
memories of half-forgotten renown haunting the present, as multitudinous and omnipresent. Chatterton's spirits are quite different, are
indeed *up*. Some are excitable busybodies, interfering, and literate,
popping out of books and swarming about writers like the sylphs that
Alexander Pope describes in 'The Rape of the Lock', or Shakespearean
fairies whipping up a storm in a teaspoon; others are hellish disem-
bodied curses; some are colonial slavers. They come from no single
orthodox model of inspiration; they are, it transpires, anti-inspirational.

Inspiration is a degraded concept for Chatterton. His lengthy satire
'Kew Gardens' includes an elaborate if rather ramshackle passage on
inspiration. National celebrities and local Bristolians are connected

through a satirical rhapsody on their common enervation, a dunce-like darkness that smothers all:

> Hail Inspiration whose Cimmerian Night,
> Gleams into Day with every flying Light. . . .

Empty invocations to Inspiration's 'mysterious Wings', 'sooty Pinnions', and so forth pile up by the hatful. It motivates politicians:

> By Inspiration North directs his tools,
> And [Bute] above by Inspiration rules

and even makes you sneeze. 'Kew Gardens' proposes a purely physio-logical or mechanical form of inspiration when describing a faltering preacher, who takes snuff on his handkerchief of 'lawn' (cambric) in order to rekindle his imagination:

> He stammers; instantaneously is drawn,
> A bord'red Piece of Inspiration Lawn;
> Which being thrice unto his Nose apply'd,
> Into his Pineal Gland the Vapors glide

and so he's roaring off again. Meanwhile, Chatterton is unable to resist savaging his own most intense work, most sustained inspiration: one of the more popular brands of herb snuff in the 1760s was called . . . 'Rowley's'.

This self-parodic puncturing which provides the high octane self-hate in his satires also lies behind Chatterton's more extended quotations from – or allusions to – Ossian, in which the reader is duped into an Ossianic pose. The effect in 'Ælla', for instance, is to imply retreat at the point of attack:

> Ælla rose lyche the tree besette wyth brieres;
> Hys talle speere sheenynge as the starres at nyghte,
> Hys eyne ensemeynge as a lowe of fyre;
> Whanne he encheered everie manne to fyghte. . . .

This is no King Harry exhortation. Incongruously, he speaks with a soft low voice, 'Hys gentle wordes dyd moove eche valourous knyghte', and his warriors respond as gently:

Lyche slowelie dynnynge of the croucheynge streme,
Syche dyd the mormrynge sounde of the whol armie seme.

The Ossianic voices have regressed so infinitely into an ambient reverb that the past now speaks the present as a quiet and demented reiteration mumbling away at the brink of sense and audibility. The effect in 'Battle of Hastings II' is more stark. The mighty army blasts forward, while simultaneously seeming inert, half-asleep, as if they are already exhausted by having to carry an Ossianic burden on top of their cladded Rowleyan armour:

As when the erthe, torne by convulsyons dyre,
In reaulmes of darkness hid from human syghte,
The warring force of water, air, and fyre,
Brast from the regions of eternal nyghte,
Thro the darke caverns seeke the reaulmes of lyght;
Some loftie mountaine, by its fury torne,
Dreadfully moves, and causes grete affryght;
Now here, now there, majestic nods the bourne,
And awfulle shakes, mov'd by the almighty force,
Whole woods and forests nod, and ryvers change theyr course.

So did the men of war at once advaunce,
Linkd man to man, enseemd one boddie light;
Above a wood, yform'd of bill and launce,
That noddyd in the ayre most straunge to syght.
Harde as the iron were the menne of mighte,
Ne need of slughornes to enrowse theyr minde;
Eche shootynge spere yreaden for the fyghte,
More feerce than fallynge rocks, more swefte than wynd;
With solemne step, by ecchoe made more dyre,
One single boddie all theie marchd, theyr eyen on fyre.

And when in 'Hastynges I' Wales is described as the destination of bewitched souls – very similar to the Lake of Lego, the haunt of the dead, in *Temora* – it does not elevate Mervyn ap Tewdore to the misty stature of an Ossianic brave, but belittles him to the status of an elf. He revenges himself upon the Normans for the slaying of Howel ap Jevah:

As furious as a Mountain Wolf he ran,
As Ouphant Faeries whan the Moon shine bryght,

In little Circles daunce upon the Green,
All Livynge Creatures flie far from their Syghte,
Ne by the Race of Destinie be seen –
For what he be that Ouphant Faeries strike,
Their Souls will wander to King Offa's Dike –*

So what we have here then is not the storm-racked Highlands or the magnificence of Fingal's Cave of basalt pillars, but English ethnicity and English eccentricity. Chatterton was a poet of English identity: his two, unfinished versions of the 'Bloudie Battle of Hastynges', for instance, are clearly attempts at early English epic, translated by Rowley, he says, from an eleventh-century eye-witness poem by Turgot, and Rowley's own 'Englysh Metamorphosis' is an Anglo-Ovidian attempt to circumscribe a national topography. Chatterton describes the birth of the Severn from Sabrina, the creation of St Vincent's Rocks, another Bristol landmark, from Sabrina's mother Elstrid, and most impressively the spontaneous conflagration of a giant whose mountainous ashes become Snowdon:

The bawsyn gyaunt . . .
Whanne, as he strod alonge the shakeynge lee,
The roddie levynne glesterrd on hys headde;
Into hys hearte the azure vapoures spreade;
He wrythde arounde yn drearie dernie payne;
Whanne from his lyfe-bloode the rodde lemes were fed,
He felle an hepe of ashes on the playne:
Stylle does hys ashes shoote ynto the lyghte,
A wondrouns mountayne hie, and Snowdon ys ytte hyghte.†

This is certainly an eccentric conclusion to the poem, but both 'Hastynges' and 'Englysh Metamorphosis' are also about English *ethnicities* as well. 'Hastynges' is extremely partisan in favour of the Saxons. They inflict four times as many casualties on the Normans as they sustain themselves, and their enemy is generally portrayed as either cowardly or incompetent. The Saxons are defeated not so much by Norman prowess as by themselves: by their generosity of spirit and headstrong rashness; and by their unquenchable thirst for beer, consumed on the

---

* 'Ouphant': elfin.
† 'Bawsyn': huge, bulky; 'levynne': lightning; 'dernie': gloomy, solitary; 'lemes': flames, rays, lights.

eve of battle while the Normans remain in strategically sober prayer. Elsewhere too, Chatterton is avidly pro-Saxon, and so it is perhaps surprising – or admirably perverse – that in 'Extracts from Craishes Herauldry' he invented a pedigree for himself that traced his family to one 'Chateau Tonne', an invading Norman knight.

If 'Hastynges' poses questions about historical ethnicities, 'Englysh Metamorphosis' makes the same point about regional identity. As much as they are Saxon, the Rowley works are also a Bristolian cultural enterprise. A piece like 'A Discorse on Brystowe' is effectively Bristol's *Britannia*. Rowley, like Edmund Gibson to William Camden, translates and emends Turgot's Latin notes, and Chatterton does not therefore figure in the work. But Rowley is also a Camden of the district of Redcliffe, which is stuffed with such an embarrassment of churches, friaries, inscriptions, and relics of Kings Arthur and Alfred as to make it the crucible of Bristolian, if not national, identity. This then is the ground on which to have the Rowley debate: a place where the ground shifts both literally ('As when the erthe, torne by convulsyons dyre') and politically (between Saxons and Normans, Redcliffe and Bristol, York and Lancaster, Government and Opposition). It is not a stable space: nowhere is. Even in Africa, the River Tiber [*sic*] 'crumbles mountains down and shakes the world'. The power of Chatterton's poetry is to make a principle of flux, and to allow it to cast long shadows.

On 21 September 1819, John Keats wrote to John Hamilton Reynolds: 'I always somehow associate Chatterton with autumn. He is the purest writer in the English Language. He has no French idiom, or particles like Chaucer – 'tis genuine English Idiom in English Words.' He perhaps should be saying 'I always somehow associate Chatterton with "To Autumn" ', as he had just composed that ode, and as Andrew Motion remarks, Chatterton is the 'presiding figure' of the poem, a mixture of 'fulfilment and finality', and the verse is suffused both with Chatterton's own lines and those of his elegists. Indeed it appears, for reasons that will become clear, that the very genius of 'To Autumn',

> sitting careless on a granary floor,
> Thy hair soft-lifted by the winnowing wind . . .
> Drows'd with the fume of poppies . . .

is itself a portrait of Chatterton.

But there is more to Keats's identification, I think, than the myths
of neglected genius. Keats was actually reading Chatterton rather than
simply adopting him as an archetype of youth and neglect. Like the
'peasant poet' John Clare, who 'lookd in to the Poems of Chatterton
to see what he says about flowers' and then made natural history notes
from his poems ('have found that he speaks of the Lady smock'), Keats
recognized in Chatterton a profound poet of nature, using a language
apparently uncorrupted by modernity and the agrarian and industrial
revolutions. If there is any certainty in Chatterton's chaotic imagined
worlds, it lies almost unregarded on a bank, in the beauty of flowers.
One of Chatterton's 'Mynstrelles Songes' from 'Ælla' begins on a spring
dawn:

> The boddynge flourettes bloshes atte the lyghte;
> The mees be sprenged wyth the yellowe hue;
> Ynn daiseyd mantels ys the mountayne dyghte;
> The nesh yonge coweslepe bendethe wyth the dewe;
> The trees enlefed, yntoe Heavenne straughte,
> Whenn gentle wyndes doe blowe, to whestlying dynne ys brought.

Every word chimes in a concatenation, an incantatory mix of rhyme
and assonance, both verbal and visual. The effect is not dissimilar to
the poems of Gerard Manley Hopkins a century later: 'Degged with
dew, dappled with dew / Are the groins of the braes that the brook
treads through.'

In this way, then, the 'Mynstrelles Songe' is the answer to Keats's
question in 'To Autumn',

> Where are the songs of Spring? Ay, where are they?

Keats poses the essential question not just about the seasons, or Chatterton, but about the dim confusion of history: where has it gone, can
nostalgia ever be satisfied? The past – whether it be the Middle Ages,
the 1760s, 1819, or the songs that were sung to spring – has passed,
but it leaves its own elusive poetry, a poetry that is inseparable from
language – the English language.

> O! synge untoe mie roundelaie,
> O! droppe the brynie teare wythe mee,
> Daunce ne moe atte hallie daie,

> Lycke a reynynge ryver bee;
> Mie love ys dedde,
> Gon to hys death-bedde,
> Al under the wyllowe tree.

This 'Mynstrelles Songe', also from 'Ælla', was a favourite of Keats's, who used to delight in chanting it and apparently took special pleasure in the stanza:

> Comme, wythe acorne-coppe and thorne,
> Drayne mie hartys blodde awaie;
> Lyfe and all yttes goode I scorne,
> Daunce bie nete, or feaste by daie.
> Mie love ys dedde,
> Gon to hys death-bedde,
> Al under the wyllowe tree.

Keats, recognizing that his own death, whenever it would occur, was as inevitable as Chatterton's, manages in 'To Autumn' to supersede the Chattertonian commonplace of forgery and suicide by revealing an autumnal harmony of nature and death, by a timeliness that is necessarily untimely. As Chatterton puts it in 'Narva and Mored', an eclogue of the passing of the African golden age:

> Their lives were transient as the meadow flow'r,
> Ripen'd in ages, wither'd in an hour.

Keats had 'ramped' through Spenser 'like a young horse turned into a spring meadow', but he reads Chatterton as a harvest: as a gleaner steadying his laden head across a brook, watching the last drops wrung from cider apples, peering through the autumnal mist.

> And sometimes like a gleaner thou dost keep
> Steady thy laden head across a brook;
> Or by a cyder-press, with patient look,
> Thou watchest the last oozings hours by hours.

Once glimpsed in this way, Chatterton seems to saturate Keats's verse like a sunset, gilding the waters of oblivion and twisting wolf's-bane, tight-rooted 'for its poisonous wine'; haloing the flitting faeries that scamper among his flowers and through the land.

On the same day that Keats wrote to Reynolds describing Chat-

terton as 'the purest writer in the English Language', he made a similar
remark to brother George and wife Georgiana:

> The purest english I think – or what ought to be the purest – is
> Chatterton's. The Language had existed long enough to be entirely
> uncorrupted of Chaucer's gallicisms, and still the old words are
> used. Chatterton's language is entirely northern. I prefer the native
> music of it to Milton's cut by feet.

This English purity rests, then, not in history, the medieval, not even
in Spenser or Shakespeare (or Ossian or Milton), but in the beginnings
of a blend of folk and autodidact traditions that never sleeps in evading
stultifying homogeneity, and above all still sings with the strange and
intense onomatopoeia of its own passing. Against the inconstant prose
of the world the language of flowers has a native poetry, and Keats can
be no more concerned with whether the Rowley poems are authentic or
not than with whether there really are fairies living at the bottom of
his garden.

> There is no language site outside bourgeois ideology. . . .
> The only possible rejoinder is neither confrontation nor
> destruction, but only theft: fragment the old text of culture,
> science, literature, and change its features according to for-
> mulae of disguise, as one disguises stolen goods.
>
> Roland Barthes, *Sade, Fourier, Loyola*

In 'Ælla', Rowley boasts that he will 'soare 'bove trouthe of hystorie'.
So just as his use of ghosts rejects the stability of a single supernatural
cosmology for a more fluid and improvisatory otherness, infusing the
bloody dreams of Stonehenge or the hunting of the reeking tiger with
a reality, Chatterton is also denying that history is a system. Both his
spirits and his Rowley parchments are like quotations – fragments of
other books, other places – and are therefore discontinuous, irreconcilable, even opaque.

   This is clear in his repudiation of the model of an author as a
single, knowable, and knowing entity, whether as a musing Ossianic

bard or as the 'author-function', devised and derived by Michel Foucault from St Jerome's canons of authenticity in *De viris illustribus*:

> (1) if among several books attributed to an author one is inferior to the others, it must be withdrawn from the list of the author's works . . . ; (2) the same should be done if certain texts contradict the doctrine expounded in the author's other works . . . ; (3) one must also exclude works that are written in a different style, containing words and expressions not ordinarily found in the writer's production . . . ; (4) finally, passages quoting statements that were made or events that occurred after the author's death must be regarded as interpolated texts. . . .

On such criteria Chatterton would fragment into a score of different authors. In addition to signing work with his initials T.C., C., and D.B. ('Dunhelmus Bristoliensis'), and the dozen or so Rowley writers,* Chatterton also wrote poetry and prose under the names Asaphides, Astrea Brokage, Celorimon, Decimus, Q., Libertas, Probus, A Hunter of Oddities, [Paul?] Vamp, Harry Wildfire, Menenius, Z.A., and Hasmot Tnchaorett. 'A character is now unnecessary', he wrote to his mother from London on 6 May 1770; 'an author carries his character in his pen.' In this flurry of names, then, the signature has itself become another, travelling quotation; a way of bringing word.

Quotation is in any case a way of making history: that which is quoted becomes part of the terrain of the past, and hence is plotted by the present in art and literature – something quite evident in Chatterton's intense layering in the Rowley works. Early commentators, both pro- and anti-Rowleyan, wrote hundreds of pages tracing sources and parallels: in the case of Jeremiah Milles, it was to demonstrate the Homeric parallels that Chatterton, who spoke no Greek, could not be aware of, but to which Rowley was consciously alluding;† in the case of George Steevens it was to ransack Shakespeare to find sources for as many Rowleyan lines as possible and thereby prove that Chatterton

---

* Turgot, The Abbatte John, Seyncte Baldwynne, Seyncte Warburgie, John de Burgham, The Rawfe Chedder Chappmanne, Syr Thybbot Gorges, Syr Wm. Canynge, Carpenter (Bishoppe of Worcester), Ecca (Bishoppe of Hereforde), Elmar (Bishoppe of Selseie), John Ladgate, and John à Iscam.
† Milles's edition is useful for quoting classical parallels to argue that Rowley had read the classical authors of whom Chatterton was ignorant; strangely, he uses Homer in Pope's translation.

had effectively 'Rowleyized' the Bard. Quotation was a way of affirming a writer's place in the canon (no one searched for lines filched from poets like Thomas Tickell or Edward Chicken), but it is significant that the taboo of forgery poisoned Chatterton's entire literary technique: he was not 'imitating', he was 'plagiarizing'.

So, a line like 'O, for a muse of fire!' (*Henry V*) is Rowleyized (according to Steevens) in 'Ælla' as 'O forr a Spryte al Feere!'.* Likewise,

> Mie Honnoure yette somme *drybblet Joie* maie fynde

seems to be from *Othello*:

> I should have found in some place of my soul
> A drop of patience.

And:

>   To the Skyes
> The dailie Contekes of the Londe ascende,
> The Wyddowe, Fahdrelesse, and Bondmennes Cries,
> Acheke the mokie Aire, and Heaven astende.

from Rowley's unfinished drama 'Goddwyn', Steevens claims is taken from *Macbeth*:

>   Each new morn,
> New widows howl: new orphans cry; new sorrows
> Strike heaven on the face.

Further 'parallels' were drawn from Milton, Dryden's Virgil and Pope's Homer, Gray, and so forth. Admittedly elsewhere Chatterton, as a mid-eighteenth-century poet, did imitate explicitly. His 'Elegy on the Demise of a Great Genius', for one, opens with the lines, 'Begin my Muse the imitative Lay / Aonian Doxys sound the thrumming String', and he wrote Horatian imitations, one of which includes the love-lorn and strangely familiar lines:

> Yet, ah! too soon th'extatic vision flies,
> Flies like the fairy paintings of a dream.

He also of course imitated Ossianics. But this attack claiming that the Rowley works are plagiarized is clearly an attempt to close down

---

* Quotations are taken from Steevens's own edition of Shakespeare (1778).

the text as an unlawful racket in stolen (if disfigured) words, because
his offences seem all the more criminal because the plagiarism occurs
within forgery. And yet these disparities can also sing. Chatterton
is turning the tide of literary history back on itself and radically
demonstrating T. S. Eliot's subsequent argument in 'Tradition and the
Individual Talent' that the historical and aesthetic order of the literary
canon is completely modified whenever a major new work appears:
the present rewrites the past.* But Rowley does not merely imitate
those writers who actually succeed him, like Shakespeare and Milton:
he even collages his own work from that of his followers. So Shelley's
opening of 'Ghasta':

> Hark! the owlet flaps her wing,
> > In the pathless dell beneath,
> Hark! night ravens loudly sing,
> > Tidings of despair and death –

is rewritten by Rowley, in the course of Keats's favourite 'Mynstrelles
Songe', thus:

> Harke! the ravenne flappes hys wynge,
> > In the briered delle belowe;
> Harke! the dethe-owle loude dothe synge,
> > To the nyghte-mares as heie goe. . . .

And Chatterton's own lines from 'Narva and Mored',

> So when the splendor of the dying day,
> Darts the red lustre of the watry way,

might be in imitation of Byron's 'Monody on Sheridan':

> When the last sunshine of expiring day
> On summer's twilight weeps, despite itself away.

Whichever way we decide to read Rowley, the prevalence of quotation also erases the figure of the author-as-author, replacing it with
a sifter, a collector and selector, or a curator, residing in the fragments
of another's work. Such making is a craft – and in this model of
literary influence, writers are artisans who imitate and mix earlier –

---

* The point is also made by Jorge Luis Borges in 'Kafka and His Precursors', which
deliberately cites Eliot. 'The fact is that every writer properly *creates* his own precursors.
His work modifies our conception of the past as it will modify the future.'

and also in the case of Rowley, later – linguistic gestures. The prewar
German critic Walter Benjamin boasted a collection of over 600 quotations when he was working on his study of German tragedy: as
Hannah Arendt suggests, they 'constituted the main work, with the
writing as something secondary', and she compares his technique to
surrealistic montage.* But eighteenth-century history writing, of which
Rowley is both precursor and exemplum, is characterized by a more
capacious and communal ambition. In Warton's, Gibbon's, and Burke's
histories, the work, according to David Fairer, incorporates prior texts
into itself not as 'sources', but 'so as to articulate an inherited language'.
It is how the nation is narrated, how culture actually works.

Such a meticulous and territorial craft is evident too in Blake's
definition of natural genius – on which he had immediate second
thoughts: 'Invention depends Altogether upon Execution *or Organiz-
ation*; as that is right or wrong so is the Invention perfect or imperfect';†
and Roland Barthes has controversially described the text as 'a tissue
of quotations drawn from the innumerable centres of culture'. As
Baudelaire said of Thomas De Quincey's lexicon of ancient Greek,
Chatterton too had 'created for himself an unfailing dictionary [in his
case the red pocket-book], vastly more extensive and complex than
those resulting from the ordinary patience of purely literary themes':
a dictionary for translating modern ideas and images into Middle
English. Hence, the Rowleyan language is the vehicle for translating
the contemporary into the archaic, for moving the present into the
past, just as his spirits are quotations from elsewhere to destabilize
the central figures in his verses.

Rowley's language in this medieval never-never land is itself based
on a principle of fragmentation. Chatterton compiled some 1,800
words from glossaries and dictionaries that he transliterated into his
extravagant spelling (he coined none himself). As Warton suggested
in his *History of English Poetry*: 'In counterfeiting the coins of a rude
age, he did not forget the usual application of an artificial rust: but
this disguise was not sufficient to conceal the elegance of the workmanship.' In other words, Chatterton copies (counterfeits) a word taken
from a medieval text and supplements it with lyttell allusions to
medieval orthography. But he quotes more widely still: Chatterton

---

* In his essay on surrealism, Benjamin does compare surrealism with 'forgery'.
† My emphasis.

distributes history, architecture, and myth like words in a mighty, uncoiling sentence; arranging these elementary signs, made up of his garbed quotations, in a new cultural language – one subject only to the ironic order of authenticity. A piece like 'The Rolle of Seyncte Bartlemeweis Priorie' shows Chatterton, as Taylor puts it, as 'an anti-quary of the broadest competence, expert in medicine, books, and plays, and in popular, ecclesiastical, architectural, and artistic antiqui-ties'. The generation of new forms within his framework of authenticity – that is, the casting of more and more Rowleyana – can therefore continue indefinitely and in infinite permutations, without the possi-bility of summary, without order, and whether they have any literary value or no.

This could of course be related to the intimations of dementia in Ossian: Rowley now figures as a mouthpiece for previous enunciations. But what is significant in any comparison of these lunatic forgers is Macpherson's cool clarity of ambition compared with Chatterton's boast in his 'Will' that he was known in Bristol by the title of 'Mad Genius'. Although eighteenth-century writers should not be psychoana-lysed as if they were twentieth-century Americans, there might be a shared condition of disturbance: there are mad people and there are sane people, even after Foucault's book *Madness and Civilization*. Chat-terton's Rowley language could be called an idioglossia, such as those private languages shared between twins; moreover, the intense creation of personal mythologies, the interest in maps, writings, genealogies, and the physical cramming of detail – whether in dates, names, and historical events, or simply filling every available space on parchment with words, diagrams, heraldic shields running up to the edges – are characteristics evident, in part, not only in the works of other contemporary writers who were also excluded from the canon, like Christopher Smart and William Blake, but also by twentieth-century 'Outsider' artists.

Thomas Rowley was dreamt into being to utter the fictions of an invented world, inspired by multitudinous instances of quotation translated into a new tongue. But he was just one of the host of signatories that possessed Chatterton like the devils that possessed the Gadarene: 'My name is Legion: for we are many.' In Chatterton's posterity, however, later poets, in particular the Romantics, neither hold the work at the distance of citation by admitting Rowley to be a forgery, nor are they themselves overcome by the clamorous voices of

Chatterton's writing that bark like a sounder of devilish swine swarming down a steep place to choke in the sea. Instead, these writers refashion Chatterton into the herald of inspiration, shape him out of a scattering of what Barthes calls 'charms' – those telling episodes in a writer's life and legend that combine to make a biography. We have encountered some of these charms already, such as our man falling into a fresh grave, but the next chapter, guided by Romantic theories of the imagination, will cast many more.

V. DAEMON

For a Poet is indeed a thing ethereally light, winged, and sacred, nor can he compose anything worth calling poetry until he becomes inspired, and, as it were, mad, or whilst any reason remains in him.

Plato, *Ion* (translated by Percy Bysshe Shelley)

I have rather made up my mind that I am a mere apparition.

Samuel Taylor Coleridge to John Thelwall, 1796

Chatterton
Rose pale, his solemn agony had not
Yet faded from him

Percy Bysshe Shelley, *Adonais*

Francis Thompson was a studious and serious child who appeared destined for the ministry until he read Thomas De Quincey's *Confessions of an English Opium Eater.* He was corrupted with almost supernatural speed, and was subsequently discovered living as a poet in London: scribbling verses on scraps of paper, eking out a living selling matches, addicted to opium. He was utterly destitute and slept rough under the arches of Covent Garden; in fact, he slept very rough – every quarter of an hour he was kicked awake by the police and moved along. Doped up, starving to death, and unable to get a decent night's sleep, Thompson sunk into a suicidal mood. One night, he spent his pathetic fortune on one large dose of laudanum, and went to the rubbish tip behind Covent Garden Market to kill himself. But he had only swallowed half his poison when he felt an arm laid on his wrist, and looking up he saw Thomas Chatterton standing over him. Chatterton forbade him to drink the other, fatal half, and Thompson obeyed. Chatterton had saved Thompson's life, *but Thomas Chatterton had been dead for over a century.*

Thompson was certain it was the 'marvellous Boy': 'I recognised him from the pictures of him – besides, I knew that it was he before I saw him – and I remembered at once the story of the money which arrived for Chatterton the day after his suicide.' Thompson survived, had his ragged lines published, and was soon cured of his opium addiction.

How can one make sense of such an experience? Soon after his mysterious death, Chatterton embarked on a long and uncanny afterlife. As a literary forger, or disguised writer, he had already been living the life of Rowley, but the subsequent controversy openly pitted the one against the other. A dead boy confronted his archaic daemon twin, and was briefly undone by this mask, his persona, Thomas Rowley. Chatterton's own meteoric life, which left only intangible trails of doubt and uncertainty, was far less believable than that of the copiously archived fifteenth-century monk. But when by 1782 the controversy had settled and it was established that Chatterton had indeed forged Rowley, their two lives – one historical, one fictional – merged into a hybrid, a myth. Henceforth, the 'marvellous Boy' commenced his posthumous career as an unparalleled, archetypal, and precocious genius. This became the ground ('with its vague connotations suggesting superhuman talent and qualities of the mind', as Eric Hebborn says of the precondition, 'genius'), on which his poems were read: as early as 1780, Herbert Croft in *Love and Madness* perceived Chatterton as an incarnation of Apollo, the god of poetry. Even Milton was beneath him.

If Chatterton's transformation from history into myth required his death, then so did his return, his recurrence. Chatterton could be a ghost only by the mystery of his passing, but the stories about his death created such optimum conditions for his 'spectrification' that his return became necessary and then inevitable. His status as a genius and the mythologization of his suicide created a ghost-shaped hole through which Chatterton re-entered the world.

Spectrality, essential to the idea of 'Romantic authorship', finds its apotheosis in Chatterton – although with some notable exceptions recent author theory has shied away from ghosts, and busied itself with accounting the economic and legal conditions that supposedly produced authorial identity. Martha Woodmansee and Peter Jaszi, for instance, argue that the emphasis on authorial originality and creativity in this period, 'far from being timeless and universal, is a relatively recent formation', and in the words of the Marxist critic Terry Eagleton, 'it is just when the artist is becoming debased to a petty commodity producer that he or she will lay claim to transcendent genius'. Admittedly, the tangled relationship of law and property does present contexts within which instances of culture are recorded, by which I mean writers writing books or painters painting pictures, but such materialist approaches ultimately tend to do to all of culture what has previously been reserved as the fate of forgeries, counterfeits, and plagiaries. Traditionally, by analysing paper and ink rather than reading the poetry, criticism has reduced literary forgeries to cases of forensic evidence as a way of excluding such works from the canon. Materialist critiques operate in a similar fashion: they reduce texts to their material conditions of production, to the workings of the literary marketplace – which may indeed be insightful, but is only one step. At the crucial moment they lose faith and fail to rise to the challenge of poetry: they jettison criticism in favour of other discursive action, such as economic fetishism and political special pleading, which results in similar effects of exclusion.

So rather than mimic this activity and reduce all culture to a species of fraud, I will instead explain how a poetics of forgery arose in the Romantic period. This entails tracing the appearances of ghosts and other repetitions of the ineffable, and thinking about how literature accounts for itself. In the later years of the eighteenth century, literary self-awareness abandoned its intertextual preoccupation with imitation, allusion, and satire for an exploration of the irrationality of the imagination, and particularly of the nature of inspiration.

Yet here, there is perpetual recession and mystification: Coleridge famously misplacing the lion's part of 'Kubla Khan' somewhere in the opiated mistiness of his mind after being interrupted by 'a person on business from Porlock' – who, to thicken the plot, was probably Wordsworth (if we can really believe any part of this creation myth at all). Or Percy Bysshe Shelley bemoaning the poverty of poetic composition in *The Defence of Poetry*: 'When composition begins, inspiration is already on the decline, and the most glorious poetry that has ever been communicated to the world is probably a feeble shadow of the original conceptions of the poet' – which presumably makes poets themselves pretty 'feeble', as well as 'unacknowledged', 'legislators of the world'. Inspiration, however irreproduceable or unrepresentable, is consistently presented as being very much outside of the self. According to Tim Clark, it is a

> scene of composition . . . in which the writer recognizes in his or her emergent material with such apparent force that it seems to be coming from another and to be part of a work which is somehow both already-read and also yet to emerge. The work thus announces itself as a certain compulsion-to-be.

These features will soon fall into recognizable lineaments. In the meantime, it is worth noting that Shelley himself translated Plato's *Ion*, which as I have already indicated celebrates the obliviousness of inspiration, to the extent of perhaps satirically suggesting that the inspired production has not been individually created at all: 'The God seems purposely to have deprived all poets, prophets, and soothsayers of every particle of reason and understanding, the better to adapt them to their employment as his ministers and interpreters.' Poets are properly not *responsible* for their work; they are merely the 'interpreters of the divinities – each being possessed by some one deity'. This quality of interpreting or administering or of being spoken through perfectly captures the sense that poetry is a repetition of what is still yet to come, that the poet is a ghost-in-waiting.

For many writers Chatterton was not merely an inspiration, but a more literal spirit: a guardian angel, a ghostly presence, a force from outside. So his ghost did not simply await the advent of these supernatural theories of poetry; it shaped them, breathed life into them. The autodidact George Gregory, for example, translated Robert Lowth's *Lectures on the Sacred Poetry of the Hebrews* (1787; first published in Latin in 1753), which dwelt upon the mysticism and revelation of Hebraic poetry in contrast to the imitative composition of the Greeks. Hebraic poetry was 'something sacred and celestial, not produced by human art or genius, but altogether a divine gift'; it was composed under stress: 'When, as it were, the secret avenues, the interior recesses of the soul are thrown open; when the inmost conceptions are displayed, rushing together in one turbid stream, without order or connexion.' The same George Gregory subsequently wrote an influential biography of Chatterton (1789) and in 1797 published a sermon on suicide: ghostly theories of irrational inspiration and composition were continuous with the mystery of Chatterton's life and death.

Chatterton's poetic afterlife among later eighteenth-century poets has been examined by David Fairer, who finds him invoked in lyrics, in satiric attacks on a society that fails to nurture poverty-stricken genius, and also at moments of Gothic horror. The verses of Mary 'Perdita' Robinson and Ann Yearsley have Chatterton flowering as respectively a primrose or harebell, whose petals 'o'er the precipice by winds are cast'. Although he remains elusive and transcendent in these images, Keats and Clare were to find much in this association of Chatterton with flowers. But the more usual invocations were morbid or macabre, brooding upon the horrors of his extinction or the haunting of his spirit. 'The Poet's Garret' (1804) by 'Perdita' Robinson, who had by then already penned her 'Monody to the Memory of Chatterton', evokes the impending deathbed scene and the sacramental, fatal, use of laudanum:

> All around
> Small scraps of paper lie torn, vestiges
> Of an unquiet fancy.
> . . .
>
> On a shelf
> (Yclept a mantle-piece) a phial stands,
> Half fill'd with potent spirits! – spirits strong,
> Which sometimes haunt the poet's restless brain,
> And fill his mind with fancies whimsical.

A more ghoulish image of Chatterton freshly risen from the grave also haunts much poetry and painting of the period. James Thistlethwaite, writing as early as 1770 – the year of Chatterton's death – had a particularly terrible vision: 'See! see! he comes! . . . How pale and wan those lifeless cheeks appear.'

Pursuit, traumatic repetitions or doubles that seek to supplant the self, devilry (too much devilry): this is typical off-the-peg Gothic. Indeed, inspiration was commonly described as a haunting, and it was Gothicized and vulgarized as the spawning of self-engendered monsters: bad repetitions of the self that were counterfeit and illegitimate. This is seen most obviously in *Frankenstein* (1818), but many other stories of the time were likewise based on pursuing and/or being pursued by one's Doppelgänger.* But the discourse of inspiration is much more complex than these fanciful cases of the internalization of desire. Inspiration now emerges from other, ancient, and esoteric texts. A figure takes shape: not a ghost or a monster, still less the Muse, but a 'daemon'.

HAUNTING

The brother of death daily haunts us with dying mementos.

Sir Thomas Browne, *Hydriotaphia* (*Urne Buriall*)

Sentimental poets are 'haunted' by Chatterton; Thistlethwaite sees his dead friend arise. What is meant by this haunting, which is both a memento mori and a moment of inspiration (that is, finding oneself not oneself but part of some other coherence)?

Chatterton is seen as a ghost; haunting is the historical condition of his (non)-existence, moreover ghosts are revenants, from the past or from the future, or from a place of dreams and visions; inbetween, neither. We have already tasted some of the morbid uncanniness of Chatterton's life and death, but if he really did commit suicide, as it was believed, such an offence remained in the eighteenth century an irredeemable sin against God, and a treason against the monarch. Unless a coroner's verdict of *non compos mentis* could be reached, a suicide's corpse would be likely to be buried at a crossroads, naked, face down, and impaled on a stake, in an attempt to prevent a ghost or vampire rising. Having rejected both this world and the next, the suicide was cursed to be forever interjacent and could only wander the hereafter, literally a 'sleepless soul'. In the seventh circle of Dante's *Inferno* the suicides' shades are likewise bound as trees, though in a

---

* The word was coined at the end of the eighteenth century in the novels of Jean-Paul Richter to describe a double, or facsimile, or counterfeit self.

cruel perversion of the grove of Dodona they continue to talk, and to bleed.

Moreover, until the beginning of the eighteenth century, suicide was also, like witchcraft, a diabolical crime, considered to be an effect of possession. In that sense it is a form of devilish fraud, or counter-feiting, and the dual insistence on possession and ghostliness constitutes what could be called the infernal sublime of the suicide. Self-transforming and self-obliterating, suicide is evidently a form of inspir-ation. So shaped under the myth of suicide, Chatterton is possessed and inspired, mad, and ghostly. But ghosts are usually merely fright-ening, and if sometimes seductive or prophetic they are not themselves the direct agents of inspiration. Chatterton metamorphosed into a more complex and poetic entity: a daemon. Many tenets of daemon-ology were incorporated into mainstream theology, as well as mystical and heretical schools, in theories of good and evil spirits, but the Church insistently demonized the daemon. A little rehabilitation is necessary.

'Daemon' has two clear semantic arcs: it is the fiend or devil, the demon of Christian eschatology, but it is also the ancient Greek *daimon* (δαίμων), a presiding genius, or demi-god, between the mortal and immortal, between the earthly and the divine. Daemons are suprasen-sible and suprahuman creatures, intermediate between gods and men; they are messengers and agents, beyond good and evil: 'if it is not yet itself a "god",' writes Rudolf Otto in *The Idea of the Holy*, 'it is still less an anti-god, but must be termed a "pre-god".'

The root δαίω is two verbs, meaning to kindle a fire or to burn with life, and to divide or be torn asunder – both seem oddly pertinent to Prometheus: stealing fire, and having his liver recurrently ripped out by an eagle. A fiery daemonic flicker is a glimpse of the presence of the divine, whether in the atmosphere of a place, in the gift of madness, or even in the shy of a horse. The word *daiomai* also has a sense of the divine, referring to how the Gods divide and distribute blessings and curses upon humans. In *Cratylus*, however, Plato derives *daimon* from δαήμων, meaning 'knowing or skilled', which could indeed refer to Prometheus's other work: crafting humans and tricking Zeus over the sacrifice. In Homer, δαίμων refers to a manifestation of a god, often in a fateful fashion (δαιμόνιος means 'strange' or 'incomprehensible'); the word has no feminine form and no plural. In Hesiod, the passed of the Golden Age are referred to as *daimones*, who in the *Theogony* are 'invisible and wrapped in mist'. In Heraclitus (Fragment 69), translated as 'A man's character is his guardian divinity [δαιμων]', the *daimon* is present as an individual's personal 'law' and his destiny. This guardian divinity was called by Socrates his δαιμονιου (*daimonion*) – a divine voice that addressed uniquely him.* Later Neoplatonists often referred to Aristotle as *daimonios*, the mediator with the 'divine' Plato.

By Plato, *daimon* was used to describe the intermediaries between the gods and humans, messengers between the secular and sacred realms, like Eros, and also to semi-divine humans, like the blind seer and transsexual Tiresias. Not simply the erotic but the condition of '*falling* in love' is an instance of daemonic possession, and in Plato's famous passage on Love in the *Symposium*, Diotima indeed describes Love itself as 'A great Daemon [δαιμων] . . . and everything daemonical holds an intermediate place between what is divine and what is mortal.' Shelley's translation of 'Plato's Banquet' then continues:

> He interprets and makes a communication between divine and human things, conveying the prayers and sacrifices of men to the Gods, and communicating the commands and directions concerning the mode of worship most pleasing to them, from Gods to men. He fills up that intermediate space between these two classes of beings, so as to bind together, by his own power, the whole universe of things. Through him subsist all divination, and the science of sacred things as it relates to sacrifices, and expiations, and disenchantments, and prophecy, and magic. The divine nature cannot immediately communicate with what is human, but all that intercourse and converse which is conceded by the Gods to men, both whilst they sleep and when they wake, subsists through the intervention of Love; and he who is wise in the science of this intercourse is supremely happy, and participates in the daemonical nature; whilst he who is wise in any other science or art, remains a mere ordinary slave. These daemons are, indeed, many and various, and one of them is Love.

The wise woman then says that *Eros* is only one name for this daemon;

---

* In *Human, All Too Human*, Nietzsche dismisses this as a disease of the ear.

another is poetry. This is recognizably the same poetic philosophy that
has been discussed thus far, but now the fine frenzy of lovers and poets,
lunatics and prophets has been cosmologized, and even sanctified. The
mysterious harmony of these daemonic states is the preliminary state
of holiness.

In Plato's *Timaeus*, the daemon is more characterful, more homely,
more *heimlich* (perhaps punning on *eudaemon*, meaning happiness):
'God has given to each of us, as his daemon, that kind of soul which
is housed in the top of the body and which raises us – seeing that we
are not of an earthly but of a heavenly plane – up from earth towards
our kindred in the heaven.' In the *Statesman*, Plato uses the word for
a heavenly shepherd; in *Epinomis*, for a creature of aether, a meditator
and interpreter. Contrastingly in *Cratylus*, he invokes Hesiod's golden
men:

> But now that Fate has closed over this race,
> They are holy daemons upon the earth
> Beneficent, averters of ills, guardians of mortal men.

Socrates claims that good and wise men become daemons after they
die, and so there is a sense of the daemon (as there is in haunting
more generally) being 'even here'. The ethereality of the daemon is
also evident in looser usages of the term. Weather is daemonic: 'the
elements are the gods' arsenal', as Ruth Padel puts it, 'The gods both
use and are inherent in the weather.' One may be tempted to suggest,
especially in the context of this book, that Ossian is daemonic, but
the interminable sense of inertia, perpetual loss, and abysmal failure
really makes it dysdaemonic. Ossian does not have the activity, the
force, the power of the daemonic; his daemon has, catastrophically,
fled.

Later readers of Plato (the Neoplatonists) found daemons enticing
as divine mediators, messengers, and advocate interlocutors; they were
angelic and therefore also diabolical spirits of inspiration and of possession. For the third-century philosopher Plotinus, daemons were the
lower order of divine beings. 'Every being above the moon is a god',
but daemons had sublunary power. William Ralph Inge glosses this,
'They are everlasting, and can behold the spiritual world above them;
but they have bodies of "spiritual Matter," and can clothe themselves
in fiery or airy integuments; they can feel and remember, and hear
petitions.' In Plotinus, this cosmological ascent still carries with it a

sense of homeliness: 'But if a man is able to follow the spirit [δαιμων] which is above him, he comes to be himself above, living that spirit's life, and giving the pre-eminence to that better part of himself to which he is being led; and after that spirit he rises to another, until he reaches the heights.'

It is a sentiment echoed by William Blake in *All Religions Are One* (1788) when he declares, 'PRINCIPLE 1st: That the Poetic Genius is the true Man, and that the body or outward form of Man is derived from the Poetic Genius. Likewise that the forms of all things are derived from their Genius, which by the Ancients was call'd an Angel & Spirit & Demon.' Iamblichus, who studied under Porphyry, the editor of Plotinus, had reiterated this more extravagantly in his *On the Mysteries*: 'Good daemons permit us to survey, in conjunction with themselves, their own works, and the benefits which they impart.'

It was this same Iamblichus who began to erect a Neoplatonic superstructure by proposing four daemonic levels, and Proclus, a devotee of the *Mysteries*, refined this in his commentary on Plato's *Timaeus* into a tripartite division of daemons with two levels of soul. For Proclus, daemons are again characterized by power, are intermediaries between the imperfect and the perfect, and also patrons of the arts: Hephaestus, the forger is, thereby, a daemon. Great philosophers too are daemonic powers: 'first they attach themselves to the daemons above them. . . . Next they are presented by these daemons to certain angels and gods, for it is through the daemons, as Diotima tells us, that all the fellowship and converse takes place between men, whether awake or sleeping, and the gods.' Hence Proclus's daemonic architecture is, as Lucas Siorvanes puts it, a classification according to the metaphysical function of daemons: 'to abide ("angels"), to proceed ("daimons proper") and to revert ("heroes")'. This model eventually developed into the 'celestial hierarchy' described by Dionysius the Areopagite, supposedly the Dionysius converted by Paul on the Athenian Areopagus. From Diotima's description of 'Venerian daemons', Dionysius clarified the Catholic and Orthodox angelic order, devolving angels into three triads: Seraphim, Cherubim, Thrones, Dominations, Virtues, Powers, Principalities, Archangels, and Angels. In doing so, he coined the word 'hierarchy' and his model held celestial sway for a thousand years. In 1457, however, the texts of Dionysius the Areopagite were belatedly exposed as forgeries and henceforth he was known as Pseudo-Dionysius; but it was too late to rebuild the heavens.

The pedigree of this complicated classical and Christian daemonic stock as it is understood in the eighteenth century is summed up in R. D. Stock's study, *The Holy and the Daemonic*. The daemon is the unruly part of the numinous, which is the *mysterium tremendum*: aweful mystery, monstrous dread, the wholly other fascination of divine presence; the daemon is what Rudolf Otto calls 'the numen at a lower stage, in which it is still trammelled and suppressed'. It is what makes the holy authentically holy: 'The most authentic form of the "daemon" may be seen in those strange deities of ancient Arabia, which are properly nothing but wandering demonstrative pronouns.' 'Daemon' is also applied to the human character, indicating an ineffable individuality, defying interpretation, and they do not arise 'as a collective produce of crowd-imagination,' writes Otto, 'but were the intuitions of persons of innate prophetic powers.' The daemonic, either person or transcendence, is 'mysterious, energetic, non-rational, non-moral', manifesting in a Dionysiac rapture 'the Numen's horrendousness and ethically ambiguous vitality'.

There is a dark side to this. Empedocles suggested each person has two daemons in attendance, one of these may be the 'evil genius' (κακος δαίμων). Plutarch subsequently developed the model of the evil daemon, and the tradition of the fallen angels ultimately derives from an essay by Apuleius on the Socratic *daimonion*. More strikingly, Iamblichus (*On the Mysteries of the Egyptians, Chaldeans, and Assyrians*) considered that daemonic revenge is manifested as an allegorical, reflective, doubling attack: 'avenging dæmons exhibit the species of punishments [which they inflict]'. But there are worse things, monstrous things: 'such other dæmons as are depraved are surrounded by certain noxious, blood-devouring, and fierce wild beasts.' In the eighteenth century, Thomas Blackwell warned against the release of such fearsome passions in *Letters concerning Mythology* (1748): 'A STRAIN of Poetry stretched beyond its due Bounds turns into a Strain of Madness; and that same soft Vein of native Music, which when the Mind is in its natural State, breathes nothing but Harmony and Love, if raised to an extravagant unnatural Pitch, racks the lab'ring overburthened Breast, and breaks loose in Rage and foaming Ecstacy.' In this case there is no inspired communion, rather a bestial metamorphosis:

Wild Looks, amazing Postures, Soul-rousing Sounds commonly

ushered the furious dithyrambic Song; and when heightened by
Wine and processional Worship were as so many Steps that led
to the tortured bacchanal State of tossing and roaring; and, like
ravening Wolves or enraged Bears, rending in pieces whatever
came in the way; driven to the Desarts and wandering in the
Woods, Danger was their Delight, and Mischief their Pastime.

So the definition of daemon is, literally, bedevilled. As Nietzsche
brilliantly recognized in *Dawn* (aphorism 76), this might explain the
Church's reluctance to accommodate the erotic:

> The passions become evil and malignant when regarded with evil
> and malignant eyes. It is in this way that Christianity has suc-
> ceeded in transforming Eros and Aphrodite – sublime powers,
> capable of idealisation – into hellish genii and phantom goblins,
> by means of the pangs which every sexual impulse was made to
> raise in the conscience of believers. Is it not a dreadful thing
> to transform necessary and regular sensations into a source of
> inward misery, and thus arbitrarily to render interior misery neces-
> sary and regular *in the case of every man*! Furthermore, this misery
> remains secret. . . .

By the later part of the eighteenth century, all these connotations of
daemon had been blended together. In John Lemprière's *Classical
Dictionary* (first published in 1788), his entry for 'Daemon' is confusedly
ambivalent: 'a kind of spirit which, as the ancients supposed, presided
over the actions of mankind, gave them their private counsels, and
carefully watched over their most secret intentions'. So far, so good. But
then this corrupts into a version of the Socratic *daimonion* described in
Plato's *Laws*:

> Some of the ancient philosophers maintained that every man had
> two of these Daemons; the one bad and the other good. These
> Daemons had the power of changing themselves into whatever
> they pleased, and of assuming whatever shapes were most subser-
> vient to their intentions. At the moment of death, the Daemon
> delivered up to judgment the person with whose care he had been
> entrusted; and according to the evidence he delivered, sentence
> was passed over the body. The Daemon of Socrates is famous in
> history. That great philosopher asserted that the genius informed
> him when any of his friends was going to engage in some unfortu-
> nate enterprise, and stopped him from the commission of all

crimes and impiety. These Genii or Daemons, though at first reckoned only as the subordinate ministers of the superior deities, received divine honour in course of time, and we find altars and statues erected, *Genio loci, Genio Augusti,* &c. *Cic. Tusc.* I. – *Plut. de Gen. Socr.*

'Genius' is the Latin translation of daemon. The artistic representation of this *Genius loci*, the genius of the place or guardian spirit like the *Genius libertatis* erected on the site of the Bastille in revolutionary France, was based on classical figures. It was an *ephebe*: a young man.

So, there is much to characterize the daemonic here: the sense of genius, of between-ness and the morally ambiguous, of a binding force, of the domestic space, of doubleness and doubt and vengeance, of shape-changing, of inspiration, of power. And as we know, Thomas Chatterton was a precocious genius who seems to preside over the empowerment of the word 'genius' from eighteenth-century salon usage to its Nietzschean peak. As indicated above, the 'genius' was figured as an *ephebe*, a young man. Furthermore, Chatterton was a morally ambiguous writer, a forger of the hallucinated works of a fictional medieval, a multivalent talent and shape-shifter; a writer whose space of writing is oddly contained – in chests and boxes, in muniment rooms and garrets: in the place of home.

And Chatterton was indeed lauded as the paradigm of Romantic genius. Young, brilliant, poverty-stricken, proud, mad, suicidal – he served as an inspiration. Yet this inspiration was not 'intentional imitation', in Coleridge's phrase – powerful as Chatterton was as a model for rebellious autodidact poets, his Icarus-like flight was not to be emulated as far as teenage arsenic-poisoning. Rather, it seems, Chatterton manifested himself to Coleridge and to Keats and to other poets and writers as a recognizable figure returned: as a daemon. This was his authenticity, his power; breathing into them, like God into Adam, *pneuma* (the breath of life) and *pnoe* (the promise of immortality). Chatterton impregnated these readers in a form of parthenogenic reproduction, and they gave birth to the beings of their imaginations.* In other words, the female Muses were displaced by the male daemon, hetero- was succeeded by homo-psychosexual reproduction, and elsewhere, Coleridge and Keats articulated the anxieties and terrors of

* Frankenstein's monster: a crafted, forged person would of course make another case study – the novel is a sort of user's guide to parthenogenic reproduction.

imaginative possession by the feminine in poems such as 'Christabel' and 'La Belle Dame Sans Merci'.

Other beings were being daemonized too, if for different reasons. Goethe in talking to J. P. Eckermann agreed that Napoleon was daemonic, on account of the force that emanated from him – a quality Goethe was particularly alive to, and which he felt as Promethean, 'who, separated from the gods, peopled a world'. German transcendentalist philosophy too was seeking to make the daemonic more secular, more cultural, more political, and less mystical. Friedrich von Schiller declared that there was a 'lofty *daemonic* freedom' in the human breast that becomes active through contemplation and a sense of self. This process of meeting the self is numinously turbulent, characteristically daemonic, and of course sublime:

> Fearlessly and with a terrible delight he now approaches these ghastly visions of his imagination and deliberately deploys the whole force of this faculty in order to represent the sensuously infinite, so that even if it should fail in this attempt he will experience all the more vividly the superiority of his ideas over the highest of which sensuousness is capable.

Schiller follows Immanuel Kant's view that the sublime is produced by the mind's attempt to know itself. Reason projects itself out of itself, but returns alienated: the self cannot comprehend its own being, but in attempting to do so at least receives a sense of the infinite, and the abysmal. The daemonic thus utterly characterized the sublime for Schiller:

> The beautiful is valuable only with reference to the *human being*, but the sublime with reference to the *pure daemon* in him; and since it is certainly our vocation, despite all sensuous limitations, to be guided by the statutes of pure spirit, the sublime must complement the beautiful in order to make *aesthetic education* into a complete whole and to enlarge the perceptive capacity of the human heart to the full extent of our vocation; beyond the world of sense in any case.

It is this sort of daemonically idealizing mix of paganism, Christianity, and contemporary philosophy that irradiates Coleridge's perception of Chatterton.

❦ ❦ ❦

COLERIDGE

Idly talk they who speak of Poets as mere Indulgers of Fancy,
Imagination, Superstition, &c – They are the Bridlers by
Delight, the Purifiers, they that combine them with *reason*
& order, the true Protoplasts, Gods of Love who tame the
Chaos!

Samuel Taylor Coleridge, *Notebook* II (2355)

On 19 November 1796, Coleridge purchased Marsilio Ficino's edition
of the daemonic texts of Iamblichus, Proclus, Porphyry, Michael
Psellus, and Hermes Trismegistus. He was familiar with some of these
writings already – even if Charles Lamb's remembrance of Coleridge
discoursing upon Iamblichus and Plotinus while a bluecoat schoolboy
at Christ's Hospital ('for even in those years thou waxedst not pale at
such philosophic draughts') is a trifle exaggerated. But this '*vade mecum*
of Neoplatonic daemonology' is identified by John Livingston Lowes
as instrumental to the supernaturalism of 'The Rime of the Ancient
Mariner', a poem written between November 1797 and March 1798.
The fateful Albatross has daemonic qualities – Coleridge himself
described it in 1817 as a 'Spirit . . . one of the invisible inhabitants of
this planet, neither departed souls nor angels . . . They are very
numerous, and there is no climate or element without one or more' –
which are transferred to the Mariner himself, compelled to repeat his
story, his fall.

Around this time, Coleridge was also borrowing a series of fantastical books from Bristol Library, a trawl that included a paper
by John Ferriar, 'Of Popular Illusions, and particularly of Medical
Demonology', which contained a disquisition that began, 'It is an
opinion of considerable antiquity, that the bodies of deceased men
were sometimes reanimated by demons . . .'. Later in his poem, Coleridge glosses the animation of the dead crew as being 'inspirited . . .
not by the souls of the men, nor by dæmons of earth or middle air,
but by a blessed group of angelic spirits'. Livingstone Lowes makes the
point that these are all forms of revenant, all ways of coming back.

If 'The Ancient Mariner' is the first serious indication of the daemonic attentions of Coleridge's imagination, there are repeated indications in the literature of Neoplatonism that daemons are 'secondary gods', and one is inevitably reminded of Coleridge's theory of the imagination, eventually and most concisely expressed in *Biographia Literaria*. The 'secondary imagination', that is, the imagination of the artist who echoes, shadows, repeats God's ultimate act of imagining the creation into being,

> dissolves, diffuses, dissipates, in order to re-create; or where this process is rendered impossible, yet still at all events it struggles to idealize and to unify. It is essentially *vital*, even as all objects (*as* objects) are essentially fixed and dead.

This dissolving, diffusing, dissipating quality is a characteristic feature of the daemonic (daemons take on new forms as rapidly as the clouds change); it also distinguishes the copy from the composition. Coleridge noted that 'If the Artist . . . began by mere perfect copying, he would produce Masks only, not forms breathing Life' – the breath of Life being daemonic fire. In trying to express how to master the *'essence'* of artistry, Coleridge unites the compositional distinction between poetry as an art and forging as a craft, by comparing them against non-productive art activities. In *Biographia Literaria* (chapter 18), poetry is defined as *poesis*, the masculine principle of imitative creating, and distinguished from the mechanical and feminine process of fashioning, copying, *morphosis*, which is counterfeit:

> Could a rule be given from *without*, poetry would cease to be poetry, and sink into a mechanical art. It would be μόρφωσις [*morphosis*: a process of shaping], not ποίησις [*poesis*: a process of making]. The *rules* of the IMAGINATION are themselves the very powers of growth and production. The *words*, to which they are reducible, present only the outlines and external appearance of the fruit. A deceptive counterfeit of the superficial form and colors may be elaborated; but the marble peach feels cold and heavy, and *children* only put it to their mouths.

It is precisely in crafting (forging), then, that the daemonic resides, like the fire in the forge, and it is in the visionary poem 'Kubla Khan' that this daemonic mode of production is most effectively described.

❖

As Mark Allen has shown, 'Kubla Khan' (probably written 1797, published 1816) stands in close proximity to Neoplatonic allegory, and if
complicated by radical ambiguities surrounding, centrally, the daemonic figure, it is still a powerfully daemonic poem. 'Kubla Khan'
enacts (or rather, repeats) the creative work of the secondary imagination, in which 'the supernatural possibilities of the holy are restored
by conjunction with the enchanted':

> A savage place! as holy and enchanted
> As e'er beneath a waning moon was haunted
> By woman wailing for her daemon lover.*

It also blends daemonic inspiration with a figure of the Muse:

> A damsel with a dulcimer
> In a vision once I saw.

It is a poem of a creative genius, Kubla Khan, of language and letters,
of time past and time future:

> And 'mid this tumult Kubla heard from far
> Ancestral voices prophesying war!

'Kubla Khan' is also a poem inspired by two of Chatterton's 'African
Eclogues'. In 'Norva and Mored' there are 'mystic mazes of the
dance':

> Three times the virgin swimming on the breeze,
> Danc'd in the shadow of the mystic trees:
> When like a dark cloud spreading to the view,
> The first-born sons of war and blood pursue . . .

and a cave and workshop are located beneath the plummeting waves:

> Where howls the war-song of the chieftain's ghost
> Where the artificer in realms below,
> Gilds the rich lance, or beautifies the bow.

Also, in Chatterton's 'The Death of Nicou', the Tiber

> Rushes impetuous to the deep profound;
> Rolls o'er the ragged rocks with hideous yell;

---

* The Crewe MS of the poem specifically reads 'daemon lover'.

> Collects its waves beneath the earth's vast shell:
> There for a while, in loud confusion hurl'd,
> It crumbles mountains down and shakes the world

before flowing into the sultry heat of Arabia.

But it is no surprise that Coleridge should have been reading Chatterton alongside his daemonology at this time: his very first published verse was a 'Monody on the Death of Chatterton', written while Coleridge was still a bluecoat boy at Christ's Hospital, close by the Brooke Street garret in which Chatterton died. Coleridge's 'Monody' was prefixed to the 1794 Cambridge edition of the Rowley poems, and Robert Southey badly wanted to reprint the verses in his own edition of Chatterton's works, finally published in January 1803. Coleridge's 'Monody' is an interestingly 'anthological' poem – it is allusive, imitative, crafted, light-fingered – and also perhaps the only verses that he consistently reworked throughout his life. So, where might Chatterton come in the perceptual universe of Coleridge? He is a historical figure who has become numinous, who has transformed his suffering into sublimity. In the 1794 'Monody', Chatterton is imagined as an uncanny wanderer:

> With wild unequal steps he pass'd along,
> Oft pouring on the winds a broken song:
> Anon upon some rough Rock's fearful Brow,
> Would pause abrupt – and gaze upon the waves below.

His steps across a sublime landscape are 'wild' and 'unequal', as if he passes, in asymmetrical deambulation, between different worlds as a trickster, or as a ghostliness. He is a genius. In later versions, Coleridge added a vision in which Chatterton accompanied himself, Southey, and their wives, the Fricker sisters, across the sea to the banks of the Susquehanna, where they planned to found an idyllic Pantisocratic society. Coleridge vowed he would build a locus to Chatterton, to worship and purify the dead. One is reminded, fleetingly, of the Albatross following the Mariner's boat.

But if Coleridge never built his Pennsylvanian Platonopolis, he maintained his faith in Chatterton as a guardian divinity throughout the 1790s as he studied his daemonic texts. He had of course moved to Bristol, and married Sara Fricker at St Mary Redcliffe on 4 October 1795 in a service that was itself haunted: 'poor Chatterton's Church,' wrote Coleridge of the *genius loci* three days later. 'The thought gave me a tinge of melancholy to the solemn Joy, which I felt.'

He lived with his new wife in Clevedon, overlooking the Bristol Channel, but the melancholy did not leave him, and in December 1796 the Coleridges left for Nether Stowey, a village on the edge of the Quantock Hills. What sent them there? Coleridge went at the invitation of Thomas Poole, after Poole had become alarmed at his friend's hallucinatory state. Coleridge was haunted by 'the phantasms of a Wife brokenhearted, & a hunger-bitten Baby!' He was pursued by 'The evil Face of Frenzy"!' And he was *literally* haunted, he hysterically complained, by 'the Ghosts of Otway & Chatterton'. Coleridge could no longer distinguish the inspirational from the avenging daemons. . . .

George Dekker has suggested that 'At Nether Stowey . . . Coleridge simply outgrew the identification with Chatterton: the *Monody* became a literary embarrassment, and as a husband and father in his middle twenties he could no longer picture himself as a "wond'rous boy".' But Wordsworth's later poem 'Resolution and Independence' (1802) appears to be addressed to Coleridge, still helplessly drawn by the daemonic pull of Chatterton's genius.

> I thought of Chatterton, the marvellous Boy,
> The sleepless Soul that perish'd in its Pride.*

This is a warning against Coleridge's morbid infatuation:

> We Poets on our youth begin in gladness;
> But thereof comes in the end despondency and madness.

Such nightmares were anyway a contagion: a year later, Thomas De Quincey was writing in his *Diary* of his 'Chattertonian μελαυχολια [melancholia] state of mind' returning. Within the month he has had a daemonic dream of Chatterton:

> Last night too I image myself looking through a glass. 'What do you see?' I see a man in the dim and shadowy perspective and (as it were) in a dream. He passes along in silence, and the hues of sorrow appear on his countenance. Who is he? 'A man darkly wonderful – above the beings of this world; but whether that shadow of him, which you saw, be yᵉ. shadow of a man long since passed away or of one yet hid in futurity, I may not tell

---

* Note the word 'its' – some versions have 'his'.

you. There is something gloomily great in him; he wraps himself up in the dark recesses of his own soul; he looks over all mankind of all tongues – languages – and nations "with an angel's ken"; but his fate is misery such as y^e. world knoweth not; and upon his latter days (and truly on his whole life) sit deep clouds of mystery and darkness and silence; –

> Amazement in his van with flight combin'd
> and sorrow's faded form and solitude behind!!*

I imaged too a banquet or carousal of feodal magnificence – such (for instance) as in Schiller's Ghost-Seer, in y^e. middle of which a mysterious stranger should enter, on whose approach hangs fate and the dark roll of many woes, etc. I see Chatterton in the exceeding pain of death! in y^e. exhausted slumber of agony[.] I see his arm weak as a child's – languid and faint in the extreme' . . . stretched out and raised at midnight – calling and pulling (faintly indeed but yet convulsively) some human breast to console him whom he had seen in the dreams of his fever'd soul.

This melancholia, characterized by Chatterton, is patently daemonic, and hints at the more mysterious and creative vistas that would later characterize De Quincey's fervid writings; meanwhile, Chatterton himself is dreamt of as dreaming; as if he too has shared – or become – the dream of the 'man darkly wonderful – above the beings of this world'.

Coleridge's 'Kubla Khan', probably written a few months after his arrival at Nether Stowey and in the immediate aftermath of the Ireland Shakspeare controversy, also emerges out of a dream. Among many other things, it is a poem about Chatterton; Chatterton is the very genius of the work. For while 'Kubla Khan' certainly echoes the 'holy dread' of the 'African Eclogues', there is a recognizable presence here as well. Chatterton was always pictured as a youth with shoulder-length hair rather than as a young buck in a peruke; he was pictured as bright-eyed, even goggle-eyed in one posthumous portrait; of course there was his opium eating and, like Adam in Eden, his vegetarianism. The portrait is worth fleshing out a little for it owes something to William Henry Ireland's exactly contemporary account, gleaned from

* The lines are from Thomas Gray's 'The Bard'.

Bristol gossip. Chatterton was thin and neat, striking rather than
handsome, with startling eyes of a piercing grey; the left eye was (like
Lord Byron's) of a paler brilliancy than the other and would 'flash fire',
as his sister put it, whenever his temper flared. William Barrett
described his eyes, 'You might see the fire roll at the bottom of them,
as you sometimes do in a black eye, but never in grey ones, which his
were', and his landlady later remembered, 'he would often look steadfastly in a person's face, without speaking, or seeming to see the person,
for a quarter of an hour or more, till it was quite frightful.' One is
reminded of the Ancient Mariner's 'glittering eye'. 'Christabel' too is a
poem about seeing, envisioning, eyes, and possession – when Sir
Leoline is inspired to revenge, 'He spake: his eye in lightning rolls!'
But the most emphatic vision is in 'Kubla Khan':

> His flashing eyes, his floating hair!
> Weave a circle round him thrice,
> And close your eyes with holy dread,
> For he on honey-dew hath fed,
> And drunk the milk of paradise.

The eyes, the hair, the supernaturalism, the 'holy dread' of the daemonic, the Edenic honey-dew, the opiated milk of paradise . . . 'See!
see! he comes!'

KEATS

> O Chatterton! how very sad thy fate!
>   Dear child of sorrow – son of misery!
>   How soon the film of death obscur'd that eye,
> Whence Genius mildly flash'd and high debate.

John Keats, 'To Chatterton'

John Keats's Chatterton has 'Melted in dying numbers . . . A half-
blown floweret . . . among the stars / Of highest Heaven', but this

'camelion' poet takes his place within a daemonology that differs from Coleridge's: Keats was less sophisticated, more fanciful than Coleridge. He believed in a 'theory of natural inspiration' cobbled together from Christoph Martin Wieland's *Oberon*, Lemprière's *Classical Dictionary*, Milton, and of course Shakespeare.* But Keats did appear to have learnt a version of the Platonic theory of daemonic inspiration from his friend Benjamin Robert Haydon, although he persistently uses the spelling 'demon'. Charles Patterson argues that Keats meant by the demonic 'a special mode of intense perception . . . [and] the extraordinary qualities of the objects when known through that mode'. This mode is characterized by a focused trance, and it is clearly related to that weirdly characterless state, or perhaps supercharacterful condition, of negative capability, itself ambiguous and Chattertonian: '*Negative Capability*, that is when man is capable of being in uncertainties, Mysteries, doubts, without any irritable reaching after fact & reason.' For Keats the imagination is a mode of knowing which is higher than Reason: it therefore has its own authenticity.

And in Keats too, Chatterton comes again as a daemon. He haunts Keats's verse – indeed in the words of Richard Woodhouse to Keats in 1818, Chatterton died of 'unkindness and neglect' almost in order for Keats to be able to expiate this 'vast debt to Genius'. In the idiosyncratic Hellenic hodgepodge of the 'Ode on Indolence', Keats dreams of 'Three Ghosts' ('Shadows', 'Phantoms'): Love (recalling Diotima), 'my demon Poesy' (a 'maiden most unmeek'), and, between them, 'Ambition, pale of cheek, / And ever watchful with fatigued eye'.

Chatterton may also have haunted Keats in the voice of the nightingale, which obviously played a prominent and complex part in Keats's personal mythology. The traditional reading is that the nightingale sang Philomel's haunting song of loss and mortality. While reading *King Lear*, as he did many times in his short life, Keats once paused over the line: 'The foul fiend haunts Poor Tom in the voice of a nightingale.' He underlined 'Poor Tom'; his brother Tom died shortly afterwards; and the 'Ode to a Nightingale' seems partly inspired by his death. But Poor Tom is also apparently possessed:

---

* Keats read Spence's *Polymetis* and Tooke's *Pantheon* for Greek myth, and was also reading Robert Burton in 1819.

Five Fiends have been in poor Tom at once; of lust, as *Obidicut*; *Hobbididance*, prince of dumbness: *Mahu*, of stealing; *Modo*, of murder; and *Flibbertigibbet*, of moping and mowing, who since possesses chamber-maids and waiting-women.

And there is another Tom, another youth who 'grows pale, and spectre thin, and dies', as indicated by Shelley in his lament for Keats, 'Adonais':

> Midst others of less note, came one frail Form,
> A phantom among men; companionless
> As the last cloud of an expiring storm
> Whose thunder is its knell; he, as I guess,
> Had gazed on Nature's naked loveliness,
> Actæon-like, and now he fled astray
> With feeble steps o'er the world's wilderness,
> And his own thoughts, along that rugged way,
> Pursued, like raging hounds, their father and their prey.

This archetype of the doomed young poet is, of course, Chatterton, obscurely pursued by his own daemonic force, staggering, as he does 'With wild unequal steps' in Coleridge's 'Monody', as faint as he is in De Quincey's dream, chased by the knowledge of some forbidden revelation. In his youth, Shelley had invoked Chatterton in the opening stanza of 'Ghasta or, The Avenging Demon!!!', and later in that poem the prototype of this archetype briefly emerges:

> At last the thin and shadowy form,
> With noiseless, trackless footsteps came, –
> Its light robe floated on the storm,
> Its head was bound with lambent flame.

And for Shelley too, poetry sang as marvellously as the nightingale:

> A Poet is a nightingale, who sits in darkness and sings to cheer its own solitude with sweet sounds; his auditors are as men entranced by the melody of an unseen musician, who feel that they are moved and softened, yet know not whence and why.

In Keats, this youth, this genius figured as an *ephebe*, keeps returning. In his famous letter to Benjamin Bailey, 'I am certain of nothing but of the holiness of the Heart's affections and the truth of Imagination', we tend to forget the glimpse of the daemonic world given by a boy:

O for a life of Sensations rather than of Thoughts! It is 'a Vision
in the form of Youth,' a shadow of reality to come.

In the 'Ode to a Nightingale' again, the Chattertonian presence is
palpable for the story is about becoming immortal and cheating death,
hinting at an escape ('I cannot see what flowers are at my feet'), into
a countryside of 'near meadows', 'still stream', and 'valley-glades'. This
'draught of vintage' Keats even begins by echoing the death of Chatterton:

> My heart aches, and a drowsy numbness pains
>   My sense, as though of hemlock I had drunk,
> Or emptied some dull opiate to the drains
>   One minute past, and Lethe-wards had sunk. . . .

Endymion was explicitly 'inscribed to the Memory of Thomas Chatterton', and had originally been dedicated to Chatterton as 'the most
english of Poets except Shakespeare'; he was, as we know Keats twice
called him, 'the purest writer in the English Language'. He seems to
haunt the unfinished epic, *Hyperion*, as well, in which according
to Andrew Bennett, death figures as the very precondition for inspiration: 'it is a poem crucially concerned with the notion of dying into
poetic creation, a mortal creativity'. The deification lines recall the
medieval parchments, poems, and plays that Chatterton claimed to
have discovered in the muniment room of St Mary Redcliffe:

> Knowledge enormous makes a God of me.
> Names, deeds, gray legends, dire events, rebellions,
> Majesties, sovran voices, agonies,
> Creations and destroyings, all at once
> Pour into the wide hollows of my brain,
> And deify me, as if some blithe wine
> Or bright elixir peerless I had drunk,
> And so become immortal.

'Names, deeds, gray legends, dire events, rebellions, / Majesties, sovran
voices, agonies, / Creations and destroyings': these are the Rowley
works.

As John Beer has pointed out, Keats was anxious to be influenced
in meet fashion, turning first to Spenser and then to Milton and
Shakespeare in his search for a 'presider': 'The word was well chosen:
while avoiding the subservience of discipleship it combined the sense

of an identifiable great writer with the more general one, familiar from Socrates and others, of a daimonic presence which could inspire while not dictating the form into which inspiration was to fall' – indeed, it evades connotations of authority. Beer quotes Keats's belief stated in the poem 'Great Spirits' that there were new agencies in the world, giving it 'another heart, and other pulses'.

There were evidently also other inspirations. The lines from *Hyperion* quoted above shadow *Paradise Lost* in their delight of falling into knowledge, and also in the cadence of 'sovran voices': the word 'sovran' (sovereign) is contested by God and Satan in a microcosm of the angels' rebellion. More generally, as Lucy Newlyn points out, the very experience of reading and re-reading *Paradise Lost* is deifying: 'the reader becomes increasingly god-like, because more in touch with the Providential plan which Milton's epic narrator discloses'. If he was first attracted to Spenser, it became primarily Milton who provided Keats with a mechanism for binding his daemon into the English countryside, and suggested a model of originality, composition, and repetition that could help to justify the ways of Chatterton to man. Chatterton was therefore foremost in his mind when he admitted he had abandoned *Hyperion* as the heavy hand of Milton began to stifle it. 'I wish to give myself up to other sensations,' he wrote to John Hamilton Reynolds – and composed 'To Autumn' instead.

But it is worth pausing awhile with Milton, who spins another strand in the web of originality and inspiration, and whose reception underscores the shifting meaning of authenticity. In the eighteenth century, Milton was a byword for originality: from Isaac Watts's encomium 'The Adventurous Muse' (*Horae Lyricae*, 1709) to Samuel Johnson's 'Life of Milton' (1779). But while Watts praises the exploits of Milton's (female) Muse, claiming 'He talks unutterable things', Johnson damns him for it. He writes wearily, 'reality was a scene too narrow for his mind. He sent his faculties out upon discovery, into worlds where only imagination can travel, and delighted to form new modes of existence, and furnish sentiment and action to superior beings, to trace the counsels of hell, or accompany the choirs of heaven' – and then carps at Milton's use of the agency of spirits. Johnson argues that it is all muddled up, mixing materiality with immateriality.

This is Johnson the arch-pragmatist again. He is bent against the

vanities of writers, and pooh-poohs the account of Miltonic inspiration
retold by Jonathan Richardson in his 1734 *Life*:

> he would sometimes lie awake whole nights, but not a verse
> could he make; and on a sudden his poetical faculty would rush
> upon him with an *impetus* or *œstrum*, and his daughter was
> immediately called to secure what came. At other times he would
> dictate perhaps forty lines in a breath, and then reduce them to
> half the number.

Johnson does not quote this approvingly.

> These bursts of lightning and involutions of darkness, these tran-
> sient and involuntary excursions and retrocessions of invention,
> having some appearance of deviation from the common train of
> Nature, are eagerly caught by the lovers of a wonder. Yet some-
> thing of this inequality happens to every man in every mode of
> exertion, manual or mental. The mechanick cannot handle his
> hammer and his file at all times with equal dexterity; there are
> hours, he knows not why, when 'his hand is out.'

The image of the artisan with which this concludes shows just how
weedy Johnson believes Milton's neurotic mystification of composition
to be, especially against the hale and hearty reliability of a writer like
himself. Johnson belittles Milton at every opportunity. He says, for
example, that he looked like a girl and was spanked at college, and
even repeats as true the claim that Milton succeeded in libelling
Charles I as a plagiarist by inserting into *Eikon Basilike* a verse by
Sir Philip Sidney. Johnson's source? No less a man than the forger
of plagiarism, William Lauder. Equally, Johnson ridicules Milton's
claim that he felt an increase in his poetical power with the arrival
of spring:

> This dependance [*sic*] of the soul upon the seasons, those tem-
> porary and periodical ebbs and flows of the intellect, may, I
> suppose, justly be derided as the fumes of a vain imagination. . . .
> The author that thinks himself weather-bound will find, with a
> little help from hellebore, that he is only idle or exhausted; but
> while this notion has possession of the head, it produces the
> inability which it supposes.

Johnson concludes by declaring that Milton is 'to be admired rather than imitated', before the rather hollow judgement that 'The highest praise of genius is original invention.'

Yet despite Milton's notorious originality, his epic *Paradise Lost* really is what Coleridge called 'a repetition in the finite mind of the eternal act of creation'. It is a grand imitation, and it is also a comprehensively contingent work – contingent upon the continuing existence of the world. Milton writes of beginnings, origins, creations: first things – but to do so he repeats, reiterates, gives accounts of accounts, and begins his epic with the Fall rather than with Genesis. Indeed, the dependence of the poem on the Bible, primarily, makes the whole work a hymn of repetition and remembering, of real resemblance. These typological correspondences also penetrate the persistent, if sometimes wry, allusions to other literatures: for instance, the boast to pursue 'Things unattempted yet in prose or rhyme' is a translation of the second line of Ariosto's *Orlando Furioso*. For many eighteenth-century readers the work was a monument of imitation, a view with which Hazlitt later concurred: 'Milton has borrowed more than any other writer, and exhausted every source of imitation, sacred and profane; yet he is perfectly distinct from every other writer.' Even Satan is repetitiously wicked. He calls for a specialized form of repetition – revenge – that will compound his 'reiterated crimes', and his devils are condemned precisely to *repeat* their error, much as the shades in Dante's inferno endlessly and repeatedly endure their allegorical torments. Hence repetition is made cosmological, and creative. Coleridge's formula for authentic repetition likewise allows abundant and repeated creativity; only in the hands of Satan can repetition be made original: original in the wrong way, original as sin.

Hence Milton's Muse is not Calliope (classical Muse of the heroic epic) but the Holy Spirit, who

> with mighty wings outspread
> Dove-like sat'st brooding on the vast abyss
> And mad'st it pregnant: what in me is dark
> Illumine, what is low raise and support.

This ultimately inspiring spirit that first filled the body of Adam will, like the classical Muses, 'Instruct me, for thou know'st'. But although Milton is presuming upon the divine, apparently without an intermediary, the daemonic is there too precisely in the almost ritualistic act of repeating the Creation.

Milton's poem *Lycidas* also begins with repetition: 'Yet once more, O ye laurels, and once more', and ends with the transformation of the dead Lycidas into a spirit of place. This allows the lament for Lycidas's untimely death to end precisely because it is eternally repeated. His supernatural presence will persist:

> Now, Lycidas, the shepherds weep no more;
> Henceforth thou art the Genius of the shore.

Such daemons also animate the natural world of 'Il Penseroso', where they are imagined as hermetic forces distributed among the elements:

> And of those daemons that are found
> In fire, air, flood, or under ground,
> Whose power hath a true consent
> With planet, or with element.

Chatterton inhabits Keats's poetry precisely as this sort of presiding autumnal daemon. Milton also wrote of the nightingale in ways that Keats could adopt as Chattertonian, for instance in his sonnet, 'O nightingale' ('Whether the Muse, or Love call thee his mate'), and again in 'Il Penseroso' ('Most musical, most melancholy'). Finally, Milton also invoked the tragic figure of the Christ-like Orpheus in 'L'Allegro', and in *Lycidas* too. This poet-prophet could charm wild beasts, trees, and rocks, but could not save his own life. Like a ritually sacrificed fertility god, he was torn limb from limb by the Bacchanals, who were jealous that he no longer loved women after he had lost Eurydice. His dismembered parts were cast into the Hebrus, but his head, floating on the waters, continued to sing. Orpheus's end is a hideously daemonic revenge. It is literally diabolical, for as 'symbolic' means to put elements together, the 'diabolic' means slander, fraud, dissension, strife: to tear asunder. But the death of Orpheus does not silence poetry: it abstracts it from the broken body, turns dying voice to living breath. Orpheus now sings from beyond the grave. Uncannily; daemonically.

❖

Let us now return to Chatterton. Death, the past, ghosts haunt his family history and his childhood: he was a posthumous child, constituted by the dead, and after death he left no remains. There is no final resting place for Chatterton, no body. He was perfectly qualified to become a ghost: between the material states of life and death; inbetween, neither.

As if in celestial chorus, there are angels here as well. When his uncle William gave the young Chatterton a Delft cup and offered to decorate it for him with a lion, Chatterton asked: 'Paint me like an angel with wings and a trumpet, to trumpet my name over the world' – he was, his landlady remembered, 'as proud as Lucifer'. It was she, Mrs Angell, who presumably discovered his corpse and so indeed trumpeted his name up and down Holborn. Shoe Lane burying ground was overlooked by the Angel Inn and more trumpeting angels: his body passed beneath a bas-relief of the Last Judgement which stood over the archway.

Although some of these anecdotes are doubtless untrue, they do exhibit the mythographic tenacity of a ghost-becoming-daemon. The stories told about Chatterton already figured him as possessed. William Smith remembered his walks with Chatterton when he was working on Rowley:

> There was one spot in particular, full in the sight of the church, in which he seemed always to take a particular delight. *He would frequently lay himself down, fix his eyes upon the church, and seem as if he were in a kind of ecstasy or trance.* Then on a sudden and abruptly, he would tell me, 'that steeple was burnt down by lightning; that was the place where they formerly acted plays'.

Another friend later said of him, 'He was one of the most extraordinary geniuses I ever knew. The most extraordinary I ever heard of.'

Mrs Ballance, his first landlady in London, supported the stories of Chatterton's wraith-like existence: 'he never touched meat,' she claimed, 'and drank only water, and seemed to live on the air'. Curiously, seventeenth-century bestiaries describe the chameleon – a sort of forger's, or indeed poet's, mascot – as living on air. Chatterton himself survived on two or three hours' sleep a night, resting only between four and six in the morning: 'he was a *spirit*,' she said, 'and never slept.'

The life of Chatterton was unusual enough already, without supernatural dimensions accumulating as well – which is another reason why Thomas Rowley, fifteenth-century monk, poet, and antiquarian, seemed a safer bet. Yet within fifteen years Chatterton had completely overshadowed Rowley, and later writers, who were so fond of fictional characters like Hamlet and Faustus (both entangled with ghosts and daemons themselves), have very little to say about Rowley at all – indeed Coleridge warned Southey, 'Rowley's poems were never popular ... [never] generally read.' So Romantic poets forged their theories of the imagination around Chatterton: he gave contours to their thoughts, gave body to 'all the images [that] rose up ... as *things*'. Chatterton passed easily into myth, became an authentic haunting, and had his mendacious writings accommodated within the holy reveries of inspiration. In daemonic cosmology, where repetition has a magical and poetic quality, forgery is a form of repetition that repeats what never happened. In that sense, it is original and authentic. Moreover, forgery presupposes, dialectically, an ideal of entirely pure originality. Thus Coleridge's introduction of Plotinus (Ennead V) in his *Biographia Literaria* (chapter 12) marks a moment at which forgery becomes daemonic. Coleridge repeats Plotinus's Socratic suspicion of origin, in this case of the highest intuitive knowledge:

> it is not lawful to inquire from whence it sprang, as if it were a thing subject to place and motion, for it neither approached hither, nor again departs from hence to some other place; but it either appears to us or it does not appear. So that we ought not to pursue it with a view of detecting its secret source, but to watch in quiet till it suddenly shines upon us; preparing ourselves for the blessed spectacle as the eye waits patiently for the rising sun.

The accommodation of forgery within the inspirational discourse of Romantic writing is enabled by making it daemonic, part of the divine harmony of repetition, authentic and original, breathing poetic fire and yet of the body, close to the creating sun.

Whither has the daemon since flown? Thomas Carlyle's loquacious account of the 'Great Man', from his 1840 lecture 'The Hero as Prophet', describes an '*original* man' as recognizably daemonic:

> he comes to us at first hand. A messenger he, sent from the Infinite Unknown with tidings to us. We may call him Poet, Prophet, God; – in one way or other, we all feel that the words he utters are as no man's words.

Some of these elements may be reckoned in the typology of the forger as described in the remaining chapters of this book: 'in one way or other, we all feel that the words he utters are as no man's words'. A few years later, Rudyard Kipling described his daemon in his autobiographical *Something of Myself* (published in 1937), a daemon who had brought him the *Jungle Books, Puck of Pook's Hill*, and *Kim*. Kipling's advice? 'When your Daemon is in charge, do not try to think consciously. Drift, wait, and obey.'

In a different context, Sigmund Freud's paper 'The "Uncanny" ' (1919), already a presence here, psychologized elements of the daemonic into the *unheimlich* (literally: the 'unhomely'):

> this uncanny is in reality nothing new or alien, but something which is familiar and old-established in the mind and which has become alienated from it only through the process of repression. This reference to the factor of repression enables us, furthermore, to understand Schelling's definition of the uncanny as something which ought to have remained hidden but has come to light.

Freud's uncanny is a quality that is inherent in a secret never to be told, at least never told by oneself to oneself. The ensuing feeling of feverish dislocation works like a weird possession and stems from self-alienation – mistaking an automaton for a human being, or from experiences of doubling, or 'it is marked by the fact that the subject identifies himself with someone else, so that he is in doubt as to which his self is, or substitutes the extraneous self for his own'.

The crisis of writerly identity experienced by Macpherson–Ossian and much more profoundly perceived in the multiplicity of identities along the Chatterton–Rowley axis could then be psychoanalytically glossed as uncanny, but this would present the argument back-to-front, and would be anachronistic. Freud has really proposed a psychoanalysis of the daemonic. His comments might appear inescapably relevant to that shadow of the authentic, forgery, but that is because he is writing in a discourse in part shaped by forgers, and forged; forgery returns.

The philosopher Jacques Derrida helpfully glosses this quality of return in his meditation *The Post Card* (1987):

> there is not a return *of the* demonic. The demon is that very thing which *comes back* without having been called by the Pleasure Principle from one knows not where ('early infantile influences,'

says Freud), inherited from one knows not whom, but already persecutory, by means of the simple form of its return, indefatigably repetitive, independent of every apparent desire, *automatic*.

Forgery too, once construed as daemonic, is the very thing that comes back: inescapably, erotically, seductively. So 'finally', Freud notes, inexpertly alluding to Nietzsche, 'there is the constant recurrence of the same thing'. This does not merely consist of the involuntary repetition of surrounding events, but is a 'compulsion to repeat . . . a compulsion powerful enough to overrule the pleasure principle, lending to certain aspects of the mind their daemonic character . . .' This compulsion to repeat is potentially self-annihilatory. It later led Freud to propose Thanatos, or the 'death instinct', which also has a certain piquancy when thinking about the posthumous Ossian or the suicide Chatterton, but more immediately explains their lovely persistence in Romantic aesthetics.

Others have been more explicit in trying to restore the daemonic to a structure of thought, feeling, or indeed of living. Derrida has followed his post-*Post Card* work on Martin Heidegger with *Specters of Marx* (1994), a meditation on Karl Marx's ghostly metaphors for money via what he calls 'hauntology'. Hauntology analyses the 'logic' of haunting, its extreme alterity and alienation and illusion. Some would deny that such an enterprise can be called analysis: hauntology, Derrida claims,

> would harbor within itself, but like circumscribed places or particular effects, eschatology and teleology themselves. It would *comprehend* them, but incomprehensibly . . . Can the extremity of the extreme ever be comprehended?

In a moment, perhaps it can, but not from Derrida's perspective. Working alongside Derrida is Ned Lukacher, whose study of conscience, *Daemonic Figures* (1994) – in a sense a companion volume to *Specters of Marx* – proposes a daemonology derived from Derrida's hauntology. Lukacher argues that Shakespeare plays 'a daemonic and uncanny role' in our reading of texts such as Plato's *Republic*, the Pauline Epistles, or the writings of Freud and Heidegger, dwelling on the uncanniness of the ancient Greek *daimon* (which I hope will by now be familiar, even homely): 'between the human and divine world, which is to say between the world of consciousness and that which, unseen and uncomprehended, underlies the forms and expressions of consciousness and sustains its very existence'. Despite himself, Lukacher divines something of the essential in the daemon: 'The daemon is the cipher, the name, and the figure for the incontrovertible ghostliness, the familiar strangeness, that dwells between the perceptions and reflections of consciousness and the enigmatic ground of Being itself.' This, of course, is Neoplatonic daemonism varnished with a little post-structural theory. And Lukacher goes on to spell out the poetic, productive, and inspirational function of hauntings from, and possession by, the daemon. 'The daemon is a figure for the god that dwells in language and, by virtue of this daemonic function of language, allows human beings to be called into their humanity or, inversely, allows them to fail to respond to the call.'

Both Lukacher and Derrida, then, are using ghosts and daemons as metaphors for the inexpressible qualities of expression; sombre rather than ludic metaphors; they are traces of otherness, hauntings that trouble; they are dislimners, if not deconstructors. But this hauntology is itself haunted by the objective qualities of the daemonic. The ghosts are haunted by a sense of their own being. What I mean by this is that ghosts and daemons for Derrida and Lukacher are more strictly metaphors than are words like, say, 'Nietzsche', or 'Europe', or 'Shakespeare'. They don't believe in them. And yet to describe daemons they use the same terms as those who have done so in the past precisely to confirm a sense of their supernatural being, both in language and in the world.

This is the problem with talking about daemonic inspiration, although it is no problem if you can believe in spirits – as William Blake did – or simply believe what poets say about spirits. Blake, perhaps unsurprisingly now, modelled himself on Chatterton. They were both autodidacts, children who forged themselves. Blake was known as 'English' Blake, he certainly never left England, indeed he barely left London; Chatterton lived only in Bristol and London. Blake famously annotated his copy of Wordsworth with the line, 'I believe both Macpherson & Chatterton, that what they say is Ancient Is so.' For Blake, national history was a spiritual exercise that unified mythology, typology, and typography by the sixth sense – imagination – which was a life-force, having the power to synthesize, transcend, and reveal history. Imagination was truly revolutionary, a Promethean theft from God, and thus the poet was a myth-maker (of *poesis*), a true creator: 'forms must be apprehended by Sense or the Eye of Imagination'.

Coleridge, who had a similarly arduous philosophy of the imagination, a comparably dialectical and revelatory knowledge of the divine work of poetry, was seen by contemporaries as an angelic counterpart of Blake. When they met towards the end of Blake's life, as he was painting his glorious and transcendent 'Vision of the Last Judgement', they kept company like 'congenial beings of another sphere, breathing for a while on our earth'. And like Coleridge, for Blake to be able to state his mystical insights in simple and direct words and images would have been a repudiation of them: his philosophy was pitted against reductive systems – including systems of language and logic.

Blake was endeavouring to braid together the mighty threads of being: the antiquarian reinvention of history and the symbolic potential of the world, the subversion of every system of understanding that was a means of control and a philosophy of restraint, and the elevation of the poet-scholar-artist into a prophet, a sorcerer, a god. 'Knowledge', in this new brave new Blakean world, 'is not by deduction, but Immediate by Perception or Sense at once'. It was an immediate way of seizing and synthesizing complex identity – even voices as various and contradictory and irreducible as Chatterton's. But for Blake this involved a comprehensive plan to figure his life and make his art in a sacred pilgrimage that carried with it the destiny of the nation, and the future of humankind. The magnificent difficulty in his work is summed up by Mark Schorer: 'He wished, in a system of ever-widening metaphorical amplification, to explain his story, the story of his England, the history of the world, prehistory, and the nature of all eternity.' It was a form of Edenic nationalism, to cleanse the doors of perception and see things as they really are: infinite. Blake was compelled to find a form of writing beyond the purely written; this was made possible by Chatterton.

Consider Chatterton's manuscripts – his idiosyncratic orthography and calligraphy, his mix of visual and textual forms; consider Chatterton's verses – his epic medievalism, and the vivacious, chaotic flux of his vision; consider Chatterton's lives – as child, genius, ghost, angel . . . William Blake had caught some flicker of Chatterton's fire. His illuminated books, from *Songs of Innocence and Experience* to the turbulent Outsider Art of major prophecies like *Milton*, seem to breathe the same air as Chatterton's works. If Blake almost certainly saw the Rowley manuscripts only in facsimile, the tangible form proclaimed to him the possibility of a unity of human vision. Accordingly, his brother taught him the printing technique of 'relief etching' – or rather the ghost of his late brother taught it to him in a dream – a technique that combined 'Poet, Painter, Philosopher, & Musician' in forging designs copied not from a paper original, but worked directly onto the plate: printing was productive rather than reproductive. Blake could begin production without a fair copy or completed manuscript, because he used the medium to generate his ideas. This synthesis of the artist and the craftsman became a metaphor and a metonym for the new synthesis that Blake considered the righteous occupation of the imagination, so printing itself was a spiritual exercise – analogous to the divine work of creation, which it sought to repeat.

Originality was for Blake too, an act of repetition. Perfect repetition being physically impossible (and in a sense undesirable), each of his relief-etching impressions was different, and had to be different. The inks were laid on anew for each printing, so it became the very accidents and happenstance in pressing and colouring that proved to be his aids to meditation and revelation. As one contemporary noted, 'The accidental look they had was very enticing.' This mutability was a way to glimpse the infinite through the finite: there was no original – or rather every copy was an original – and this feat dissolved the restrictive forms of thinking that had dismissed Macpherson and Chatterton for forgery; indeed, it restored forgery. Blake took inspirational theories of ghostly composition as a way of returning forgery to the art and craft of physical making.

William Blake's gorgeous illuminated books are the most sublime fruits of Chattertonian daemonic inspiration. Other writers were less coherent and much more sentimental, unread in Thomas Taylor's translations of Orphic and Neoplatonic literature, or even in Lemprière's *Classical Dictionary* – but they nevertheless responded to the call of the daemonic Chatterton figure. Literary culture was saturated with him. One destitute Grub Street hack wrote on 28 October 1796: '[I] now am left to little better than a state of Starvation I plainly see what the World is & little am I astonished at poor Chatterton's fate.' This writer later penned a fragmentary sentimental novel, *Effusions of Love from Chatelar to Mary Queen of Scotland, Translated from a Gallic*

manuscript, *In the Scotch College, at Paris* (1805), the supposed con-
fessional journal of the lovesick Chatelar. It is an amalgam of songs,
ballads, unmediated diary entries, brokenness, lacunae – all elucidated
with a series of sober historical footnotes supplied by a supposed
antiquarian editor. It is evidently much influenced by Chatterton –
and the writer had also looked into the first few pages of Bartholomeus
Anglicus's *Proprietibus de Rerum*, a Platonic encyclopaedia published
in the fifteenth century that describes the properties of daemons. But
Chatelar goes far beyond Rowley in the sheer extremity of his sentimental expression: this is writing in the face of death, writing unto
death. *Effusions* begins:

> – – – WHAT are sublunary considerations to the mind of fire?
> – What has this world to do with love? All – all is vanity, nothing
> but the neglected chaff wafted on the rude wings of the northern
> blast – – – Avaunt – fly from me power and riches, and give me
> love, nought else but love. – It shall be my state, my fortune, and
> I will be proud with it though robed in the garments of worldly
> wretchedness, – – – Love knows not want – he has no such
> inmate as Poverty; if he smiles, he has but one dread foe; if he
> frowns, he has but one true friend; and both concentrate on the
> oblivion of death, – But must we die? Is there not in love sufficient
> fire to keep this earthly frame from marble coldness?

This febrile projection of love is a daemonic return. And in a later
fragment, love is now a dark, melancholy presence:

> Why am I? Wherefore was Chatelar created? To whom are his
> praises due? – scarce nineteen summers yet have mark'd my pil-
> grimage life, and I am doom'd to love, and love in vain. – Oh!
> That I could drive the demon, melancholy, from me; that fiend,
> who now sits hovering o'er my soul, affrighting every gleam that
> might afford me comfort. – – – No! not even the air-fram'd
> phantom of my queen can chace the gloom away. – Life is all a
> blank to me; for reason bids me cease to hope. – Better be warm'd
> by madness, than chill'd by coward fear; better burn with jealousy,
> than die the silent fool of black despair –

Such lines could be an epitaph for Thomas Chatterton; they are in
fact an epigraph for their author, the subject of the next chapter:
William Henry Ireland.

VI. BASTARD

Thy Willye syncere ande moste trewe

William Shakspeare, *Verses to Anna Hatherrewaye*

Let me not burst in ignorance! but tell,
Why thy canoniz'd bones, hearsed in death,
Have burst their cearments? why the sepulchre,
Wherein we saw thee quietly in-urn'd,
Hath op'd his ponderous and marble jaws,
To cast thee up again? What may this mean –

William Shakespeare, *Hamlet*, i. iv

Spectres may speak, – and *speak* I WILL!

Anon., *Familiar Verses, from the Ghost of
Willy Shakspeare to Sammy Ireland*

Since finishing his monumental *Life of Johnson*, James Boswell had
been an exhausted and broken man. He was vilified by society for his
paparazzo tenacity in seizing and publishing every anecdote about
Samuel Johnson he could lay his hands upon, and his own highly
mottled lowlife was intoned as a terrible cautionary tale and a spectacular fall from grace: a promising young lawyer who dined at the
tables of some of the greatest men of the century began eavesdropping,
then tale-telling. Impertinence led to bigotry, hypocrisy, drunkenness,
lechery, whoring, adultery, and lunacy – and seemed every day to
presage a miserable death. In 1793, aged an elderly fifty-three, Boswell
was mugged while staggering about in the street intoxicated. Although
he recovered sufficiently to promise he would drink less, he continued
to gad about the city. Over the next two years, James Boswell was

frequently unwell. It appears that having dogged Johnson's heels for some twenty years, and then wrecked his health writing his great biography of the man, Boswell now drifted without purpose. He was searching for a literary omen, a sign of cultural assent, to confirm that his work was done. That call came on 20 February 1795. Boswell was invited to Norfolk Street to examine an extraordinary literary find. One Samuel Ireland was exhibiting the manuscripts of one William Shakspeare. Here were deeds and business receipts, verses to Anna Hatherrewaye (enclosing a lock of hair), letters and memoirs, paintings and sketches, annotated books, and holographs of the 'Tragedye of Kynge Leare' and 'Hamblette'. Most spectacularly, there were rumours that new plays had been uncovered: 'Vortigern and Rowena', 'Henry II', and 'The Virgin Queen'. Boswell fell to his knees in reverent disbelief, murmuring, 'I now kiss the invaluable relics of our bard: and thanks to God that I have lived to see them.' He left Norfolk Street in a daze, and almost immediately became 'weak and languid'. James Boswell was dead within a few weeks.

Two months previously, at 8 o'clock in the evening of 16 December 1794, William Henry Ireland had delivered to his father a mortgage deed between William Shakspeare* and Michael Fraser. The deed came from a collection of papers he was in the process of obtaining from a gentleman in the country, or so he said. Bearing in mind that there were only three known signatures of Shakespeare, the appearance of a fourth – and the possibility of others being discovered – set Samuel Ireland and then the whole of London agog with anticipation. And sure enough more papers appeared: legal documents, his library, then letters, verses, and even eventually two new plays. Samuel Ireland exhibited the papers and transcripts at his house, charging visitors the outrageous entrance fee of a guinea, and had the manuscripts engraved onto plates for facsimile publication at the end of 1795. The new play of *Vortigern* went into production at Drury Lane.

By the time of the play's performance on 2 April 1796, however, the new Shakspeare was in shambles. Sceptics and scoffers had filled the newspaper columns and now crammed into the theatre. Just two days

---

* I use the spelling 'Shakspeare' when referring to William Henry Ireland's man, spelling the other one 'Shakespeare'.

before the play hit the stage a definitive and damning critique had
been published by Edmond Malone, the leading Shakespeare editor
and scholar of the age. His demonstration that the papers were forged
was utterly devastating. The performance of *Vortigern* was packed with
his rowdy supporters and although there were many others opposing
the contention that the play was a forgery, things disintegrated into
bedlam when it became clear that even John Kemble, the actor playing
Vortigern, thought the production laughable. The play collapsed and
did not return to the stage for over two centuries; the Irelands were
ridiculed.

A kangaroo committee was set up to investigate the papers, and
extracted an astounding confession from Samuel Ireland's teenage son,
William Henry, who admitted the works were his. He then fled. The
father entirely refused to accept this information, and he and his
cronies, like the woefully misguided antiquarian George Chalmers,
continued to defend the Shakspeare papers in a series of ludicrously
hair-splitting books, printing numbing selections of hitherto unpublished (and deservedly unpublishable) Elizabethan manuscripts. Despite
this heroically futile rearguard, Ireland senior died an unhappy man
in 1801. His wayward son spent the remainder of his life as a Grub
Street hack; the only things of note he produced were a madcap
autobiography, *Confessions* (1805) – at best an idiosyncratic account of
the Shakspeare debacle, at worst a pack of lies* – and counterfeit
forgeries of his Shakspeareana for bibliomaniacs. Ireland junior eventually died in 1835.

This, in a nutshell, is the common account of William Henry
Ireland's career and constitutes the critical ground on which he is
assessed. In other words, Ireland has suffered in precisely the same way
as the 'marvellous Boy' Chatterton: he is identified with one dubious
cultural project (Shakspeare), which then eradicates his subsequent
œuvre and effectively removes him from the canon. One critic, for
example, suggests that Ireland 'might have made an honourable name
for himself as a contemporary of Coleridge and the other romantic
writers', but that 'it is scarcely to be wondered at that nobody took an
impostor seriously as a writer'. But Ireland *was* a contemporary of

---

* In Malone's copy of *Confessions*, he notes on an endpaper: 'There is as much *falsehood*
in this Rogue's *Account* of his impudent forgery, as there was in the forgery itself; for
scarcely a single circumstance is represented truly in all its proofs. EM.'

Coleridge and the others, and he did have his successes and certainly influence. A striking case can be made for the rehabilitation of Ireland, not least in assessing his position in the genealogy of forgers, and the Romantic canonization of Shakespeare.

As a poet, novelist, playwright, satirist, historian, translator, revolutionary librarian, bookbinder, and bigamist, Ireland is potentially as remarkable as Chatterton, though his works lie idle and uncollected and probably no one has yet read the whole lot. The redoubtable Montague Summers has given the best account of Ireland's range in *The Gothic Quest*, focusing on his novels, in particular *Gondez the Monk* (1805). But Summers has little truck with Ireland's poetry; about which the best one can say is that it is an acquired taste. He is, for instance, the first English writer to describe the preparation of fish and chips. In the georgic *The Fisher Boy* (1808), the eponymous hero prepares his mother (Jane the maniac's) supper:

> And for his parent's eating dab supplies,
> Which cleans'd – in dripping pan he dextrous fries;
> Then adds potatoes slic'd, thin, crisp, and brown,
> Whereto he sets his silent mother down;
> Praises the dish, to coax her to the meal,
> The highest earthly transport he can feel.

Evidently there is much more to Ireland than forgery, and forgery should not be allowed to tyrannize his writing – although admittedly Ireland himself was seldom far from the subject, repeatedly and unrepentantly confessing his guilt in a process of self-mythologization. Even late in life he would occasionally sign his name 'W^m. H^y. Ireland otherwise Shakspeare', buttressing himself with the bard. He penned other dubious and semi-fraudulent texts, such as *A Ballade Wrotten on the Feastynge and Merrimentes of Easter Maunday Laste Paste* (1802), and *Effusions of Love from Chatelar to Mary Queen of Scotland* (1805, quoted at the close of the last chapter), and blistering auto-fictions about the Shakspeare papers. Ireland's first novel, *The Abbess* (1799), is prefaced with an amazingly arrogant attack on 'the world' for being duped by the forgeries:

> how could they suffer themselves to be thus deceived? Men of
> superior genius, of common understanding, truly, sincerely, and
> firmly believed, that Shakspeare alone, and no other, wrote those

papers. I knew they would believe it. I knew how far the credulity
of mankind might be imposed upon. The number of plagiarisms
which I collected from all Shakspeare's plays did not deter me –
I knew this would be the last subject of investigation. I brought
forth this not-undigested, not unconnected medley – and success
crowned my bold attempt. I have deceived the world, you say.
No; the world have deceived themselves. Whose fault is it? . . .
mine, or the world's?

It may be that part of the reason for not admitting Ireland to the
honourable company of Coleridge et al. is that his writing does not
easily fit into recognizable critical traditions or notions of Romantic
authorship. In this outburst against the world for not recognizing his
plagiaristic form of composing the Shakspeare papers, Ireland presents
himself as a sort of radical *bricoleur.* Although *bricolage* perhaps unfortunately became a byword of postmodernism, Claude Lévi-Strauss
defines it in *The Savage Mind* as something more magical and primitive
than the pretentious cross-cultural cutting and pasting it later served
for: a *bricoleur,* says Lévi-Strauss, is 'someone who works with his
hands and uses devious means comparable to those of a craftsman' –
which chimes nicely with the manual craft and craftiness of forgery.

An examination of Ireland, then, discloses a complex of forgery
motifs that prodigiously and paradoxically power his writing. The
ghosts and daemons are still here, but are compounded with other
questions of authenticity and legitimacy and truth, especially how these
imponderables might be proven. Craft too remains a defining concept.
Shortly after *Vortigern's* collapse, *Precious Relics; or the Tragedy of Vortigern Rehearsed* was anonymously published. In this farce, the forger's
name was – Craft.*

The last years of the eighteenth century concentrate the mind
wonderfully on forgery. 1796, the year of *Vortigern's* performance and
publication, was also the year of James Macpherson's death and interment in Westminster Abbey, and the year in which Coleridge published
his *Poems* – including his 'Monody on the Death of Chatterton' and
imitations from 'Ossian'. In 1797, Coleridge wrote 'Kubla Khan'. In
1798, *Lyrical Ballads* was published by Biggs & Cottle of Bristol; within
three years, they had published Ireland's own book of ballads. By then,

* *Fortune's Fool,* a comedy on the affair by Frederick Reynolds, was also published and
performed.

at the advent of the new century, Ireland was wandering and writing in search of paternity and posterity (and salt 'n' vinegar).

THE SECOND CHATTERTON

C ALE and neglectedd slombers Fancie's bard,
H ys mortalye parte entremed wythe the duste;
A irie the mysterk sprytes pace o'er the sward,
T o joyne theyre laments wyth eche passente gust.
T hrillinge's the owlett's screech, wyth bat's combin'd,
E mbolleing lethalle horrours off nyghte's howr;
R ede, swotelie stealynge onn thee sorrowyng mynde,
T riomphaunte cryes – Dethe has ne longerr power;
O 'er erthe's frayle parte hys aderne bronde had swaye,
N owghte cann atteynte hys *fame* that glemes forr aye.

William Henry Ireland, 'Acrostic'

Young boy fools elderly amateur antiquarians before professional critics join the fray and crush the imposture. The merest glance reads the Ireland forgery as a retelling or repetition of the Chatterton story, and Ireland cultivated the identification in his *Confessions*. Like Chatterton, he had an ambiguous and difficult paternity. Like Chatterton, he was slow at school, describing himself as 'very backward' and 'averse to every thing like study and application'. Like Chatterton, he was articled in his mid-teenage years and found himself spending long days alone and with nothing to do in an office full of ancient deeds and documents. Like Chatterton, he read Percy's *Reliques* and imitated his ballads. Like Chatterton, he was admired by a housemaid who said *'that it was very odd that I could do such unaccountable strange things'*. He even claims that 'the fate of Chatterton so strongly interested me, that I used frequently to envy his fate, and desire nothing so ardently as the termination of my existence in a similar case'.

In the aftermath of the Shakspeare forgery, Ireland fled to Bristol.

There, he interrogated Chatterton's sister, inspected the poet's letters, 'which she styled the only remaining relics of her dear Thomas', interviewed a Bristol bookseller, and of course visited the muniment room:

> I paus'd – methought his spirit wander'd near.

When these recollections were published, they greatly enhanced the Chatterton myth, and cannily shaded Ireland's own *Confessions* in an enigmatic shadow.

If nothing else, all this was certainly an inspiration: Ireland wrote reams of verse on Chatterton. 'Elegiac Lines to the Memory of Thomas Chatterton' is the opening poem in Ireland's collection *Rhapsodies* (1803). It ends:

> Farewell, sweet youth, one bosom still can melt,
>> Still gaze with anguish, and thy woes deplore;
> Still vainly sooth the suff'rings thou hast felt,
>> Those agonies which thou canst feel no more.

A decade later, the same lines appeared again in *Neglected Genius* (1812), among a dozen or so of Ireland's other verses on, and in imitation of, Chatterton; yet more, including 'Chatterton: A Tragedy', remained unpublished. Elsewhere, references and allusions abound. For instance, in the pseudonymous *Chalcographimania* (by 'Satiricus Sculptor', 1814) he twinned himself with his hero:

> In autographs as ably vers'd,
> As *Chatterton* the poet erst;
> Or he that later wielded fire-brand,
> The impudent and forging *Ireland.*

Others remarked on the similarity too. Ireland was another precocious teenager who had discovered another hoard of manuscripts in another chest. The fearsome antiquarian Joseph Ritson christened Ireland the 'second Chatterton', and Chatterton was immediately recognized as the aesthetic model for the Shakspeare forgeries, the touchstone of newspaper correspondents and pamphleteers. John Wyatt, for instance, asked, 'Would a forger incumber himself with unnecessary letters after the *fatal model* of Chatterton? – Would he not rather have studiously avoided the rock on which that youth split?', and Francis Godolphin Waldron ended his *Free Reflections . . .* (1796) with the melancholy remark,

> I conclude with a sincere wish, that, should *Vortigern*, or any other play imputed to Shakespeare, possess merit enough to warrant the assumption; yet, by critical process be proved a forgery: the ingenious impostor may be ranked with Chatterton in fame; but find better fortune than did that ill-fated, and ever-to-be-lamented youth!

The first Chatterton possessed this second Chatterton, and experienced a sort of resurrection in the controversy over the Shakspeare papers, as if Ireland was reforging Chatterton, rather than forging Shakespeare. And in inspiring Ireland, the condemnation of Chatterton's own work as inauthentic, as forged – however authentically inspirational – was inevitably renewed.

Unlike Chatterton, however, Ireland lived well past his forgery, and his identification with Chatterton risks being over-cultivated, if it was equally self-fictionalized. Ireland's problems with his father began *after* the Shakspeare Controversy; Chatterton never knew his own father, who died before he was born. Ireland may have been slow at school but was also educated in France and spent periods of his life there; Chatterton of course was a bluecoat boy. Ireland came from a wealthy background and was being groomed for the legal profession; he lied about his age in his *Confessions* to make himself appear younger, more Chattertonian; and his forgery was of the canonical literary figure – the National Poet – rather than of a complete unknown. Having admitted to the forgery, he continued to forge Shakspearean signatures for collectors – including Joseph Cottle in Bristol, who like a berk had him add several autographs to the back of a Chatterton manuscript. Neither could Ireland bring himself to commit the ultimate Chattertonian and authenticating act of suicide, and by the time of his death in 1835, the sixty-year-old William Henry Ireland had published at least sixty-seven works.

Ireland's knowledge of Chatterton came from his father, who one evening read aloud from Herbert Croft's sentimental epistolary novel *Love and Madness*, which contains an account of Chatterton's suicide and many of his own letters pilfered from the poet's mother and sister by Croft. The effect on Ireland was electric. A decade later, writing in the smug radiance of self-mythologization, he mused: 'Little did I then imagine that the lapse of a few months was to hold me forth to public view as the supposed discoverer of the Shaksperian manuscripts.' But *Love and Madness* is not primarily about Chatterton: as noted above, it is actually a story about the murder of Martha Reay by the lovelorn Revd James Hackman. Reay was an extremely accomplished singer and mistress to John Montagu, fourth Earl of Sandwich. As it would turn out, William Henry Ireland would be haunted as much by these as he was by Chatterton.

Samuel Ireland's reading from *Love and Madness* seems to have been a rare exception to his insistent habit of post-prandial family readings from the plays of Shakespeare. He was a serious collector of Shakespeareana, and for some time had been in great expectations of acquiring Shakespearean manuscripts. Already in about March 1785, Samuel Ireland had told his friend John Nichols that there was a cache of Shakespeare papers, wills, and other documents in an attorney's office at Measham. Naturally the cupboard was bare, but Nichols later opined, 'I have no doubt but that the origin of the fictitious *Shaksperian MSS.* may be dated from this early period.' William Henry would therefore have been hearing rumours about lost Shakespeare papers from at least the age of nine.

Samuel Ireland was daily extolling the genius of the Bard – 'there was no divine attribute which Shakespeare did not possess' – and the son took to regularly reading Shakespeare and quietly absorbing his father's enthusiasm. By the time he was sixteen and idling in his conveyancing chambers at New Inn, Ireland had become the oblivious agent of a greater imagination, possessed by the spirit of poetry, the genius of Shakespeare: 'the idea of imitating the hand-writing of Shakspeare gradually took *possession* of my mind, without my having been aware of the fact'.*

Apart from Shakespeare and Chatterton, Ireland read Chaucer, Horace Walpole's Gothic novel *The Castle of Otranto*, and Thomas Percy's collection of ballads *Reliques of Ancient English Poetry*. But it was not enough merely to read such stuff, and Ireland also shared his father's enthusiasm for collecting antiquarian books. In this activity, the language of material possession is exactly the same as that of imaginative inspiration: 'Although not partial to modern printed books, the subject matter of Dr. Percy's Relics of Ancient Poetry was a suf-

* Emphasis added here and in succeeding paragraph.

ficient inducement for my becoming its *possessor*.' Inspired by Francis
Grose's taxonomy *Ancient Armoury* (1786–9), Ireland also collected
helmets and breastplates, which he hung from the walls of his bedroom.
'I had hourly opportunities of remarking the satisfaction which the
possession of any rarity gave Mr. Ireland. This naturally impressed itself
on my mind: and in consequence I became a follower of similar
pursuits: which was soon a source of the greatest emulation.'

So Samuel Ireland was a collector, and he had a cabinet of curiosities that included mummy wrappings, parts of Wyclif's vestment
and Charles I's cloak, gloves given by Mary Queen of Scots to Elizabeth
I, Shakespeare's purse, the jackets of both Philip Sidney and Oliver
Cromwell, Joseph Addison's gold fruit-knife, and locks of Edward IV's
and Louis XVI's hair.* This antiquarian obsession with bits and pieces
is a secularization of the sacred theory of holy relics that has been
parodied for centuries but still remains a fascination today. Chaucer
cannily notes of his Pardoner that he 'hadde a croys of latoun, ful of
stones, / And in a glas he hadde pigges bones'; today at Samuel
Johnson's birthplace in Lichfield one may see Johnson's armchair, tea
service, and even a book on which he cack-handedly spilt his
tea. Association objects, from Sigmund Freud's cigar to Catherine the
Great's dildo, still exert a prurient fascination. They are both worthless
and priceless; touched by genius, or its contemporary formation, celebrity, they become objects of a pseudo-religious veneration. In the
case of the Irelands, though, the concept of *possession* dovetails pure
physical acquisition and ownership with inspiration: the material meets
the supernatural. In a sense, William Henry Ireland identified the
'impulse buy' as the condition of the consumer being possessed in
order to possess. Not spirits to enforce, art to enchant, but commodities to go. In the hands of Ireland, inspiration was industrialized, and
Shakespeare was commodified.

Shakespeare and Percy and Chatterton, manuscripts and book-
collecting, antiquities and curios, the revealing recourse to the word
and concept 'possession', Ireland's self-confessed passivity and sug-

---

* Among Sir Walter Scott's '*Treasures*' were Queen Mary's seal, Napoleon's clasps for
his cloak, his pen case and blotting book, a pair of seventeenth-century thumbscrews,
and a toadstone amulet. Among the curiosities exhibited at Don Saltero's coffeehouse
(*c.* 1785) were Chinese chopsticks, a dried chameleon, the pizzle of a raccoon, a surprisingly large moth from Constantinople, an Indian hubble-bubble pipe, a basilisk, and
'Unknown'.

gestibility ... there is yet more to add to the brew: performance. Ireland had always relished the stage, and as an infant he had scampered about at Drury Lane and built his own pasteboard theatres. He had even played in private performances of *The Gentle Shepherd* and *Bon Ton* at Richard Brinsley Sheridan's house, and also appeared in a production of *King Lear*. Later, his forgeries would take on the character of an improvised performance, and his alibis too were elaborately acted out. Ireland said at the height of his production, 'My reason for appearing so much in public, was to make the world think me a giddy thoughtless young man, incapable of producing these papers', and as we have seen elsewhere, forgery embodies a sense of performance and gesture in craft and making.

So William Henry Ireland blended two strains of bardolatry – the ardour of the amateur antiquarian with the fashionable taste of the stage – and it was in this context, in the summers of 1792 and 1793, that the Irelands father and son visited Stratford to pay homage to Shakespeare and acquire any relics, any news, anything at all. These trips are recorded in Samuel Ireland's *Picturesque Views on the ... Avon* (1795), because in addition to everything else, Samuel Ireland was an amateur artist and engraver, specializing in aquatint, a technique used to reproduce wash drawings and sketches. It was an easy and efficient process, 'so expeditious a method of etching, that it will produce, on a large plate, in one week, the effect of two months labour at some kinds of engraving'. He put it to good use in *Picturesque Views on the ... Avon*, which duplicated his sketches of many Shakespearean sites.

Initially, all went well. The Irelands spent the first week of their tour of Shakespeare country in the company of the Stratford Poet, John Jordan: wheelwright, autodidact, rumour-monger, and bullshitter. The man was a mine of useless speculation, but seemed willing to help the Irelands to whatever Shakespeareana might still be about. Encouraged, Samuel Ireland straightaway tried to buy John Harte's house, the Shakespeare birthplace, but the only way he could take possession of the building was by a minute description and drawing, later reproduced in his book. And he was too late too for Shakespeare's chair. Sadly, this wonder had been sold just a couple of years earlier to a Polish princess, Czartoryska, with 'a proper certificate of its authenticity on stamped paper' – all for just 20 guineas. The legendary mulberry tree planted by the green-fingered Bard at his house, New

Place, had been chopped down long ago by the irascible Revd Gastrell, who had subsequently demolished New Place as well. Samuel Ireland described this as a 'sacrilegious act' – although it did provide timber for souvenir tobacco stoppers, tooth-pick cases, goblets, and other nick-nacks, which he snapped up as not unconsidered trifles: verily, 'pieces of the *real cross*' as his son later described them.

Their treasure hunting met with more success, however, at the cottage of 'Anna Hatherrewaye'. Fired by the knowledge that it was here that the actor David Garrick had obtained Shakespeare's inkstand and his pair of fringed gloves, Samuel purchased the chair on which Shakespeare had decorously sat whilst courting Anne, and 'a purse that had been likewise his'. He recorded, with pathetic credulity, 'From the best information I was able to collect at the time, I was induced to consider this account as authentic' – then he tried to buy the bed. What dreams may come, in such a bed? The poet Mark Akenside had in the mid-century been made a present of John Milton's bed:

> Whose Bed is undefil'd and chast pronounc't,
> Present, or past, as Saints and Patriarchs us'd.

A paradisical resting place, a place to muse, dream, compose – although it seems Akenside simply snored in it. And no bed at all for the Irelands, but the Shakespearean chair was still a great prize. It was installed in Norfolk Street; later, guests come to read the Shakspeare papers would be enthroned thereon as part of the bardic ritual.

The obliging John Jordan could not, however, provide them with manuscripts, and so father and son went to Clopton House, apparently the destination of documents removed from New Place. Ireland later described this famous visit:

> We visited *Clopton House*, about a mile from *Stratford*, the gentleman who occupied it, behaved to us with much civility. On my father saying, he wished to know any thing relative to our *Bard*? the gentleman replied, that had he been there a few weeks sooner, he could have given him a great quantity of his, and his family's letters. My father, much astonished, begged to know what was become of them? The gentleman's answer was, that having some young partridges which he wished to bring up, he had, for the purpose, cleared out a small appartment wherein these papers lay, and burnt a large basket of them, he said they were all rotten

as tinder, but to many of them, he could plainly perceive the signature of *William Shakspear.*

He appealed to his wife for confirmation; Samuel Ireland was thunder-struck, and exclaimed, 'Good God, Sir! You do not know what an injury the world has sustained by the loss of them.'* He was mortified. But when news of this episode came to the ever-open ear of Edmond Malone, he rapidly established that there had been no papers, no bonfire, and no injury to the world.

Jordan then regaled the despondent duo with the unedifying tale of an inebriated Shakespeare falling asleep under a certain crab apple tree. They gloomily repaired to Stratford Church, which, declared the pious boy, 'then took possession of my soul'. Clearly, a more sober, more saintly Shakespeare was needed – and in manuscript.

What Ireland implies in his *Confessions* is that a sequence of events and influences caused him to surfeit on Shakespeare and start forging. Everything culminated at Stratford: the trip 'greatly conduced to the subsequent production of the papers, by riveting on my mind a thousand little anecdotes and surmises respecting the sublunary career of our dramatic lord'. In effect, Ireland bestowed a genealogy and thereby a legitimacy on his Shakspeare papers and his inspiration to forge. His narrative was an attempt to legitimize the illegitimate act of forgery, and, as will become apparent, it was also an attempted legitimation of Ireland himself. This might explain why he changed his original story, in which he claimed that he had already presented his first forgery, a handwritten dedication in a presentation copy of an Elizabethan tract, at the ripe old Chattertonian age of seventeen and before he and his father ever visited Stratford.

Ireland then explains the physical composition of his manufactured Shakespeare, how the lines took shape under his fingers. He gives detailed, if again sometimes contradictory, instructions. First he tried a watered ink, but a bookbinder's journeyman mixed him one that wrote pale until held against a flame, when it took on a dark brown

---

* Ireland's version is from the *Authentic Account.* His later *Confessions* gives an expanded version of events, in which the gentleman farmer is now a bluff Squire Western sort of chap. A little over a page is extended to three pages: there is more direct speech, more characterization, more fiction.

and antique appearance.* This absolves Ireland of a little more responsibility, but surely he had access to his father's etching workshop: the
house was probably littered with brushes, quills, and engravers' tools,
not to mention paints, inks, and chemicals – and his sisters were
of an artistic bent too. According to *The Cabinet of the Arts* (1805), for
etching one needs asphaltum, gum-mastic, virgin-wax, mastic, resin,
shoemaker's pitch, common pitch, varnish, amber, beeswax, Burgundy
pitch, turpentine, tallow, and olive oil, and for aquatint the ingredients
include aqua-fortis (nitric acid), ground sulphur, and silver (though
there were also sweeter preparations involving ink and treacle). Hand-
books such as *Valuable Secrets Concerning Arts and Trades* (1775),

> A guide to the techniques, secrets, and formulas used by artists,
> artisans, and others for engraving, metalwork, varnishing, glass
> and paste gemstones, paints and painting, gilding, staining, inks,
> wines, vinegars, liquors and oils, foods and fruits, snuff, removing
> stains, etc,

contained recipes for all sorts of ink. It is likely, then, that Ireland
mixed up the stuff himself.†

He claims too that even as he prepared to forge, he was still
assiduously hunting for genuine Shakespearean deeds among the
mouldering manuscripts in his conveyancing chambers, but without
success. So the inevitable happened: 'For mere frolick and diversion,
I soon after formed the plan of attempting to imitate his hand, and
for that purpose copied out as nearly, as I could, the fac similes of his
name . . .'. Then, taking as a template the mortgage deed reproduced
in the Johnson–Steevens–Malone edition of the complete Shakespeare,
Ireland cut a piece of parchment from the end of an old rent roll and
wrote out a lease between William Shakspeare and John Heminges,

* In the *Authentic Account* he claims he mixed 'a few drops of acid with some other
liquid (used in marbling the covers of books)', whereas *Confessions* describes 'three
different liquids used by bookbinders in marbling the covers of their calf bindings. These
ingredients being shaken up produced a fermentation; when, the froth having subsided,
the liquid was of a dark brown colour.'
† The twentieth-century forger Eric Hebborn naturally had a large number of ink
recipes, from willow soot to cuttlefish ink and oak galls. Ireland had a little laboratory
at hand and certainly would not have been required to go out and about for his
concoctions of ink. Like Hebborn, Ireland adopted another classic forger's technique of
adapting his work to fit with the paper he found, and not attempting to find the right-
sized paper for the work.

with Michael Fraser and his wife Elizabeth. Ireland's deed was so close
to that printed that he calls it an 'obvious plagiary'. But even so, he
did not consider Shakspeare's written signature sufficiently authentic
on its own – 'a law instrument was assuredly the most calculated to
stamp validity on the signature produced' – so he manufactured a seal
as well, which supplemented the signature. The law, rather than the
body, was now the guarantor of authenticity; the legal discourse had
overtaken the literary, and so the physical hand and its trace, the
signature, was haunted by its own insufficiency, its threatened nonexist-
ence. When the papers were eventually published, the title announced
that they were verified by Shakspeare's 'Hand and Seal'. Such was the
deed that was presented to Samuel Ireland one December night in
1794.

FROMM THE OAKEN CHEƒTE ATT OURE GLOBE THEATRE

> Different questions require different evidence, and are tried
> by different senses; but on questions concerning certain
> visible and material instruments, inspection is the only stan-
> dard to which reference is to be made. The eye alone
> examines into the evidence, because it is only by the eye,
> that minute analogies can be remarked, and comparisons of
> colors, shades, and resemblances fairly and accurately made.
>
> Samuel Ireland, *An Investigation of Mr. Malone's
> Claim . . . Of the Shakspeare Manuscripts, &c.*

Ireland claimed to have obtained the Shakspeare papers from a man
only ever known as 'Mr. H.'. He had met the gentleman of fortune at
dinner (later this became a coffeehouse) and after discussing old books
and manuscripts, was invited to call upon him, rummage through his
papers, and take anything he wished. Ireland said he delayed a few
days before paying this visit, but eventually called – whereupon he was

shown into a room housing 'a vast collection of old deeds and papers tied up in bundles'. He was offered his pick – and discovered the deed drawn up between Shakspeare and Michael Fraser. As Mr H. was an honourable man, Ireland was allowed to keep that and anything else he might discover. Ireland later claimed that the gentleman's stupendous generosity was also in thanks for help in tracing documents that had settled a long property case in his favour.

This concoction is a fairy tale: a mysterious tryst between a good benefactor and a resourceful young lad who draws up treasures to the wonder of the world. It is a story of secrecy and complicity, of a surrogate father figure, of an intense, if imaginary, homoerotic relationship. The young Mr H. seemed to take a more than paternal interest in the boy William Henry: he was lavishing priceless gifts on him, entered a very familiar correspondence with Samuel Ireland (this too was audaciously forged by his son), but he refused to reveal his name or his face or his title. Samuel Ireland observed at one point that Mr H. had a very *'feminine'* hand – what might that imply? – but any debauching of his son in return for Shakspeare papers does not appear to have troubled him too much – although he rejected H.'s sound recommendation that William Henry should be allowed to wear his hair 'with flowing locks'.

It is worth pointing out that Ireland developed the character of Mr H. not, as one might expect, from the 'onlie begetter' of Shakespeare's sonnets, 'Mr. W. H.', but by implying that H. might be the descendent of John Heminges. In the forged 'Deed of Trust to John Hemynge', it becomes apparent that Heminges had failed to execute Shakspeare's will properly, hence a possible reason for dissimulation and disguise. But there was more. H. was possibly descended from a bastard scion of Shakspeare's *sang real*, as the deed also mentions 'thatt Chylde of whom wee have spokenn butt who muste nott be named here'. Shakespeare gives this brat, 'ye eyghte Playes thatt bee stylle inne s^d. Cheste as allso mye otherr Playe neverr yett Imprynedd called Kynge Vorrtygerne'. This simple expediency immediately cast insoluble doubt over who might actually own the papers.

The legal documents that Ireland initially produced were formulaic and nugatory, difficult to prove true or false, and of more interest to sensation-seekers than literary historians. But he then turned to much more inventive and interfering work, the first such being Shakspeare's 'Profession of Faith'. Ireland had a straightforward motive – 'thereby to prove *Shakspear* a Protestant' – and as with the mortgage deed, he had a template – what Malone would later call an 'archetype' – in the shape of John Shakespeare's 'Profession of Faith'. This recently discovered, possibly spurious document printed in the Johnson–Steevens–Malone edition seemed to indicate that the dramatist's father was Catholic; it has since disappeared. So Ireland selected some old paper,* and placed the facsimile signatures before him to guide his hand through a twelve-letter alphabet, 'forming every letter in his name as he might have written them' – the other letters he simply made up. 'I kept the tracings from Shakspeare's original autographs before me, and so penned the epistle, without making any studied transcript, but merely committing my thoughts to paper in the disguised hand as they occurred to my mind.'

In other words, Ireland claims to be composing his texts using words primarily spelt with the letters W, i, l, a, m, S, h, k, e, s, p, r. Presumably this animated his entire corpus with the sibilant name of the bard: in essence signing it. Evidently one of the early defenders, 'Philalethes' (Francis Webb), was quite correct when he stated: 'these papers bear not only the signature of his hand, but also the stamp of his soul, and the traits of his genius. His *mind* is as manifest as his *hand*.' In lieu of inspiration, Ireland wrote rapidly and spontaneously, and thoughtlessly: 'the effusion was altogether unstudied, being committed to paper, in the disguised hand and redundancy of letters in the spelling, just as the thoughts arose in my own mind, without any previous transcript or subsequent alteration whatsoever.' This feat of direct expression is a parody of Romantic inspiration, a wilful self-abandonment to some 'other' – or something or other. As the Irelands' housekeeper Mrs Freeman later put it to William Henry's friend Montague Talbot: 'he says that of late he has been inspired with all the Furor of a Divine Poet . . . [he] has deserted his office (for a genius like his, he says, cannot condescend to sit at a desk) and does nothing but lounge about the streets, or drive about. . . .'

A breakneck speed of composition, a text formed out of the material of an autograph and resonating with the signature, an extravagance of cod-Elizabethan spellings, consisting of doubled consonants

* He paid 5s. to take all the flyleaves from the old books in a shop in St Martin's Lane, taking care to avoid watermarked paper, though later he had a preference for 'the *Jugg*' watermark. These early leaves may, however, have come from Samuel Ireland's library.

and added 'e's wherever at all possible: this was a risky business. But it produced some notable results: 'O cherishe usse like the sweete Chickenne thatte under the coverte offe herre spreadynge Wings Receyves herre lyttle Broode ande hoevynge oerre themme keepes themme harmlesse ande in safetye.'* And when Drs Samuel Parr and Joseph Warton visited and inclined an ear to this 'Profession of Faith', one of them declared: 'Sir, we have very fine passages in our church service, and our litany abounds with beauties; but here, sir, here is a man who has distanced us all!' Later, they disagreed as to which one had made this encomium, but at the time they were both so impressed they drew up a Certificate of Belief that was eventually signed by a score of the papers' most eminent supporters – 'the whole nest of ninnies', as George Steevens hailed them. Meantime, young Ireland staggered out of the room, intoxicated with the praise: vanity 'took possession' of his mind. He adopted a pose of poetic rapture, cooling his burning forehead against the windowpane, 'fired with the idea of possessing genius to which I had never aspired'. He was an untutored genius, possessed with the spirit of Shakespeare, and possessed of the papers of Shakspeare; he was Shakespeare's natural successor and heir; he set to work.

Ireland now dashed off a succession of masterpieces: a letter from Queen Elizabeth ('this letter was produced to make our *Bard* appear noticed noticed [*sic*] by the greatest personage of his time'), a love letter and verses to Anne Hathaway together with a lock of bardic hair tied with red silk ('I laid great emphasis on the workmanship of the silk, as if executed by the hand of Shakspeare'), a promissory note to John Heminges ('Shakspeare, in addition to his other good qualities, was very punctual in all pecuniary transactions'), and so forth. Ireland soon realized that 'nothing could possibly come from the hand of Shakspeare which did not possess some sterling good'. This was the gold standard, the whole basis of English cultural confidence.

Yet already Ireland was tired and dissatisfied. He had exhausted himself with his own brilliance; he now moved into a new phase of workmanlike activity, filling out the corpus:

> As I heard it unceasingly stated that 'the more bulky the papers were, the more probable would their authenticity appear,' I began

---

* 'O cherish us like the sweet chicken that under the cover of her spreading wings receives her little brood and heaving over them keeps them harmless and in safety.'

to consider what would be the best expedient to accomplish this end without much labour of the brain; for as my muse was not so very prolific as to 'spin and weave' poetry as fast as it was required, I really began to loathe the very idea of the manuscripts, which became to me an insufferable burden.

Thus he wrote memoranda, receipts ('to prove *Shakspear* correct in matters of the most trivial nature'), and more legal documents ('it was generally allowed that law documents were the most convincing evidences of the validity of manuscripts'). All contributed to the authenticity of the corpus – some by their very banality.

If Ireland's Shakspeare was acclaimed and valued, uxorious and loving, honest, meticulous, and Protestant, little of this really affected his plays. To reinvent Shakespeare fully as a decent English gentleman, Ireland really had to tackle the works and show that Shakespeare was not responsible for the faults attributed to him: 'if the original manuscript of one of his printed plays should be found, it would prove whether he wrote all the ribaldry attributed to him in the first quarto's.' He had to cultivate impeccable manners in the bard – a form of interventionist editing that anticipated the Bowdlers by only a few years. To this end, Ireland obtained from his father a Quarto edition of *King Lear* (1608) and applied himself to removing bawdiness, solving cruces, cutting characters like Oswald, and amplifying sentimental moments such as Kent's exit speech at the close of the play (although he retained Edmund's 'bastard' speech). Except for a few leaves that were missing from his copy, he completed the play, and next commenced work on 'Hamblette'. But he was soon bored by this as well and rather than repeat and reinscribe the whole play, abandoned the work after only a few pages and struck out in a new direction. Ireland entered what was to be the final period of his life as a Shakspeare. He wrote two new plays, *Vortigern and Rowena* and *Henry II*, and planned *The Virgin Queen* and a new sequence of histories.

One of the consequences of producing new works was the renewal of possible copyright problems if a real heir appeared. As indicated above, Ireland deftly confused the legacy by suggesting that John Heminges had not diligently followed Shakspeare's will. It was a subtle solution to an indeterminate problem; he then tried to solve it more decisively and in the crassest way imaginable: by making himself the heir. William Henry Ireland wrote himself into Shakspeare's life. The extraordinary 'Deed of Gift to Ireland' described the daring rescue of Shakspeare from drowning in the Thames. The company's boat is overturned by drunken bargemen and all manage to swim to the shore, all except Shakespeare:

> Masterre William henrye Irelande notte seeynge mee dydd aske for mee butte oune of the Companye dydd answere thatte I was drownynge onn the whyche he pulledd off his Jerrekynne and jumpedd inn afterre mee withe muche paynes he draggedd mee forthe I beynge then nearlye deade and soe he dydd save mye life.*

In return for this th'immortal, if waterlogged, Swan of Avon gave Ireland and his heirs (who must always be called 'William Henry Ireland') a purse of ten pounds sterling, plus the rights to *Henry IV, Henry V, King John, King Lear*, and *Henry III*, and he wrote the hitherto lost eulogy, 'Tributary Lines to Ireland'. This is a very elaborate thank-you note, adorned with patterned shields and Ireland's house and Coat of Arms, as sketched by Shakspeare:

> Inne life wee wille live togetherre Deathe shall forre a lytelle parte usse butte Shakspeares Soule restelesse inne the Grave shalle uppe Agayne ande meete hys freynde his IRELAND Inne the Bleste Courte of Heavenne.†

The sense here of Ireland resurrecting the nonexistent dead – both his ancestor and Shakspeare – is absolutely palpable. There is also a sense that inspiration is historical, as well as being a form of lineal repetition, and even that it is uncanny – a repetition rather than a remembering. But again all has a legal dimension: the documents are establishing the ownership of plays. And with this in mind, Samuel Ireland was now eager to publish, and publish in his own way.

---

* 'Master William Henry Ireland not seeing me did ask for me but one of the Company did answer that I was drowning, on the which he pulled off his jerkin and jumped in after me. With much pains he dragged me forth I being then nearly dead and so he did save my life.'
† 'In life we will live together, death shall for a little part us, but Shakespeare's soul, restless in the grave, shall up again and meet his friend, his Ireland, in the blessed court of Heaven.'

Samuel Ireland fancied himself to be numbered among the cognoscenti. By the mid-1790s, he was already halfway through engraving an ambitious series of topographical tours, produced in the most lavish of formats at the remarkable rate of virtually a book a year. These ten folio volumes are super-connoisseur copies: 'a rivulet of text trickles down the middle of the page,' as Sheridan might have remarked, ambling like Samuel Ireland himself along the banks of English rivers or weaving through the streets and alleys of European towns and cities. He describes environs, history and antiquities, artworks, lives of artists, details of travel, and reproduces many of his aquatint engravings; most of his scenes are cool landscapes or architectural studies, in just a few are lonely figures dispersed.

The first of these enterprises was the mildly salacious *A Picturesque Tour through Holland, Brabant, and part of France* (1790), dedicated to the antiquarian and sot Francis Grose – possibly because it included a passing account of a visit to a brothel. Samuel Ireland then embarked on a series of national *Picturesque Views*, following the Thames (1792), the Medway (1793), the Avon (1795), the Wye (1797), and the Severn (posthumously published in 1824). His treks up and down these rivers were psychogeographical peregrinations mapping sources and fountain-heads, searching for origins and originality in the mystical waters that irrigate the English imagination – and in this they were mirrored by his cultural works. Just as his volumes of Hogarth's sketches (1794 and 1799) constituted the artistic wing of this grand enquiry into the state of the country, Samuel Ireland's volume of Shakspeare papers (dated 1796, issued 1795) was the literary equivalent of his thirst for national authenticity and legitimacy. Even his ultimate views of the Inns of Court (published 1800) might be seen as trying to establish the finer points of the origin of the characteristic English legal mind.

The discovery and exhibition of the Shakspeare papers occurred therefore during an extremely prolific decade, in which the Irelands engaged in a sort of family enterprise in patriotic connoisseurship. Moreover, the engravings for *Graphic Illustrations of Hogarth* (1794) were made ('*fecit*') by Samuel and his two daughters, who in the same year were helping their brother William Henry to transcribe the Shakspeare papers – papers that seemed peculiarly suited to a facsimile edition.

Miscellaneous Papers and Legal Instruments under the Hand and Seal of William Shakspeare was sold by subscription at 4 guineas a copy –

about £175 today. The volume is a voluptuously lavish folio, copiously
illustrated with facsimile engravings of almost all the papers, paired
with generously spaced parallel transcriptions, printed very scrupulously, on one side of the paper only. Samuel Ireland could barely
contain his gleeful self-vindication in making prefatory remarks,
declaring that he had 'incessantly laboured', consulting 'the Scholar,
the Man of Taste, the Antiquarian, and the Herald', and that 'he has
been equally anxious that the whole should be submitted to the practical experience of the Mechanic, and be pronounced upon by the
papermaker, &c.'. It is worth noting this appeal to the craftsman,
'the practical experience of the Mechanic'. Samuel Ireland, an erstwhile
weaver and semi-professional engraver himself, places a considerable
anti-intellectual emphasis on practical skill. To validate his project,
Ireland wants not the book-learning of the antiquarian scholar, but
craft. This is precisely what characterizes forgery as a mode of production.

Yet simultaneously he was anxious to reprieve Shakspeare of his
own immediate mechanicals: his troupe had marred the plays. *King
Lear* had evidently been corrupted by the Globe's actors, and these
errors had been perpetuated in every performance and edition since
1608. For example, Edgar's lines:

> Blanket my loines *else* all my hair with knots
> And *with presented* nakednes out-face
> The winde, ande persecution of the skie.

are fallacious adulterations, for Shakspeare actually wrote:

> Blankette mye loynes *twiste* alle mye hayre in Knottes
> And *inne Adam lyke* Nakeddenesse oute face
> The Winde ande persecutyonne o the Skye [.]*

Even on such feeble evidence as this, the point was that Shakespeare's
genius lay in individual composition rather than the collaborative work
undertaken by a company of players. Authentic meant physical legal
remains. Indeed, the word 'authentic' had shifted in meaning from the
seventeenth century, when it indicated an axiomatic truth, to the later

---

* Not all agreed with the beauties of the ur-*Lear*, however – James Boaden described
the text as 'this WORM, this *irregular, writhing*, and *creeping* inhabitant of the *old*
TRUNK'.

eighteenth century, when it came to mean the resident properties of actual documents. In other words, to be properly authentic, Shakespeare did not need plays and performances and scholars and jubilees and Stratford-upon-Avon, but an archive of official records, signed and sealed by his own hand. Hence the prerequisite of authenticity was the legally endorsed autograph manuscript.

Before publication, the manuscripts had been reverently passed among visitors to Norfolk Street, who each took it in turns to perch on Shakespeare's courting chair when consulting the papers. Although they could probably read no more than Shakspeare's autograph (which did appear with gratifying frequency*), the extra-textual elements of smell and touch, and the rustle of antique paper, were all part of the experience of authenticity. As John Wyatt excitedly pointed out, 'It is a circumstance very favourable to the MSS. that the *sight* of them has seldom failed to produce at *least a conviction* of their authenticity.' Hence Samuel Ireland's exertions to publish the manuscripts as scrupulously as possible: *Miscellaneous Papers* proposed itself as a perfect copy in its very medium.

Etching, particularly copper-plate engraving, was the supreme eighteenth-century craft of copying. A typical account (given by Hodson and Dougall in *The Cabinet of the Arts*) claims that engraving is more effective in describing scenes than poets or historians because engraving takes a direct physical impression: 'We are transported to ancient scenes, view, as if actually present, the devastation which reigned in ancient fields of slaughter, enter into the contest, and for a moment forget we are beings of a posterior generation . . .'. That phrase, 'as if actually present', is the key to understanding how an eighteenth-century connoisseur would inspect an engraving: it was considered an entirely mechanical reproduction. Exhibitions of Old Masters were infrequent, and many virtuosos, let alone artists like William Blake, whose tutor was considered one of the best facsimilists in London, knew much of the work of, say, Raphael and Michelangelo mainly through such prints. Indeed, because prints were considered a transparent medium, they were not classed as an art form, but a secondary, imitative, and subordinate craft. Even in its credits, the print itself articulates this opposition between art and craft: *delineavit, invenit,* or *pinxit* (drawn, designed, or painted) appears at the leading

* The recent and infamous Hitler Diaries were also signed on almost every page.

edge, *sculpsit, incisit,* or *fecit* (engraved, incised, or made) is at the tail end. Despite the extraordinary skill and patience involved in making a plate, engravers were treated as copyists, artisans, and were not eligible for membership of the Royal Society. Their work was almost akin to the eerie image on the Shroud of Turin – or indeed a photograph – that is, not made by the hand of man; as Roland Barthes says, '*acheiropoietos*'.

In some cases, the connoisseur could also view, 'as if actually present', the very process of artistic composition. Samuel Ireland's volume of sixty Hogarth engravings focused on sketches and drafts, capturing composition at its most raw and immediate, in its most pure and original state. Genius was believed to be especially recognizable in first thoughts, for first thoughts embodied inspiration and sincerity. Shakespeare's genius especially was characterized by 'that spontaneous flow of soul and simple diction, which so eminently distinguish this great Author of Nature', and this natural brilliance was confirmed by the clean, unblotted lines of his manuscripts.

Some artists, like Edwin Landseer, understandably objected to this fetishization of working practices: 'It is not the painter's *sketches* that it is most desirable to multiply, but his *finished performances*.' But connoisseurs remained particularly keen to obtain facsimiles of pen and ink sketches and drafts – indeed, the demand for drawings was far greater than that for paintings. The signature was implicit in every piece, so the emphasis on the *sprezzatura* of the hand, the identification of individual idiosyncrasies of gesture and composition, became characteristic of connoisseurship and authentication. Again we have the legal prerogatives of signature (image) and seal – literally the impression of the plate onto the paper. To mystify this construction of authenticity, the medium of engraving is understood to be utterly transparent, carrying no trace of the mode of production: the engraver's hand.

So Samuel Ireland published *Miscellaneous Papers . . . under the Hand and Seal of William Shakspeare* in order to rout the sceptics, claiming that it was his 'earnest desire to give such a variety of fac-similes of the hand writing as to enable the reader to form a complete judgment of the general character of the manuscript'. But the translation of manuscript into print transformed the enticing, if empty, subtleties of William Henry Ireland's stunt-Elizabethan penmanship into stark black and white. The engravings had an unremitting, pornographic precision; they made the Shakspeare papers too explicit, obscene even, and their mysterious seductiveness drained away. Moreover, the typeset transcriptions, 'verbatim et literam from the originals', rather than bestowing any aura on the original manuscripts by emphaizing how unique they were, simply exposed all the caprices and imbecilities of spelling and style. These copies did not confirm the status of the original manuscripts, but revealed that any imagined authenticity they possessed had been a projection of the bewitching material conditions under which they were presented. Authority now lay with the engravings – and the papers were deemed fake. In the case of Rowley, only one manuscript had been widely disseminated in print; in the case of Shakspeare, it was virtually the entire corpus. This was a fatal miscalculation. The papers were killed stone dead.

So, *Miscellaneous Papers* was less a portable cabinet of curiosity than a systematic gallery of fraud. The Shakespearean scholar George Steevens, for instance, examined the engravings in preference to the originals, and discovered the most minute traces of forensic palaeographical evidence. He noted his findings in a memo of March 1797:

> The hair strokes that are so frequent in the real signatures of Shakspeare, are undiscoverable in the forged ones, which are given in what the Clerks at the Post Office (when they mean to distinguish true from fictitious Franks) most significantly style – a *painted hand*; i.e. a hand that sluggishly and elaborately traces letters and words, which, had they been of genuine manuscript, would have been expressed by lines of different thickness, and other unequivocal denotements of easy and familiar penmanship. In the Plates belonging to the Publication of Mr Ireland the elder, this stiff and dull uniformity is, in some instances, avoided; and, perhaps, through the skill of the engraver, who must have been convinced that no scribe, except one who was employed in the servile task of imitating a hand unnatural to him, would have proceeded so slow as to have dwelt, in the equal pressure of quill, on every part of every letter.

The publication of *Miscellaneous Papers* without a doubt hastened the calamitous end of the affair: the papers shifted from manuscript to print, from the private to the public space, and ultimately from the authentic to the inauthentic. But, as suggested by Steevens's recourse to criminal terminology, the publication also decisively shifted the debate from the literary to the legal discourse. Literary authenticity needed to be underwritten by the authority of the law; now the Shakspeare papers became a quasi-legal case, tried at the public bar.

Newspaper articles and pamphlets commonly described the Shakspeare controversy as a 'trial' in which the public were acting as judge and jury, lawyers and witnesses – for example James Boaden declared of the papers, 'their authenticity is now on trial at the bar of the publick, and every one is free to give evidence'. Boaden's newspaper *The Oracle* was an early supporter of the Irelands; he subsequently defected to the other side and wrote *A Letter to George Steevens, Esq* (1796), which opened with legal quibbles. Henry Bate-Dudley's contribution was entitled *The Great Literary Trial . . . of Vortigern* (1796), and he continued the analogy in his social satire, *Passages selected by Distinguished Personages, on the Great Literary Trial of Vortigern*. This proceeded as a mock trial hearing in numbered days. Even at the performance of *Vortigern*, the MP Charles Sturt was heard to yell in drunken exasperation at the heckling from the pit, 'Give the thing a fair trial!'

The most professionally legalistic assessment was, of course, Edmond Malone's gigantic and comprehensive assault, *An Inquiry into the Authenticity of Certain Miscellaneous Papers and Legal Instruments*. This was strategically published two days before the performance of *Vortigern*. It sold 500 copies before the curtain went up and transformed a theatrical evening into a crazy vendetta, a cultural riot. Malone had trained as a barrister before a private pension allowed him to devote his life to editing Shakespeare, and Paul Baines notes that 'the rhetoric of the courtroom hangs over the whole *Inquiry*'. Malone makes it quite clear that it is only proper legal procedure and not critical or aesthetic values that will settle this case. He elects himself Shakespeare's Counsel, and, in order to establish what might constitute admissable literary evidence, cites specific cases from *Select Trials* and quotes William Blackstone's *Commentaries on the Laws of England*. It is worth emphasizing how very few of the commentators remarked on the literary quality of the forgeries – certainly not Malone.

His gruelling argument then proceeds by inches, grinding through:

> 1. the Orthography, 2. the Phraseology, 3. the Dates given or deducible by inference, and 4. the Dissimilitude of the Handwriting, [to prove] that not a single paper or deed in this extra-

ordinary volume was written or executed by the person to whom
it is ascribed.

The *coup de grâce* was an appendix on the 'Origin and History of
Promissory Notes and Paper-Credit', establishing that paper-credit
postdated Shakespeare. In particular, Malone revealed that Shakespeare
had no title to his plays: they belonged to the playhouse, and therefore
he personally could not grant rights to them to anyone else. Bearing
in mind the number of financial documents and bequests among the
papers, the argument proved conclusive.

By publishing so encyclopedically, Samuel Ireland had evidently
provided abundant ammunition for the sceptics. Nevertheless, his son
had indeed tried to authenticate the papers by making them, at least
initially, legal rather than literary. There was a persistent expectation
that Shakespearean legal papers were about to be discovered (even the
former lawyer Malone held this view), if only because such documents
would have been more likely to have survived than literary ephemera.
And if such formulaic documents were relatively easy to forge, it
actually proved extraordinarily difficult for Malone to establish conclusively that the papers were not genuine – his *Inquiry* runs to over
400 pages. Even then he considered publishing a second edition in
response to counterblasts from the Ireland camp, some of which were
unnervingly accurate in their evidence, and telling in their accusations that Malone had appointed himself to police Shakespeare studies
and censor debate. Samuel Ireland accused Malone and his supporters
of being 'Bow-street runners in literature', and he is called 'the public
accuser' throughout George Chalmers's *Apology for the Believers in the
Shakspeare-Papers* (1797). Jonathan Bate believes that Samuel Ireland
'undoubtedly has the better of these arguments'.

The sheer vindictiveness of Malone's attack stems, Bate suggests,
from an anxiety that his methods of exposing the Shakspeare papers
as fraudulent could as easily be used against any construction of
Shakespeare – they were all fictitious – but the detection of the forgery
depended itself on creating an alternative Shakespeare to the 'Irish'
one: an expedient and coherent Shakespeare for the present age. In his
1790 edition of the *Works*, Malone had elegantly shaped his Shakespeare
out of legal remains and presented him as a successful and respectable
businessman and property-owner, a thoroughly decent English gent.
And arguably Ireland was providing some clinching evidence that his

thoroughly decent plays had been corrupted by ribald and licentious
actors: in *Vortigern*, Edmunda recovers her sanity and the villainous
king is merely exiled rather than being royally butchered. Many other
aspects of Ireland's Bard also seemed to confirm him as being as
bourgeois as Malone could wish for; to Malone, however, this presented
an unforgivable trespass. His prosecution came down to a defence of
what he considered to be both his and Shakespeare's property rights,
vested in what he legally considered to be authentic.

Malone had already warned forgers 'to deter from invading the
rights or property of others by any kind of fiction'. The phrase resonates
with echoes of recent social upheaval, for the *Inquiry* was also a
veiled political attack against republicanism in literary studies. Malone
supposed that the Irelands were trying to seize the Bard's literary estate
and corrupt his pedigree. He accused them of no less than revolutionary
Jacobinism in suggesting that Shakespeare was anything less than an
absolute monarchist, in even daring to lay hands upon him. Malone
sent a copy of his *Inquiry* to his friend Edmund Burke, a man who
reflecting on the recent revolution in France had also associated literary
forgery with the historical distortions of radicalism. Evidently the law
that legislated over literature was itself ultimately answerable to, and
in the service of, other interests. As soon as authenticity ceased to be
a matter of literary criticism and was instead determined as a legal
absolute, so the function of literature ceased to be social or spiritual
and began to be based on another practice – that of politics.

The condition of literary forgery as theft, indeed as treason, was
therefore reasserted. This expectation, that literary forgers were all
economic forgers in waiting, was melodramatic to say the least, but
now all of a sudden it had apparently been proven by Ireland's
hamfisted attempts to lay claim to the Shakespeare canon. Horace
Walpole had claimed he feared that Chatterton would graduate to
financial forgery, and Malone rather maliciously decided that it was at
least worth threatening the latest marvellous boy with the gallows,
jotting down among his notes: 'The *Professors* of this *art*, which at the
Old Bailey goes by another name, it has been observed are seldom
long lived: too sedulous an application to it frequently ending in
sudden death, generally by suffocation.'

Ireland himself rightly found these threats absurd:

should literary imposture be rendered cognisable to a criminal court of judicature, Would it be credited, that such men have proceeded to the ridiculous length of ranking my offence on a par with the forgery of a bank-bill; and, I am thoroughly convinced, would have felt infinite delight in witnessing my exit as a delinquent at the Old Bailey. If an untruth in literary manners were so heinous an offence, whence comes it that the late Sir Horace Walpole, afterwards Lord Orford, escaped the lash of reproof, for palming off his 'Castle of Otranto' as the translation from an old Italian MS.? and why were not a long list of others, guilty of similar literary misdemeanours, dragged forth to public execration? No! the whole, except in the instance of poor Chatterton, to whose memory the world has since done justice, was reserved for my devoted head; every burthen was accumulated on my shoulders; this I have endured with stoicism, until I conceive my penance fully achieved.

But the question of legal proceedings came as a direct result of Ireland's forgeries, many of which were precisely *Legal Instruments*, signed and sealed: receipts, indenture agreements, a mortgage lease, deeds of gift and deeds of trust, and so forth. In other words, these were just the sort of documents that, were they contemporary, really would have sent young William Henry Ireland to the gallows. How close to indictable forgery did he come with the ill-advised 'Deed of Gift to Ireland'? The deed is dated 25 October 1604. It would have been preposterous for Ireland to have pursued the claim; undoubtedly, it would also have been fatal to him. So, true to the paradigm of the felon, Ireland did what thousands had done before him: he confessed, twice in fact.

An apology, as it lately came from IRELAND.—
'I confess I am an impostor, and therefore I expect you will be prepared to believe every word I say.'
Another. – ['] *Shakespear* did not write these plays, *therefore* I did. – I imposed upon you before, *therefore* I speak truth now. – You have detected me already, *therefore* I am above suspicion at present.'

Ridicule aside, the Shakspeare forgery briefly exposed writing as the instrument and evidence of ideological control. Ireland would presently make the case more emphatically: rethinking and redefining authorship as a drastic remedy for another desperate disaster.

✤ ✤ ✤

NOW GODDES ∫TANDE UPPE FORRE BA∫TARDES

SOME Authors gratify their fancies
By writing novels and romances;
Some rise to fame on loftier themes,
On poems, prophecies, and dreams;
Some launch a frigate, some a shallop,
Some 'prime – bang up' – start off full gallop;
While other Bards, whose wits are scanter,
Go gently on the road, a canter;
Some write to *fill*, some *fill* to write,
Some write thro' frolic, some thro' spite;
Some write to gain the world's applause,
And others, to employ their – jaws;
My Muse and I disdain such follies,
We write to banish melancholies,
To sooth the rugged brow of Care,
To drive away the fiend Despair,
T'expose hypocrisy and crimes,
And lash the Follies of the Times.

'Cervantes', *The State Doctors.*
or *A Tale of the Times*, canto III

The ancient Greek for fakes is *nothoi*, literally *bastards*, and counter-feiting especially is an abiding Shakespearean metaphor for illegitimacy. 'We are all bastards,' declares Posthumus in *Cymbeline*,

And that most venerable man, which I
Did call my father, was I know not where
When I was stamp'd; some coiner with his tools
Made me a counterfeit.

Illegitimacy casts long shadows over the Shakespeare industry too. William Davenant, leader of the Duke's Men and a semi-fictitious character himself (his name means 'Charming'), cultivated rumours that he was Shakespeare's bastard son, conceived in an Oxford pub, the Crown. Meanwhile, the surname 'Shakespeare' was often in the eighteenth century given to foundlings and orphans as a way of encouraging them to aspire. But more specifically, illegitimacy suddenly cast a long and very sobering shadow over William Henry Ireland.

Despite Shakspeare's 'Deed of Gift' to 'William henrye Irelande', our William Henry Ireland still failed to become his heir. As the debate surrounding the authenticity of the papers grew in intensity, gossip about the Irelands became acute, and the first revelation was that Samuel Ireland had been born 'Samuel Irwin' – so that put paid to claiming any descent from Shakespeare's pal. What was more terrible, however, was that during the rows that blazed in Norfolk Street following the catastrophic performance of *Vortigern* and Ireland's claim to have forged the papers, tempers snapped and something dreadful was hinted at. William Henry Ireland was not even an Irwin. He began calling himself William Henry Freeman.

This needs disentangling. Mrs Freeman was the housekeeper at Norfolk Street, and had handled domestic affairs since the death of Mrs Ireland, shortly after William Henry's birth. According to a theory first advanced by Bernard Grebanier and half-confirmed by the diary of John Farington, Mrs Freeman was the onetime mistress of a dissolute rake, John Montagu, 4th Earl of Sandwich. Even in his sixties, Sandwich maintained his reputation for licentious living – seducing young women and siring bastards – and so in his fifties, one of his mistresses may well have been a young girl called Anna Marie de Burgh Coppingen. She had two or three children and was eventually passed on to Samuel Ireland and lived with him as his housekeeper under the (rather ironic) name of Mrs Freeman. This might explain how this Spitalfields weaver rose to writing master, artist, engraver, publisher, and connoisseur; how he became a Hogarth collector to rival Horace Walpole and the author and illustrator of almost a dozen large-paper virtuoso folios. He took Anna Marie Coppingen to the tune of £12,000 a year.* There never had been a Mrs Ireland.

Samuel Ireland raised the three children Anna Maria, Jane, and William Henry as his own, claiming that the original Mrs Ireland had died some years previously. This speculation has since been partly

---

* It is also worth noting the evident wealth of the young William Henry Ireland: here was a boy able to collect antiquarian books and ancient armour: one of his purchases for his 'Shaksperian Library' was a copy of Spenser's *Faerie Queene* for 30 guineas, a small fortune. Clearly he was not debarred from sharing in the Coppingen dowry.

proven by the discovery of the Ireland family Bible, which confirms that the children were indeed Mrs Freeman's.* What is not clear from this record, of course, is who fathered the children: Sandwich, Ireland, or indeed someone else – and did all the children have the same father anyway? William Henry was apparently always treated differently, but then he was the youngest, and apparently an older son named Samuel had died in infancy. And did Sandwich – if it were he – continue to visit his erstwhile mistress at Norfolk Street?

This Sandwich was the selfsame John Montagu who had kept another mistress: 'thy Nightingale', the singer Martha Reay – before she was murdered by Revd Hackman. And of course this is the story told by Herbert Croft in *Love and Madness*, from which William Henry Ireland learnt all about Chatterton. So: Chatterton, illegitimacy, and death suddenly reacted together at a defining moment for Ireland – an equation, if you like, that forgery is precisely a bloody bastard way of writing. This compound of psychological associations was shattering, and indeed Ireland seems to have had some sort of breakdown in the immediate aftermath of the Shakspeare fiasco. He never restored his relationship with his father, who now refused to own him at all. Hence, while Ireland's *Confessions* is, like his first stab at coming clean (*An Authentic Account*, 1796), a trauma-riddled attempt to bestow a genealogy and therefore a legitimacy on the Shakspeare papers, it is also an attempted legitimation of Ireland himself: a self-validation to counter the threat, and perhaps the ensuing desire, that he is illegitimate, without a story of his own cause and effect, except as a felon. If the death of Chatterton ensured that he evanesced into a daemon, taking forgery into the ether of the imagination, Ireland, the forger who lived on, became, like his writing, illegitimate. Yet maybe this was also a liberation: Ireland was untrammelled, could now lead not one life but several, and so was strangely original.

All this may have been in Ireland's mind when he wrote three poems on his base condition, published in his collection *Rhapsodies* (1803). He magnificently vindicates himself, describing the eponymous Bastard as

---

* It also incidentally proves that William Henry Ireland was born on 2 August 1775, making him nineteen years old at the publication of the Shakspeare papers – two years older than he would claim throughout the rest of his life.

> A child of chance – a being uncontroll'd,
> A glowing creature form'd in passion's mould;
> Whose soul unshackled soars above mankind,
> And leaves the world and all its cares behind:
> Thou mind of fire upon creation hurl'd!
> Thou sun amid the children of the world!
> Thou noon-tide blaze, whose all-absorbing light
> Astounds of lineal men the drowsy sight!
> Thou mortal with immortal thoughts inspir'd,
> With energy akin to madness fir'd!

There is a wild ambition here to be super-original, singular, wholly authentic, and inspired by virtue of an accident of birth. But ironically, Ireland seems less possessed by genius and more by what one might call *savagery*:

> Blest be the *Bastard*'s birth! through wondr'ous ways,
> He shines eccentric like a Comet's blaze.
> No sickly fruit of faint compliance he;
> He! stampt in nature's mint of extasy! . . .
> He, kindling from within, requires no flame;
> He glories in a *Bastard*'s glowing name.

These lines are from another poem called 'The Bastard', written by Richard Savage and published seventy-five years earlier in 1728. This one believed himself to be the bastard offspring of Lady Macclesfield and the 4th Earl Rivers. Ireland is not exactly plagiarizing – and he does not lay any explicit claim on Montagu – but he is certainly engaged in a spirited imitation of these sentiments of originality: ventriloquizing, reiterating, repeating Savage.

Ireland's next, 'The Bastard's Complaint', is less exulting. The Bastard is now 'Dejected, helpless, wretched, and forlorn' – rejected, solitary, and haunted – and the poem ends with a threat to commit suicide. But this is merely an interlude and the ensuing 'Reply to the Bastard's Complaint' recalls the former Savage strain of inspiration:

> Thou hast no fetter to enchain the soul,
> 'Tis godlike will each action must control;
> 'Tis to be more than mortal, more refin'd,
> To be in form the man, the God in mind.
> Arouse the dormant feelings of thy breast,

> In every action stand thyself confess'd;
> Mar not the will supreme, but lustrous shine,
> Prove thyself foster'd by a God Divine.

Ireland equates genius with freedom, and desires to escape the gravity of literary influence, inheritance, and pedigree.

> Born to himself, by no possession led,
> In freedom foster'd, and by fortune fed;
> Nor Guides, nor Rules, his sov'reign choice controul,
> His body independent, as his soul.
> Loos'd to the world's wide range – enjoyn'd no aim;
> Prescrib'd no duty, and assign'd no Name:
> Nature's unbounded son, he stands alone,
> His heart unbiass'd, and his mind his own.

As Richard Savage put it.

An obvious point about this relationship with Savage is that it questions Ireland's insistence on his professed inspiration, Thomas Chatterton. Ireland's reliance on Savage is a poetic innovation, identifying a radical tradition of illegitimate writing in which forms of authenticity and inauthenticity are twisted together with issues of life and work – a tradition that incorporates Chatterton too, and Ireland.* In Samuel Johnson's *Life of Savage*, arguably the first English literary biography, far more compelling than his work is Richard Savage's life – the thrilling tale of a dispossessed aristocratic poet, a neglected genius who 'unfortunately killed a man in a drunken frolic', as Ireland once put it. Johnson is determined to investigate whether the fraudulence of Savage's writing can be a way of judging the morality of his life.

There is also a general sense in which an endemic concern with legitimacy and posterity can be identified among eighteenth-century literary forgers and forgeries. Macpherson refused to accept the gift of his old clan estates because it would have perverted clan laws of succession; he sired five bastards, but Ossian has lost his son – and indeed, his entire race; the land is evacuated of history and myth, and lineage and inheritance are halted. Boswell compared Ossian to a

---

* Hazlitt remarks in his *Conversations of James Northcote*, that 'Savage, in my mind, was one of those writers (like Chatterton) whose vices and misfortunes the world made a set-off to their genius, because glad to connect those ideas together.'

bastard child.* Chatterton was a posthumous child, and Rowley is a celibate monk. Shakspeare's donation of various plays to a Renaissance chap called William henrye Irelande precipitated Samuel Ireland's disclosure to his son that he was not his son at all, but Shakespeare too had 'thatt Chylde . . . who muste nott be named here' – what might better be termed a *natural* offspring.

While it may be tempting to explain away some of Ireland's later extravagancies such as his bigamous marriages, as evidence of his psychological compensation for being illegitimate, his writing is actually in the tradition of a Savage–Chatterton plurality. In one dramatic dialogue he called them his 'two angels'. It is this multifariousness that enables Ireland to challenge emergent notions of authorship. The name of the author cannot function as a useful means of classification here, because Ireland used at least sixteen different pseudonyms throughout his writing life.† The name is not containing, separating, defining, identifying the text – instead, the writer is engaged in espionage against such authorial principles, either by habitually masking himself, or going about with no name at all.

Ireland's writing tends to go about all over the place. The *Confessions*, for example, is a text entirely out of joint, mixing Shakespeare, critical quotations, and his own poetry in a compendious confusion only consistent in its inconsistency. The range of his publication is equally erratic. He wrote *Mutius Scævola*, a Roman play in which Mutius thrusts his hand into a fire to prove his honour, and he edited a children's chapbook, *Youth's Polar Star or The Beacon of Science*. He composed 'Lines' on a balloon flight, 'Johannes Taurus, the Don Juan of England by Byronus Secundus',‡ and at the request of Princess Elizabeth, daughter of George III, he provided under the name of 'Cervantes' a pantomime for Frogmore Fete. He wrote *Gondez the Monk*, a celebrated Gothic novel of thirteenth-century Inquisitorial torture and execution, and attacked patriotism in *The State Doctors*. In *France for the Last Seven Years*, he wrote a history of the country interlaced with personal reminiscences, satires and street songs, and

* 'The *Filiation* of a literary performance is difficult of proof; seldom is there any witness present at its birth.'
† Such as 'Paul Persius', 'Henry Boyle', 'Charles Clifford', 'Flagellator', 'Satiricus Sculptor, Esq.', 'Anser-Pen-Drag-On, Esq.', and 'Baron Karlo Excellmanns' – perhaps like Pessoa these are better described as heteronyms.
‡ Byron had reviewed Ireland's *Neglected Genius*.

society conversation, and as 'Henry Boyle', editor of *The Universal Chronologist* (a history of the eighteenth century), he suggested that the performance of *Vortigern* 'caused the greatest ferment in the world of literature'. As 'Anser Pen-Drag-On, Esq.' he satirized Robert Southey, Robert Burns, Walter Scott, Lord Byron, Samuel Taylor Coleridge, and William Wordsworth in *Scribbleomania* (he also included himself, as Ireland, for good measure), and, in a similar compendium of folly, *Stultifera Navis* (*The Modern Ship of Fools*), he described everyone from 'Venal Fools' to 'Fools who do not understand a Game, and yet will play', and ultimately 'The Folly of all the World'. He translated Voltaire's *La Pucelle d'Orléans* into English verse (at the end of the century this was edited and revised by Ernest Dowson), and as 'Satiricus Sculptor' in *Chalcographimania* he charted 'Infatuations of Every Description', taking a cross-section of print-selling and connoisseurship. This panorama runs from pornography to 'Nicknackatarian Mania':

> Samples we have of some, whose hopes
> Concentrate in the *hangman's* ropes:
> One rusty *armour* buys amain,
> Or painted window's shatter'd pane;
> The skins of birds, of beasts, and fishes,
> Cups, saucers, tea-pots, old Delft dishes.

Every collector, from the erotic print hoarder to the archivist of the gallows, was footnoted – including his own Hogarthian father, and himself again:

> That *Ir–l–nd*, fam'd for picturesque,
> And fond of *Hogarth's* keen burlesque . . .
> To parent now the *son* let's add,
> Of ancient lore, *impostor lad.* . . .

Evidently Ireland moonlighted as his own gang of Boswells, adding one version of himself as the Shakspeare forger to the satires and histories he penned in other names, as other people. But Ireland was not even his real identity – just the monicker of the Shakspeare forger, only about a twentieth of his eventual identity. Ireland's is a defeatist form of egotism. He dissolves himself as an author-function just at the moment at which the Wordsworthian figure of 'the Poet' was beginning to dominate Romantic models of authorship and confer proprietorial rights. Henceforth, the author was increasingly defined as a legal entity. What authorship Ireland claimed for himself was irrepressibly illegal.

It is supposedly the repetition of the self, whether in law or psychiatry or artistic composition, that makes the self legal, sane, and authentic: in signatures and lineage, personality function, style, and so forth, although the *perfect* copy is considered counterfeit in the case of the signature, a monstrous clone in the case of breeding, in psychiatry neurosis and dementia, or in literature plagiarism. Ireland was a man of repetitions, but the wrong sort of repetition – not of his self, but of an other: 'the *second* Chatterton', or '*Shakspeare* Ireland', he was nicknamed 'Sam' after a dead older brother and after his stepfather, he effectively copied out *Lear* and parts of *Hamlet*, he wrote his autobiography twice. In contrast, in the breadth of his writing and the catalogue of his names, he only rarely maintains any coherency across more than a few works. This might be deemed illegal, insane, inauthentic, unliterary, and indeed unselfish, but in bastardy, repetition becomes a particularly hectic anxiety: what is being repeated? Where can the original, the patriarch, the pedigree ever be? If he was not going to fall prey to the same cultural logic that made his illegitimate writing a forgery, Ireland needed to reinvent his bastard self perpetually through a succession of names and writing identities. This was not a conservative and fairy-tale wish to discover himself a nobleman, but rather a revolutionary creative force that could repudiate history and inheritance. Indeed, in the context of the revolution in France, the bastard might be seen as a post-apocalyptic model of creativity and radical cultural succession. That said, it will still come as a surprise to learn that Ireland once served as Napoleon Bonaparte's librarian.

Ireland's forgery of Shakespeare had a sense of inevitability about it. There was a secular cult of bardolatry at the theatre supported by pageants and jubilees, the thriving trade in relics, and a dynasty of multi-volume complete works. Shakespeare was the National Poet forming the national character and the national literature, and yet, like so many of the orphans who might bear his name, he had passed without leaving much physical trace. John Heminges and Henry Condell had published the 'First Folio' of Shakespeare's Plays in 1623, 'Published according to the True Originall Copies', but none of those true original copies had survived. And despite almost incessant references to manuscripts, signatures, deeds, documents, letters, and forgeries in his plays, there was very little remaining physical evidence of the Bard: no extant literary manuscripts, and only a handful of verifiable signatures; his theatres and houses had disappeared, and even the mulberry tree had been chopped down. Shakespeare seemed oddly intangible.

For both Malone and Ireland, the hand Shakespeare offered was predominantly a legal quantity: a way to recognize, greet, and *have* Shakespeare – a way of taking possession, legal possession, of him. But from the outset, Ireland was also aware of the mystery that breathed through Shakespeare's work, and he identified this as a supernatural dimension of possession, a dim daemonism. Some years later, Ireland did describe his forgery commencing at the moment 'the demon seized his opportunity to place temptation in my way'. Indeed, possession in Ireland is a hapless form of inspiration in which he becomes the mere instrument of the imagination of another, more powerful – and angelic – poet, be it Shakespeare, Chatterton, or Savage. And as if under pursuit, Ireland ultimately became a wanderer, incapable – perhaps rightly so – of locating a singular poetic voice. His multifarious but almost invisible post-Shakspearean career is a campaign of irregular skirmishes against hegemonic models of identity and authenticity, which he saw as based on the fictions of the law. Throughout the nineteenth century, the assumption that literary forgery was a crime was gradually internalized, generally unexamined, and became purely ideological; routinely advocated by such influential writers as Charles Dickens, as will become evident.

In the same way, then, that the impulse to possess a materialized Shakespeare drew attention to his persistent ghostliness, the Ireland papers, once shown to be forged, became another profound reminder of Shakespeare's shadowiness. How could one grasp the wraith? Again, by repositioning the 'author function' in a different discourse, one that made a virtue of ghostliness. Shakespeare shifts from being the subject of eighteenth-century legal scrutiny seeking to authenticate and verify the life and works by physical evidence, to becoming the negatively capable Bard of the Romantics. So, much as the daemon Chatterton haunts Romanticism, the spectre Shakespeare – through the forgeries of Ireland – is there also, reinscribed in possession and imagination. Less an empirical entity captured in the meticulous multi-volume editions that culminated in James Boswell the younger's edition of

1821, than the 'myriad-minded' genius half-glimpsed by Coleridge. Shakespeare becomes less tangible, a gone 'Shakspeare' at the edges of fiction and legitimacy. This Shakespeare, a Shakespeare who writes insistently on forgery, is thereby fully forged.

VII. NO ONE

The one duty we owe to history is to rewrite it.

Oscar Wilde, 'The Critic as Artist'

Lex est quodcumque notarius

Notarial motto*

What is your substance, whereof are you made,
That millions of strange shadows on you tend?

William Shakespeare, Sonnet 53

On 27 June 1837, Charles Dickens visited the Newgate prison with John Forster (his eventual biographer), his illustrator 'Phiz' (Hablot Browne), and the actor William Macready. As he had done throughout his life, he was compiling notes on the inmates and the conditions of the gaol, researching. One aristocratic prisoner awaiting transportation seemed rudely familiar. His grey eyes were more accustomed to poring over exquisitely cut gemstones and fine ink etchings than staring at the dead walls of a prison ward; his small, white hands, softened by the pelts of purring cats, were becoming engrimed. Still, the other prisoners treated him with respect, as a gentleman.

'My God! There's Wainewright!'

In the words of John Forster:

In the shabby-genteel creature, with sandy hair and dirty moustache, who had turned quickly round with a defiant stare at

---

* 'Whatsoever we write is the Law.'

our entrance, looking at once mean and fierce, and quite capable
of the cowardly murders he had committed, Macready had been
horrified to recognize a man familiarly known to him in former
years, and at whose table he had dined.

The chance meeting inspired Dickens to use Wainewright as the model
for Jonas Chuzzlewit (1843–4), as the villain Rigaud alias Blandois alias
Lagnier in *Little Dorrit* (1855–7), as the poisoner Mr Julius Slinkton in
the short story 'Hunted Down' (1859), and for elements of Magwitch
in *Great Expectations* (1860–1).* He also published Walter Thornbury's
short biography of Wainewright too (*All the Year Round*, 1867).

But Thomas Griffiths Wainewright was a man of so many lives:
some are fictions composed by himself, others were mythologizations
imagined by others like De Quincey and Dickens. He was an art critic,
a poisoner, and a con-artist; a lion in sheep's clothing who dined
with the Lambs Charles and Mary, murdered his kinfolk, and was
transported for forgery. As a writer, a painter, and a connoisseur he
demonstrates the internalization of the forged self through multiple
pen names, lives, and crimes.

Dickens was haunted by Wainewright, but Wainewright was
haunted and hunted by himself – by his dead selves. Just as Thomas
Chatterton lived beyond his own mortality in a series of myths and
ghostly appearances, so did the multiple personality Wainewright. But
there are crucial differences. Wainewright was not so much daemonized
as demonized. He provided a template for the evil genius, a fiendish
inspiration for a literature increasingly coming into conflict with moral
responsibility and legal dogma. Wainewright snakes through the work
of Dickens as a theatrical baddie, as a shorthand for wickedness,
although his contemporaries were not so morally erect. In *Lucretia;
or, The Children of Night* (1846), Edward Bulwer Lytton claims that
Wainewright is incorporated straight into the plot of his novel as the
horribly evil Gabriel Varney, to which end Bulwer Lytton had obtained
Wainewright's own papers. But such 'Newgate Novels' were heavily
criticized for glamorizing criminals and crimes, and in his afterword
to the 1853 edition, Bulwer Lytton was prompted to quote the Neoplatonist Proclus in his defence:

* Dickens accepted the enormous, record-breaking advance of £1,000 for 'Hunted
Down' while he was working on *Great Expectations*.

whatever is tragical, monstrous, and out of the common cause of nature in poetical fictions, excites the hearers in all imaginable ways to the investigation of the truth, attracts us to recondite knowledge, and does not suffer us through apparent probability to rest satisfied with superficial conceptions, but compels us to penetrate into the interior parts of fables, to explore the obscure intention of their authors.

There is the shadow of daemonism here – a notion that studying paragons of wickedness may reveal psychological mechanisms.

This fascination with evil becomes more decadent as the century falls away. Oscar Wilde specifically took the amphibian Wainewright as the prototype of the dandy aesthete and the genius of a diabolical and seductive version of 'art for art's sake'. The poet laureate Andrew Motion was unable to resist writing his biography of Wainewright as a mendacious first-person confession; and Wainewright is even there haunting *The Blue Suit*, the auto-fiction of novelist, book thief, credit fraudster, and burglar, Richard Rayner. In all three, the supernatural Romanticism of the daemonic sublime has been replaced by a seductive self-destructiveness, in which identity is moulded from the legal puzzles that try to define identity, forgery, and possession – perhaps as masking, lying, and stealing. Wilde's prototype of this amoral artist draws on the dynasty of Macpherson, Chatterton, Ireland, and Wainewright. In other words, the aesthete is modelled on the forger.

So the otherworldly and inspirational quality of the forger shifts decisively in the nineteenth century to a predominantly legal issue of fraud, dealt with in material and bodily ways of incarceration and transportation. Money becomes the defining object: one of Bulwer Lytton's declared intentions was to depict 'the influences of money upon modern civilization'. Wainewright is a transitional figure here: a shape-shifter, but also a felon. Art, forgery, and crime dovetail. The legal implications of literary composition, criticism, and reception introduced in the 1790s in the debate over William Henry Ireland's forged Shakspeare papers become fixed values in the nineteenth century, locking together literature, authenticity, and authorship. As Oscar Wilde would himself learn, writers could now be charged in the dock for writing the wrong sort of thing.

✦ ✦ ✦

WAINEWRIGHT

These are no men, but apparitions,
Ignes fatui, glowworms, fictions,
Meteors, rats of Nilus, fantasies,
Colosses, pictures, shades, resemblances.
Seest thou yon gallant in the sumptuous clothes,
How brisk, how spruce, how gorgeously he shows?
Note his French herring-bones: but note no more,
Unless thou spy his fair appendant whore.

John Marston, 'Cynic Satire', in *The Scourge of Villainy*

It was actually quite a feat for Macready to have recognized Wainewright after so many years and under such unexpected conditions. He
had grown a beard in the interim, but clearly there was something
about his physique or demeanour that picked him out. 'He seemed a
somebody – not a somebody of conventional rank, but a somebody
of personal individuality – an artist perhaps, a poet, or a soldier in
some foreign service, but certainly a man whose name you would
expect to have heard of.'* Perhaps his 'huge head . . . and square solid
jaw', perhaps his hair curled and parted down the middle – Thornbury
suggests he had it curled every morning, and Julius Slinkton has
oppressively centre-parted hair. His hair had been blond, but he usually
dyed it black – like Rigaud's in *Little Dorrit* – presenting a foppish
appearance. Indeed, Barry Cornwall presents a very pretty picture of
his erstwhile friend: 'absolutely a fop, finikin in dress, with mincing
steps, and tremulous words, with his hair curled and full of unguents
and his cheeks painted like those of a frivolous demirep'.† Cornwall goes on to describe him as 'thoroughly effeminate', were it not
for his 'thick and sensual lips'. . . . According to the prison description of Wainewright in Tasmania, he was only 5ft 5½in, with brown
hair and grey eyes; Cornwall called him 'short and rather fat, with a

---

* Bulwer Lytton on Gabriel Varney.
† Barry Cornwall was the pen name of Bryan Waller Procter.

fidgety, nervous manner and sparkling twinkling eyes, that did not readily disclose their meaning'. Hazlitt described Wainewright as dark haired and having an 'elegant lisp'; Cornwall, his voice sounded 'like a whisper, wanting in firmness and distinction'. He seems, as Charles Baudelaire said of the dandy, to have had 'a facial expression of a very special kind', although Robert Crossland concludes from all this that Wainewright suffered from the dandy's pathological complaint of disseminated sclerosis!

Byron seems to have been entranced by Wainewright, purportedly saying to Lady Blessington that Wainewright 'was the first man I ever saw wear pale yellow-coloured gloves, and devilish well they looked'. He wore them with an exquisitely blue military coat 'all braided and befrogged down the front', as Thornbury later surmised. He was also fond of sensual pleasures, and was described by a contemporary as presenting himself 'with a sort of undress military air and the conversation of a smart, lively, clever, heartless, voluptuous coxcomb'. Hazlitt referred to Wainewright as a 'dandy scribbler' of the 'Dandy School', and De Quincey noted 'the dandyism which overspread the surface of his manner'. De Quincey thought him tawdry too: 'he was a *parvenu*, not at home even amongst his second-rate order', whereas Wilde judged him 'a true virtuoso, a subtle connoisseur' with 'that curious love of green'. John Clare, meanwhile, found Wainewright a 'very comical sort of chap':

> he is about twenty-seven & wears a quizzing-glass & makes an excuse for the ornament by complaining of bad eyes. . . . He is a very clever writer & some of his papers in the Magazine are very entertaining & some very good.

Thomas Griffiths Wainewright was a poseur and a shape-shifter; his portrait fizzes with artifice – and such features of trickery, confusion, and frippery pervade not only his writing, but also his shadowy life, his afterlife, and his reputation. As such, his character dissolves. It is marked only by deep duplicity and revision and play, a performance that glides across genres. One could say he lacked firm and distinctive character traits; or one could say he internalized and then played out the subtle contradictions of his artistry, and ultimately his life. He is dust shaped by others, into which a hollow puff of reputation is blown. Even Andrew Motion's *Wainewright the Poisoner* refuses Wainewright the dignity of a full-fig biography; like the others in this book, he is marginalized and fictionalized, too challenging to be fully accommodated. Although Wainewright's character was literally tried in the courts, being multifarious was considered no defence for breaking the law. Oscar Wilde was outraged at this example of the shifting – indeed shiftless – character of the artist being pinned down by inflexible legal definitions of identity: 'The permanence of personality is a very subtle metaphysical problem, and certainly the English law solves the question in an extremely rough-and-ready manner.' This would be proven to Wilde himself, to his own great disadvantage.

As far as any of these biographies are factual, Thomas Griffiths Wainewright was the maternal grandson of Ralph Griffiths, editor of the eighteenth-century journal the *Monthly Review* and publisher of John Cleland's erotic escapade *Memoirs of a Woman of Pleasure, by Fanny Hill* (1749). His mother died in childbirth, his father followed her shortly afterwards, and Thomas and two stepbrothers were brought up by a paternal uncle, Arnold Wainewright. The Wainewright clan tended towards the Unitarian Church, the Whig party, and the legal profession, but the young Wainewright showed an early aptitude at sketching and painting, was apprenticed to John Linnell and then, aged nineteen, to the portrait painter Thomas Phillips. He made friends of Henry Fuseli and John Flaxman, and painted Byron, before, in an apparent fit of listlessness, joining the 16th, or Bedfordshire, Regiment of Foot. Military life in County Cork and Portsmouth did not, however, suit his delicate sensibilities. Wainewright sold off his commission to return to the art world and the Royal Academy. He later claimed that it was the poetry of Wordsworth that had converted him from the life of a soldier – an indication of his precocious taste. So Wainewright returned to painting and ambitions to be a Royal Academician, and began writing idiosyncratic art criticism. He was published by the *London Magazine*, the dazzlingly fashionable monthly journal edited by John Scott – who was unfortunately shot on 16 February 1821 in a duel with a representative of the *London*'s arch-rival, *Blackwood's*.

Thomas Griffiths Wainewright assiduously cultivated the most discerning artistic sensibility of his generation, manifested as a colossal dandyism poised over the finest points of impeccable and voluptuous discrimination. He was one of the select few who read Keats and Shelley, and an early admirer and patron of 'our great Genius' Blake:

His Dante is the most wonderful emanation of imagination that
I have ever heard of. His fate is a national disgrace; while his
pious content is a national example[.] I have asked him to let me
have a coloured copy of the '*Songs of* Innocence' & ['] *The Marriage
of Heaven & Hell*'.

He wrote a tour de force Preface to an edition of Christopher Marlowe's
Hero and Leander (1820), and wild, witty, and splendidly erudite art
essays for the *London*, written under an elaborate variety of flamboyant
pseudonyms: 'Janus Weathercock', 'Cornelius Van Vinkbooms', 'Bevil
Seymour', one 'Senex', and possibly 'Egomet Bonmot'.* Contrary and
affected, he then referred to his artists by their real names, rather than
their titles: to him, Julio Romano was Julio Pippi, Paul Veronese was
Cagliari, Titian was Vecelli. Wainewright alternately crept and strutted,
like a cross between a chameleon and a peacock. Did the *London*'s
readership recognize these signatures as so many pranks of a single
author? One essay by 'Janus Weathercock' is shot through with a
sudden malice when he informs the reader that 'Cornelius Van Vinkbooms' 'now lies in Horsemonger jail under sentence of death for a
M. Antonio [*sic*] robbery in the British Museum!!' 'Weathercock',
however, finds it in his heart to excuse the theft, because 'Love of art
swayed him, not lucre'. Money, in the very act of denying its place in
the economy of taste, is admitted.

Wainewright had married Eliza Frances Ward in 1817. They
lived off the interest on her marriage settlement, and kept rooms in
Great Marlborough Street. He was fond of sparkling dinner parties,
entertaining the aforementioned Macready, as well as Charles Lamb,
Thomas Noon Talfourd, John Clare, and others. His rooms were
exquisite, fascinating. His taste ran from antiquarian objets d'art to
the bizarre and grotesque to intriguing natural curiosities: Ann
Boleyn's Book of Hours, a Norman prick-spur, 'A little ugly grinning
stone monster', pickled hummingbirds. He had a penchant for proof
impressions of botanical engravings, for classical intaglios and cut
gemstones, and for indulging the languorous tortoiseshell cats that
stretched over his deep rugs and rich couches and quizzically examined

---

* Wainewright has been considered responsible for the 'Bonmot' papers since W. C.
Hazlitt's edition (1880), but serious doubt has recently been cast on the attribution by
Marc Vaulbert de Chantilly.

the occasional watercolours he occasionally dashed off. With such élan, he was fast exhausting his fortune.

Wainewright ran out of money. This was in part due to his posing as a gentleman. He refused to accept payment for his *London* contributions, or to sign or sell his own pictures. Was this just an issue of gentility, or is there a sense that money, that all such character, is essentially counterfeit? Whatever the case, he became a forger not for any artistic satisfaction but purely for financial gain. He executed the simplest and most rewarding frauds. With the objective eye of a connoisseur blurring copies into originals, he took to faking engravings – not by reproducing them, but by exchanging authentication certificates:

> Mr Westall [later Queen Victoria's art tutor] and I [his 'friend' Barry Cornwall] found that he had recently contracted intimacies with some German art-students, and that he had been buying and dealing with scarce old prints and etchings to a great extent. Among these were some very costly engravings after Marc Antonio and Bonasoni, which he had purchased from Mr Dominic Colnaghi upon trust, and parted with by mortgage or sale immediately afterwards. Subsequently he purchased very cheap copies of the *same* prints, and placed these on the card-boards, which had large prices noted on them in Mr. Colnaghi's writing, and from which the expensive specimens had been removed. These he sold for various sums far exceeding their value.

It is provenance that sells these pictures: they are endorsed by a signature that is as good as gold.

Nevertheless, things still declined. Rather than declare himself bankrupt and witness the dispersal of his treasures, Wainewright executed a more audacious forgery. His money was frozen in annuities, invested so as to provide a comfortable – though by no means extravagant – annual interest. But on 15 July 1822 (less than a month after 'Janus Weathercock' had exulted over the fate of 'Cornelius Van Vinkbooms') Wainewright forged the signatures of his uncle Robert Wainewright, and cousins Edward Foss and Edward Smith. In doing so he released £2,250 of his money – and spent it. Such a forgery on the Bank of England still carried the death penalty; it was also, as Bulwer Lytton pointed out, 'an offence it was impossible to disprove'. Wainewright, however, treated the offence with nonchalant disparagement and on 17 May 1824 took the remaining £3,000 – and spent that as well. As it was, he proved to be so subtle and successful at the fine art of forgery that his crime was not even noticed for more than a decade. Yet it did not halt his collapse into catastrophic debt. From 1826, he began borrowing money at crippling rates; he could no longer afford to keep their rooms, and so Wainewright took his pregnant wife and moved in with another uncle, George Edward Griffiths, who had inherited both the editorship of the *Monthly Review* and Linden House, the mansion purchased by Ralph Griffiths.

Uncle George was dead within the year. He died intestate and Wainewright inherited everything – including the mansion – but he was now much worse off. He had a tiny estate, an expensive house to run, further debts, as well as a son to raise. The baby had portentously been born on the day that George Griffiths died, and there is an echo of William Henry Ireland here: Wainewright's 'friend' Barry Cornwall noted that the child Griffiths '(scandal whispered) was the son of a dissipated and impoverished peer'.* While Wainewright lived upon credit, he shared his unexpected windfall by inviting his mother-in-law, Mrs Abercromby, and his wife's two half-sisters, Helen Frances Phoebe and Madeleine Abercromby, to join his family at Linden House. On 22 August 1829, soon after their arrival, Mrs Abercromby died.

Things now become very dark. Wainewright began taking out a series of life policies on the hale and healthy Helen Frances Phoebe Abercromby, who reached the age of twenty-one on 12 March 1830. Her life was colossally insured: at The Palladium (£3,000 for three years), The Eagle (£3,000 for three years), The Imperial (£3,000 for two years), The Pelican (£5,000 for two years), The Hope (£2,000 for two years), and The Provident (£2,000 for two years – though this premium was never paid). And another £12,000 of insurance had been refused on the grounds of misrepresentation.† She had also written two wills, appointing Wainewright as the executor in both. The whole enterprise stank – Wainewright, already in dire need of money, had committed himself to paying premiums of over £220 for at least the

---

*   George Griffiths died on 16 January 1828; Griffiths Wainewright was baptized on 4 June.

†   The Globe (£5,000 for two years), The Alliance (£5,000 for two years), and The Eagle (another £2,000 for two years).

next two years for the dependent Helen Abercromby. It was an inordi-
nate amount. On the other hand, on Helen's demise he stood to make
£16,000 (some three-quarters of a million today). As it was, immediately after a trip to the theatre and a celebratory supper of oysters and
beer, Helen caught a cold, went into an amazing and agonizing decline,
was struck blind, and within a few days was dead.

Despite two sound autopsies, the insurers, after having compared
notes, refused to pay, and in order to establish a precedent for all of
his claims, Wainewright entered a suit against the Imperial in the
Court of Exchequer. But he was cripplingly in debt, hounded by
adverse gossip, and it was rumoured he might be tried for murder. In
October 1831, he moved to France under a false passport in the name
of 'Theodore G. Williams' – ostensibly to stall his creditors. Although
he had lost from the death of Uncle George and only made some £100
out of the demise of Mrs Abercromby, Wainewright's flight seemed to
pin further suspicion on him, while simultaneously removing it from
his abandoned wife, Eliza Frances, who may have been party to the
treatment of her half-sister. Wainewright's actions were evidently those
of a desperate man.

He now all but disappears. Wainewright's time in France is a
particularly murky passage in his life. Several things might have happened. Wainewright himself later claimed to have written a number
of studies, some of which must have dated from this time on his
travels:

> 'A Philosophical Theory of Design, as concerned with the *Loftier*
> Emotions, showing its deep action on Society, drawn from the
> Phidean-Greek and early Florentine Schools', (the result of
> 17 years study) illustrated with numerous plates executed with
> conscientious accuracy, in one vol. Atlas folio. 'An Aesthetic
> and Psychological Treatise on the *Beautiful*, or the Analogies of
> Imagination and Fancy, as existed in *Poesy, Verse, Painting, Sculp-
> ture, Music* or *Architecture*', to form four Vols folio; with a
> profusion of Engravings by the best Artists of Paris, Munich,
> Berlin and Wien. 'An Art Novel' in 3 vols. and a collection of
> Fantasie, Critical Sketches &c. selected partly from *Blackwood,
> the Foreign Review* & the *London Magazine*. All these were nearly
> ready for, *one* actually at press.

He lived in a lonely country house with an elderly Frenchman.

According to Barry Cornwall, he fell in love with a married woman in Calais, 'whom fear of detection or some other strong motive induced him to poison'. Her sister then fell in love with him. He was starving in Paris and pawned his shirt to pay for a stamp to send a begging letter to Cornwall: 'His letter exhibited great depression. He spoke of the crowds of gay and careless people – gamblers and prodigals and others, all of whom passed him by – whilst he was without a meal, without a single acquaintance, and not knowing where he could apply with the smallest chance for help.' He stayed with an English family from Norfolk in Boulogne, and insured his host's life for £5,000 at The Pelican, following which the poor man died. Wainewright consoled himself by seducing his daughter. Perhaps it was here that he was visited by the Forrester brothers, who were investigating the Bank of England forgery that had now been uncovered; they had a warrant for his arrest. He wandered, was arrested for going under a false name, and imprisoned for six months for the possession of *nux vomica*, the poison strychnine: according to Thornbury, 'a poison almost tasteless, difficult of discovery, and capable of almost infinite dilution'.*

Wainewright's case for the validity of his policies was tried in 1835. His former servants testified against him and it was clear to everyone, says Thornbury, that there had been foul play. Nevertheless, the jury was split. Wainewright ordered a retrial, they almost immediately found against him. The money was lost. In May 1837, he secretly returned to London – and was swiftly arrested for the Bank of England forgery he had committed fifteen years earlier. The *Morning Advertiser* carried the report of his arrest on 10 June 1837, *The Times* on Monday 12 June:

> MANSION HOUSE. – On Saturday a man of respectable appearance, named Thomas Griffiths Wainwright [*sic*], was brought up, charged with having used a power of attorney for the sale and transfer of 2,250*l.* in the stock of the New 4 per Cent. Annuities, standing in the names of Robert Wainwright, of Gray's inn, Edward Smith Foss, of Essex-street, Strand, and Edward Foss, of Bernard-street, Russell-square, with intent to defraud the Governor and Company of the Bank of England.

---

* Bulwer Lytton suggests he used an organic poison to deplete Helen's health (perhaps antimony) and then the lethal *aqua di Tufania* (Tufania water) – a colourless and tasteless liquid.

John and Daniel Forrester, the officers, have had a warrant against the prisoner since 1835, and having gone over to Bolougne after him at that time, but without being able to accomplish anything except the object of seeing him, were rather particular in their enquiries as to the probable time of his return to this country. On Friday evening Daniel Forrester having observed a female whom he knew to be a friend of the prisoner in the neighbourhood of Howland-street, cautiously looked about, followed her, and soon saw her joined by a person, whom, notwithstanding the addition of a large tuft of mustachios and beard, he knew to be the prisoner; he ran up, and tapping him smartly on the arm, said, 'Ah, Mr. Wainwright, how do you do? Who would have thought of seeing you here?' The prisoner started upon being thus addressed, and was what is called completely flummexed [sic], did not deny that he was the man, and was locked up in the Compter. He had about him a small dirk in a sheath, and appeared to be without money or friends.

Sir PETER LAURIE (who sat for the Lord Mayor) asked the prisoner what he was?

Prisoner. – I am nothing. I have been an independent gentleman, and had considerable property, and I was originally an officer in the 16th Foot.

Sir PETER LAURIE. – Have you been here long? I see you are described in the warrant as an artist.

Prisoner. – I am no artist. I belong to no trade or profession, and I have been in France these six or seven years. I arrived here about six weeks ago.

Mr. Freshfield, solicitor to the Bank of England, called witnesses to prove the case so far as to justify the Alderman in remanding the prisoner.

Mr. Jonas Rogers Woodford, a clerk in the Bank of England, produced the bank ledger, in which was kept the account of Robert Wainwright, Edward Smith Foss, and Edward Foss, from which it appeared that 5,000l. Navy Five per Cents. had been converted into the New 4 per Cent. Annuities on the 5th of July, 1822; that the amount in the Four per Cents. was 5,250; that on the 15th of July, 1822, 2,250l. of that sum had been transferred; and on the 17th of May, 1824, the remaining sum of 3,000 l. [Here the witness produced the transfer-papers, which were witnessed by a Mr. Catterton [*sic*], a clerk in the bank, since deceased, and on which appeared the signature, 'T. G. Wainwright.']

Mr. Edward Foss stated that he was one of the trustees of the stock described. His father, who was now dead, had been another, and Mr. Robert Wainwright was a third trustee. The signatures of witness and his father were forged.

Sir P. LAURIE. – Prisoner, do you wish to ask any questions?

Prisoner. – None at all at present; I am not yet steady in my head. I was arrested but yesterday, and have not had time to communicate with my friends.

Sir P. LAURIE. – The charge is a serious one; do you wish for time?

Prisoner. – I shall have to send to France for documents, and wish to be remanded.

Sir P. LAURIE. – You shall be remanded till the latter end of next week. Sir P. Laurie said he thought the Bank might prevent losses such as they had sustained in the present instance by writing to the joint trustees in all cases of transfer.

– Remanded.

This is a rich document. First, it confirms that the Forrester brothers had visited Wainewright in France once there was a warrant for his arrest. They clearly expected him to return, had established who were his contacts, and could even recognize him under a thick beard and moustache. He was of respectable appearance and they were gentlemanly in taking him.* There is a pathetic note in Wainewright being betrayed by a kiss (the lady vanishes – the same Mademoiselle whose sister or father he had poisoned?), and an almost hapless charm at being 'completely flummoxed' at his arrest. There is a dreadful desperation at his evident lack of money and friends, and his abject misery in the dock: 'I am nothing ... I am no artist. I belong to no trade or profession ... I am not yet steady in my head.'

There were actually five indictments against Wainewright; he managed to plea-bargain, pleading guilty to two charges, and thereby escape with his life and what he expected to be a lenient sentence.

* Barry Cornwall describes a slightly different, deferential greeting: 'Mr. Wainwright ... I have been looking after you for a considerable time.' When the forger and criminal mastermind 'Jim the Penman' was similarly taken a few years later, a Runner found him in a public House in Oxford Market, London, and introduced himself: 'Mr. Hopkins, I have been looking for you.'

The last forger had been hanged in 1829, and although the capital statute would be repealed later in the year, it was still active: Wainewright could technically go to the gallows. On 5 July 1837 he was sentenced to transportation for life to Van Diemen's Land (now Tasmania) for forging and uttering a Bank of England bill for £2,250. It was a ghastly fate, a far harsher punishment than he expected. But if the Bloody Code was only an incarnadine memory, the law was still savage – as Motion notes, Wainewright was transported in the company of one felon who had done no more than steal a hat.

It was while in Newgate that Wainewright was recognized by Macready, although that unrepentant villain, 'with a defiant stare at our entrance, looking at once mean and fierce', appears entirely at odds with the cowed creature here. He proliferates again into many different characters, dogged by myths and slanders. Wainewright was lionized by visitors to the Gate as a celebrity, and revered as a master criminal by fellow felons. The extent of his forgery grew in size and audacity, and there were still the stories of murder. Indeed, before he left, Wainewright was informally questioned by his insurance agents about the murder of Helen Abercromby. They upbraided him. He allegedly replied,

> Sir ... you city men enter on your speculations and take the chances of them. Some of your speculations succeed; some fail. Mine happen to have failed; yours happen to have succeeded; that is the difference, sir, between my visitor and me. But I will tell you one thing in which I have succeeded to the last. I have been determined through life to hold the position of a gentleman. *I have always done so.* I DO SO STILL. It is the custom of this place that each of the inmates of a cell shall take his morning's turn of sweeping it out. I occupy a cell with a bricklayer and a sweep. But, by God, they never offer me the broom!

This breathtaking example of frightful snobbery made a deep impression on Dickens, who rehearsed it in the first chapter of *Little Dorrit* to indicate the character of Rigaud Blandois: 'Have I ever done anything here? Ever touched the broom, or spread the mats, or rolled them up, or found the draughts, or collected the dominoes, or put my hand to any kind of work?'

In any case, Wainewright would not admit that he had done Helen in for the money; there appeared to be a better reason for killing her:

' "I scarcely know myself," replied he, with a yawn and a sneer, "unless it was that her legs were too thick." ' This scandalous remark also spread like wildfire – and seemed to run faster on 'thick ankles' than 'thick legs' – though its provenance is even less sound than the other anecdote. Indeed, it seems to have arisen from nowhere – a ghost to haunt the living, breathing, dying Wainewright. Disgusted, the insurance officers then seized his effects from France, which included his diary. Thornbury describes it as written with 'voluptuous cruelty and a loathsome exultation worthy of the diseased vanity of such a masterpiece of evil'; and this gorgeous testament of wickedness went through the hands of Bulwer Lytton before it disappeared. It appears to have been a chilling chronology of the decline and extinction of Helen Abercromby: a timetable for poisoning.

Wainewright was already being forged as a monster of depravity, combining Gothic terror with social horror: the sadism of the vampire with the suffocating self-absorption of the decadent. There is another Wainewright, however, unearthed by the scholar Marc Vaulbert de Chantilly, a Wainewright whom it is worth bearing in mind. This Wainewright wrote in desperation to the Home Office even as he was awaiting imminent deportation on the *Susan*. In return for a pardon, he was prepared to give 'a full account and revelation of the circum-stances connected with the sudden or somewhat sudden end of x x [i.e. Helen]', declaring 'I am ready & can point out the places where Medicines were procured &c &c'. He was also perhaps prepared to implicate his wife as well: 'My evidence will touch two Persons and the Warrants should be got at once to stop farther Proceedings in Equity', that is, pursuing claims on Helen's policies. But by now, Van Diemen's Land was clearly the best place for him. Although Waine-wright was merely a forger, he had effectively confessed to murder and was treated there with the severity reserved for a murderer: condemned to a chain gang. It was only much later that he won a reprieve, became a hospital orderly, and could practise his portraiture again.

Even in Van Diemen's Land, rumours were rife. Thornbury says (in 1867) that it is 'now well known' that he carried a supply of strychnine about with him, concealed in a hollowed-out Borgia-like signet ring, and a version of this ring is also described by Bulwer Lytton. He attempted murder twice with poison, once with a knife, and once with a sharpened file; he also threatened to return to England to murder his cousin Edward Foss, who had testified against him. He

made salacious remarks to women sitting for their portraits, and
even made one sitter scream by sharpening his pencil so ravenously.
He was a demon:

> There is a terrible story told of his savage malignity towards a
> fellow-patient in the hospital, a convict, against whom he bore
> a grudge. The man was in a state of collapse – his extremities were
> already growing cold. Death had him by the throat. Wainewright's
> snakish eyes kindled with unearthly fire. He saw at once the fatal
> sign. He stole softly as a cat to the man's pallet, and hissed in
> exultation into his dying ear:
>
> 'You are a dead man, you – In four-and-twenty hours your
> soul will be in hell, and my arms will be up to that (touching his
> elbow) in your body, dissecting you.'

Wainewright eventually died in 1847, an opium addict, his only friend
a supercilious cat, and in the words of Barry Cornwall, 'raving mad'.
Dead and buried. But again there is another Wainewright, in contrast
to this dastard: Wainewright the society painter who still refused to
sign his portraits, and whose good conduct record eventually won him
some freedoms, and eventually a pardon. It came in the same month
he succumbed to a fatal stroke.* From the Antipodean perspective,
he certainly succeeded in reinventing himself. In the Macmillan *Dictionary of Art*, Andrew Sayers gives Thomas Griffiths Wainewright the
following entry:

> Australian painter and writer of English birth . . . drawing of
> amorous couples in a landscape [in BM] . . . reminiscent of Fuseli,
> whom he described as 'the God of his worship.' . . . reputed to
> be a poisoner and embezzler . . . despite his convict status and
> poor health, he made an important contribution to the early art
> of Australia. He was, with Thomas Bock (1790–1855) the most
> skilful convict portrait draughtsman in Hobart in the mid-19th
> century. . . . His elegant elongation of his subjects and poised
> line owed much to the style of English portrait painters such
> as Thomas Lawrence, who was among the artists he most
> admired. . . .

Lest we forget, it was for forgery, not murder, or embezzlement

---

* He also supposedly made engravings of Henry Dowland's *Pickwick Papers*, and collaborated with Marcus Clarke in writing *For the Term of His Natural Life*.

for that matter, that Wainewright was transported.* Wainewright *sans* murder might perhaps still have been transported, but would he still have been so enthusiastically vilified, and with such a mixture of abhorrence and fascination; would he still have painted his diabolical portraits? It was Wainewright's reputation as a poisoner rather than a forger that so excited Thomas De Quincey, for instance, who had been invited to dinner with the man some years before. De Quincey had not been able to keep the appointment, much to his subsequent dismay, but remembered with ghoulish delight that he had indeed once sat down to dinner at the Lambs' with the ogre: 'Amongst all the company, all literary men, sat a murderer.' For De Quincey, this retrospective context becomes deliciously pregnant:

> if I had known this man for the murderer that even then he was, what sudden loss of interest, what sudden growth of another interest, would have changed the face of the scene! Trivial creature, that didst carry thy dreadful eye kindling with perpetual treasons – dreadful creature that didst carry thy trivial eye mantling with eternal levity, – over the sleeping surfaces of confiding household life, – oh, what a revolution for man wouldst thou have founded, had thy deep wickedness prospered!

It is as if Wainewright himself is poisonous, or amorally contagious. Barry Cornwall concludes his reminiscence with the warning: 'He was like one of those creatures, seemingly smooth and innocuous, whose natural secretions, when once excited, become fatal to those against whom they are accidentally directed.' But De Quincey's sinister desire for a 'revolution for man', led by the forger-poisoner Wainewright, deserves further consideration. He exemplifies the proposition, already argued by De Quincey, and subsequently by Jean-Paul Sartre, that murder is a fine art.

Some years earlier, Keats had written in response to Hazlitt's essay on *Coriolanus* to the George Keatses (February–May 1819) about power and aesthetic pleasure:

> Is it a paradox of my creating that 'one murder makes a villain millions a Hero!' or is it not true that here, as in other cases,

---

* Neither was it, as Wilde archly remarked, for 'his fatal influence on the prose of modern journalism'.

the enormity of the evil overpowers and makes a convert of the imagination by its very magnitude?

Keats believes that 'The language of poetry naturally falls in with the language of power' – an idea that fills the *Hyperion* poems like a sonorous daemonic purr. Hazlitt concludes his *Coriolanus* essay, 'We may depend upon it that what men delight to read in books, they will put into practice in reality', and this too reverberates through the nineteenth century: in the moral debate around the 'Newgate Novels', in Dickens's pragmatic sentimentality, and in the countercultural decadence of Art for Art's Sake and *fin de siècle* movements. Literature may have fatal consequences.

The Wainewright case also confirms that forgery – writing – is potentially more dangerous than murder – as noted above, it was impossible to dispute that the actual offence had occurred, and so Wainewright could not defend himself. Writing leaves a body of evidence much more legible than the faint traces of strychnine and morphine in a young girl's body. Moreover, William Carew Hazlitt, the first and so far only editor of Wainewright's works, was clearly troubled by a criminal succession that put forgery ahead of homicide: 'First came Forgery. Then followed Strychnine.' Forgery is the unnamed crime, and yet it is ultimately the crime that exposes Wainewright. The Wainewright case reaffirms the contagious criminality of forgery: Wainewright, who unites a trinity of writing, lying, and killing that challenges the distinction between the aesthetic and the criminal, is hunted down by a forgery he had committed a decade before. Writing fictions and poetry is a form of forgery, and forgery is always haunted by death: the self-destruction of a Chatterton, or the murder of a Wainewright. And yet at the same time, W. C. Hazlitt recognized that there was an excess that was not defined by either forgery or murder: 'Still, when all has been said, does not the man, like all such men, remain a sort of enigma and bewildering contradiction?' There remains a daemonic residue here. It is worth looking further at Wainewright's complications of the self and establishing how he shaped the typology of the forger in later literature.

JANUS

> Why does it disturb us that Don Quixote be a reader of
> the *Quixote* and Hamlet a spectator of *Hamlet*? . . . these
> inversions suggest that if the characters of a fictional work
> can be readers or spectators, we its readers or spectators, can
> be fictitious.
>
> Jorge Luis Borges, 'Partial Magic in the Quixote'

Wainewright popped onto the cultural scene in the *London Magazine*,
perhaps first in the bouncing persona of 'Egomet Bonmot', a supremely
egotistical nom de plume ('I myself, witticism'), who announced
himself with a consummate sense of his own personal worth: 'in a
word, Sir, I hereby pronounce myself to be, not one, but all mankind's
epitome.'

Or perhaps not. Long attributed to Wainewright, the 'Egomet
Bonmot' papers, including *'Some Passages' in the Life, &c. of Egomet
Bonmot, Esq. Edited by Mr. Mwaughmaim* [moi-même], *and now first
published by ME* (1825), are more likely to be the work of Edward
Gandy. Odd, that such a masterly display of self-obsession has helped
to write the myths of the wrong man. 'Bonmot', however, has an
extravagant faith in himself, justified by his sensitivity and susceptibil-
ity to the inspiration of dead poets and artists. They become manifest
as inspirational forces for current writing – although his account
of inspiration is presented so satirically that it does little to excuse or
explain his critical megalomania: 'dead things with inbreathed sense I
am able to pierce, and, by windy suspiration of oracular breath, pour
into any reader's mind the genuine characteristics of the great and
good of every kindred and nation under heaven.'

Whether 'Bonmot' was Wainewright or Gandy, this properly *inspirational* quality of good art becomes the touchstone of Wainewrightian
criticism. He styles the critic as an artist who takes the earlier artistic
conception of Longinan inspiration for a further creative flight. Hence
his brilliantly inventive reading of Correggio's *The Descent from the
Cross*:

This picture is truly of the spirit, spiritual. – Corregio's [*sic*] mind must have been full to saturation, of the honey-dew of Christianity, when he gave birth to this mysterious conception. – A holy love swims over the surface of the deep, dead sea of grief, in which every object is immerged, – like the floating mist-wreaths, with which Ossian clothes his ghosts. The women dissolve in the very '*luxury of woe*'.

The references here are significant: 'the honey-dew of Christianity' is clearly an allusion to Samuel Taylor Coleridge's 'Kubla Khan', and an attempt either to Neoplatonize a Catholic painting or to Christianize that suggestively Neoplatonic meditation on divine creation. Likewise, the reference to Ossian is not simply a reminder of the antiquity of those supposed third-century epics, but also an invocation of the intangible vatic momentum of Ossian's muse. Wainewright is mystifying the work of the literary commentator as a form of inspired *sprezzatura*. Criticism is not just craft; it has pretensions to art.

It is also crucial that this essay appears under the name 'Janus Weathercock': we have already moved on from 'all mankind's epitome', 'Egomet Bonmot' – if indeed we ever started there. 'Weathercock' is a gourmet and a connoisseur; he has sensitive skin; he takes the reader on an objet-by-artefact tour of his private rooms:

Fancy, comfortable reader! Imprimis, A very good sized room. Item. A gay Brussel's carpet, covered with garlands of flowers. Item. A fine *original* cast of the Venus de Medicis. Item. Some choice volumes in still more choice old French *maroquin*, with water-tabby-silk linings! Item. Some more vols. coated by the skill of Roger Payne, and '*our* Charles Lewis.'* Item. A piano, by Tomkisson. Item. A Damascus sabre. Item. One cat. Item. A large Newfoundland dog, friendly to the cat. Item. A few hot-house plants on a white-marble slab. Item. A delicious, melting love painting, by Fuseli: – and last, not least in our dear love, *we*, myself, Janus!

'*We*, myself, Janus': this Wainewright–Weathercock composite character mixes fact and fiction in an attempt to materialize taste: he

---

* Barry Cornwall remembered that 'he had two or three old books on poisons. These were richly bound (by Roger Payne).' Vaulbert de Chantilly has found no evidence that such volumes were in Wainewright's library.

needs things to lavish his critical temperament upon, he celebrates consumption for consumption's sake. Or rather he infuses the commodities of the connoisseur with spirit, with life, with authenticity. Wainewright–Weathercock also, as Oscar Wilde admired and recognized, developed his essays into consumer manifestoes for readers of the *London* – 'he never lost sight of the importance of reproductions of the greatest masterpieces of the past, and all that he says about the value of plaster casts is quite admirable.' He fizzed with advice: what exactly is art? how and where do you purchase it? what are the best strategies for filling a cabinet with the choicest etchings? meanwhile, here are the top ten Royal Academy pictures.

Wainewright's own taste was for the freshest proof engravings on heavy paper: copies masquerading as originals. For him these were not mechanical facsimiles at all; they have a midnight artistry all of their own. He was particularly fond of the work of Marcantonio Raimondi, the engraver of such nightmare fantasies as *Raphael's Dream*, and Raimondi is in fact known only for his engravings. These tend to be after other artists, but in cases such as *Raphael's Dream* the original is missing, and so they are ghost prints – shadows of images lost, or never even recorded. Wainewright had a taste too for the erotic, such as Fuseli's 'delicious, melting love painting' inventoried above. He painted such amorous scenes himself, in which, as Charles Noon Talfourd enticingly put it, 'the voluptuous trembled on the borders of the indelicate'.

'Janus Weathercock' is alive as a critic because he is inspired by the finest arts. Yet this is at the expense of Wainewright's own identity; Wainewright wanes, becomes intangible, because he is articulated and mediated through the art, craft, and criticism of others: painters, engravers, and 'Weathercock'. His very name is in doubt. When he signs – whether for the *London Magazine* or for the Bank of England – he is not simply producing a written and repeatable sign of simultaneous presence and absence, but something much more elusive. So the signature, the seal of the critic, like the art that moves the spirit and the spirit that moves the pen, begins to disappear: it becomes ghostly. And it is precisely such ghostliness that diffuses Wainewright's readings, for example of Correggio's *Descent from the Cross*. 'Kubla Khan' conjures the daemonic imagination, Ossian catches misty presences which float only on the Highland breeze, but 'Janus Weathercock' is patently an imaginary signature that looks both hither and thither and shows which way the wind is presently blowing.

In other words, as a signature, 'Janus Weathercock' does not authenticate a work with a physical presence, but rather leaves the writing open and unfinished for further interpretation. Seán Burke argues that 'The primary ethical function of the signature [is] to set up a structure of resummons whereby the author may be recalled to his or her text. As with the legal signature, the textual mark is addressed to the future; to mortality and to the afterlife of the written sign'.* But a *fictional* signature either leaves any 'structure of resummons' empty and evacuated of presence, or commits a forgery. If this fictional self is performed on a legal document, it becomes an ultra-remunerative way of writing: half a dozen words, a couple of signatures, can release thousands of pounds. What is characteristic about Wainewright's forgery, then, is its consistency with his artistic method. Similarly, his murder, at least of Helen, was conducted with the precision and craft of a painting: mixing poisons as one might grind pigment, gradually executing the subject, and effacing the means of production in the very moment of completion. In Romantic aesthetics, such crimes are moments of transcendence.

Such a character-critic is also what Keats said of the 'poetical Character' – that it is 'every thing and nothing' – and Wainewright indeed aims at every thing and nothing, both through his Shandyan self-infatuation and his hallucinatory art criticism. 'Weathercock' writes on deadlines, for instance:

> I felt my vigorous personal identity instantly annihilated, and resolved, by some mystic process, into a part of that unimaginable plurality in unity, wherewithal Editors, Reviewers, and, at present, pretty commonly Authors, clothe themselves, when, seated on the topmost tip of their top-gallant masts, they pour forth their oracular dicta on the groaning ocean of London spread out huge at their feet.

---

* Jacques Derrida says in 'Signature, Event, Context': 'To write is to produce a mark that will constitute a kind of machine that is in turn productive, that my future disappearance in principle will not prevent from functioning and from yielding, and yielding itself to, reading and rewriting. . . . For the written to be written, it must continue to "act" and to be legible even if what is called the author of the writing no longer answers for what he has written.'

His critical picaresque, 'Janus's Jumble', is an eccentrically self-obsessed catalogue of fictional selfhood, while his essay 'The Academy of Taste for Grown Gentlemen, or the Infant Connoisseur's Go-Cart' takes two epigraphs from *Tristram Shandy* before careering off on another imaginative roller-coaster. There are also closer sources than Sterne to hand. William Henry Ireland, himself an expert on engravings and fine bindings, had published *Chalcographimania; or, the Portrait-Collector and Printseller's Chronicle* in 1814. It is impossible to imagine a waspish gossip like Wainewright being ignorant of this satire on the world of London print collecting, especially as he probably compiled the lists of artists and print shops in London for Leigh Hunt's *Literary Pocket Book* of 1819. *Chalcographimania* mentions friends of Wainewright's such as Flaxman, Fuseli, and Francis Douce, and the giddy, hare-brained style would have appealed to him.

While 'Weathercock', of whom we have a complete inventory of furnishings and even the delights of his 'favourite tortoiseshell cat stroked into a full and sonorous *purr*', is Wainewright's most developed persona or mask; this entails that he is simultaneously the persona who is most comprehensively obliterated by his critical method. Wainewrightian criticism is about the extinction of the self in the face of great art – despite this sacrifice of identity being at one level merely ironic when one remembers that Wainewright always writes through fictional voices, begging the question whether the effect of art can be measured against the calibrated annihilation of a forged or pseudo-self.

The most notable example of this is 'Weathercock' on Rembrandt's engraving of the Crucifixion, 'this fearful exhalation (we cannot call it *print*) of Rembrandt's brain'. Wainewright's technique is a precursor of that used by Walter Pater for his reading of Leonardo's *La Gioconda* (the Mona Lisa) in *The Renaissance* (1873), a seminal piece of aesthetic criticism that Wilde quotes at length in 'The Critic as Artist' (and which Evelyn Waugh echoes again in *Scott-King's Modern Europe*). Wilde quotes the following passage from Wainewright as extensively in his essay 'Pen, Pencil and Poison', except in this case, it is not Wainewright (or indeed Pater), but 'Janus Weathercock' who is supposedly writing:

> Darkness – sooty portentous darkness – shrouds the whole scene;
> only above the accursed wood, as if through a horrid rift in
> the murky ceiling, a rainy deluge, 'sleety-flaw, discoloured water'

streams down amain, spreading a griesly spectral light, even more horrible than that palpable night. Already the Earth pants thick, and fast! The darkened Cross trembles! The winds are dropt – The air is stagnant – A muttering rumble growls underneath their feet, and some of that miserable crowd begin to fly down the hill. The horses snuff the coming terrors, and become unmanageable through fear. . . .

His head sinks, and the Sacred Corpse 'swings senseless of the Cross.' – A sheet of vermillion flame shoots sheer through the air, and vanishes: the rocks of Carmel, and Lebanon cleave asunder; the sea rolls on high from the sands its black weltering waves. Earth yawns, and the graves give up their dwellers. The dead and the living are mingled together in unnatural conjunction, and hurry through the Holy City. New Prodigies await them there – . . .

Rembrandt never *painted* this sketch; and he was quite right. It might have delighted the cold connoisseur, and have brought 3000 guineas at Christie's; but to the accomplished Artist and Poet (such a man as Fuseli for instance), it would have lost nearly all its charms, in losing that perplexing veil of indistinctness which affords such ample range wherein the doubting imagination may speculate. – – At present it is like a thing from another world. A dark gulf is betwixt us. – – – It is not tangible by the body. We can only approach it in spirit.

Again we have 'Kubla Khan', which comes at moments of crisis in Wainewright's work; again there is a ghostly imaginative scene, dark and murky, and an alarming mix of the living and dead, a metaphor for his citations, forged selves, and commune with Rembrandt; and again Wainewright stresses the intangibility of the engraved vision which is elevated to the level of revelation: 'it is like a thing from another world'. The etching has, in a real Blakean sense, an aura of mysticism. And by *not* being himself, Wainewright-as-Weathercock is submerged in empathy and has intensified the individual's engagement with art. Or, to put it another way, Wainewright's use of forged personas poses the same sort of ethical and critical problems as opium does: it collapses authentic identity into intensified imaginative experience. Opium is, as De Quincey claims in *Confessions of an English Opium Eater*, which first appeared in the *London* alongside

Wainewright's work, a perfect counterfeit of the self; opium is, as
Coleridge called it, the 'avenging Dæmon'.

To go from the sublime to the ridiculous, we may return to 'Egomet
Bonmot', who describes himself, whoever he might be (certainly, for
a time, Wainewright), in the third person, thus:

> he is *the* strangest melody, *the* maddest wag it was ever our fate
> to cope withal! It is not known in what a variety of shapes he has
> been figuring away through our pages . . . one revolving hour
> shall find him critic, fidler, poet, and buffoon. *He cannot last
> long.* . . . Who can be wise, frolicsome, temperate, furious, tragical,
> comical, helter skelter – one thing down and another come on,
> – in a moment, without damage? No man! And yet such is
> Bonmot.

'No man!' here is significant. It looks forward obliquely to Wainewright's weary abnegation of himself, 'I am nothing'. He seems to have
turned naming, or nomocentricity, into nemo-centricity, making a
virtue of the nameless: to have too many characters is to have none
at all. Wainewright's condition is echoed by Roland Barthes in his
'autobiography', *Roland Barthes par Roland Barthes*. The narrator speaks
from all places, all persons – first, second, third – and therefore in no
person: '*no one – personne*, as we say in French'. So Wainewright
is simply, spectacularly, meticulously growing weary of the inherent
fictionality of writing and of the writer. Even in private journals or
diaries every phrase risks being inauthentic – not only because it might
be insincere, but because at best it is only simulating the sincerity of
the idea of a phrase in a journal. Barthes again:

> for every emotion being a copy of the same emotion one has read
> somewhere, to report a mood in the coded language of the
> Collection of Moods is to copy a copy: even if the text was
> 'original,' it would already be a copy; all the more so if it is
> familiar, worn, threadbare: 'The writer, by his pains, those dragons
> he has fondled, or by a certain vivacity, must set himself up, in
> the text, as a witty histrion' (Mallarmé). What a paradox! By
> choosing the most 'direct,' the most 'spontaneous' form of writing,
> I find myself to be the clumsiest of ham actors.

And yet there is perhaps a fleeting, evanescent authenticity in Wainewright, a glimmer of transcendence emerging from his recognition of

the fictional condition, a justification for his studied frivolity. 'Janus' describes it thus: 'Those niceties and particularities of narration which are to be found in myself – and all other authors of value and credibility, are the tests, the witnesses, the vouchers, for the authenticity of the tale – for every tale is or ought to be (after a fashion) historically true. . . .'

NEMO

'Friends, Noman is murdering me by craft, not by force'

Polyphemus's blind lament, *The Odyssey*

If we now turn towards an avowedly fictional work, Charles Dickens's *Bleak House* (1852–3), we find many of the same themes and images that seem characteristic of the writing of Thomas Griffiths Waine-wright. While Joep Leerssen, for instance, has already indicated the Ossianic nature of the opening of *Great Expectations*, the point can be much more powerfully made for the opening of *Bleak House*.

> Fog everywhere. Fog up the river, where it flows among green aits and meadows; fog down the river, where it rolls defiled among the tiers of shipping of a great (and dirty) city. Fog on the Essex marshes, fog on the Kentish heights.

This, as we later learn, is a 'London particular'. But Ossianic wind, rain, and mist pervade the whole book: for example, in the descriptions of the Ghost's Walk at Chesney Wold: 'if there be a little [fancy] at any odd moment, it goes, like a little noise in that old echoing place, a long way, and usually leads off to ghosts and mystery'; and there is more ghostliness while Guppy and Weevle are waiting to see Krook:

> One disagreeable result of whispering is, that it seems to evoke an atmosphere of silence, haunted by the ghosts of sound – strange cracks and tickings, the rustling of garments that have no

substance in them, and the tread of dreadful feet that would leave no mark on the sea-sand or the winter snow.

At a more domestic, and indeed Wainewrightian level, Esther falls asleep with Caddy Jellyby on her lap:

> I began to lose the identity of the sleeper resting on me. Now it was Ada; now, one of my old Reading [reading] friends from whom I could not believe I had so recently parted. Now it was the little mad woman worn out with curtseying and smiling; now, some one in authority at Bleak House. Lastly, it was no one and I was no one.

This reference to nobody alerts us, on a second reading, to the extinguished character Nemo, who actually advertises himself in an advert as Nemo, care of Mr Krook, or, to put it another way, *no-one, c/o criminal*: a perfect description of a forger. Miss Flite says of him:

> The only other lodger . . . is a law-writer. The children in the lanes here, say he has sold himself to the devil. I don't know what he can have done with the money. Hush!

And Snagsby and Tulkinghorn have the following conversation about the mysterious writer:

> 'Nemo, sir. Here it is. Forty-two folio. Given out on the Wednesday night, at eight o'clock; brought in on the Thursday morning, at half after nine.'
> 'Nemo!' repeats Mr. Tulkinghorn. 'Nemo is Latin for no one.'
> 'It must be English for some one, sir, I think,' Mr. Snagsby submits, with his deferential cough. 'That's the person's name.'

Snagsby goes on:

> 'The advantage of this particular man is, that he never wants sleep. He'll go at it right on end, if you want him to, as long as ever you like.'

Nemo is, then, a machine for writing, effacing his own identity with the copying and reproduction of text. At one level, he is a metaphor for the entire novel. As Hillis Miller has put it, '*Bleak House* is a document about the interpretation of documents', and he goes on to list letters, wills, parchments, scraps, and the contents of Krook's shop; he describes Miss Flite's papers and Richard Carstone's gradual poisoning by an ever-increasing dosage of debilitating documents, even if he misses the crucial and apparently matrimonial correspondence between Esther and John Jarndyce. Of course, much of the action of *Bleak House* unfolds in papers or letters, or hinges on documents – and many of them are either misread, or not read at all and simply inferred, such as the symbolic status of Tulkinghorn's files with *Jarndyce and Jarndyce* inscribed on the spines. The pivotal character, Krook, boasts:

> 'I have so many old parchmentses and papers in my stock. And I have a liking for rust and must and cobwebs.'

But Krook is illiterate, and can only transcribe letters, devoid of meaning. Elsewhere, Caddy Jellyby's penwomanship becomes entirely a matter of personal hygiene, Esther teaches Charley to read and write but not to express herself grammatically, and the final evacuation of paper from the court is a grotesque sort of vomiting:

> presently great bundles of papers began to be carried out – bundles in bags, bundles too large to be got into any bags, immense masses of papers of all shapes and no shapes, which the bearers staggered under, and threw down for the time being, anyhow, on the Hall pavement, while they went back to bring out more.

But if there is very little reading in this novel of reading, there are new kinds of reading proposed. The wily, Odyssean Nemo – 'no one' – is the most literate of characters, not least because he reveals his true self through the forensic comparison of his hand with that of Capt. Hawdon. Yet nearly all we experience directly of Nemo is through his death – and what a deathbed scene he presents to Mr Tulkinghorn:

> He comes to the dark door on the second floor. He knocks, receives no answer, opens it, and accidentally extinguishes his candle in doing so.
> The air of the room is almost bad enough to have extinguished it, if he had not. It is a small room, nearly black with soot, and grease, and dirt. In the rusty skeleton of a grate, pinched at the middle as if Poverty had gripped it, a red coke fire burns low. In the corner by the chimney, stand a deal table and a broken desk; a wilderness marked with a rain of ink. In another corner, a ragged old portmanteau on one of the two chairs, serves for

cabinet or wardrobe; no larger one is needed, for it collapses like the cheeks of a starved man. The floor is bare; except that one old mat, trodden to shreds of rope yarn, lies perishing upon the hearth. No curtain veils the darkness of the night, but the discoloured shutters are drawn together; and through the two gaunt holes pierced in them, famine might be staring in – the Banshee of the man upon the bed.

For, on a low bed opposite the fire, a confusion of dirty patchwork, lean-ribbed ticking, and coarse sacking, the lawyer, hesitating just within the doorway, sees a man. He lies there, dressed in shirt and trousers, with bare feet. He has a yellow look in the spectral darkness of a candle that has guttered down, until the whole length of its wick (still burning) has doubled over, and left a tower of winding-sheet above it. His hair is ragged, mingling with his whiskers and his beard – the latter, ragged too, and grown, like the scum and mist around him, in neglect. Foul and filthy as the room is, foul and filthy as the air, it is not easy to perceive what fumes those are which most oppress the senses in it; but through the general sickness and faintness, and the odour of stale tobacco, there comes into the lawyer's mouth the bitter, vapid taste of opium.

As Tulkinghorn says, 'Here's poison by the bed.'

This is a recognizable portrait of Thomas Chatterton, who was discovered dead in his Brooke Street garret, poisoned with arsenic and opium. Brooke Street is within the half-mile of London's Inns of Court where much of the action in *Bleak House* takes place; William Henry Ireland the 'second Chatterton' was also based here in the 1790s. Like Chatterton, it is debatable whether Nemo's death is a suicide or an accident. The surgeon called to Krook's recognizes Nemo: 'he has purchased opium of me for the last year and a half', much as Mr Cross the Brooke Street apothecary admitted selling drugs to Chatterton. Both writers have their pathetic possessions inventoried, and coroners' inquests are held at adjacent public houses. Chatterton ended up in a pauper's grave in Shoe Lane burial ground; Nemo's body is deposited in 'a hemmed-in churchyard, pestiferous and obscene'. Of course, eighteenth-century representations of Chatterton's death tended to dwell upon the poverty of his London existence: he was a byword for the poet starving in a garret. Moreover, Chatterton had trained as a legal scrivener or copier in Bristol, and if Nemo did not, like

Chatterton, cover the floor of his room with shredded manuscripts, he does have letters – letters spirited away by Krook – which are, like Chatterton's Rowley forgeries, read with a particularly forensic eye in order to establish who Nemo (like Rowley) really was. Chatterton would also stay up all night writing, and even the twice-repeated rumour that Nemo has sold himself to the Devil has a Chattertonian source.

Dickens's fraught set piece influenced Henry Wallis's seminal painting, *The Death of Chatterton*, first exhibited four years later in 1856. As Holman Hunt said, 'The cruelty of the world towards poor Chatterton, whose only offence was that he asked to be heard as a poet under a feigned name, will never henceforth be remembered without recognition of Henry Wallis the painter, who first so pathetically excited pity for his fate in his picture of the death of the hapless boy.' Dickens greatly admired the painting, and one could be forgiven for imagining that he had forged the *locus classicus* in his blending of elements in *Bleak House*. In fact, a startlingly similar image had been published as early as 1794, coincidentally the year in which Wainewright was born, as an engraving by Edward Orme. From this, Wallis took the central figure athwart the bed, and telling minor details such the empty laudanum bottle lying on its side, and one shoe on, one off – Chatterton limping into another world. Dickens must have seen the Orme engraving too.

Elsewhere in *Bleak House*, Chatterton perhaps emerges in more subtle similarities: Chatterton, like Esther and Inspector Bucket, rode through snow storms, and endured the hottest city summer for years. Chatterton was, like Richard Carstone's child, posthumous – and indeed the novel is teeming with orphans and bastards. On the other hand, of course, Nemo, for all his Chattertonian inflections, is an ex-soldier with wild black hair and whiskers, and aged forty-five. So I am not after a *Bleak House* 'original' here; rather I am proposing a typology of the forger – or what Dickens's contemporary reviewers called a 'daguerrotype'. Nemo, a middle-aged bewhiskered ex-soldier who expires in a fog of opium, also owes something to Wainewright the poisoner – an orphan who moves in with his guardian, who has an interest in a Chancery suit, who is diabolical: 'I don't know what he can have done with the money.' Nemo is not Chatterton, and neither is he Wainewright: he is formed from a hybrid of their respective myths of forgery, which lace the novel.* Ossian is there too as the banshee, and perhaps even Ireland, scribbling away in the Inns of Court. Bizarrely, Ireland's family motto was *Nemo sine vitiis*: 'No one without his faults'!

Indeed, the emphasis on the materiality of writing instruments in *Bleak House* is reminiscent of legal attempts in the eighteenth century to detect forgeries by ink, quill, idiosyncrasies of handwriting, and paper. Chapter X, 'The Law-Writer', opens with Mr Snagsby the stationer among his stock, legal stock for legal cases that could quite easily double as the cabinet of a forger:

> In the shade of Cook's Court, at most times a shady place, Mr. Snagsby has dealt in all sorts of blank forms of legal process; in skins and rolls of parchment; in paper – foolscap, brief, draft, brown, white, whitey-brown, and blotting; in stamps; in office-quills, pens, ink, India-rubber, pounce, pins, pencils, sealing-wax, and wafers; in red tape and green ferret; in pocket-books, almanacks, diaries, and law lists; in string-boxes, rulers, ink-stands – glass and leaden, penknives, scissors, bodkins, and other small office-cutlery.

It is amongst Krook's crooked stock, amidst 'so many old parchmentses and papers', that the new Will is discovered, though Dickens deliberately refuses to disclose whether the document is authentic and valid. This is because the novel ultimately rejects questions of textual value in emphasizing the totalitarianism and self-sufficiency of legal systems of order and interpretation.

The same generation of a composite forger figure is evident in *Little Dorrit* (1855–7). Charles Swann has already pointed out Blandois Rigaud's smooth, white, Wainewrightian hand, his fingers full of rings, his refusal to sweep his cell, his insistence on being treated as a gentleman. There's more, of course: in his moustache, slouched hat, and cloak, the tricks of his eyes, he bears a striking similarity to Theodore von Holst's rakish portrait of his friend, later purchased by Bulwer Lytton and therefore available to Dickens, and 'Phiz' was in any case numbered among the Dickens party that had discovered Wainewright in Newgate. His use of three aliases – Rigaud, Blandois,

---

* John Beer notes that 'The tendency to take a rigid moral position and marginalize anyone who did not live up to its standards into the posture of a Dickensian character was typical of the period' (*Romantic Influences*, 1993).

Lagnier – means we never learn his real name, and he also manages to obliterate Affery's identity. Like Wainewright, he leaves crucial papers in France, eventually retrieved by representatives of the law. More generally, *Little Dorrit* is a novel of doubles and parentage, problems with wills and codicils, papers and signatures – and most significantly money, or rather the lack of it. The universally admired and respected Mr Merdle turns out to be 'simply the greatest Forger and the greatest Thief that ever cheated the gallows'; he commits suicide, taking laudanum as a painkiller as he opens his jugular with a paperknife. Some of these elements overlap with William Henry Ireland's career: he not only ran a prison for French prisoners of war, but was several times incarcerated and at least once (*c.*1820) imprisoned for debt and locked in a sponging house by his publisher ('because I could not get my MS. executed on time'); he wrote begging his friend George Virtue for £1. But it is of more significance that Ireland lived the last years of his life in the stews of Southwark, and could conceivably have been known to Dickens, who also tramped those streets. In 1835, Ireland was buried in the common ground of St George the Martyr, the closest church to the Marshalsea, where many who died in the prison were buried. Little Dorrit sleeps in St George's when she is locked out, and eventually marries Arthur Clennam there.

The ultimate victory of the legal over the literary is exemplified by an unfortunate writer whose very christening invoked the forgeries of James Macpherson. His mother wrote to her friends in November 1854 to announce the birth of her son: 'He is to be called Oscar Fingal . . . Is not that grand, misty, and Ossianic?' He lectured on Thomas Chatterton in 1886, wrote a short story on the literary and artistic forgery of Shakespeare, and an essay on Thomas Griffiths Wainewright. He was ultimately imprisoned for his failure to convince the law of the incompatibility of legal and literary identities.

Oscar Wilde's essay 'Pen, Pencil and Poison', originally published in the *Fortnightly Review* for January 1889 and derived from W. C. Hazlitt's edition of Wainewright's writings (1880), offered Wilde the opportunity to develop his subject into a prototype of the aesthete: 'One can fancy him', said Wilde, 'lying there in the midst of his books and casts and engravings, a true virtuoso, a subtle connoisseur . . .' Wilde admired Wainewright's taste for fine art, and also for his prescient appreciation of his contemporaries Keats and Shelley, but he saw in Wainewright an opportunity to 'other' the dandy artist-forger and his exotic tastes. Wainewright is made strange and uncanny in Wilde's essay. He epitomizes the artist who knows no limits, whose extension of artistic method into forging and poisoning makes the world into a decadent canvas. From this, Wilde proposes an aesthetics of crime, which is brought to life by the inspired complicity of the critic.*

This was a position Wilde had already explored in 'The Decay of Lying'. In this fanciful dialogue, Vivian describes 'the temper of the true liar, with his frank, fearless statements, his superb irresponsibility, his healthy, natural disdain of proof of any kind! After all, what is a fine lie? Simply that which is its own evidence.' Vivian quotes from his fictitious article:

> Lying and poetry are arts — arts, as Plato saw, not unconnected with each other — and they require the most careful study, the most disinterested devotion. Indeed, they have their technique, just as the more material arts of painting and sculpture have their subtle secrets of form and colour, their craft-mysteries, their deliberate artistic methods. As one knows the poet by his fine music, so one can recognise the liar by his rich rhythmic utterance.

Having dissolved the ethical dimension of the literary by admitting that all literature is fiction, and therefore lies, Wilde concludes 'Pen, Pencil and Poison' with the observation: 'There is no essential incongruity between crime and culture. We cannot rewrite the whole of history for the purpose of gratifying our moral sense of what should be.' He ends the essay with a statement of Wainewright's true worth as the villain of both 'Hunted Down' and *Lucretia*: 'To be suggestive for fiction is to be of more importance than a fact.' Wilde forges Wainewright as a decadent martyr. As Lawrence Danson describes Wilde's reading, 'Wainewright is not only a forger but, as an artist, he is himself a forgery', and this is essentially the Wildean credo: that the artist necessarily stretches invention far enough to make, to forge, his (or her) self.

---

* The Wildean influence is clear in Andrew Motion's *Wainewright the Poisoner* in details of how Wainewright's possessions were dispersed and his lovely clothes auctioned off, like Christ's cloak, to be replaced by a coarse grey suit: the tone is of *De Profundis*.

This position is developed in Wilde's story 'The Portrait of Mr. W. H.', which begins with a discussion about 'Macpherson, Ireland, and Chatterton'. With regard to Chatterton, the narrator declares

> I insisted that his so-called forgeries were merely the result of an artistic desire for perfect representation; that we had no right to quarrel with an artist for the conditions under which he chooses to present his work; and that all Art being to a certain degree a mode of acting, an attempt to realise one's own personality on some imaginative plane out of reach of the trammelling accidents and limitations of real life, to censure an artist for a forgery was to confuse an ethical with an æsthetical problem.

The story itself concerns the identity of the addressee of Shakespeare's sonnets, Willie Hewes, a young actor or 'shadow', whose existence is deduced from the poems, and then proved by a portrait – though this turns out to be a forgery. Wilde tells us all this in the first couple of pages, however, the remaining thirty-odd thousand words are devoted to an attempt to convince the reader that Willie Hewes is indeed the subject of the sonnets, despite the fact the reader already knows that: a) the clinching evidence has been forged, and b) the story is a piece of fiction.*

Wilde manages to make the principle of forgery central to his aesthetic philosophy – rather as Ireland had proposed in treating Chatterton as a creative genius instead of a forger: through performance, self-invention and reinvention, his insistence on masks and truth and lies, and during his trial by his refusal to allow any reading of his letters, poems, or stories that was not purely aesthetic. Putting literature in the dock was a trial for Macpherson, critical for Chatterton, metaphorical for Ireland, transitional for Wainewright, and literal for Wilde.

Wilde was not of course the only writer to write about Wainewright. Charles Algernon Swinburne, in his book on Blake (1868), had anticipated Wilde's own position, as Wilde himself pointed out. For Swinburne, Wainewright is

---

* The first serious editor of Shakespeare's sonnets was Ireland's nemesis, Edmond Malone, in 1780. He noted that the sonnets were likely to have been addressed to one Will Hewes; the idea was suggested to him by Thomas Tyrwhitt, who edited the first edition of Chatterton's Rowley poems in 1777.

admirable alike as a painter, a writer, and a murderer. In each
pursuit, perhaps, there was a certain want of solid worth and
fervour, which at times impeded or impaired the working of an
excellent faculty; but in each it is evident there was a noble sense
of things fair and fit; a seemliness and shapeliness of execution, a
sensitive relish of excellence, an exquisite aspiration after goodness
of work, which cannot be overpraised. With pen, with palette, or
with poison, his hand was never a mere craftsman's.

Swinburne's final remark 'his hand was never a mere craftsman's' is
interesting, because it distinguishes artistic forgery above mere criminal craft, discriminates between the gentleman poisoner and the
journeyman murderer, suggesting that 'his articles and his crimes
are both too often wanting in the most delightful qualities of
which finished art is capable; qualities which a more earnest man of
lesser genius might have given them'. So inspiration still hovers
about here in the guise of criticism, and ethical considerations are
of course completely ignored: 'Too often the murderer is not an
artist; and the converse defect is no doubt yet more unhappily frequent.'
'To fake out and out' was actually nineteenth-century slang for
murder.

Likewise, Wilde's lecture on Chatterton, a relatively early piece
(1886), dismisses the ethical nature of the problem of forgery thus:

> Was he a mere forger with literary powers or a great artist? The
> latter is the right view. Chatterton may not have had the moral
> conscience which is truth to fact, but he had the artistic con-
> science, which is truth to Beauty. He had the artist's yearning to
> represent and if perfect representation seemed to him to demand
> forgery, he needs must forge. Still his forgery came from the desire
> for artistic self-effacement.

But Wilde was forever teasing out the implications of forgery. Despite
this lecture's success, it was never published – and it was never published because it was heavily plagiarized. Certainly the problems of
originality and plagiarism haunted Wilde and provided his enemies
with much ammunition, but plagiarism is essential to Wilde's citational
or 'anthological' style. He welcomes different voices into his writing,
internalizes the contradictions of the forger, and like 'Janus Weathercock' in Wilde's own analysis, 'saw that it was quite easy by continued
reiteration to make the public interested in his own personality'. For

Wilde, this form of repetition was also a cascade of apt quotations that
provided a running aesthetic commentary on life, much as Walter
Pater proposes in the controversial Conclusion to *The Renaissance*.
This is the 'revolution for man' De Quincey recognizes: an artistic revolution of the everyday that dissolves the dichotomies of romance and
realism, invention and imitation, art and life, and most importantly
of character.

The case of Thomas Griffiths Wainewright, as it is variously received
through the nineteenth century, involves issues of original and engraved
works, art and craft, counterfeiting and forgery, dandyism and posing,
murder and literature. As with Chatterton, the life and myth of the
forger, poisoner, and archetypal aesthete tends to overtake the works,
except that the life is now seen as an œuvre, a body of works rather
than a myth, and therefore every act within it, including murder, can
be read as a work of art. *Bleak House* firmly, if covertly, delineates the
forger by considering craft and copying, lack of character (Nemo),
illegitimacy (Esther), the law, suicide, and so forth – and Dickens
thereby *buries* forgery in the law courts, even as he is implicitly
attacking the fraudulence of the law, by half-hidden allusions to
forgery. When Oscar Wilde tries to revive the art of the liar or the
Wainewrightian forger, he himself eventually ends up in the dock –
imprisoned for writing the wrong sort of letters. The Wainewright
case, after Ireland's, confirmed that forgery was a legal misdemeanour
rather than a literary practice. It insisted on the criminality of forgery,
on forgery as the first resort of the murderer – much as posing was
the first resort of the '*somdomite*' – and so today our current notions
of authenticity are underwritten by the mythology of Wainewright,
and the trials of Oscar Wilde.

   Within a decade of his death, an anonymous columnist in the
Hobart Town Courier had predicted that 'a famous novel' would be
based on Wainewright's life, and in the following years Wainewright
was comprehensively mythologized, taking on the expression of sadistic
and unrepentant gentlemen drawn from annals like the *Newgate Calendar*. But this process does not culminate in Wilde's 'Pen, Pencil and
Poison'. Tracing the contours of Wainewright's sacrifice so delicately,
Wilde suicidally anticipated the catastrophe of his own life by fulfilling
his own aesthetic claim that life imitates art. His future suffering

followed the contours of the redemptive Wainewrightian pattern: from artistic acclaim and luxury to crime, public humiliation, suffering, and obscure death, before mythologization and restoration. Even now, we can still see something Promethean there.

After

There is a concept which corrupts and upsets all others. I
refer not to Evil, whose limited realm is that of ethics; I refer
to the infinite.

Jorge Luis Borges, 'Avatars of the Tortoise'

Authenticity is the abiding perversion of our times. It is indulged as
a vice, worshipped as a fetish, embraced as a virtue. Like a deity it is
pervasive, rapacious, and demanding: authenticity is the underwriter
of history and culture, the guarantor of social legitimacy and personal
integrity; it is the theorist of truth. Everything it touches turns to gold
– or at least is burnished with a scrape of lustre – and in that sense it
is the mark of genius, the Midas touch, the apotheosis of capitalism.

As a vehicle of thought and critical idiom, authenticity carries to
the very heart of culture the aesthetics of Romantic authorship – the
conceits of genius, creativity, and especially that of originality. As
we have seen, in doing so it also carries falsehood and fraudulence
there as well. This is a straightforward ideological contradiction, a
contradiction that maintains the primacy of the authentic, and so
authenticity shimmers rather than falls. Hence the streets are packed
with counterfeit goods; the galleries are replete with forged paintings
and their archives threaded with fraudulent documents; copyright law
is entranced by the worldwide web; a sheep is cloned (and neatly turns
out to be a fake); resting actors find work posing as citizens on
television chat shows, documentaries are revealed to be staged fictions
or, perhaps worse, comedy shows; a troupe of impostors don clerical
vestments and charitably cock their ears to confession; Faux Art is
cooed over by faux women; prize-winning writers shrug off accusations
of plagiarism; theme parks replace museums and the cinema rewrites

history; credit card fraud is booming; and on the internet and else-where, everywhere, identities are blurred, swapped, falsified, multiplied, invented, dissolved.

The thirst for authenticity is in nowise slaked by this superfluity of copies. Jeans and software now carry the same security measures as paper money – from signatures to holograms – false signs; artists make cults of themselves and register as trademarks; television turns to protracted fly-on-the-wall documentary soap operas; the issue-memoir becomes the degree-zero of literature, judged primarily not by any quality of writing but by the truth of the writer's testimony; politicians cock-a-doodle-doo their personal provenance to confirm policy and win votes.

In art criticism, the authentic becomes the synonym for taste – a taste-test that cannot be empirically proven but is imagined as an intrinsic quality, recognized as a secret handshake among the cog-noscenti who enigmatically glide about like the Illuminati. Such connoisseurship is a brazen admission that the most reliable judgements are made rapidly and intuitively – that is to say, superficially and sentimentally. This is what David Phillips identifies in the fine arts as the 'connoisseurs' paradox': 'If the point of the whole exercise is to identify artefacts that give rise to experiences of a kind that other objects cannot offer, why should identification depend on properties of the artefact that play a minor role in evoking the experiences?' The most conclusive evidence is often scientific and documentary – entirely invisible to the naked eye as it surveys a work.

But authenticity is nevertheless, necessarily, internalized. Thomas Hoving begins his book *False Impressions* with the claim that 'fake-busters' have a 'sixth or seventh sense . . . a pull in the gut or a warning cry from a voice deep inside them' (ahh, taste). He goes on to describe one art historian and connoisseur who could not articulate his objec-tions to an iffy work, though his body was marvellously eloquent:

> [Bernard] Berenson was able to say only that his stomach felt wrong. He had a curious ringing in his ears. He was struck by a momentary depression. Or he felt woozy and off balance.

Another art critic describes a Swiss art dealer who buys an Egon Schiele, with which she had been 'head over heels in love'. Later she reads a book casting doubt on its authenticity and feels 'physically sick'.

It is at this vulgarized outpost on the road of inspiration, which
has led us from the pre-Socratics to the postmodern, where we now
rest. Art is sacred here, and the connoisseur is a prophet inspired by
truth. Art is also medicalized here, and the connoisseur is an aesthesodic
surgeon, tapping the nerves. Art is being literally consumed here, and
seasoned with authenticity provides the bodily symptoms and physical
effects of well-being. The inauthentic, in contrast, taints and poisons,
is disorderly and abnormal, and requires vigilance to guard against it.
But the sick, the halt, and the lame do not need herbs or curative
waters, or be immersed in magnetic bathtubs filled with mesmeric
fluid to recover their health. They need a good dose of aesthetics –
aesthetics that soothe like anaesthetics.

As pain gives authenticity to illness, fakes have given authenticity
to art. Likewise, if the role of the doctor is to remove pain, which is
ironically a patient's most manifest proof of being authentically ill, the
role of the connoisseur and the scholar has been to remove fakes,
ironically a canon's most manifest proof of being authentically valued.
And likewise too, the healer and the critic both claim to have powers
of control and scrutiny and description – powers of naming – over
internal sensations and sensibilities. The forger is treated, then, much
as the villain, the lunatic, the bastard, even the ghost are treated: as a
social abnormality to be excluded, to be literally treated as if sick.

One consequence of this 'an-aesthetic theory' is that when faced
with those enigmatic contemporary diseases that exhibit in a patient
no external signs – no sores, wounds, or other physical symptoms –
the healer may switch from science to the parallel discourse of the arts.
Painting is regarded as therapeutic, music plays an holistic role, writing
releases 'hidden' or 'suppressed' (apocryphal?) memories. And so in
this culture that returns everything to the supposed authenticity of
body, whither art? In the past, it was the dead who provided the richest
sources of succour: the body-parts of the martyred, or more gruesomely
in 'mummy', or the sweat of a corpse, which was often collected from
unfortunate criminals hanging from gibbets at the fag end of the moral
hierarchy, and also in real mummy's hands bottled and sold by the
apothecary. It would be enough if we now just gobbled up works of
art, but in the contemporary present it is the sign and not the referent
that is consumed to salve the soul.

Hence the works of Cornelia Parker (mountainous molehill relics),
Tracey Emin (the cult of celebrity voyeurism), and Damien Hirst

(genius reduced to a signature), and why all such contortions are profoundly conservative. These artistes [*sic*] embrace the familiar logic of the authentic, and that logic is the logic of artistic and social authority, the logic that maintains dead distinctions, the logic in which authenticity is traced to establish purity. In such scenarios of cultural order, genealogy is the master-plot and authenticity is a model for eugenics. Even the Appropriation Art of Sherri Levine, who appropriated *After Mondrian* from a forgery of Mondrian, or Kathy Acker, who pirated 1,500 words from Harold Robbins's 1974 novel *The Pirate* into her 1975 work *The Adult Life of Toulouse Lautrec by Henri Toulouse Lautrec*, fall victim to the same logic – although at least the problem of authenticity is sized up here before it implodes. Other saboteurs are perhaps more subtle. Cindy Sherman's suggestively derivative photographs have no real referent: like the meticulously presented artefacts in the Museum of Jurassic Technology, they are signs taken for wonders. The MJT itself presents such incongruous curiosities that its exhibitions tip the discreet conformity of museum display into the splendidly comic.* J. S. G. Boggs, in contrast, redesigns bank notes and performs transactions as part of his artwork. Boggs was actually prosecuted by the Banks of America and England for *forging* (as opposed to counterfeiting) currency.† The episode crystallizes the commercial inefficiency of authenticity, because Boggs dismantles the illusion that authenticity is an inherent quality in an object such as a five-pound note; it is rather a mere supposition briefly shared between buyer and seller – the convention of a certain economic genre.

I have already argued further than this. In literature, what might be called the 'essential relativism' of the sign – the written word – has

* Among the microminiature sculptures suspended in the eyes of needles, human horns, and anthropological dioramas of trailer parks, the MJT has displays on the Deprong Mori or 'Piercing Devil' (*Myotis lucifugus*), a small bat able to fly through solid objects by increasing the frequency of its echo-locations until they reach the threshold of X-rays (a single example was captured by Donald R. Griffith in 1952 using an ingenious pattern of radial lead walls – it remains 'eternally frozen in a mass of solid lead'); also the Stink Ant of the Cameroon (*Megolaponera foetens*), which, upon inhaling a microscopic spore, has its brain gradually consumed by the invading fungus (*genus Tomentella*) until the ant starts confusedly climbing trees, and reaching a certain height, grips the plant with its mandibles – whereupon the fungus gradually grows out of the head of the ant and produces more spores; and a heliotropic sunflower clock, in which a sunflower is attached to a cork and floated in a reservoir of water: as the blossom rotates to face the sun, a pointer through its centre tells the time along the side of a suspended dial. . . .
† Boggs's notes are originals, not copies.

likewise been contested and defined by legal definitions of right and wrong, and this has expelled supposedly illegitimate forms of fiction – most notably literary forgeries – from cultural history. These eliminated forgers return, however, either as good daemons or evil demons: either as dematerialized transfusions of inspiration for rapt poets, or as typological components in a criminal figure who embodies the multifarious contradictions of textual transgression. This then activates the work of later writers.

Robert Jamieson, probable author of the early Anti-Stratfordian essay 'Who Wrote Shakespeare?' (1852) proposed that Shakespeare hired a poet: 'some pale, wasted student ... who, with eyes of genius gleaming through despair, was about, like Chatterton, to spend his last copper coin on some cheap and speedy means of death.' The image is so familiar, so frictionless, it is almost a cliché.* On 4 July 1880, the heady Pre-Raphaelite champion of Chatterton, Dante Gabriel Rossetti, wrote to his brother William regarding portraits of the boy: 'They seem to acquire additional attraction from a certain resemblance to the type of Keats.' This is myth delightfully winding back upon itself – precisely the fantastic ambition of the Pre[sic]-Raphaelites to turn back and recapture history. And it is a history written by forgeries: monks 'piously' fabricated backdated charters, Richard of Cirencester's map of Roman Britain (published in 1757) gave cartographers the name of the Pennines, and if we might remain suspicious of the eighteenth-century Würzburg professor Johann Adam Beringer, whose collection of fossils included spiders in their webs and Hebrew letters spelling out the name of God, 'Druidical' eisteddfods are still regularly celebrated in Wales. They were entirely invented by the eighteenth-century antiquarian Iolo Morganwg.

We now need to arrest authenticity, by breaking open history – revealing that the many histories that nestle together to form our pasts and our memories as well as proper 'History' should not then govern us by consenting to oppressive but barely discernible laws. Friedrich Nietzsche (and later Michel Foucault) have argued that history is discontinuous, composed of a gigantic mass of tiny and irreconcilable detail, opaque to interpretation and analysis: 'What is found at the

* I must say here that since I commenced this book Bristol has erected a statue to the memory of Thomas Chatterton.

historical beginning of things is not the inviolable identity of their origin; it is the dissension of other things. It is disparity.'

If history is theorized in this way, the historian exists merely to conjure up a version of events that buttresses certain political or deductive credos like 'progress', or 'cause and effect', or 'human values'. Other histories exist beyond these frames, although they are likely to be unutterable. This is not a way of disposing of the real; rather it is perhaps the way to approach that most complex and sensitive historical issue of the time: the Holocaust. How can that untellable story be told? How can a history be written that resists imposing an incondite moral pattern on the extermination? Should genocide even be a topic for aesthetic representation, or theoretical discussion in a book about forgery?

Holocaust historians have sought to establish truth by recording witnesses. These archives form a colossal monument, but one which is diverse and disparate. Truth here is not one story but many. It is not a totalitarian aspiration, but is often confused and contradictory, for multiplying witnesses multiplies error, and there is a human validity in that imperfection. The Holocaust was in any case unbelievable to its victims – that word 'unbelievable' reverberates through testimonies. The Holocaust goes beyond the limits of representation; as Aharon Appelfeld has described the predicament, 'Everything that happened was so gigantic, so inconceivable, that the witness even seemed like a fabricator to himself.' Witnessing and testifying thus collapse into each other, as if the witness is simply an instrument to record and replay those atrocities witnessed. But though language and literature are not objective, testimony has still become the paramount literary genre. Elie Wiesel has remarked that 'our generation invented a new literature, that of testimony'. This overstates the case – early Christian martyr-doms, seventeenth-century spiritual autobiography, eighteenth-century conversion narratives are all testimonial literature, as is witchcraft confession and evidently the popular crime literature of rogues' histories and trial reports – but the claim is insistent, and discloses a self-conscious ambition precisely to establish testimony as the authentic literature of the Shoah.

That this state of affairs cannot last was shown most spectacularly in the recent case of Binjamin Wilkomirski's book *Fragments* (1996). This searing memoir of a childhood spent in concentration camps received almost universal praise from critics who were often, like Wilkomirski in his public appearances, moved to tears. Wilkomirski was compared to Primo Levi; Wilkomirski won prizes. The book, despite being childlike and otherworldly and at times even intangible, is an extraordinary testament and a desperately harrowing read. It is also a literary forgery. The exposure of Wilkomirski as Bruno Dössekker, a Swiss clarinet-maker (in other words, a craftsman), provoked intemperate condemnations from the very readers who had so extravagantly praised it, even shrill demands that the book be withdrawn – or at the very least reclassified: they felt, yes, sickened. But is the Holocaust a sacrosanct subject that must be policed by censorship? Is literary value subordinate to the authenticity of an individual? Frankly, I thought we already knew that writers can often spin a bewitching yarn.

The Wilkomirski affair has generated a massive and wide-ranging debate; it does, however, exemplify the dangers that readers and writers face in being enthralled by a simplistic understanding of authenticity, and the possibility (and dangers) of overcoming authenticity in literature, such as *Fragments*, or in pseudo-history, such as *The Protocols of the Elders of Zion*. Nietzsche turns to literature for his own antidote to nihilism, the Superman and prophet Zarathustra: there are no historical examples for this visionary rebel, no prior authenticity of the spirit, and Nietzsche wonders whether there is instead a literary paradigm for how art can lead to authenticity. True, human society unfolds its greatest talents in telling stories about itself, in narrating its own adventure, and today we live through rare moments in a way inaugurated by Nietzsche: there is no predominant obeisance to one overriding grand narrative, mythological or religious, that wholly defines one symbolic order. Stories are told in many ways today, and in many voices – from news stories to fiction to issue-memoirs to video games to digital cinema – and all claim to be believable and authentic, true on their own terms. They all 'construct' a little bit of reality for us, and yet even so it remains tenuous. The distinctions of genre between truth and lies have become so slight that there is an ever-increasing fear of transgression: the postmodern iconoclasts are perpetually juggling signs and mixing codes, questioning all faith in representation. The risk of this 'play' is estrangement from one's own humanity – becoming a viewer of, rather than a participant in, one's life. Watch the telly: is this entertainment, or information, or infotainment, docusoap, or satire . . . ? How are you enjoying it? Why are you watching it anyway?

But if there is no master-narrative for contemporary society, the very idea of story itself – and the force to recognize it – is literary, and so the world is built on the pattern of literature. Hence the power of literary forgeries. Add to this power their supernaturalism, and forgeries become the new metaphysics. Thus we return. The clock winds back to the very dust of genesis and the Promethean creation of man. So pause before you read on. The cries echo.

In the sixth chapter of the Book of Genesis there is an alternative story of the Fall:

> There were giants in the earth in those days; and also after that, when the sons of God came in unto the daughters of men, and they bare children to them, the same became mighty men which were of old, men of renown.

These 'sons of God' are beings half-divine, and their brood – the giants and mighty men fathered upon the 'daughters of men' – are, in Hebrew, the Nephilim. Their story is told in the lost and apocryphal Books of Enoch, Jubilees, and Giants (this last, recounting their dreams, remains but in fragments). The Watchers, or 'sleepless ones', or angels, lusted after the daughters of men. Led by Semjaza, two hundred Watchers descended to earth and 'went a-whoring'. They took wives 'and they began to go in unto them and to defile themselves with them'; 'And they begat sons the Naphidim [*sic*]': 'great giants, whose height was three thousand ells'. The Watchers also taught men in the arts of the forge, as well as writing, medicine, astrology, and magic; but they corrupted them too, and presently their giant offspring devoured mankind: 'And they began to sin against birds, and beasts, and reptiles, and fish, and to devour one another's flesh, and drink the blood.'

God was wreaking his revenge. He sent the Edenic prophet Enoch to reprimand the rebel Watchers and describe to them their fate: condemned to the abyss of fire. Yet the most sustained torture is preserved for Azazel, who has corrupted the whole earth: 'to him ascribe all sin'. It is Azazel who taught men smithying and forging; he is cast out into the darkness. Meanwhile, the giant sons are provoked into slaying each other, but being semi-divine, an intermix of spirits and flesh, they will linger on earth as demons:

> Evil spirits have proceeded from their bodies; because they are born from men and from the holy Watchers is their beginning and primal origin; they shall be evil spirits on earth, and evil spirits shall they be called. . . . And these spirits shall rise up against the children of men and against the women, because they have proceeded from them.

Finally, the Flood will cleanse the land:

> the Lord destroyed everything from off the face of the earth; because of the wickedness of their deeds, and because of the blood which they had shed in the midst of the earth He destroyed everything.

Yet the knowledge of the Nephilim remained.

This founding myth of destruction is a piece of Mosaic propaganda designed to expropriate the multifarious fables of gods, demi-gods, and super-heroes that pre-dated Scripture (one of the Nephilim is supposedly called Gilgamesh). It really derives from such sources as Hesiod, however, and in doing so establishes a counter-Fall, another paradise lost, a riddle murmuring at the heart of genesis – nothing less than a fundamental rupture, or rapture, in the story of humankind.

So it is no coincidence that Plato tells a similar story. Another story wrapped about with questions of essence and being. In his radical dialogue the *Sophist*, the Stranger from Elea begins his discourse with the very anxiety of this very book you have been reading: 'no one when he speaks of false words, or false opinion, or idols, or images, or imitations, or apparitions, or about the arts which are concerned with them, can avoid falling into ridiculous contradictions'. This leads the Stranger, rapidly if obliquely, into a discussion about the being and not-being of things; he draws a mythical analogy:

> There appears to be a war of Giants and Gods going on among them; they are fighting about the nature of essence. . . . Some of them are dragging down all things from heaven and from the unseen to earth, and seem determined to grasp in their hands rocks and oaks . . . and will hear of nothing but body. . . . [But] their opponents cautiously defend themselves from above, out of

an unseen world, mightily contending that true essence consists
of certain intelligible and incorporeal ideas.

This contention of matter and essence lies at the heart of Platonic
philosophy, and evidently Christian theology too. Plato half-answers
his problem in the succeeding dialogue, the *Statesman*, by describing
the divine hierarchy and the origins of humanity. Unlike the first earth-
born race, the children of Kronos did not come into being through
the agency of greater beings, but somehow generated themselves and
grew in imitation of the world around them, and in competition with
other animals. But this left them 'in a great strait': sundered from the
gods, who had failed them. Hence the intervention of daemons: 'fire
was given to us by Prometheus, the arts by Hephaestus . . .' Rebellious
spirits bring knowledge of forging and writing. Prometheus was indeed
considered the inventor of writing.

Dovetailing Genesis and Plato like this is a vertiginous activity,
but the implication seems to be for Plato that *both* 'giants' and 'gods'
are misled. There is no adequate philosophy for distinguishing the
divine from the material, the world of essences from the world of appearances, the idea from the image – and there is no adequate philosophy
because that sort of philosophy is ultimately redundant. Neither the
fallen world nor the divine suffices; it explains why he is haunted by
daemons.

Deep in the *Dialogues*, then, Plato admits that there is an argument that questions his abiding binaries of, say, original and copy. For
Gilles Deleuze this is a constitutive philosophy: 'God made man in
his [*sic*] image and resemblance. Through sin, however, man lost the
resemblance while maintaining the image. We have become simulacra.'
Maybe. But if so we need to reinvent the simulacrum as a post-Platonic
entity. This simulacrum is our reality, but in our being we remain
haunted by the chimaera of authenticity. We can overcome this authenticity by craft and by making, and in rebellion, and in becoming
inspirational; and we can overcome it too in that poetry which is all
this and still more. Is the simulacrum the postmodern word for the
daemonic? It has returned. It dwells herein: a flicker, a recurrent beat;
whatever stirs the heart:

the progeny immortal
Of Painting, Sculpture and rapt Poesy
And arts, though unimagined, yet to be.

This is how it called to me in a dream, a dream of fire and writing, of the breath of life:

> The wandering voices and the shadows these
> Of all that man becomes, the mediators
> Of that best worship, love, by him and us
> Given and returned, swift shapes and sounds which grow
> More fair and soft as man grows wise and kind,
> And veil by veil evil and error fall.

Prometheus, Shelley's Prometheus Unbound, Act III

And the heart beats . . .

Bibliography

One that feeds
On objects, arts, and imitations

William Shakespeare, *Julius Caesar*, IV. i

As an alternative to numbered footnotes listing sources and authorities, which I felt to be inappropriate for a book about authenticity, there follows a summary of the main works consulted. Where a title is given in the text or the source is obvious, it is generally omitted from the bibliography in the interests of brevity, but publication details of all direct critical quotations are given. I apologize for any omissions, oversights, or inadvertent plagiarisms.

Abbreviations

BJECS	*British Journal for Eighteenth-Century Studies*
DNB	*Dictionary of National Biography*
CR	*Critical Review*
ECS	*Eighteenth-Century Studies*
ELH	*English Literary History*
JHI	*Journal of the History of Ideas*
LRB	*London Review of Books*
NLH	*New Literary History*
NQ	*Notes and Queries*
OED	*Oxford English Dictionary*
PMLA	*Publications of the Modern Language Association of America*
PQ	*Philological Quarterly*
SBT	*Studies in Burke and His Times*

SJC   *St James's Chronicle*
SSL   *Studies in Scottish Literature*
TLS   *Times Literary Supplement*

Before

The standard life of Thomas Chatterton is by E. H. W. Meyerstein, *A Life of Thomas Chatterton* (London: Ingpen and Grant, 1930). Since then, a handful of scholars and critics, including Donald Taylor (in his incomparable edition of the *Complete Works*, Oxford: Clarendon Press, 1971), Richard Holmes ('Thomas Chatterton: The Case Reopened', *Cornhill Magazine* 178 [1970], 200–51: an essay reprinted in *Sidetracks: Explorations of a Romantic Biographer*, London: Harper-Collins, 2000), and Michael Suarez (' "This Necessary Knowledge": Thomas Chatterton's Understanding of the Bristol and London Book Trades', in Nick Groom [ed.], *Thomas Chatterton and Romantic Culture* [London: Macmillan, 1999], 96–118), have contributed certain details and interpretation. A further two biographical studies, Linda Kelly's *The Marvellous Boy: The Life and Myth of Thomas Chatterton* (London: Weidenfeld and Nicolson, 1971) and Louise J. Kaplan's *The Family Romance of the Impostor-Poet Thomas Chatterton* (Berkeley: University of California Press, 1989), proved valuable. Peter Ackroyd has dramatized the biographical questions in a novel, *Chatterton* (London: Hamish Hamilton, 1987), and my preface is in part a homage to Holmes and Ackroyd. Bristol Public Library has a file of cuttings of the Chatterton statue, and Revd Cartwright's memoirs are available from St Mary Redcliffe. For a bibliography of Chatterton, see below ('Lunatic and Daemon').

Quotations are taken from Jorge Luis Borges, 'Tlön, Uqbar, Orbis Tertius', in *Labyrinths: Selected Stories and Other Writings*, ed. Donald A. Yates and James E. Irby (Harmondsworth: Penguin, 1970), and Joseph Cottle, *Malvern Hills, with Minor Poems, and Essays* (4th edn, London: Cadell, 1829). The myth of Prometheus appears in Hesiod's *Theogony* and *Works and Days*.

1. WRIGHT

The bibliography of forgery is very large and very uneven: rogues' galleries of hoaxers and conmen, forensic guides to identifying fakes (especially among the fine arts and antiques), legal histories of fraud, and ultra-specific studies of particular cases. But there is very little on what might be called the 'theory' of forgery (as opposed to the practice and history), and very little too on literary forgery. Susan Stewart, *Crimes of Writing: Problems in the Containment of Representation* (Durham, NC: Duke University Press, 1994) and, less so, Anthony Grafton, *Forgers and Critics: Creativity and Duplicity in Western Scholarship* (Princeton: Princeton University Press, 1990) are the only notable monographs in the field; Ian Haywood's two books, *The Making of History: A Study of the Literary Forgeries of James Macpherson and Thomas Chatterton in Relation to Eighteenth-Century Ideas of History and Fiction* (London: Associated University Press, 1986) and *Faking It* (Brighton: Harvester, 1987) are also useful; however I have tried to think around the issues raised in different ways to these approaches. (K. K. Ruthven's *Faking Literature* [Cambridge: Cambridge University Press, 2001] appeared too late for consideration.) Certain essays on authorship laid the foundations: Roland Barthes's 'The Death of the Author' (*Image – Music – Text*, trans. Stephen Heath [London: Fontana, 1977], 142–8); Jean Baudrillard's 'Gesture and Signature: Semiurgy in Contemporary Art' (*For a Critique of the Political Economy of the Sign*, trans. Charles Levin [New York: Telos Press, 1981], 102–11); Walter Benjamin's 'The Work of Art in the Age of Mechanical Reproduction' (*Illuminations*, ed. and trans. Hannah Arendt [New York: Schocken, 1969], 217–51); Jacques Derrida's 'Signature-Event-Context' (*Margins of Philosophy*, ed. and trans. Alan Bass [Chicago: University of Chicago Press, 1982], 307–30); and Michel Foucault's 'What Is an Author?' (*The Foucault Reader*, ed. Paul Rabinow [Harmondsworth: Penguin, 1984], 101–20). Seán Burke has compiled a useful canon in the reader *Authorship: From Plato to the Postmodern* (Edinburgh: Edinburgh University Press, 1995), which includes Donald Pease's handy essay 'Author', and Burke has also written a meditation, *The Death and Return of the Author: Criticism and Subjectivity in Barthes, Foucault and Derrida* (Edinburgh: Edinburgh University Press, 1998). The related debate about artistic intention has also offered ways of thinking, especially W. K. Wimsatt and M. C. Beardsley, 'The Intentional Fallacy' (reprinted in the collection *On Literary Intention*, ed. David Newton-De Molina [Edinburgh: Edinburgh University Press, 1976]); E. D. Hirsch, *The Aims of Interpretation* (Chicago: University of Chicago Press, 1976); Edward Said, *Beginnings: Intention and Method* (New

York: Basic Books, 1975); Geoffrey Strickland, *Structuralism or Criticism? Thoughts on How We Read* (Cambridge: Cambridge University Press, 1981); and most recently Patrick Swinden, *Literature and the Philosophy of Intention* (London: Macmillan, 1999).

Cultural materialist analyses of authorship appear in Martha Woodmansee and Peter Jaszi (eds), *The Construction of Authorship: Textual Appropriation in Law and Literature* (Durham, NC: Duke University Press, 1994); see also Woodmansee's *The Author, Art, and the Market: Rereading the History of Aesthetics* (New York: Columbia University Press, 1994), and essays such as Linda Zionkowski, 'Aesthetics, Copyright, and "The Goods of the Mind" ' (*BJECS* 15 [1992], 163–74). For the implications of passing in postcolonial thinking see Henry Louis Gates, Jr, *Figures in Black* (Oxford: Oxford University Press, 1989) and Homi Bhabha, 'Of Mimicry and Man: The Ambivalence of Colonial Discourse' (*October* 31 [Spring 1984], 125–33), and in gender studies see Judith Butler, *Excitable Speech: A Politics of the Performative* (London: Routledge, 1997). Barthes, however, remains the most suggestive critic, and I have particularly returned to *Criticism and Truth* (trans. Katrine Pilcher Keuneman, London: Athlone, 1998), *Sade, Fourier, Loyola* (trans. Richard Miller, London: Cape, 1976), *Camera Lucida* (trans. Richard Howard, London: Fontana, 1984), the essay 'Deliberation' (in *Barthes: Selected Writings*, ed. Susan Sontag, London: Fontana, 1983), as well as guides such as Jonathan Culler's *Barthes* (London: Fontana, 1990). John Sturrock's review of Alan Sokal and Jean Bricmont (*LRB*, 16 July 1998, 8–9) was refreshing in a Barthesian manner. Finally, Umberto Eco has provided a structural taxonomy of forgery ('Fakes and Forgeries') in *The Limits of Interpretation* (Bloomington: Indiana University Press, 1994, 174–200), and, like Baudrillard, is fascinated by 'hyper-reality' and the dissolution of the real in simulation; see also Eco's *Faith in Fakes* (London: Secker and Warburg, 1986); Fredric Jameson, *Postmodernism, or, The Cultural Logic of Late Capitalism* (London: Verso, 1991); and Baudrillard's work that followed his pioneering essay, 'The Beaubourg Effect: Implosion and Deterrence', first pub. 1977, trans. Sheila Faria Glaser, *Simulacra and Simulation* (Ann Arbor: University of Michigan Press, 1994), 61–73. Threads of such thinking have become part of the texture of this book; they began to weave in *Narratives of Forgery*, ed. Nick Groom (*Angelaki* 1.2, 1993–4), discussed by Greg Clingham in 'Chatterton, Ackroyd, and the Fiction of Eighteenth-Century Historiography' (in Clingham [ed.],

Making History: Textuality and the Forms of Eighteenth-Century Culture [Lewisburg, Penn.: Bucknell University Press, 1998], 35–58).

The *Oxford English Dictionary* has been invaluable in plotting the arcs of the different terms I evaluate. Two major books have also been excellent sources of ideas and examples: Terence Cave, *The Cornucopian Text: Problems of Writing in the French Renaissance* (Oxford: Clarendon Press, 1979), and Hillel Schwartz, *The Culture of the Copy: Striking Likenesses, Unreasonable Facsimiles* (New York: Zone Books, 1996). I have also made much use of Harold White's *Plagiarism and Imitation During the English Renaissance* (Cambridge, Mass.: Harvard University Press, 1935); as well as Reuben Brower, *Alexander Pope: The Poetry of Allusion* (Oxford: Clarendon Press, 1959), and Roger Lonsdale, 'Gray and "Allusion": The Poet as Debtor', in *Studies in the Eighteenth Century IV*, ed. R. F. Brissenden and J. C. Eade (Canberra: Australian National University Press, 1979), 31–55. Certain articles, such as Helen Deutsch, 'The "Truest Copies" and the "Mean Original": Pope, Deformity, and the Poetics of Self-Exposure' (*ECS* 27 [1993], 1–26) and Donald W. Nichol, 'On the Use of "Copy" and "Copyright": A Scriblerian Coinage?' (*Library*, 6th ser., 12 [1990], 110–11) provided illustrations.

Originality is analysed by Thomas McFarland, *Originality and Imagination* (Baltimore: Johns Hopkins University Press, 1985); Françoise Meltzer, *Hot Property: The Stakes and Claims of Literary Originality* (Chicago: University of Chicago Press, 1994); and David Quint, *Origin and Originality in Renaissance Literature: Versions of the Source* (New Haven: Yale University Press, 1983); it is surveyed by Patricia Philips, *The Adventurous Muse: Theories of Originality in English Poetics, 1650–1760* (Uppsala: Almqvist and Wiksell, 1984). The history of plagiarism is surveyed by Thomas Mallon in *Stolen Words: Forays into the Origins and Ravages of Plagiarism* (New York: Ticknor and Fields, 1989); it is theorized by Stewart Home in *Neoism, Plagiarism and Praxis* (Edinburgh: AK Press, 1995), as well as Bernard Dupriez, *A Dictionary of Literary Devices*, trans. Albert W. Halsall (New York: Harvester Wheatsheaf, 1991); Center for Advanced Studies in the Visual Arts, *Retaining the Original: Multiple Originals, Copies, and Reproductions* (Hanover, NH: University Press of New England, 1989); and Ed Baxter, 'A Footnote to the Festival of Plagiarism' (*Variant* 5, 1988, 26–30); see also Robert Burchfield, 'Dictionaries New and Old' (*Encounter*, Sept.–Oct. 1984, 10–19). Both Jonathan Bate, *The Genius of Shakespeare* (London: Picador, 1997) and Paulina Kewes, *Authorship and Appropri-*

ation: Writing for the Stage in England, 1660–1710 (Oxford: Clarendon Press, 1998) have helpful discussions on the topic, as does Laura J. Rosenthal, *Playwrights and Plagiarists in Early Modern England: Gender, Authorship, Literary Property* (Ithaca: Cornell University Press, 1996). K. R. St Onge has written an idiosyncratic polemic, *The Melancholy Anatomy of Plagiarism* (Lanham, Md: American University Press, 1988), situating the gross anxieties inspired by plagiarism within the structure of American academia – indeed, the topic has perhaps predictably attracted Americans: for example, Maurice Salzman, *Plagiarism: The 'Art' of Stealing Literary Material* (Los Angeles: Stone and Baird, 1931), Alexander Lindey, *Plagiarism and Originality* (New York: Harper, 1952), and most recently, Lise Buranen and Alice M. Roy (eds), *Perspectives on Plagiarism and Intellectual Property in a Postmodern World* (New York: State University of New York Press, 1999); see also Peter Shaw, 'Plagiary' (*American Scholar* 51 [1982], 325–37), and as a practical exercise, Norman Fruman's *Coleridge: The Damaged Archangel* (New York: Braziller, 1971). Fresh insights are offered by A. D. Nuttall's *A New Mimesis: Shakespeare and the Representation of Reality* (London: Methuen, 1983) and Stephen Orgel, 'The Renaissance Artist as Plagiarist' (*ELH* 48 [1981], 476–95). For a more comprehensive consideration of plagiarism see my essay, 'Forgery, Plagiarism, Pegleggery', in Paulina Kewes's forthcoming collection, *Plagiarism*.

Classical texts used include Plato, *The Republic*, trans. H. D. P. Lee (Harmondsworth: Penguin, 1955); see also Eric Havelock, *A Preface to Plato* (Cambridge, Mass.: Belknap Press, 1963); *Classical Literary Criticism*, ed. T. S. Dorsch (Harmondsworth: Penguin, 1965); D. A. Russell, *On Sublimity* (Oxford: Clarendon Press, 1965); *Classical Literary Criticism: Translations and Interpretations*, ed. Alex Preminger, Leon Golden, O. B. Harrison, Jr, and Kevin Kerrane (New York: Frederick Ungar, 1974); and Stephen Halliwell, *The Poetics of Aristotle: Translation and Commentary* (Chapel Hill: University of North Carolina Press, 1987). I checked these against Benjamin Jowett's and the Loeb translations, but also used contemporary editions when it seemed meet to do so (see below). Göran Sörbom's *Mimesis and Art: Studies in the Origin and Early Development of an Aesthetic Vocabulary* (Uppsala: Scandinavian University Books, 1966) is a useful compendium of citations; see also Richard P. McKeon, 'The Concept of Imitation in Antiquity', in *Critics and Criticism: Ancient and Modern*, ed. R. S. Crane (Chicago: Chicago University Press, 1952, 147–75). Erich Auerbach's

Mimesis: The Representation of Reality in Western Literature (Princeton: Princeton University Press, 1953) remains an inaugural study. For a sensitive rendering of elements contextual to my reading, see Ruth Padel's two books, *In and Out of the Mind: Greek Images of the Tragic Self* (Princeton: Princeton University Press, 1992) and *Whom Gods Destroy: Elements of Greek and Tragic Madness* (Princeton: Princeton University Press, 1995). Timothy Clark's *The Theory of Inspiration: Composition as a Crisis of Subjectivity in Romantic and Post-Romantic Writing* (Manchester: Manchester University Press, 1997) effectively brought such material up to date.

Among the too-many books written on sindonology (study of the Turin Shroud) are Peter Jennings (ed.), *Face to Face with the Turin Shroud* (Great Wakering, Essex: Mayhew McCrimmon and A. R. Mowbray, 1978); Lynn Picknett and Clive Prince, *Turin Shroud: In Whose Image? The Truth behind the Centuries-Long Conspiracy of Silence* (New York: HarperCollins, 1994); David Sox, *The Shroud Unmasked: Uncovering the Greatest Forgery of All Time* (Basingstoke: Lamp, 1988); and most recently Ian Wilson, *The Blood and the Shroud* (London: Weidenfeld and Nicolson, 1998); the most useful is J. Nickell, *Inquest on the Shroud of Turin* (Buffalo, NY: Prometheus Books, 1987). For a more general survey, see David Sox, *Relics and Shrines* (London: George Allen and Unwin, 1985).

Eric Hebborn, *Drawn to Trouble: The Forging of an Artist* (Edinburgh: Mainstream, 1991) is both indispensable and mischievously entertaining, although Thomas Hoving in *False Impressions: The Hunt for Big-Time Art Fakes* (New York: Touchstone, 1997) discounts much of what Hebborn says – including the Michelangelo story; see also Alice Beckett, *Fakes: Forgery and the Art World* (London: Richard Cohen, 1995). Surveys such as Frank Arnau, *Three Thousand Years of Deception in Art and Antiques* (London: Cape, 1961) and studies such as Lord Kilbracken, *Van Meegeren: Master Forger* (New York: Charles Scribner's, 1967) have also been consulted, as have researches into practical artistic technique: for example, Joseph Viscomi, *Blake and the Art of the Book* (Princeton: Princeton University Press, 1993). Copying and sacred art are described by Gary Vikan, 'Ruminations on Edible Icons: Originals and Copies in the Art of Byzantium' (*Studies in the History of Art* 20: *Retaining the Original: Multiple Originals, Copies, and Reproductions* [1989], 47–59), and Roger Benjamin, 'Recovering Authors: The Modern Copy, Copy Exhibitions and Matisse' (*Art*

History 12 [June 1989], 176–201). Among the art theorists who have written on the subject are Arthur Danto (*Philosophizing Art: Selected Essays,* Berkeley: University of California Press, 1999), Norman Bryson, Michael Holly, and Keith Moxey (eds), *Visual Culture: Images of Interpretation* (Hanover, NH: Wesleyan University Press, 1994), Erwin Panofsky, *Meaning in the Visual Arts* (Chicago: University of Chicago Press, 1983), and E. H. Gombrich (*Art and Illusion,* Princeton: Princeton University Press, 2000). Discussion of Rembrandt is in Jakob Rosenberg, *Rembrandt the Draughtsman, with a Consideration of the Problem of Authenticity* (Cambridge, Mass.: Harvard University Fogg Museum, n.d.[1956]), and more topically Hubert von Sonnenburg et al., *Rembrandt/Not Rembrandt* (New York: Metropolitan Museum of Art, 1995) and Christopher White and Quentin Buvelot (eds), *Rembrandt by Himself* (London: National Gallery, 1999); Egbert Haverkamp-Begemann's *Creative Copies: Interpretative Drawings from Michelangelo to Picasso* (New York: Drawing Center, 1988) is also helpful.

The auction house Sotheby's has a 'black museum' of art and antique fakes, and the Musée Contrefaçon, Paris, includes counterfeits and half-fakes of commodities: from Levi 501s to roses, automobile parts to ketchup. Many galleries have held such exhibitions, most notably the British Museum, see Mark Jones (ed.), *Fake? The Art of Deception* (London: British Museum, 1990) and *Why Fakes Matter: Essays on the Problems of Authenticity* (London: British Museum, 1992); see also *Vraiment faux* (Paris: Fondation Cartier pour l'art contemporain, 1988); William Olander, *Fake: A Meditation on Authenticity* (New York: New Museum of Contemporary Art, 1987); and Hillel Schwartz, 'Appropriationism' (*Journal of Unconventional History* 2 [Spring 1991], 82–91). The Vinland Map has been republished by Thomas Marston, George Painter, and Raleigh Skelton as *The Vinland Map and the Tartar Relation* (New Haven: Yale University Press, 1996). Spoof names include Batson D. Sealing, 'Three Unrecognized Demotic Texts' (*Discussions in Egyptology* 19 [1991], 53–68) (see Nick Groom, 'Forgery or Plagiarism? Unravelling Chatterton's Rowley', *Angelaki* 1.2 [1993–4], 41–54) and William Boyd's *Nat Tate, An American Artist: 1928–1960* (Cambridge: 21 Publishing, 1998). The comment about Chatterton was made by George Steevens (*SJC,* 2 March 1782) and is reproduced by Arthur Sherbo, *The Achievement of George Steevens* (New York: Peter Lang, 1990). Wyndham Lewis's *The Revenge for Love* (Santa Rosa:

Black Sparrow, 1991) and William Gaddis's *The Recognitions* (Harmondsworth: Penguin, 1993) are the most interesting novels on the subject of forgery.

II. VILLAIN

Some material in this chapter was published in a rudimentary form as 'Forgery and Plagiarism' in David Womersley (ed.), *Companion to Literature from Milton to Blake* (Oxford: Blackwell, 2000); I have also auto-plagiarized my introduction to *The Bloody Register* (London: Routledge, 1999).

Studies in the cultural history of literary property and copyright have gained in popularity over the past few years, creating a wide field that covers ground from history of the book to legal theory, and provides a historical foundation for current challenges in intellectual property law. An exemplary study is David Foxon, *Pope and the Early Eighteenth-Century Book Trade*, rev. and ed. James McLaverty (Oxford: Clarendon Press, 1991); see also Roger Lonsdale's introduction to *The New Oxford Book of Eighteenth-Century Verse* (Oxford: Oxford University Press, 1984). Also useful is John Feather, *Publishing, Piracy and Politics* (London: Mansell, 1994), Mark Rose, *Authors and Owners: The Invention of Copyright* (Cambridge, Mass.: Harvard University Press, 1993), and David Saunders, *Authorship and Copyright* (London: Routledge, 1992). Among essays and articles, three in Woodmansee and Jaszi (eds), *The Construction of Authorship* (1994) proved helpful: Peter Lindenbaum, 'Milton's Contract' (175–90), John Feather, 'From Rights in Copies to Copyright: The Recognition of Authors' Rights in English Law and Practice in the Sixteenth and Seventeenth Centuries' (191–209), and Mark Rose, 'The Author in Court: *Pope v. Curll* (1741)' (211–29). Michael Treadwell's 'On False and Misleading Imprints in the London Book Trade 1660–1750', in Robin Myers and Michael Harris (eds), *Fakes and Frauds: Varieties of Deception in Print and Manuscript* (Winchester: St Paul's Bibliographies, 1989, 29–46) provided material, and also of interest is Michael Harris, 'Trials and Criminal Biographies: A Case Study in Distribution', in Robin Myers and Michael Harris (eds), *Sale and Distribution of Books from 1700* (Oxford: Oxford Polytechnic Press, 1982, 1–36). Among the more useful articles are David Hunter's 'Copyright Protection for Engravings and

Maps in Eighteenth-Century Britain' (*Library*, 6th ser., 9 (1987), 268–73) and Don Nichol's 'Warburton (Not!) on Copyright: Clearing up the Misattribution of *An Enquiry into the Nature and Origin of Literary Property* (1762)' (*BJECS* 19 (1996), 171–82). A sound selection of the relevant source material is collected in *Freedom of the Press and the Literary Property Debate: Six Tracts, 1755–1770, The Literary Property Debate: Six Tracts, 1764–1774*, and *The Literary Property Debate: Eight Tracts, 1774–1775*: all ed. Stephen Parks (New York: Garland, 1974).

Eighteenth-century crime is also a rich field for historians and literary critics. William Blackstone's founding *Commentaries on the Laws of England* was consulted in the edition annotated by John Taylor Coleridge, the poet's brother (London: A. Strahan, 1825). Historical surveys of the field include J. M. Beattie, *Crime and the Courts in England, 1660–1800* (Oxford: Clarendon Press, 1986); John Brewer and John Styles (eds), *An Ungovernable People: The English and their Law in the Seventeenth and Eighteenth Centuries* (London: Hutchinson, 1980); J. S. Cockburn (ed.), *Crime in England, 1550–1800* (Princeton: Princeton University Press, 1977); Clive Emsley, *Crime and Society in England: 1750–1900* (London: Longman, 1987); Douglas Hay, Peter Linebaugh, John G. Rule, E. P. Thompson, and Cal Winslow, *Albion's Fatal Tree: Crime and Society in Eighteenth-Century England* (Harmondsworth: Penguin, 1975), especially chapters by Hay ('Property, Authority and the Criminal Law') and Thompson ('The Crime of Anonymity'); James Heath, *Eighteenth Century Penal Theory* (Oxford: Oxford University Press, 1963); Sir William Holdsworth, *A History of English Law* (London: Methuen, 1938); Frank McLynn, *Crime and Punishment in Eighteenth-Century England* (London: Routledge, 1989); Leon Radzinowicz, *A History of English Criminal Law and its Administration from 1750* (London: Stevens, 1956); and J. A. Sharpe, *Crime in Early Modern England, 1550–1750* (London: Longman, 1984).

With regard to counterfeiting and forging, *Documents in English Economic History: England from 1000 to 1760*, ed. H. E. S. Fisher and A. R. J. Jurica (London: G. Bell and Sons, 1977) provided some source material, and *Counterfeit Detection* (reprinted from *The Numismatist* 2, 1988) provided some examples. The most entertaining survey, among very many, is perhaps Murray Teigh Bloom, *Money of Their Own: The Great Counterfeiters* (London: Weidenfeld and Nicolson, 1957). A *Financial Times* article by Nicholas Leonard ('Scourge of the Counterfeiters', *FT* 11–12 Apr. 1998, *Weekend* XXII) prompted me to look at

Isaac Newton: see Sir John Craig, *Newton at the Mint* (Cambridge: Cambridge University Press, 1946); Frank E. Manuel, *A Portrait of Newton* (New York: Da Capo, 1968); and Michael White, *Isaac Newton: The Last Sorcerer* (London: Fourth Estate, 1997). Other specific cases are detailed by Daniel T. Ames, *Ames on Forgery: Its Detection and Illustration with Numerous Causes Célèbres* (New York: Ames-Rollinson, 1900); and in articles by Randall McGowen ('Forgery Discovered or the Perils of Circulation in Eighteenth-Century England', *Angelaki* 1.2 (1993–4), 113–29), John Powell ('The Birmingham Coiners: 1770–1816', *History Today* 43 [July, 1993], 49–55), and John Styles (' "Our Traitorous Money Makers": The Yorkshire Coiners and the Law, 1760–83', in John Brewer and John Styles [eds], *An Ungovernable People* [1980], 172–249). A meditation on money rather more relevant than Marxist accounts is John Buchan's *Frozen Desire: An Inquiry into the Meaning of Money* (London: Picador, 1997), which supplied me with the lines from Edward Gibbon (the sentiment is also suggested by Adam Müller, *Versuche einer neuen Theorie des Geldes* [Attempts at a new theory of money], 1816). Peter Lamborn Wilson's 'The Sacred and Profane History of Money' (*Whole Earth* 92 [Spring 1998], 41) is thought-provoking, as is Ralph Rugoff, *Scene of the Crime* (Cambridge, Mass.: MIT Press, 1997).

Literary sources include the various *Newgate Calendars* and similar compendiums of crime: there is a good bibliography in Lincoln B. Faller, *Turned to Account: The Forms and Functions of Criminal Biography in Late Seventeenth- and Early Eighteenth-Century England* (Cambridge: Cambridge University Press, 1987). Editorial and antiquarian implications are raised by Joseph M. Levine (' "Et Tu Brute?" History and Forgery in 18th-Century England', in Robin Myers and Michael Harris [eds], *Fakes and Frauds* [1989], 71–97). Bentley is discussed by William Empson in 'Milton and Bentley: The Pastoral of the Innocence of Man and Nature' (*Some Versions of Pastoral* [London: Chatto and Windus, 1935], 149–91); Levine again in *The Battle of the Books: History and Literature in the Augustan Age* (Ithaca: Cornell University Press, 1991); and Marcus Walsh, *Shakespeare, Milton and Eighteenth-Century Literary Editing: The Beginnings of Interpretative Scholarship* (Cambridge: Cambridge University Press, 1997). The career of Ademar is described by Richard Landes in *Relics, Apocalypse, and Deceits of History* (Cambridge, Mass.: Harvard University Press, 1995); Lauder has received attention from James L. Clifford ('Johnson and

Lauder', *PQ* 54 [1975], 342–56) and Michael J. Marcuse ('The Lauder Controversy and the Jacobite Cause', *SBT* 18 [1977], 27–47); Psalmanazar from Rodney Needham (*Exemplars*, Berkeley: University of California Press, 1985). James Boswell's remarks are in *Boswell's Column*, ed. Margery Bailey (London: William Kimber, 1951). Having said all this, the best monograph by far on literature and the law in the period is Paul Baines's *The House of Forgery in Eighteenth-Century Britain* (Aldershot: Ashgate, 1999).

III. Ghost

For two centuries, Ossianic studies have been an undercurrent in English [*sic*] literary criticism and Macpherson has received little serious attention, apart from a surprisingly sound biography by Bailey Saunders (*The Life and Letters of James Macpherson*, London: Swan Sonnenschein, 1894), and a clutch of articles on poetic influence (such as John Dunn, 'Coleridge's Debt to Macpherson', *SSL* 7 [1969], 76–89; Robert Folkenflik, 'Macpherson, Chatterton, Blake and the Great Age of Literary Forgery', *CR* 18 [1974], 378–91; and David Punter, 'Blake: Social Relations of Poetic Form', *NLH* 18 [1982], 182–205). He has been taken more seriously by Scottish literary critics; see most notably Derick S. Thomson, *The Gaelic Sources of Macpherson's 'Ossian'* (Edinburgh: Oliver and Boyd, 1952); Richard B. Sher, *Church and University in the Scottish Enlightenment: The Moderate Literati of Edinburgh* (Edinburgh: Edinburgh University Press, 1985); and a new biography by Paul deGategno, *James Macpherson* (Boston: Twayne, 1989). He has also attracted the attention of comparativists, for example Mary Margaret Rubel, *Savage and Barbarian: Historical Attitudes in the Criticism of Homer and Ossian in Britain, 1760–1800* (Amsterdam: North-Holland, 1978) and Kirsti Simonsuuri, *Homer's Original Genius: Eighteenth-Century Notions of the Early Greek Epic (1688–1798)* (Cambridge: Cambridge University Press, 1979).

The publication of Fiona J. Stafford's *The Sublime Savage: A Study of James Macpherson and the Poems of Ossian* (Edinburgh: Edinburgh University Press, 1988) inaugurated a renaissance in Ossian studies. It was followed by Howard Gaskill's collection *Ossian Revisited* (Edinburgh: Edinburgh University Press, 1991), which includes important essays by Stafford, ' "Dangerous Success": Ossian, Wordsworth, and English Romantic Literature' (49–72) and John Dwyer, 'The Melancholy Savage: Text and Context in *The Poems of Ossian*' (164–206), and then by Gaskill's edition: *The Poems of Ossian and Related Works* (Edinburgh: Edinburgh University Press, 1996). Gaskill and Stafford have since collaborated on a collection, *From Gaelic to Romantic: Ossianic Translations* (Amsterdam: Rodopi, 1998), which includes essays by Joep Leerssen ('Ossianic Liminality: Between Native Tradition and Preromantic Taste', 1–16), F. J. Lamport ('Goethe, Ossian and *Werther*', 97–106), Susan Manning ('Henry Mackenzie and *Ossian*: Or, The Emotional Value of Asterisks', 136–52), Thomas Keymer ('Narratives of Loss: The *Poems of Ossian* and *Tristram Shandy*', 79–96), and Stafford again ('*Fingal* and the Fallen Angels: Macpherson, Milton and Romantic Titanism', 162–82).

This revival was part of a wider revision of Scottish Enlightenment culture, evident in monographs such as Robert Crawford, *Devolving English Literature* (Oxford: Clarendon Press, 1992); Colin Kidd, *Subverting Scotland's Past: Scottish Whig Historians and the Creation of an Anglo-British Identity, 1689–c.1830* (Cambridge: Cambridge University Press, 1993); and Howard D. Weinbrot, *Britannia's Issue: The Rise of British Literature from Dryden to Ossian* (Cambridge: Cambridge University Press, 1993). The field remains rich, as seen in focused studies such as Kristine Louise Haugen's 'Ossian and the Invention of Textual History' (*JHI* 59.2 [1998], 309–27), Dafydd R. Moore's 'James Macpherson: Romancing the Gael. The Literary, Cultural and Historiographical Context of *The Poems of Ossian*' (Ph.D. thesis, University of Strathclyde, 1998) and 'Heroic Incoherence in James Macpherson's *The Poems of Ossian*' (*ECS* 34 [2000], 43–59), and David Punter's 'Ossian, Blake, and the Questionable Source' (Valeria Tinkler-Villani and Peter Davidson [eds], *Exhibited by Candlelight: Sources and Developments in the Gothic Tradition* [Amsterdam: Rodopi, 1995], 25–41); and ambitious accounts such as Stafford's *The Last of the Race: The Growth of a Myth from Milton to Darwin* (Oxford: Clarendon Press, 1997) and Katie Trumpener's *Bardic Nationalism: The Romantic Novel and the British Empire* (Princeton: Princeton University Press, 1997).

The story of Samuel Johnson's spat with Macpherson is taken from Sir John Hawkins, *The Life of Samuel Johnson, LL.D* (London: J. Buckland, 1787) and James Boswell, *Boswell's Life of Johnson (Together with Boswell's Journal of a Tour to the Hebrides and Johnson's Diary of a Journey into North Wales)*, ed. George Birkbeck Hill, rev. L. F. Powell

(Oxford: Clarendon Press, 1934–50). Stafford discovered the correspondence ('Dr Johnson and the Ruffian: New Evidence in the Dispute between Samuel Johnson and James Macpherson', *NQ* 234 [1989], 70–7), and Pat Rogers discusses the episode in *Johnson and Boswell: The Transit of Caledonia* (Oxford: Clarendon Press, 1995).

Of bards, material is taken from Homer's *The Odyssey*, trans. Albert Cook (2nd edn, New York: W. W. Norton, 1967), an edition that includes Charles Segal's indispensable essay, 'Bard and Audience in Homer' (356–73; first published in R. L. Lamberton and John J. Keaney [eds], *Homer's Ancient Readers: The Hermeneutics of Greek Epic's Earliest Exegetes*, Princeton: Princeton University Press, 1992); and John Dryden's translation of the *Aeneid* is used (ed. Frederick Keener, Harmondsworth: Penguin, 1997). A. L. Owen's *The Famous Druids: A Survey of Three Centuries of English Literature on the Druids* (Oxford: Clarendon Press, 1962) is supplemented by John Matthews's collection *The Bardic Source Book: Inspirational Legacy and Teachings of the Ancient Celts* (London: Blandford, 1998); Daithi O hOgain, *Myth, Legend and Romance: An Encyclopædia of the Irish Folk Tradition* (New York: Prentice-Hall, 1991); Patricia Lysaght, *The Banshee* (Dublin: O'Brien, 1996); and Sabine Baring-Gould, *Curious Myths of the Middle Ages* (New York: University Books, 1967). My own first analysis of the figure of the bard ('Celts, Goths, and the Nature of the Literary Source') appears in Alvaro Ribeiro, SJ, and James G. Basker (eds), *Tradition in Transition: Women Writers, Marginal Texts, and the Eighteenth-Century Canon* (Oxford: Clarendon Press, 1996, 275–96). Coleridge's Ossianic plans are detailed in *The Inquiring Spirit*, ed. Kathleen Coburn (New York: Routledge and Kegan Paul, 1951).

My thoughts were stimulated by Marjorie Garber, *Shakespeare's Ghost Writers: Literature and Uncanny Causality* (New York: Methuen, 1987); Peter T. Murphy's *Poetry as an Occupation and an Art in Britain: 1760–1830* (Cambridge: Cambridge University Press, 1993); and Adrian Poole and Jeremy Maule's *Oxford Book of Classical Verse in Translation* (Oxford: Oxford University Press, 1995); and I was led to Søren Kierkegaard's *Repetition: An Essay in Experimental Psychology* (trans. Walter Lowrie, London: Oxford University Press, 1942); Friedrich Nietzsche's *The Gay Science* (trans. Walter Kaufmann, New York: Vintage, 1974); and Gilles Deleuze's *Difference and Repetition* (trans. Paul Patton, London: Athlone, 1994). The concluding remark of the chapter is from Gilles Deleuze and Félix Guattari's essay 'Rhizome' (trans. John

Johnston, in *On the Line* [New York: Semiotext(e), 1983]; this piece also begins *A Thousand Plateaus: Capitalism and Schizophrenia* [London: Athlone Press, 1988]).

iv & v. Lunatic and Daemon

Like Macpherson, Chatterton has until recently been neglected by critics. Donald Taylor's monograph, *Thomas Chatterton's Art: Experiments in Imagined History* (Princeton: Princeton University Press, 1978), was for years the only substantial piece of criticism, although there have been several helpful articles published, among them T. O. Mabbot's 'Byron and Chatterton: A Parallel' (*NQ* 162 [19 Mar. 1932], 207); E. H. W. Meyerstein's 'Chatterton, Coleridge, and Bristol' (*TLS* 21 Aug. 1937, 606; see also letters to the *TLS*, 28 Aug. 1937); Wylie Sypher's 'Chatterton's *African Eclogues* and the Deluge' (*PMLA* 54 [1939], 246–60); and Donald Taylor's 'Chatterton: Insults and Gifts to the Rev. Mr. Catcott' (*Literature and Psychology* 22 [1972], 35–43). Biographical testimony from Chatterton's mother, sister, and friends is taken from Herbert Croft's *Love and Madness: A Story Too True* (London: G. Kearsly, 1780), Michael Lort's MS notes, Jeremiah Milles's edition of *Poems, Supposed to have been Written at Bristol in the Fifteenth Century, by Thomas Rowley, Priest, &c.* (London: T. Payne, 1782), and William Henry Ireland's *Confessions* (London: Ellerton and Byworth, 1805). The story about Thompson is repeated by both Holmes and Kelly. All the quotations from Chatterton's works are taken from Taylor's standard edition (1971). The introductory critical assessment of Rowley is in John Butt and Geoffrey Carnall, *The Mid-Eighteenth Century, Oxford History of English Literature*, vol. 8 (Oxford: Clarendon Press, 1969). 'The Ossiad' (*SJC*, 4 Apr. 1782) is signed 'J.N.B.I.'.

Although there is as yet no new monograph or edition of Chatterton, some recent and substantial essays have proved most helpful. Jonathan Barry ('The History and Antiquities of the City of Bristol: Chatterton in Bristol', 55–81) and John Goodridge ('Identity, Authenticity, and Class: John Clare and the Mask of Chatterton', 131–48) were published in *Angelaki* 1.2 (1993–4); and in *Thomas Chatterton and Romantic Culture* (1999) the following essays in particular contributed to this project: Carolyn Williams, ' "On Tiber's Banks": Chatterton and Post-Colonialism' (48–63), Inga Bryden, 'The Mythical Image:

Chatterton, King Arthur, and Heraldry' (64–78), Maria Grazia Lolla, 'Truth Sacrifising to the Muses: The Rowley Controversy and the Genesis of the Romantic Chatterton' (151–71), Paul Baines, 'Chatterton and Johnson: Authority and Filiation in the 1770s' (172–87), Bridget Keegan, 'Nostalgic Chatterton: Fictions of Poetic Identity and the Forging of a Self-Taught Tradition' (210–27), David Fairer, 'Chatterton's Poetic Afterlife, 1770–1796: A Context for Coleridge's *Monody*' (228–52), and John Goodridge, 'Rowley's Ghost: A Checklist of Creative Works Inspired by Thomas Chatterton's Life and Writings' (262–92) – the last of whom I am also grateful to for allowing me to read his unpublished essay, 'Keats and Chatterton: An Essay in Comparative Biography'. Gluttons for punishment might want to read further speculations of mine in 'Thomas Chatterton was a Forger' (*Yearbook of English Studies 1998*, ed. Andrew Gurr, 276–91) and 'Thomas Rowley Preeste' (in *Early Romantics: Perspectives in British Poetry from Pope to Wordsworth*, ed. Thomas Woodman [London: Macmillan, 1998], 242–55).

Accounts of Chatterton's influence appear at length in Linda Kelly's *Marvellous Boy* (1971), in Andrew Bennett's two books, *Keats, Narrative and Audience: The Posthumous Life of Writing* (Cambridge: Cambridge University Press, 1994) and *Romantic Poets and the Culture of Posterity* (Cambridge: Cambridge University Press, 1999) – the second of which also recognizes that Keats's nightingale is Chatterton, and also in Andrew Motion's biography *Keats* (London: Faber and Faber, 1997). With Keats, as elsewhere, I have preferred to use the 1778–80 Johnson–Steevens–Malone edition of Shakespeare. But while Keats possessed this edition, it was his facsimile of the First Folio he annotated – a text that omits Edgar's 'Five Fiends' speech.

More general studies of influence include John Beer's *Romantic Influences: Contemporary – Victorian – Modern* (London: Macmillan, 1993), Harold Bloom's *The Anxiety of Influence: A Theory of Poetry* (Oxford and New York: Oxford University Press, 1997), Zachary Leader's *Revision and Romantic Authorship* (Oxford: Clarendon Press, 1996), Mark Schorer's *William Blake: The Politics of Vision* (New York: Henry Holt, 1946), and Jack Stillinger's *Multiple Authorship and the Myth of Solitary Genius* (Oxford: Clarendon Press, 1991). T. S. Eliot's 'Tradition and Individual Talent' is in *The Sacred Wood* (London: Methuen, 1960), and Borges's 'Kafka and His Precursors' is in *Labyrinths* (1970). I have forgotten where the Terry Eagleton quote comes from – either *The Ideology of the Aesthetic* (Oxford: Blackwell, 1990) or *Walter Benjamin or Towards a Revolutionary Criticism* (London: Verso, 1981).

Chatterton's death has been discussed by Taylor (Chatterton's Suicide', *PQ* 31 [1952], 63–9), as well as by Holmes and Ackroyd; see also Al Alvarez, *The Savage God: A Study of Suicide* (London: Weidenfeld and Nicolson, 1971) and Michael MacDonald and Terence Murphy, *Sleepless Souls: Suicide in Early Modern England* (Oxford: Clarendon Press, 1990). The sentence from Luce Irigarary is from *Le Langage des déments* (1973), quoted by Toril Moi in *Sexual/Textual Politics* (London and New York: Methuen, 1985); see also George MacLennan, *Lucid Interval: Subjective Writing and Madness in History* (Leicester: Leicester University Press, 1992). For 'Outsider Art' see John MacGregor, *The Discovery of the Art of the Insane* (Princeton: Princeton University Press, 1992).

For my analysis of the daemon I have preferred to use contemporary translations where available – usually those by Thomas Taylor or P. B. Shelley, but some are modern: for example, *Proclus' Commentary on Plato's* Parmenides, trans. Glenn R. Morrow and John M. Dillon (Princeton: Princeton University Press, 1987). Marsilio Ficino's *Commentary* on Plato's *Symposium* has been edited and translated by Sears Reynolds Jayne (Columbia: University of Missouri Press, 1944). William Ralph Inge's comment is in his edition of *The Philosophy of Plotinus* (London: Longmans, 1918), and that of Lucas Siorvanes from *Proclus: Neo-Platonic Philosophy and Science* (Edinburgh: Edinburgh University Press, 1996). Lemprière's *Classical Dictionary of Proper Names Mentioned in Ancient Authors Writ Large*, 3rd edn, has been republished by Routledge and Kegan Paul (1984). Mark Allen's unpublished paper 'The Daemonic in "Kubla Khan" ' shaped a lot of my thinking. R. D. Stock's *The Holy and the Daemonic from Sir Thomas Browne to William Blake* (Princeton: Princeton University Press, 1982) is a useful introduction, but of greater interest are J. B. Beer, *Coleridge the Visionary* (London: Chatto and Windus, 1959); E. R. Dodds, *Pagan and Christian in an Age of Anxiety: Some Aspects of Religious Experience from Marcus Aurelius to Constantine* (Cambridge: Cambridge University Press, 1991); David Farrell Krell, *Daimon Life: Heidegger and Life Philosophy* (Bloomington: Indiana University Press, 1992); Rudolf Otto, *The Idea of the Holy* (trans. John W. Harvey, London: Oxford University Press,

1958); and Jaroslav Pelikan's elegant piece 'The Odyssey of Dionysian Spirituality', his introduction to *Pseudo-Dionysius: The Complete Works* (trans. Colm Luibheid, New York: Paulist Press, 1987). Among the many Coleridgeans who have used such material are M. H. Abrams, *The Mirror and the Lamp: Romantic Theory and the Critical Tradition* (Oxford: Oxford University Press, 1953); George Dekker, *Coleridge and the Literature of Sensibility* (London: Vision Press, 1978); Jennifer Ford, *Coleridge on Dreaming: Romanticism, Dreams and the Medical Imagination* (Cambridge: Cambridge University Press, 1997); Anthony Harding, *Coleridge and the Inspired Word* (Montreal: McGill-Queen's University Press, 1985); John Livingstone Lowes, *The Road to Xanadu: A Study in the Ways of the Imagination* (Boston: Houghton Mifflin, 1955); Lucy Newlyn, *Paradise Lost and the Romantic Reader* (Oxford: Clarendon Press, 1993): Charles I. Patterson, Jr, 'The Daemonic in "Kubla Khan": Toward Interpretation' (*PMLA* 90 [1975], 1033–42 and ensuing forum); and Mario Praz, *The Romantic Agony* (London: Oxford University Press, 1970). Lucy Newlyn also generously sent proofs of her study, *Reading, Writing, and Romanticism: The Anxiety of Reception* (Oxford: Clarendon Press, 2000). Keats's interest is evident from studies by Werner W. Beyer (*Keats and the Daemon King*, New York: Oxford University Press, 1947), and Charles Patterson again (*The Daemonic in the Poetry of John Keats*, Urbana: University of Illinois Press, 1970). See also Beth Lau, *Keats's* Paradise Lost (Gainesville: University Press of Florida, 1998) and Regina M. Schwartz, *Remembering and Repeating: Biblical Creation in* Paradise Lost (Cambridge: Cambridge University Press, 1988). In addition to Jacques Derrida's *Specters of Marx: The State of the Debt, the Work of Mourning, and the New International,* (trans. Peggy Kamuf, New York: Routledge, 1994) and Ned Lukacher's *Daemonic Figures: Shakespeare and the Question of Conscience* (Ithaca: Cornell University Press, 1994), I found stimulating the contemporary theory of Derrida (again) (*The Post Card: From Socrates to Freud and Beyond,* trans. Alan Bass, Chicago: University of Chicago Press, 1987; and *Given Time: I. Counterfeit Money,* trans. Peggy Kamuf, Chicago: University of Chicago Press, 1992) and Victor I. Stoichita (*A Short History of the Shadow,* London: Reaktion, 1997).

Chatterton's papers are mainly in the British Library (by way of William Barrett and Robert Glynn) and in Bristol Public Library (from George Catcott, Richard Smith, Samuel Seyer, Thomas Fry, and

Michael Lort, Catcott's papers being the most voluminous). There are also contemporary scrapbooks in the Bodleian Library and Cambridge University Library. The examples of plagiarism are from an unsigned letter by George Steevens (*SJC*, 31 Jan. 1782; reproduced by Sherbo, *The Achievement of George Steevens*, 1990). A selection of Rowley Controversy publications appears in *Thomas Chatterton: Early Sources and Responses* (London: Routledge/Thoemmes Press, 1993), but this is far from complete: for comprehensive bibliographies see Murray Warren, *A Descriptive and Annotated Bibliography of Thomas Chatterton* (New York: Garland, 1977) and Jean C. Rowles, 'Thomas Chatterton 1752–1770: An Annotated Bibliography' (Library Association thesis, 1981). The *Sources* collection does, however, include (for what it's worth) a reprint of John Dix's *Life of Thomas Chatterton Including His Unpublished Poems and Correspondence* (London: Hamilton, Adams, 1837).

VI. BASTARD

Ireland is a very promising subject for biographers, editors, and critics, but with the exception of his Shakspeare forgery, this writer too has received negligible attention. There is a large collection of his manuscripts and publications at the Huntington Library, and also in the collections of the British Library, the Folger Shakespeare Library, and the Bodleian Library. There is no bibliography of Ireland's miscellaneous published work of his MS forgeries, and I am not going to attempt one here. The Huntington has a lengthy checklist compiled by G. Hilder Libbis, and J. O. Halliwell[-Phillipps] published fifty copies of *A Descriptive Catalogue of a Collection of Shakespeariana . . . Including a Remarkable Series of the Ireland Forgeries* (London, 1866). Some of his books have been traced: see, for example, Robert Metcalf Smith, *The Shakespeare Folios and the Forgeries of Shakespeare's Handwriting* (Bethlehem, Penn.: Lehigh University Press, 1927).

Ireland wrote his confession as *An Authentic Account of the Shaksperian Manuscripts, &c.* (London: J. Debrett, 1796), revised to form his (pseudo-)autobiographical *Confessions* (1805). More objective accounts are in the *DNB* (albeit under the father's name), and in John Mair, *The Fourth Forger: William Henry Ireland and the Shakespeare Papers* (London: Cobden-Sanderson, 1938), F. E. Halliday, *The Cult of Shakespeare*, London: Duckworth, 1957), Bernard Grebanier, *The Great Shakespeare Forgery* (London: Heinemann, 1966), Samuel Schoenbaum, *Shakespeare's Lives* (Oxford: Clarendon Press, 1970), and most recently Jeffrey Kahan, *Reforging Shakespeare: The Story of a Theatrical Scandal* (London: Associated University Press, 1998); Grebanier and Kahan both have useful bibliographies. Among the few essays of note are pieces by William T. Hastings (' "Shakespeare" Ireland's First Folio', *Colophon* 1.4 [Dec. 1939], unpag.), and Jonathan Bate ('Faking It: Shakespeare and the 1790s', in *Essays and Studies 1993*, ed. Nigel Smith, 63–80). There is a lively discussion of Ireland in Leo Braudy's *The Frenzy of Renown: Fame and Its History* (London: Vintage, 1997), and Montague Summers's assessment appears in *The Gothic Quest: A History of the Gothic Novel* (London: Fortune, 1938). 'Bricolage' is described by Claude Lévi-Strauss in *The Savage Mind* (Chicago: Chicago University Press, 1966) and Jacques Derrida, *Writing and Difference* (trans. Alan Bass, Chicago: University of Chicago Press, 1978), and Jon Mee makes a similar point in *Dangerous Enthusiasm: William Blake and the Culture of Radicalism in the 1790s* (Oxford: Clarendon Press, 1992). Dave Hickey's essay 'Dealing' (in *Air Guitar: Essays on Art and Democracy*, Los Angeles: Art Issues Press, 1997) also suggested some points, surprisingly.

Conversely, there is a vast bibliography of the Shakespeareana of the eighteenth and early nineteenth centuries, including Jonathan Bate, *Shakespearean Constitutions: Politics, Theatre, Criticism, 1730–1830* (Oxford: Clarendon Press, 1989); Christian Deelman, *The Great Shakespeare Jubilee* (London: Michael Joseph, 1964); Margreta De Grazia's *Shakespeare Verbatim: The Reproduction of Authenticity and the 1790 Apparatus* (Oxford: Clarendon Press, 1991; see also Stephen Orgel, 'The Authentic Shakespeare', *Representations* 21 [1988], 1–25); Michael Dobson, *The Making of the National Poet: Shakespeare, Adaptation and Authorship, 1660–1769* (Oxford: Clarendon Press, 1992); and Peter Martin, *Edmond Malone, Shakespearean Scholar: A Literary Biography* (Cambridge: Cambridge University Press, 1995).

Among the controversialists, the publications referred to include James Boaden, *A Letter to George Steevens, Esq. containing A Critical Examination of the Papers of Shakspeare; published by Mr. Samuel Ireland. To which are added, Extracts from Vortigern* (1796); Henry Bate (afterwards Henry Bate-Dudley), *Passages selected by Distinguished Personages, on the Great Literary Trial of Vortigern and Rowena; A*

Comi-Tragedy (n.d.); [George Chalmers,] *An Apology for The Believers in the Shakspeare-Papers, which were exhibited in Norfolk-Street* (1797); *Chalmeriana: or A Collection of Papers Literary and Political, entitled, Letters, Verses, &c. occasioned by reading a late heavy supplemental apology for the believers in the Shakespeare Papers by George Chalmers, F.R.S.S.A.*, ed. Owen Junior and Jasper Hargrave (1800); 'Philalethes' [Francis Webb], *Shakspeare's Manuscripts, in the possession of Mr. Ireland, Examined, respecting the Internal and External Evidences of their Authenticity* (1796); F. G. Waldron, *Free Reflections on Miscellaneous Papers and Legal Instruments, under the Hand and Seal of William Shakspeare, in the possession of Samuel Ireland, of Norfolk Street. To which are added, Extracts from an unpublished MS. play, called The Virgin Queen. Written by, or in imitation of, Shakspeare* (1796); and [John Wyatt] *A Comparative Review of the Opinions of Mr. James Boaden, (Editor of the Oracle) In February, March, and April, 1795; and of James Boaden, Esq. (Author of Fontainville Forest, and of a Letter to George Steevens, Esq.) In February, 1796, relative to The Shakspeare MSS. By a Friend to Consistency* (n.d. [?1796]).

Samuel Ireland published two defences: *Mr. Ireland's Vindication of his Conduct, respecting the Publication of the Supposed Shakspeare MSS. being a Preface or Introduction to A Reply to the Critical Labors of Mr. Malone, in his "Enquiry into the Authenticity of Certain Papers, &c. &c."* (1796), and *An Investigation of Mr. Malone's Claim to the Character of Scholar, or Critic, Being an Examintion of his Inquiry into the Authenticity [sic]. Of the Shakspeare Manuscripts, &c.* (n.d.). Samuel Ireland's effects are listed in *A Catalogue of the Books, Paintings, Miniatures, Drawings, Prints, and various Curiosities, the property of the late Samuel Ireland, Esq.*, Leigh, Sotheby and Son, 7 May 1801 (see also *Treasures of Sir Walter Scott*, London: Adam and Charles Black, 1893; and *Catalogue of the Rarities, to be seen at Don Saltero's Coffee-House in Chelsea, c. 1785*). *Joseph Farington's Diary* is edited by Kenneth Garlick, Angus McIntyre, and Kathryn Cave (New Haven: Yale University Press, 1978–98). Ireland is also mentioned in John Nichols's *Literary Anecdotes of the Eighteenth Century* (London: the author, 1812–15) and *Illustrations of the Literary History of the Eighteenth Century* (London: J. B. Nichols and Son, 1817–58), and by William Cobbett in *Advice to Young Men and (incidentally) to Young Women* (London: Knopf, 1930).

The first full performance of *Vortigern* was at the Bridewell Theatre, London, 14 November 1997.

VII. No One

Wainewright's critical renaissance is burgeoning after relative neglect, even to the extent of inspiring fresh controversy. Again there has been a slow succession of biographies, principally: Jonathan Curling's *Janus Weathercock: The Life of Thomas Griffiths Wainewright, 1794–1847* (London: Thomas Nelson, 1938); John Lindsey's *Suburban Gentleman: The Life of Thomas Griffiths Wainewright, Poet, Painter and Poisoner* (London: Rich and Cowan, 1942); Robert Crossland, *Wainewright in Tasmania* (Melbourne: Oxford University Press, 1954); and most recent is Andrew Motion, *Wainewright the Poisoner* (London: Faber and Faber, 2000), a pseudo-autobiography or auto-fiction. I have quoted material from all four. Motion's book promptly provoked an unanswerable pamphlet by Marc Vaulbert de Chantilly, '*Wainewright the Poisoner*: An Example of Andrew Motion's "High Scholarship" ' (London: Vanity Press of Bethnal Green, 2000), which indicates that a comprehensive and accurate biography of Wainewright remains to be written. (Vaulbert de Chantilly also dates the first felonious transfer to 1823.) Vaulbert de Chantilly has since delivered a substantial paper, 'Property of a Distinguished Poisoner: Thomas Griffiths Wainewright and the Griffiths Family Library', for which I am grateful in its unpublished form (London: British Library, forthcoming); it provided me with such facts as Wainewright's son being born on the day of his great-uncle's death, and the alias 'Theodore G. Williams'. Other primary material continues to emerge, and I am also grateful to the John Linnell archives, Fitzwilliam Museum, Cambridge, for permission to quote Wainewright's unpublished comments on Blake. Wainewright's works have not been edited since W. C. Hazlitt's edition, with the exception of *"Some Passages" in the Life, &c, of Egomet Bonmot, Esq.*, ed. Vaulbert de Chantilly (London: Vanity Press of Bethnal Green, 2000), which Vaulbert de Chantilly convincingly attributes to Edward Gandy: this eminently plausible attribution further muddies the Wainewright canon – misattribution (and mythography) is prevalent in all pseudonymous writing and literary forgery. I have quoted Wainewright's (and Gandy's) texts as they were printed in the *London Magazine*.

Reports of Wainewright appear in John Forster's *Life of Charles Dickens* (London: Cecil Palmer, 1928); *Henry Crabb Robinson on Books and their Writers*, ed. Edith J. Morley (3 vols, London: Dent, 1938); Bryan Waller Proctor ['Barry Cornwall'], *An Autobiographical Fragment and Biographical Notes* (London: Bell and Sons, 1877) and *Charles Lamb: A Memoir* (London: Moxon and Son, 1869); Thomas Noon Talfourd's *Memoirs of Charles Lamb*, ed. Percy Fitzgerald (London: Gibbings, 1892); and Walter Thornbury's 'Old Stories Retold: Thomas Griffiths Wainewright (Janus Weathercock), The Poisoner' (*All the Year Round*, 5 Jan. 1867, 34–41). Doubt began to be cast on the Wainewright myth in discussion following an article in *Notes and Queries*, 6 Oct. 1866. Some of the fictionalizations are collected by Juliet John in *Cult Criminals: The Newgate Novels, 1830–1847* (London: Routledge, 1998). Ian Jack's book *Keats and the Mirror of Art* (Oxford: Clarendon Press, 1967) has details of Wainewright's criticism. For Dickens, I found useful Peter Ackroyd's *Dickens* (London: Sinclair-Stevenson, 1990), and J. Hillis Miller's criticism, especially *Fiction and Repetition: Seven English Novels* (Cambridge, Mass.: Harvard University Press, 1982), although the most direct source is Harvey Peter Sucksmith, 'The Melodramatic Villain in *Little Dorrit*' (*Dickensian* 71 [1975], 76–83). Holman Hunt's comment on Wallis appears in *Pre-Raphaelitism and the Pre-Raphaelite Brotherhood* (London: Macmillan, 1905). The best Wildean criticism is by Richard Ellmann in his biography *Oscar Wilde* (London: Hamish Hamilton, 1987) and Lawrence Danson, *Wilde's Intentions: The Artist in His Criticism* (Oxford: Clarendon Press, 1997). Also helpful was Mary Bittner Wiseman's *The Ecstasies of Roland Barthes* (London: Routledge, 1989), and a 'favourite tortoiseshell cat stroked into a full and sonorous *purr*'.

After

I fear I have said too much already, but I still read more: most notably for my conclusion Rosalind E. Krauss, *The Picasso Papers* (Cambridge, Mass.: MIT Press, 1999) and David Phillips, *Exhibiting Authenticity* (Manchester: Manchester University Press, 1997). Comments were taken from two books already mentioned: Hoving, *False Impressions* (1997) and Beckett, *Fakes* (1995); Kevin Dettmar's essay on Acker and appropriation is delightful ('The Illusion of Modernist Allusion and the Politics of Postmodern Plagiarism', in Buranen and Roy, *Perspectives on Plagiarism and Intellectual Property in a Postmodern World* [1999], 99–109).

The Museum of Jurassic Technology is described in Lawrence

Weschler's entertaining account, *Mr. Wilson's Cabinet of Wonders: Pronged Ants, Horned Humans, Mice on Toast, and Other Marvels of Jurassic Technology* (New York: Pantheon, 1995). Among the Museum's own publications are Valentine Worth's encapsulation of Geoffrey Sonnabend, *Obliscence: Theories of Forgetting and the Problem of Matter* (n.p., n.d.) and Sarah Simons (ed.), *No One May Ever Have the Same Knowledge Again: Letters to Mount Wilson Observatory, 1915–1935* (Los Angeles: Society for the Diffusion of Useful Information, 1993). There is a website at ⟨http://www.mjt.org/⟩. Lawrence Weschler has also written *Boggs: A Comedy of Values* (Chicago: University of Chicago Press, 1999).

Robert Jamieson's observation appears in *Chambers's Edinburgh Journal* (7 Aug. 1852), quoted by Schoenbaum in *Shakespeare's Lives* (1970), and Edward Williams is comprehensively treated by Gwyneth Lewis in 'Eighteenth-Century Literary Forgeries with Special Reference to the Work of Iolo Morganwg' (D.Phil. thesis, Oxford University, 1991). He plays only a bit part in this book because he was so little read in his time; others will doubtless make a meal of him.

I have adapted a line on Nietzsche and authenticity from Jacob Golomb, *In Search of Authenticity: From Kierkegaard to Camus* (London: Routledge, 1995), and Nietzsche's own thinking is of course in *Thus Spoke Zarathustra*, trans. R. J. Hollingdale (Harmondsworth: Penguin, 1969), while Foucault's essay 'Nietzsche, Genealogy, History' is reprinted in *The Foucault Reader*, ed. Rabinow (1984). Certain readers will also recognize that I have read Jacques Derrida's 'Che cos'è la poesia?' in *A Derrida Reader*, ed. Peggy Kamuf (New York: Columbia University Press, 1998), 223–37, as well as Foucault's *The Birth of the Clinic: An Archaeology of Medical Perception* (London: Tavistock Publications, 1976), *Discipline and Punish: The Birth of the Prison* (Harmondsworth: Penguin, 1991), and *Madness and Civilization: A History of Insanity in the Age of Reason* (New York: Random House, 1988). Hillel Schwartz recommended to me Elaine Scarry's *The Body in Pain: The Making and Unmaking of the World* (Oxford: Oxford University Press, 1987).

For the Holocaust, I recommend Saul Friedlander (ed.), *Probing the Limits of Representation: Nazism and the 'Final Solution'* (Cambridge, Mass.: Harvard University Press, 1992), a fine collection that includes Aharon Appelfeld's comment; Elie Wiesel's remark is in 'The Holocaust as Literary Inspiration' (Elie Wiesel, Lucy Dawidowicz, Dorothy

Rabinowitz, Robert Brown (eds), *Dimensions of the Holocaust*, New York: Northwestern University Press, 1977). Wilkomirski is discussed with some heat by Elena Lappin, 'The Man with Two Heads' (*Granta* 66 [Summer 1999], 7–65), and more coolly by Stefan Maechler, *The Wilkomirski Affair: A Study in Biographical Truth*, trans. John Woods (London: Picador, 2001).

The texts of *The Book of Enoch* and *The Book of Jubilees* are from *The Apocrypha and Pseudepigrapha of the Old Testament*, ed. R. H. Charles (Oxford: Clarendon Press, 1913); fragments are extant among the Dead Sea Scrolls (see Geza Vermes [ed.], *The Complete Dead Sea Scrolls in English*, Harmondsworth: Penguin, 1997); see also *The Book of Enoch the Prophet*, trans. Richard Laurence (Kempton, Ill.: Adventures Unlimited Press, 2000, first pub. 1883). Paula O'Keefe's stirring essay 'Leviathan Chained: The Legend of the Nephilim and the Cthulhu Mythos' was written for *KIA* 2 (1991) and is available at <http://www.spookhouse.net/angelynx/nephilim/tiamat.html>. Finally, Gilles Deleuze's reading of the *Sophist* and the *Statesman* is in *The Logic of Sense*, trans. Mark Lester and Charles Stivale, ed. Constantin Boundas (London: Athlone, 1990) – 'the rest is silence'.

Acknowledgements

I never thought I'd need so many people.

David Bowie, 'Five Years'

I have been extremely fortunate in the help I have received in writing this book, and have often been able to draw upon expertise, to benefit from generosity, and to forge and reforge friendships. It is a great pleasure to record my acknowledgements here.

I would like to thank institutions first: the University of Bristol, the University of Exeter, and Stanford University; the Bodleian Library, the British Library, Bristol Public Library, Bristol University Library, Exeter University Old Library, the Fitzwilliam Museum, the Huntington Library, the London Library, Stanford University Library; and the Vicar and staff of St Mary Redcliffe, Bristol. As I wrote drafts, I was fortunate to be able to air my ideas in seminars given at the University of Birmingham, 'Restoration to Reform' at the University of Oxford, the University of California at Los Angeles and University of Southern California, Wayne State University, Detroit, the University of Bristol, the University of Warwick, the University of Plymouth, Stanford University, the University of London Institute of Historical Research, and the University of Glasgow. I am grateful to the organizers and participants of these afternoons for their enthusiasm, insights, and drinks. More formal papers were given at conferences: 'Postures and Impostures' (Wolverhampton University, 1998), the British Comparative Literature Association Conference, 'Legenda' (Lancaster University, 1998), 'Culture and Economics' (University of Exeter, 1998), 'Bristol: Romantic City' (University of Bristol, 1998), the British Society for Eighteenth-Century Studies (St John's College, Oxford, 1999 and

2001), the British Association for Romantic Studies, 'Romantic Revelations' (University of Keele, 1999), 'Plagiarism in History and Theory' (University of London Institute of English Studies, 1999), 'Truth and Lies in the Enlightenment' (Princeton University, 2000), 'Spectres of Enlightenment' (Stanford University, 2000), and 'Early Romantic Poetry Revisited' (St Mary's College, 2000). Again I am grateful to energetic organizers, stimulating delegates, and sympathetic bar staff. Aside from seminars and conferences, I would also like to thank my students, in particular those classes on 'Forgery in the Arts' (1996–7 and 1997–8) and 'Romanticism' (1999–2000) at the University of Exeter; 'Eighteenth-Century English Poetry' and 'Forgery' (2000) at Stanford University; and currently at the University of Bristol and the University of Chicago. The intellectual communities at Stanford and Bristol proved especially supportive.

My more immediate debts are to individuals, and I would most like to thank Jonathan Barry, Andrew Bennett, Leo Braudy, Chris Brooks, Inga Bryden, Tim Burke, Marilyn Butler, Andy Caink, Nicholas Campion, Terry Castle, Steve Clarke, Lee Cox, Karen Daw, Dave Denford, Kelvin Everest, Roy Foster, Tim Fulford, John Goodridge, Richard Gray, Jonathon Green, Julia Griffin, Harriet Gugenheim, Donald Haase, Kevin House, Rosemary Hill, Thomas Keymer, Donna Landry, Grevel Lindop, April London, Roger Lonsdale, Paul Magnuson, Colin MacCabe, John McHale, Gerald MacLean, Rick Mather, Anne Mellor, George Melly, David Miller, Andrew Motion, Lucy Newlyn, Angus Nicholls, Chris Nicholson, Mike Pugh, Isabel Rivers, the late Gareth Roberts, Nicholas Roe, Adam Rounce, David Scrase, Fiona Stafford, Roger Starling, Michael Suarez, SJ, Toni Thompson, Katherine Turner, Timothy Webb, James Wilson, Peter Wiseman, Roger Yeates, 'Toni da Sony', and of course my chums at the Academy Club: Andrew, Mandana, Bill, Dorcas, Jo, Laura, Marie, Ralph, and Dea, Annie, and Rowan; and at the Oxenham Arms: Jim and Pat, George and Gaye, Cheri and Jamie, Nick, Norman and Jane, Pete and Helen, Ed and Jacci, Richard and Cindy, Jenny and Chris, Peter and Kate, John and Jackie, Mark and Kate, Terry, Dave and Jane, Beth and Tony, Bill and Carol, Bill and Irene, Keith and Wendy, James, Maggie, Michael and Jane, Sam and Jan, and Dave and Shirley. Musical interludes were provided by Black Sabbath, Fields of the Nephilim, and the North Dartmoor Big Band.

Mark Allen, Paul Baines, Sarah Barrett, Jeffrey Kahan, Dafydd

Moore, Hillel Schwartz, and Marc Vaulbert de Chantilly were especially obliging: they read chapters, made keen comments and suggestions, and corrected mistakes. My most heartfelt thanks go to Mary Mount and Peter Straus (and more lately Anya Serota), Michael Nath, Zoë Waldie, and Marina Warner: they very generously took time to read the entire manuscript and I hope that I have answered their astute and penetrating criticisms; what errors, infelicities, and nonsense that remain I claim as my own. Finally, I am deeply indebted to the Leverhulme Trust, without whom this book would never have been written; to Marina, without whom this book would never have been finished; to Michael, without whom this book would never have been a book; to Annie, forever keeping my spirits up; but most enduringly to my family, who have steadfastly supported my work with an extraordinary persistence and rare indulgence. Thank you, all.

Index